Poor Relief and Welfare in Germany from the Reformation to World War I

This account of poor relief, charity, and social welfare in Germany from the Reformation through World War I integrates historical narrative and the theoretical analysis of such issues as social discipline, governmentality, gender, religion, and state formation. It analyzes the changing cultural frameworks through which the poor came to be considered as needy; the institutions, strategies, and practices devised to assist, integrate, and discipline these populations; and the political alchemy through which the middle classes attempted to reconcile the needs of the individual with those of the community. While the Bismarckian social insurance programs have long been regarded as the origin of the German welfare state, this book shows how preventive social welfare programs – the second pillar of the welfare state – evolved out of traditional poor relief, and it emphasizes the role of Progressive reformers and local, voluntary initiative in this process and the impact of competing reform discourses on both the social domain and the public sphere.

Larry Frohman is assistant professor of history at State University of New York at Stony Brook. He received his Ph.D. from the University of California, Berkeley.

Poor Relief and Welfare in Germany from the Reformation to World War I

LARRY FROHMAN
State University of New York at Stony Brook

CAMBRIDGE UNIVERSITY PRESS
Cambridge, New York, Melbourne, Madrid, Cape Town, Singapore, São Paulo, Delhi

Cambridge University Press
32 Avenue of the Americas, New York, NY 10013-2473, USA

www.cambridge.org
Information on this title: www.cambridge.org/9780521506038

© Larry Frohman 2008

This publication is in copyright. Subject to statutory exception
and to the provisions of relevant collective licensing agreements,
no reproduction of any part may take place without
the written permission of Cambridge University Press.

First published 2008

Printed in the United States of America

A catalog record for this publication is available from the British Library.

Library of Congress Cataloging in Publication Data
Frohman, Larry.
Poor relief and welfare in Germany from the Reformation to World War I / Larry Frohman
  p. cm.
Includes bibliographical references and index.
ISBN 978-0-521-50603-8 (hardback))
1. Public welfare – Germany – History.   2. Poor – Services for – Germany – History.
3. Poor – Germany – History.   4. Charities – Germany – History.   I. Title.
HV4098.F76 2008
362.5′56209430903–dc22   2008021194

ISBN   978-0-521-50603-8 hardback

Cambridge University Press has no responsibility for
the persistence or accuracy of URLs for external or
third-party Internet Web sites referred to in this publication
and does not guarantee that any content on such
Web sites is, or will remain, accurate or appropriate.

Contents

List of Tables and Figure   *page* vii
Acknowledgments   ix

    Introduction   1

1 Discipline, Community, and the Sixteenth-Century Origins of Modern Poor Relief   11
    The Desacralization of Poverty and the New Discourse on Vagrancy   12
    Work and the Reorganization of Public Assistance   16
    Confessional Differences and the Role of Religion in the New Poor Relief   24

2 The Rise and Fall of the Workhouse: Poor Relief in the Age of Absolutism   32
    Rethinking the Disciplinary Telos   32
    The Formation of the Classical Workhouse   35
    Beyond the Workhouse: Industriousness, Education, and the Prevention of Poverty in the Age of Enlightenment   43

3 Pauperism, Moral Reform, and Visions of Civil Society, 1800–1870   53
    Voluntary Associations and the Problem of Social Governance   53
    Pauperism, the Dangerous Classes, and the Social Question   58
    Protestant Social Conservatism and the Founding of the Inner Mission   64
    Mobility, Modernity, and the Liberal Response to the Social Question   71

4 The State, the Market, and the Organization of Poor Relief, 1830–1870   80
    Reform Strategies in Prussia and Southern Germany   81
    The Elberfeld System and the Formation of a Market Society, 1850–1870   87

5 The Assistantial Double Helix: Poor Relief, Social Insurance, and the Political Economy of Poor Law Reform   99

	Poor Law Reform by Another Name	100
	Old Conflicts and New Departures	109
6	New Voices: Citizenship, Social Reform, and the Origins of Modern Social Work in Imperial Germany	112
	The Inner Mission, 1870–1914	115
	The Bourgeois Women's Movement, the Spiritualization of Motherhood, and Social Work as Social Reconciliation	116
	The Caritas Association and the Reluctant Modernization of Catholic Charity	133
	Social Democracy: The Demonization of the Capitalist System and Pragmatic Cooperation at the Local Level	138
7	The Social Perspective on Poverty and the Origins of Modern Social Welfare	141
	The Social Perspective on Poverty and the Logic of Social Citizenship	141
	Familial Subjects – The Archimedean Point of Social Reform	152
8	From Fault to Risk: Changing Strategies of Assistance to the Jobless in Imperial Germany	158
	Migrant Relief, Workhouses, and the Policing of the Residuum	160
	From the Margins to the Center: The War on Labor Market Risk	172
9	Youth Welfare and the Political Alchemy of Juvenile Justice	179
	Guardianship and the Public Interest in the Private Family	180
	Juvenile Delinquency and the Socialization of Juvenile Justice	183
10	The Social Evolution of Poor Relief, the Crisis of Voluntarism, and the Limits of Progressive Social Reform	196
11	Family, Welfare, and (Dis)order on the Home Front	206
	Total War and the Transformation of Social Politics	206
	Female Dependence, Female Citizenship, and the Wartime Challenge to Deterrent Poor Relief	210
	Kriegerfrauen *and the Politics of National Obligation*	220
	Motherhood, Work, and the Grounds of Citizenship	224
	Disabled Veterans and the Contradictions of Therapeutic Welfare	230
12	Wartime Youth Welfare and the Progressive Refiguring of the Social Contract	233
	From Prevention to Promotion: Rethinking the Political Rationality of Social Assistance	233
	State, Society, and the Corporatist Turn in the Social Sector	238
	Conclusion: The End of Poor Relief and the Invention of Welfare	243

Sources and Abbreviations 249
Index 251

List of Tables and Figure

Tables

1	Adoption of the Elberfeld System, 1853–1900	*page* 97
2	Causes of Public Assistance Cases	106
3	Women's Participation in Municipal Poor Relief, 1907–16	130

Figure

1	Von Bodelschwingh at the Bethel bei Bielefeld workstation	165

Acknowledgments

Writing books can be a long, lonely undertaking. Although this one has taken longer than most, it has not always been lonely. I have received valuable feedback not only from fellow panelists, commentators, and audience members at the conferences where I presented parts of this work, but also from encounters with other friends and colleagues, whose causal inquiries about my project led me on more than one occasion to think through issues that often proved to be important to the larger argument but that, until that point, had lain dormant around the margins of this work in process. Just as important as the formal presentations – and here I am sure that I am simply giving expression to an open secret – were the long, rambling, riotous dinners that were the real high point of many a conference.

Many thanks to the Ann Arbor crowd for copious quantities of intellectual stimulation, useful feedback, pointed wit, and general merry-making over the years. I owe special thanks to Geoff Eley for supporting this project. I benefited from the intellectual labors of Ann Taylor Allen and E. P. Hennock, who both read the manuscript for the Press, as well as from Marcus Gräser, who carefully read the manuscript as it neared completion. I would also like to thank Eric Crahan and all of the people at Cambridge University Press, who have shown admirable degrees of professionalism and speed in the production of this book.

Here at Stony Brook, I have had a number of different institutional homes, and I am indebted in a variety of ways to friends and colleagues – categories that display a far higher degree of overlap than is the case at virtually any other university – in both the History Department and the Professional Education Program. I owe a special debt to the staff of the interlibrary loan office here. Without their assistance, this project would have taken much longer than it did, and it would have been a much more onerous undertaking. In addition, as everyone working in the field is well aware, such a book could not have been completed without the generous assistance of the staffs of the many archives that have become the repository of the institutional memory of many of the actors in the story told here. I would like to especially thank the staffs of the Archiv des

Deutschen Caritasverbandes, the Archiv des Diakonischen Werkes der Evangelischen Kirche Deutschlands, the Bundesarchiv, and the Landesarchiv Berlin for allowing me to plunder their valuable resources.

But my deepest thanks go, of course, to Young-sun Hong. I have benefited from her knowledge of the topic, her refusal to tolerate lax formulations and overly long sentences, and her willingness to bring her expertise to bear on every part of the – many – successive versions of a manuscript that dealt with a subject that, despite her best efforts, she has been unable to put behind her until now. We've been through a lot together over the past twenty years; her support has made the whole project possible; and her affection has made it worthwhile. It is to her that this book is dedicated.

Introduction

Poor relief and charity have often struggled to find their historiographical voice. On the one hand, their history has often been written, especially by their practitioners and advocates, either as an expression of Christian brotherly love or as a manifestation of a primal form of human interaction.[1] On the other hand, the triumph of social insurance has given the modern social state a powerful telos that privileges the rise of state-centered social insurance and social policy programs while marginalizing all those earlier institutions and strategies for assisting the needy that cannot be incorporated into the narrative prehistory of these programs, their subsequent development, or the specific vision of modernity implicit in them. However, since the 1990s those forms of assistance to the needy that were repressed in earlier narratives of the social state have returned with a vengeance from the periphery to the center of scholarly interest, and with the rise of the new social history – and, more recently, the cultural turn – this historical backwater has become a privileged site of inquiry for historians and social theorists interested in social discipline, gender, civil society, modernity, and state-formation.

The master concept in the recent literature on poor relief, charity, and welfare has been social discipline, and any study of the topic has to come to terms with this body of work.[2] Much of this literature regarded poor relief, charity, and welfare as mechanisms for marginalizing the poor and deviant and excluding them from the community, and it correspondingly stressed the disciplinary, repressive, and potentially totalitarian character of these programs. This book intervenes in this debate – whose German variant has been more directly influenced by Gerhard Oestreich and Detlev Peukert than by Michel Foucault – in a

---

[1] For this latter characterization, see Hans Scherpner, *Theorie der Fürsorge* (Vandenhoeck & Ruprecht, 1962), 122.

[2] These comments are only meant to give the reader an overview of the book, and the relevant literature will be addressed in the individual chapters.

number of specific contexts ranging from the early workhouses to nineteenth-century voluntary associations to turn-of-the-century preventive social welfare. My thesis here is that the social discipline paradigm is not so much wrong as one sided. One of the great strengths of the social discipline paradigm has been its ability to capture the logical connections between the discursive constitution of need, surveillance of the needy and endangered, measures to discipline and otherwise influence the behavior of this population, and the formation of their subjectivity. However, the stronger versions of the social discipline paradigm have been prone to take the explication of this logic of social discipline for a description of the reality of assistance practice and to conclude that this process precludes the possibility that social intervention could have strengthened the bonds of community or genuinely enhanced the rights and welfare of the needy.

It seems, though, that the interpretive pendulum is beginning to swing in a different direction, questioning both the equation of assistance with discipline, marginalization, and exclusion and the theory of modernity implicit in this work.[3] The social discipline literature has been based on the assumption that the essential features of poor relief and charity can best be understood by studying attitudes and policies toward idlers and vagrants, and it has portrayed social assistance primarily as a mechanism for the production and exclusion of social marginality. However, those who read the history of social assistance exclusively from the margins inward have often failed to recognize that the local, deserving poor were treated with much greater solicitude than were vagrants and the foreign poor, and any interpretation that fails to understand that assistance to the poor is as much about social integration, community, and citizenship as about social disciplining, marginalization, and exclusion is fundamentally flawed.

In his work, Oestreich viewed social disciplining as one key dimension of the larger process of state formation.[4] According to Oestreich, the early modern

---

[3] Lynn Lees, *The Solidarities of Strangers. The English Poor Laws and the People, 1700–1948* (Cambridge University Press, 1998), and Robert Castel, *From Manual Workers to Wage Laborers. Transformation of the Social Question*, trans. Richard Boyd (Transaction Publishers, 2003). For Germany, see Adelheid von Saldern, "Integration und Fragmentierung in europäischen Städten," *AfS* 42 (2006), 3–60, especially 28, 34. Saldern recognizes the integrative function of poor relief without losing sight of the fact that the social discrimination and political disenfranchisement entailed by its receipt fragmented the community and marginalized its recipients. I myself have explored these issues in "Prevention, Welfare and Citizenship: The War on Tuberculosis and Infant Mortality in Germany, 1900–1930," *CEH* 39:3 (September 2006), 431–81.

[4] Gerhard Oestreich, "Strukturprobleme des europäischen Absolutismus," in *Geist und Gestalt des frühmodernen Staates* (Berlin, 1969), 179–97. See also Winfried Schulze, "Gerhard Oestreichs Begriff 'Sozialdisziplinierung in der frühen Neuzeit,'" *Zeitschrift für historische Forschung* 14 (1987), 265–302; Stefan Breuer, "Sozialdisziplinerung. Probleme und Problemverlagerunge eines Konzepts bei Max Weber, Gerhard Oestreich und Michel Foucault," in Christoph Sachße and Florian Tennstedt, eds., *Soziale Sicherheit und soziale Disziplinierung* (Suhrkamp, 1986), 45–69; Robert Jütte, "Disziplinierungmechanismen in der städtischen Armenfürsorge der Frühneuzeit," in Sachße and Tennstedt, eds., *Soziale Sicherheit*, 101–18; and Norbert Finzsch, "Elias, Foucault, Oestreich. On a Historical Theory of Confinement," in Finzsch and Jütte, eds., *Institutions of Confinement* (Cambridge University Press, 1996), 3–16.

state constituted itself by gathering up the authority that had heretofore been dispersed among the diverse intermediate authorities that had governed social life since the later Middle Ages and then asserting its own internal sovereign authority in the form of police ordinances that laid down more rational, uniform codes regulating virtually every aspect of the social, economic, and religious life of the population, including poor relief. In contrast to Foucault, who depicted social discipline as a universal, anonymous process, for Oestreich agency is clearly located in municipal authorities, territorial rulers, and their bureaucracies.[5] Recent scholarship, however, has emphasized the intrinsic limits of state-sponsored social disciplining and criticized earlier writing on poor relief and social discipline for mistaking normative pronouncements for an accurate description of reality while overlooking both the real limitations on magisterial power and, in many instances, the lack of interest on the part of the magistrates in carrying out this disciplinary project. Moreover, the explanatory power of state-sponsored social disciplining is limited by the fact that neighborhood self-help, which cannot be recuperated by any theory of social discipline, always represented an important source of assistance to the needy.[6]

These criticisms of top-down social disciplining have in recent years begun to come together in the concept of social control, which has been used to describe the ongoing efforts by religious congregations, guilds, neighborhoods, and the broader community to enforce social norms. Social control thus represents an attempt to move beyond the critique of a statist model of social disciplining to a positive conceptualization of societal or communal self-regulation as the driving force behind state formation in early modern Europe.[7] Although the idea of social control does not escape from the basic question of how to conceptualize the efforts of the community to alter the values, comportment, and sense of self of those individuals who transgress against its norms, it does evince a much more direct concern for the preservation of community than does the

---

[5] Other writers on early modern poor relief, such as Sachße and Tennstedt, *Geschichte der Armenfürsorge*, I:38, have suggested that the disciplining process should be related more directly to the rise of capitalism than to that of the absolutist state.

[6] See the exchange between Robert Jütte, "'Disziplin zu predigen ist eine Sache, sich ihr zu unterwerfen eine andere' (Cervantes). Prolegomena zu einer sozialgeschichte der Armenfürsorge diesseits und jenseits des Fortschritts," *GuG* 17 (1991), 92–101, and Martin Dinges, "Frühneuzeitliche Armenfürsorge als Sozialdisziplinierung? Probleme mit einem Konzept," *GuG* 17 (1992), 5–29.

[7] It is important to note that this new concept of social control is quite different from that laid out by Frances Fox Piven and Richard Cloward, *Regulating the Poor. The Functions of Public Welfare* (Pantheon, 1971). The development of this new incarnation of the concept can be followed in Herman Roodenburg and Pieter Spierenburg, eds., *Social Control in Europe, 1500–1800*, vol. 1 (Ohio State University Press, 2004); Heinz Schilling, ed., *Institutions, Instruments and Agents of Social Control and Discipline in Early Modern Europe* (Vittorio Klostermann, 1999); Schilling, "Disziplinierung oder 'Selbstregulierung der Untertanen'? Ein Plädoyer für die Doppelperspektive von Makro- und Mikrohistoire bei der Erforschung der frühmodernen Kirchenzucht," *HZ* 264 (1997), 675–91; and Heinrich Richard Schmidt, "Sozialdisziplinierung? Ein Plädoyer für das Ende des Etatismus in der Kofessionalisierungsforschung," *HZ* 265 (1997), 639–82.

social discipline paradigm, and this insight offers a way to assess the usefulness of social discipline for writing the history of poor relief.

One way of approaching the question of the limits of social discipline is to ask how poor people came to be recognized as deserving of assistance. While the propertied often viewed charity as a means of displaying their munificence and thereby reaffirming their social status, the poor themselves also had distinct notions of justice and their own ideas about who was deserving of what kinds of assistance under what circumstances, and in their petitions for assistance the poor had to narrate their misfortunes in ways that, without violating their own plebeian notions of justice, would affirm their honor and merit. Petitioning for assistance was part of a process in which the propertied and the poor continuously renegotiated the terms of membership in the community, the notions of honor and morality on which this community rested, the social hierarchies through which it was structured, and the rights – in this case, the right to assistance – associated therewith.[8] Social integration and social exclusion were two sides of the same coin, as were assistance and discipline, and it was through the novel and distinctly modern distinction between the deserving and the undeserving poor that the borders of the community were drawn. For the poor, the most tangible symbol of membership in the community was the recognition that they displayed the qualities that rendered them deserving of communal assistance, and building community meant as much insuring that the legitimate needs of the weaker members were met as it did correcting the wayward or excluding the incorrigible.[9]

The goal here is less to jettison the social discipline paradigm than to grasp its limits and understand the mutual implication of assistance and discipline, integration and exclusion, and correction and chastisement in the various forms of social assistance developed from the early 1500s through World War I. The diverse institutions established to assist the needy all represent elements of a broader socio-corrective complex that sought alternately to provide for the deserving poor, correct the penitent, and chastise those wayward individuals whose deviant behavior (especially with regard to work, family life, and sexual morality) was regarded as the cause of their distress, all in the name of social integration. Punishment and exclusion were only invoked as an ultima ratio to protect society from those reprobates who were chronically resistant to such socialization, and the resort to such measures reflected the failure of these programs, rather than their raison d'être. Public assistance, however, was always intrinsically paternalist, and paternalistic solicitude could assume many

---

[8] Martin Dinges, "Aushandeln von Armut in der frühen Neuzeit: Selbsthilfepotential, Bürgervorstellungen und Verwaltungslogiken," *Werkstatt Geschichte* 10 (1995), 7–15, and Steve Hindle, *On the Parish? The Micro-Politics of Poor Relief in Rural England c. 1550–1750* (Oxford University Press, 2004).

[9] Katherine A. Lynch, *Individuals, Families, and Communities in Europe, 1200–1800* (Cambridge University Press, 2003), and Joel Harrington, "Escape from the Great Confinement: The Genealogy of a German Workhouse," *JMH* 71 (June 1999), 308–45.

different forms – including chastisement when it was believed to be in the best interest of the individual. Assistance was genuine, but always conditional on proper behavior, and the threat of harsher measures was always implicit in the offer of such support. The problem, though, is that it is impossible to deduce in advance how the balance between assistance and discipline, and between the rights of the individual and those of the community, would be struck in any specific case, and the book provides a historical account of the successive attempts to square this theoretical circle from the Reformation to World War I.

Poor relief and charity are historically mutable phenomena whose history is coextensive with that of the modern world, and in Chapter 1 I argue that the origins of recognizably modern forms of assistance to the poor are to be found in the desacralization of poverty and almsgiving at the end of the Middle Ages and in the emergence of poverty as the object of state social policy in conjunction with a great wave of reforms in the first half of the sixteenth century. The questions are to what extent were these reforms the product of socioeconomic change or religious reform, in what ways did the reorganization of poor relief differ in Lutheran, Calvinist, and Catholic territories, and why? The second chapter asks how the house of correction, or the workhouse, as it came to be known, emerged as the basic mechanism for responding to the diverse manifestations of the social problem as it was understood in the age of absolutism. As its name implies, the house of correction was originally a mechanism for reintegrating into the community wayward children and others who transgressed against communal values. However, between 1650 and 1750 it was transformed into a deeply repressive institution that became the cornerstone of the absolutist war on vagrancy before itself entering into a terminal crisis in the second half of the eighteenth century. This crisis was emblematic of a broader crisis of early modern forms of paternalistic social governance, and the failure of this project created a discursive space for a new liberal approach that was to dominate public perception of the social problem until the end of the nineteenth century.

Chapters 3, 4, and 5 show how the evolution of poor relief and charity across the nineteenth century both mirrored and accelerated the formation of the market economy and bourgeois civil society during this period. This new social formation was, however, haunted by the crisis of pauperism with the social problem being defined primarily in terms of cultural deficiencies and the failure of social reproduction, rather than in political or economic terms. The distinguishing feature of the social politics of these decades was the formation of moral reform organizations competing with one another to solve the social problem by socializing the asocial pauper class in accordance with their own cultural norms so as to create the providential, responsible, industrious, and disciplined subjects whose existence was presupposed by contemporary theories of civil society and the market economy. Chapters 4 and 5 shift registers from the social domain to the domain of political economy. Here, efforts to use the poor laws to promote economic development and combat the social consequences (and associated assistance costs) of greater labor mobility gave rise to chronic conflicts between the territorial and the local state and between urban industrial regions and the rural areas (primarily in the Prussian East) from which the industrial labor force was recruited. These chapters reconstruct the evolution of the poor laws at the national level from the 1840s through the first decade of the twentieth century and analyze the Elberfeld system, which became the model for deterrent poor relief in imperial Germany and the second key mechanism for producing the self-governing subjects of the bourgeois world.

The primary goal of nineteenth-century poor relief was to combat pauperism, not prevent poverty. Relief officials provided only the barest existence minimum, and, in hopes of deterring all but the truly impotent and deserving poor from relying on the assistance of others, they did so in a discriminatory manner and on a subsidiary basis only after the individual or family had fallen into utter destitution. All these policies were based on the presumption that poverty, crime, and other forms of social deviance were a matter of individual character, and they sought to combat these problems through moral reform and the deterrent promotion of self-reliance. Beginning in the 1880s and 1890s, however, this individualist, voluntaristic understanding of need and the deterrent policies to which it had given rise were challenged by the emergence of a new form of social knowledge: a social perspective on poverty that viewed the individual not as a moral free agent, but as an embodied subject constrained by the materiality of social and environmental forces to act in certain ways. From this new perspective, the solution to the social problem depended less on strengthening individual morality than on environmental and social reforms, along with popular enlightenment regarding such things as advances in hygiene and modern child-raising practices, to provide the needy with the material and cultural resources that they needed to live in accordance with the norms established by the new social and medical sciences. Although the need to secure the economic and military power of the nation provided a compelling rationale for new forms of preventive intervention to enhance the health, productivity, and political loyalty of the population, the political rationality of the new preventive social welfare (*soziale Fürsorge*) was diametrically opposed to that of deterrent relief. The development of the new interventionist strategies associated with preventive social welfare was predicated on a rethinking of the liberal social contract in terms of a complex web of social rights and social obligations whose structure and internal dynamics were theorized by Progressive reformers. These preventive social welfare programs, which represent the second pillar of the German welfare system, were as much an evolution out of traditional poor relief and charity as they were a rejection of its underlying principles. Chapters 7 and 10 reconstruct the development of these new ideas and show how the Progressive rethinking of the liberal social contract on the basis of the social perspective on poverty led to the expansion of preventive social welfare programs designed to secure the rights implicit in their solidaristic conception of social citizenship. This turn from deterrence to prevention represents the conceptual missing link connecting the history of the poor laws to that of the

Introduction

welfare state, and this broad development provides the narrative thread for the second half of the book.

Chapter 6 examines the several new players in the welfare reform field during the empire, including bourgeois women, Catholic charities, and Social Democracy, and it shows how the ensuing competition between groups seeking to shape the character of the poor in accordance with their own worldviews altered the nature of citizenship, fragmented the social domain, and shaped the provision of social assistance. The bourgeois women's movement was especially influential in this respect because it was their gendered reform strategy that gave birth to the modern social work profession. Chapters 7, 8, 9, and 10 explore the impact of this paradigm shift from deterrence to prevention and its implications for citizenship, social rights, and the role of the state as they unfolded in the primary fields of social engagement: the family, assistance to the jobless, and youth welfare. These chapters collectively show how the principle of prevention and the subsequent call for the "social evolution" of poor relief (Chapter 10) challenged, though without completely overturning, the political rationality of mid-century liberalism and deterrent poor relief in the years leading up to World War I. But they also raise the question of whether these preventive social welfare programs enhanced the welfare of the needy or simply opened the way to their more intensive disciplining.

The war, however, fundamentally altered the political parameters of social reform, and Chapters 11 and 12 assess its impact on the development of social assistance. While both the national and local states poured massive amounts of money and energy into social programs designed to stabilize the "home" front and the breadwinner family, Chapter 11 shows how these programs unintentionally raised all sorts of unsettling questions about gender roles and women's citizenship. At the same time, the mobilization of the national community for industrialized warfare, the generalization of need, and the blurring of the lines between military and society led the diverse groups of the new poor to make restitutional claims on the state that could not be satisfied through deterrent relief, which was rapidly hollowed out by the expansion of preventive social welfare programs. All these forces, together with the challenges of postwar reconstruction, combined to forge a new sense of national solidarity that endowed preventive social welfare programs with a national, military, and social significance that made it possible to break through the political barriers that had limited their acceptance before the war. The demise of deterrent poor relief, whose development since the 1500s will be traced in this book, and the corresponding breakthrough of preventive social welfare during World War I – that is, the creation of the social welfare state through the social evolution of poor relief and the ensuing "break-up" of the poor laws – make 1918 the logical place to end this story.

Methodologically, this book aspires to go beyond the all-too-numerous organizational and administrative histories of poor relief by showing relief, charity, and welfare to be forms of historically situated social practice, both symbolic and material. The heart of the book is the analysis of the cultural frameworks and discursive strategies through which the poor came to be constructed as needy, the technologies and practices devised – on the basis of these constructs – to assist, integrate, and discipline these populations, and the political alchemy through which the dominant classes sought to reconcile the interests of the needy with those of the greater community in order to justify their interventions into the lives of the former. Although it is impossible to write a history of assistance to the poor without making some assumptions about underlying demographic, economic, and social "realities," this is not a book about poverty per se or the mentality and everyday life of the poor. The book ventures into this territory only to the extent that this is necessary to illuminate the changing contemporary understanding of the social question, though it does so in an awareness that these discourses were influenced as much by what escaped them (because it could not be made sense of in the categories employed by these narratives) as by what they encompassed. As a result, the book reveals more about the propertied classes who defined need and assisted the needy than it does about the poor themselves.[10]

The book also addresses a second set of issues. The shift in focus from social insurance to relief, charity, and welfare also entails a shift from the national state and its officials to both the local level and the voluntary sector, especially for the empire. Not only did the actual administration of poor relief lie in the hands of the cities, which retained a large degree of autonomy in the field of social policy and remained the most important providers of social services throughout the period under study here. The development of poor relief, charity, and, later, social welfare programs was largely the product of the initiative of local government officials and voluntary associations, often in collaboration with each other, and the study of voluntary action at the local level raises a number of questions that will be addressed in the following chapters: How, from the early nineteenth century onward, did these associations function as mechanisms of social governance? How did these associations serve as vehicles for the constitution of middle-class identity and the assertion of middle-class hegemony? What does the changing structure of voluntary associations and the evolving relationship between these associations and the state (i.e., the relation between state and society) tell us about German political culture in the nineteenth century and the fortunes of German liberalism? And how did the proliferation of social reform associations competing with one another for predominance within the social sector shape the structure of the public sphere?

The assistantial discourses, strategies, and technologies that evolved across mid-century need to be seen as mechanisms of social governance designed to create the industrious, responsible, and thrifty familial subjects on which the stability of civil society and market economy depended. However, this was a contested process. As I argue in Chapters 3 and 6, the social reform field was populated by groups whose views on human nature, whose understanding of

---

[10] The sources available for Germany do not generally permit the same kind of detailed parish studies that are the lifeblood of poor law historiography in other countries.

the social problem, and whose strategies for combating it differed radically from one another, and the complex struggle among these groups to define the discourse on the social question and then to use this discursive authority to mold the needy in accordance with their own worldviews is one of the central threads in the history of social assistance in nineteenth- and twentieth-century Germany. While these competing views on the proper means of combating need influenced the development of assistance practice in a variety of ways, the inability to resolve these nineteenth-century culture wars, as Young-sun Hong has shown, the driving force behind the development of the corporatist organization of the social sector in twentieth-century Germany, and these conflicts ultimately played a key role in the demise of the Weimar Republic.[11]

The process of social discipline has been presented in some accounts as a totalizing, yet subjectless, process. In this book, however, I argue that it was, in fact, driven by discrete, identifiable agents, but that, rather than depoliticizing the social question, the ideological and organizational competition among the leading social reform associations simply transformed the nature of social politics and fragmented the social domain. While much of the recent literature on German social policy and the changing meanings of the welfare state in Germany has been written under the shadow of the Holocaust and in response to the debate over Germany's fateful "special path" (*Sonderweg*) to modernity, my book rests to a large degree on an alternative interpretive framework that views the national/territorial state as only one of many actors. Correspondingly, I argue that disciplinary power and discursive authority was dispersed among a number of different agencies, including not only the local state, but also the parish, the institutional churches, employers, and – most importantly – the growing number of voluntary associations active at the local and national levels.[12]

Lastly, a few words about the geographical scope of this work. It makes little sense to speak of "Germany" in the early 1500s, and this study takes a large part of central and western Europe as its initial object before telescoping in a properly nationalist manner to focus on the territories that after 1871

---

[11] "Corporatism" is a much-debated term. Here I will use the concept – more with an eye to the Weimar Republic than to the Federal Republic – to describe a system in which public responsibility for providing for the nation's needy is delegated to the social service agencies representing the major societal groups. To the extent that the work of these agencies and their strategies for combating the diverse manifestations of need reflect the political and religious values of these groups, they facilitate the reproduction of self-enclosed, often mutually antagonistic, milieus, rather than seeking to mediate these competing values in a greater conception of the higher good. This tendency for the different groups to wall themselves off from one another leads to the notional dissolution of the res publica, and democratic control over these agencies is attenuated in an inverse relation to their quasi-public status and function. See Young-sun Hong, *Welfare, Modernity and the Weimar State, 1919–1933* (Princeton University Press, 1998).

[12] Dennis Sweeney, "Reconsidering the Modernity Paradigm: Reform Movements, the Social, and the State in Wilhelmine Germany," *SH* 31:4 (November 2006), 405–34; Hong, *Welfare, Modernity and the Weimar State*; and Edward Ross Dickinson, *The Politics of German Child Welfare from the Empire to the Federal Republic* (Harvard University Press, 1996).

comprised the German Empire. Despite this geographical constriction, there is little in the story being told here that is unique to Germany. The Germans were fond of favorably comparing their own system of statutory assistance and public visiting (as organized in the Elberfeld system) with both the English poor law of 1834 and the continued French reliance on voluntary charity. However, the wide-ranging discussions that led to the formation of these different systems were framed in terms of beliefs, values, and assumptions that were the common property of the European middle classes, and the differences *between* these ideal-typical national traditions simply replicated debates and divisions that to a large degree also took place *within* each of these countries. I would like to suggest, therefore, that, despite the geographical focus on developments in Germany, the arguments advanced in this book are equally relevant for understanding the connections between poor relief, welfare, and modernity across modern Europe and the United States.

1

Discipline, Community, and the Sixteenth-Century Origins of Modern Poor Relief

The history of poor relief in the Germanies is coextensive with that of the modern world. This history began in the second half of the 1400s with the desacralization of almsgiving and the subsequent emergence of begging and vagrancy as distinct social problems, and the attitudes toward poverty and the institutions that were established in the 1500s to relieve it defined the basic framework of assistance to the needy until the first decades of the twentieth century.

During the Middle Ages, material destitution was an unavoidable fact for a substantial proportion of the population; begging was an accepted way of holding body and soul together; charity for the poor played an essential role in the Christian economy of salvation; and beggars occupied a recognized, if subordinate, place in the complex skein of social hierarchies that made up the fabric of medieval society. However, things began to change after 1450 or so. The desacralization of almsgiving reflected a growing recognition that not all beggars could be considered the proper object of Christian charity. This new attitude meant that Christian charity would have to become more systematic and discriminating and that it would have to make greater efforts to distinguish between those who were truly deserving of charity and those who would simply be encouraged in their wicked ways by such assistance. It also meant that charity would become the object of public policy in ways that it had never been before.

The last decades of the fifteenth century saw the first sustained attempts in many parts of Europe to regulate begging, especially by the able bodied and all those who did not belong to the local community. But these modest efforts to control socially disruptive begging were overtaken in the 1520s by an intense burst of legislative activity, which sought not simply to limit begging, but to put assistance to the poor on an entirely new footing. These reforms gave birth to recognizably modern forms of poor relief as the institutional embodiment of the collective commitment of the community to fulfill in a more rational manner the charitable obligations – simultaneously Christian and civic – owed to its needy members. Between 1522 and 1550 more than thirty cities in the Germanies undertook comprehensive reforms designed to integrate the many discrete forms of charitable assistance that they had inherited from past centuries into something resembling a unified, rational system under the supervision of the urban magistrates. Within the Holy Roman Empire, the framework for these municipal reforms was established by the Augsburg *Reichsabschied* issued by Emperor Charles V (1530), which also provided the impetus for the codification of public responsibility for poor relief by the nascent territorial states in the sixteenth and seventeenth centuries. Outside the empire poor relief was first made the object of nationwide regulation in the Netherlands (1531), France (1534), England (1531/6), Scotland (1535/79), and Spain (1540).[1]

The Desacralization of Poverty and the New Discourse on Vagrancy

The theory and practice of charity that had developed since the high Middle Ages provided the frame of reference for the sixteenth-century reforms.[2] In the earlier Middle Ages, poverty had been defined less in terms of material destitution than of the dependence on other, more powerful persons for protection. However, the founding of the mendicant orders in the thirteenth century as a reaction to the new wealth and worldliness resulting from the commercial revolution shifted the concept's center of gravity, and henceforth voluntary poverty was idealized as a means of spiritual perfection, even though real, involuntary poverty continued to be regarded as something ugly, base, and ignoble. Thomist social doctrine regarded property as the common patrimony of mankind that had been entrusted to the stewardship of the rich, though only on the condition that any wealth beyond that required for these persons to discharge the obligations of their social station be used for the benefit of the poor. In this schema, the poor played a pivotal, yet passive, role in the economy

---

[1] For the German cities, Robert Jütte, *Obrigkeitliche Armenfürsorge in deutschen Reichsstädten der frühen Neuzeit* (Böhlau, 1984), 44; for the other European cities and states, Catharina Lis and Hugo Soly, *Poverty and Capitalism in Pre-Industrial Europe* (Humanities Press, 1979), 87ff. Accounts of poor relief in the Germanies and Europe in the fifteenth and sixteenth centuries can be found in Robert Jütte, *Poverty and Deviance in Early Modern Europe* (Cambridge University Press, 1994); Jütte, "Poverty and Poor Relief," in Shcilagh Ogilvie, ed., *Germany. A New Social and Economic History* (Arnold, 1996), II: 377–404; Bronislaw Geremek, *Poverty. A History* (Blackwell, 1994); Christoph Sachße and Florian Tennstedt, *Geschichte der Armenfürsorge in Deutschland*, 3 vols. (Kohlhammer, 1980–92); and Hans Scherpner, *Theorie der Fürsorge* (Vandenhoeck & Ruprecht, 1962).

[2] On poverty and charity in the Middle Ages, see Michel Mollat, *The Poor in the Middle Ages*, tr. Arthur Goldhammer (Yale University Press, 1986); Miri Rubin, *Charity and Community in Medieval Cambridge* (Cambridge University Press, 1987); Volker Hunecke, "Überlegungen zur Geschichte der Armut im vorindustriellen Europa," *GuG* 9 (1983), 480–512; Scherpner, *Theorie der Fürsorge*, 23–43; Ernst Schubert, "Gestalt und Gestaltwandel des Almosens im Mittelalter," *Jahrbuch für fränkische Landesforschung* 52 (1992), 241–62; and Otto Gerhard Oexle, "Armut, Armutsbegriff und Armenfürsorge im Mittelalter," in Christoph Sachße und Florian Tennstedt, eds., *Soziale Sicherheit und soziale Disziplinierung* (Suhrkamp, 1986), 73–100.

of salvation, providing the object and opportunity for the spiritual perfection of the propertied through charitable good works that would help them accumulate a store of merit and justify themselves before God. On the other hand, the piety of the poor was manifested in their gratitude – in the form of prayer for the salvation of the donor – for the alms that they received and in their willing acceptance of "their subordinate position in the social hierarchy as a matter of divine determination.

The poor were a permanent feature in late medieval society. In the cities, fully half of the population belonged to the "potential poor." These were persons who lived from hand to mouth, who could accumulate no property or financial reserves, and who could keep their heads above water only as long as they remained healthy, found regular employment, and lived within a family structure that could shield them from those forms of poverty that are related to the life cycle (too many children, the death or other absence of a spouse, the sickness and infirmity of old age, etc.). However, only 5–10% of the population was considered to be "needy" and thus deserving of assistance.[3] In such a world, the biblical injunction that "the poor shall always be with you" (John 12:8) was a self-evident proposition. While the poor were to be helped in their momentary need, the idea of preventing need by combating its causes simply lay beyond the mental horizon of the time.

Nor was there any strong incentive to systematically distinguish those who were truly needy and deserving of assistance from the masses of poor persons appealing for alms. The reason is that there was an unresolved, and irresolvable, contradiction at the heart of the theory and practice of Christian charity. On the one hand, it is wrong to simply dismiss medieval charity as indiscriminate. Thomist social thought affirmed the obligation to support oneself through work as far as possible, and any self-respecting scholastic could easily cobble together a long list of quotations from the scriptures and the church fathers to the effect that charity should only be given to those who were worthy of assistance. However, although most theologians who concerned themselves with the problem agreed that inquiring into causes of need was injurious to the dignity of the supplicant and inconsistent with the spirit of charity, as long as need exceeded available resources there had to be some criteria for deciding who was most deserving of help.

On the other hand, the medieval theory of charity was essentially a theory of almsgiving that was rooted in a distinctly Catholic understanding of the cycle of sin, penance, and justification. In this schema, everything depended on the subjective intentions of the donor, whose actions would be considered as genuine

---

[3] Thomas Fischer, *Städtische Armut und Armenfürsorge im 15. und 16. Jahrhundert* (Schwartz, 1979), 40–58; Hunecke, "Überlegungen," especially 489; and Jütte, *Poverty and Deviance*, 45ff. Bronislaw Geremek, "Criminalité, vagabondate, paupérisme: la marginalité à l'aube des temps modernes," *Revue d'histoire moderne et contemporaine* 21 (September 1974), 337–75, suggests (374) that municipal authorities began to feel a sense of crisis when the proportion of the population dependent on charity and relief approached 10%.

works of charity if his or her intentions were pure, regardless of whether the beneficiary was deserving of this gift. Not only did this conception of charitable good works deprive Christian social thought of any rationale for systematically investigating the causes of poverty or the personal circumstances of the supplicant. The transcendent importance of charitable good works as a means of acquiring merit and securing salvation also meant that the church could not countenance unreasonable restrictions on the right to solicit or bestow alms. In practice, much medieval charity took the form of alms given directly from one person to another or distributed by religious houses, monasteries, foundations, hospitals, and individuals on Sundays, feast days, funerals, anniversaries, and other occasions as designated by the bequests that made this charity possible, while the poor themselves were constantly on the move across broader or narrower regions in search of sustenance.[4] Under such circumstances, there could be little question of inquiring into the character of the supplicant or the causes of his – or, as was more often the case, her – misfortune. Although the ability to tack between these two extremes gave Catholic polemicists and practitioners a degree of flexibility, after the Reformation it was difficult for Catholic apologists to get past the equation of salvation through works with indiscriminate, unregulated, and socially harmful charity. As a result, the doctrine of good works was to be both the strength and the weakness of Catholic charity.

The first ordinance to regulate begging anywhere within the Holy Roman Empire was issued in Nuremberg in 1370. The basic purpose of this ordinance, which undoubtedly codified a social reality and discursive shift that had evolved over the preceding decades, was to ensure that the city's charity benefited the deserving local poor. It was inspired not by any principled opposition to begging and traditional charity, but rather by a desire on the part of the magistrates to combat what might be called the abuse of such charity. The ordinance limited the right to beg in the city to persons who carried a special metal token or medallion issued by the city to those local poor whose need had been attested to by a number of upright citizens. Foreign beggars were to be expelled from the city after three days.[5]

---

[4] Following the Benedictine rule, monasteries provided "hospitality" to pilgrims, itinerant beggars, the sick, the elderly, and the local poor at their gates, while late medieval hospitals sheltered the aged and infirm, who either bought their own places through contributions to the hospital's endowment or were nominated for available openings by those persons or corporate groups that possessed patronage rights over these charitable institutions. Only in the nineteenth century did the term hospital come to denote exclusively an institution for the provision of medical treatment to the sick. For the social context and historical development of medieval hospitals, see Marie-Luise Windemuth, *Das Hospital als Träger der Armenfürsorge im Mittelalter* (Steiner, 1995); Siegfried Reicke, *Das deutsche Spital und sein Recht im Mittelalter* (Kirchenrechtliche Abhandlungen, 111/112), 2 vols. (Stuttgart, 1932); James Brodman, *Charity and Welfare: Hospitals and the Poor in Medieval Catalonia* (University of Pennsylvania Press, 1998); and Peter Johanek, ed., *Städtisches Gesundheits- und Fürsorgewesen vor 1800* (Böhlau, 2000).
[5] Willi Rüger, *Mittelalterliches Almosenwesen. Die Almosenordnungen der Reichsstadt Nürnberg* (Nürnberg, 1932). The Nuremberg ordinance is reprinted both in Rüger and, in modernized language, in Sachße and Tennstedt, *Geschichte der Armenfürsorge*, I: 63–4.

The Desacralization of Poverty and the New Discourse on Vagrancy

It is not until the second half of the 1400s that we see the first sustained attempts to channel, limit, and otherwise regulate begging. The impulse for these measures came from the growing skepticism as to whether most beggars, and especially the itinerant poor, could be considered legitimate, deserving objects of Christian charity. Although poverty may have been pervasive in the Middle Ages, as long as the basic structures of medieval society remained intact, there was no perceived contradiction between the religious obligation to perform charitable good works, the expectations of the poor, the rituals through which they sought relief, and available aid. However, the social groups that were the object of growing suspicion in the 1400s, and then the object of surveillance and discipline in the 1500s, were the products of what has long been referred to as "the transition from feudalism to capitalism," that is, the loosening of the constraints on personal liberty that had previously bound the peasantry to the soil and the spread of markets and capitalist social relations to the countryside, with all the disruptions that followed in their wake. It was this mobility – simultaneously social and geographical – that led contemporaries to brand those persons who no longer fit into established patterns of social life as "masterless men." These sturdy beggars were increasingly regarded as a quasi-criminal element because their quest for alms depended on dissimulation and defrauding the public out of charity that was the rightful inheritance of the deserving poor. Such crimes offended against both religion and social order, and it was this latter quality that brought begging within the purview of secular authorities.[6]

The 1478 Nuremberg begging ordinance became a model for similar legislation in other German cities. Like its predecessor, this ordinance was not intended as an attack on begging and almsgiving, but as an attempt to ensure that charity served its proper end. As the ordinance explained,

it has been reported often and expressly, extensively and in a credible manner, to the honorable [city] council that a substantial number of beggars of both sexes have been engaging in behavior that is ungodly, unseemly, and improper. In addition, scores come here to Nuremberg, demand our charity, and accept it, even though they do not need it. Because giving alms is an especially praiseworthy, meritorious and virtuous deed and a good work, and because those who accept such alms illicitly or without need thereof make themselves guilty of a grave and manifest act, our councilors have – for the glory of God, but also out of necessity – undertaken to prevent such dishonesty and the danger of deception in order to insure that the poor and needy do not have their charitable subsistence alienated and withdrawn from them.

The 1478 ordinance was also more specific than its predecessor. It added detailed provisions specifying when, where, and how the deserving poor could beg. Moreover, since the city had in the meantime grown so large, citizens could

---

[6] Geremek, "Criminalité, vagabondate, paupérisme"; Schubert, *Fahrendes Volk im Mittelalter* (Verlag für Regionalgeschichte, 1995), 350ff.; and Schubert, "Mobilität ohne Chance: Die Ausgrenzung des fahrenden Volkes," in Winfried Schulze, ed., *Ständische Gesellschaft und soziale Mobilität* (Oldenbourg, 1988), 113–64.

no longer be expected to have personal knowledge of the supplicant, and the ordinance required that permission to beg be predicated on the investigation of the character and circumstances of these persons by specially designated municipal employees. The ordinance also foreshadowed new attitudes toward work, poverty, and charity. Healthy, able-bodied persons were warned that they should no longer "sit lazily in front of the churches begging on workdays, but rather should spin or perform other work that they are capable of doing." This nascent concern for the prevention of poverty was also reflected in the provision that the children of beggars should not be allowed to beg but should, instead, be taught a useful occupation so that they might support themselves in the future.[7]

These more jaded attitudes toward the able-bodied poor were translated into increasingly harsh repressive measures. In addition to being expelled and banished, vagrants could be put in the stocks, whipped, branded, made to perform dishonorable public work, and sent to the galleys. At the end of the 1400s, this administrative construction of the asocial, presumptively criminal vagrant was reinforced by the emergence of a new genre of literature devoted to unmasking the ruses of the sturdy poor and cataloging their vices. The most important of these was the anonymous *Liber vagatorum*, or *The Book of Vagabonds and Beggars* (ca. 1510). This book, which was later republished with an introduction by Luther, might with a little exaggeration be said to represent the first modern poor relief manual.[8]

Work and the Reorganization of Public Assistance

The invention of vagrancy across the 1400s marked the crystallization of the early modern social question, a question that begged for both a cultural-discursive answer and a political-administrative one. The wave of reforms that began in the early 1520s was in part a continuation of the measures that had been implemented since the mid-1400s to repress fraudulent begging by the able-bodied poor. However, it was at this point that the regulation of begging ceased to be an end in itself, and the antibegging measures pioneered in previous decades were integrated into a broader reform program. During these decades, work – the ability to work, the willingness to work, the availability of work, and the gendered expectations regarding the proper roles of men and women in work and family – provided the primary criterion for distinguishing between the deserving poor, who could not support themselves (or who could

---

[7] Reprinted in Sachße and Tennstedt, *Geschichte der Armenfürsorge*, I: 64–6.
[8] *Liber vagatorum. The Book of Vagabonds and Beggars, with a vocabulary of their language and a preface by Martin Luther*... (London, 1932). Beggars and the various mechanisms (tokens or letters) for verifying the authenticity of a person's need are one of the key themes of Valentin Groebner, *Who Are You? Identification, Deception, and Surveillance in Early Modern Europe* (Zone Books, 2007).

only partially do so), and the undeserving poor. The elevation of the (in)ability to work into the organizing principle of the new poor relief also provided the rationale for a more systematic war on begging by the able bodied, which was to be combated as harmful to both these persons and the greater community.

It was the combined classificatory and coercive effect of the new discourses on the moral value of work and the assistantial practices they engendered that produced both the disciplined, honorable, and deserving object of public charity and its Other, the asocial, quasi-criminal, and clearly undeserving vagrant. Once the focus had been shifted from the salvation of the donor to the neediness of the poor and the best method for assisting them, charity became the object of a process of rationalization, bureaucratization, and professionalization described by Max Weber and, later, Michel Foucault. Although assistance to the deserving poor might have been costly and inadequate, it did not call into question the beliefs that held a society together. However, the generative contradiction underlying these policies was the inability to grasp the extent to which itinerancy and begging represented not simply a form of immorality and asociality, but a reasoned response to the inability of these persons to find a stable position in society.[9] As a result, the history of modern poor relief can, to a large degree, be written as the history of discourses on work, family, and community and of the successive attempts to devise an administrative apparatus for effectively policing a constitutive distinction between the deserving and the undeserving poor that coincided only in part with underlying socioeconomic realities.

Whether or not a person was considered deserving of support depended on whether his or her lifestyle reflected the norms of the community. Conformity to religious doctrine and deference to authority were important criteria here, while drink, fornication, and other offenses could disqualify a person, and the threat to refuse or revoke assistance to anyone who violated these norms in a persistent or egregious manner undoubtedly had a powerful disciplinary effect on the poor. However, the most important factor in determining whether persons merited assistance was their demonstrated attitude toward work.[10] It was important that persons petitioning for assistance be able to point to either a history of gainful employment to support their requests or to recognized causes of infirmity; those persons who were known for a life of dissipation could hardly expect that their requests would be looked on favorably; and magistrates regarded it as their prerogative, if not their duty, to correct those whose morals were found wanting.

---

[9] Robert Castel, *From Manual Workers to Wage Laborers. Transformation of the Social Question*, trans. Richard Boyd (Transaction Publishers, 2003), 3–5, 74–5, 79–80.
[10] Castel, *From Manual Workers to Wage Laborers*, sees the stability of employment as the hinge on which social inclusion and social marginalization and anomie pivot: "The 'social question' is a fundamental aporia through which a society experiences the enigma of its own cohesion and tries to forestall the dangers of its disintegration" (xix–xx).

This pan-European reform wave and the discursive shift that it reflected have been explained in a number of ways. The older literature was long dominated by confessional polemics. Protestant writers argued that these reforms, which were in many cases introduced as part of a broader reformation of religious practice, represented the institutional expression of Lutheran piety. They claimed that it was the Lutheran doctrine of salvation by faith alone that first made it possible to discriminate between the deserving and the undeserving poor in a way that "indiscriminate" Catholic charity simply could not. Catholic apologists, on the other hand, defended both the theological validity and the social value of good works, denied the ostensibly indiscriminate character of Catholic charity, championed the mendicant orders, and charged that the waning of the charitable spirit in Protestant lands and the rise of the modern social question more generally was irrefutable proof of the moral bankruptcy of Protestantism – a failure whose most tangible expression was, they claimed, the institution of statutory poor relief and poor rates.[11]

In contrast, modern social historians have interpreted these reforms as a response to demographic, socioeconomic, and constitutional developments. The deep substructure of much of this work was provided by Wilhelm Abel, who argued that changes in the scope of poverty from the later Middle Ages through the early 1800s could be explained in terms of long-term trends in population, wages, and grain prices.[12] Although Abel himself did not directly address the reform of poor relief, his work implied that the reforms of the fifteenth and sixteenth centuries could best be understood as a response to the expansion of poverty and the accompanying problems of disease and social disorder. Others, however, have insisted that these trends are not independent explanatory variables, but rather must themselves be understood in relation to broader changes in the social relations of production, that is, the crisis of feudalism and the impact of capitalism on both cities and the countryside.[13] This move away from strictly confessional explanations was reinforced by the work of both Natalie Zemon Davis and Brian Pullan. Davis admitted in her influential study of the reform of poor relief in Lyon in the 1520s that the reform of poor relief in that city did represent a response by the urban magistracy to such factors as rising poverty, the threat of social disorder, crime, disease, and recurrent disasters, but she insisted that the specific features of reformed poor relief were determined more by humanist political culture and

---

[11] The classic confessional histories of charity and poor relief in Germany are Gerhard Uhlhorn, *Die christliche Liebestätigkeit*, 2. Aufl. (Stuttgart, 1895); and Georg Ratzinger, *Geschichte der kirchlichen Armenpflege* (Freiburg, 1868, rev. ed. 1884).
[12] Abel, *Agricultural Fluctuations in Europe from the Thirteenth to the Twentieth Centuries* (St. Martin's, 1980); and *Massenarmut und Hungerkrisen im vorindustriellen Deutschland* (Vandenhoeck & Ruprecht, 1972).
[13] Geremek, *Poverty*; Fischer, *Städtische Armut*; Hunecke, "Überlegungen"; and Lis and Soly, *Poverty and Capitalism in Pre-Industrial Europe*, who argue that early modern social policy "was brought into being with two dominant functions: control of the relatively superfluous population and regulation of the labor market" (220).

Work and the Reorganization of Public Assistance

the economic values of the mercantile classes than by Protestantism per se. For his part, Pullan emphasized the modernity and rationality of Catholic charity while showing how these practices grew out of and sustained new forms of Counter-Reformation piety.[14] But the broad reorganization of poor relief in the 1500s has also been seen from a different perspective not as the result of socioeconomic change, but rather as one consequence of the consolidation of sovereignty in the hands of municipal authorities at the end of the Middle Ages.[15]

It seems clear that demographic and economic factors must have in some way provided the impetus or occasion for the early sixteenth-century reforms. Aside from the unceasing flow of the landless poor from the countryside to the towns in search of both employment and the charitable resources to be found there, the new urban poor of the sixteenth century were being created through processes endogenous to the cities themselves. Although the putting-out system did provide employment to many of those forced off the land, it also weakened the foundations of the guild economy and led to the impoverishment of urban workers – masters, journeymen, and wage laborers alike. The disruptive impact of population growth and the spread of capitalism in the cities was also magnified by the great inflation of the sixteenth century, resulting from the influx of colonial silver into the European economy. As a result, real wages of urban workers fell precipitously across the sixteenth century, declining by 30–50% in the German cities as increases in grain prices far outstripped the rise in nominal wages, and this poverty was often concentrated among unskilled wage laborers in the textile and building industries and in the dishonorable occupations.[16]

The origins of the new attitude toward work that underlay these reforms can be traced in different ways to Lutheranism and humanism. Luther rejected the Catholic belief that the path to spiritual perfection lay in the contemplative life, arguing instead that the fall from grace had imposed on all people the obligation to earn their bread by the sweat of their brows, and he regarded the assiduous fulfillment of the duties associated with the individual's position in civic and social life – what he called their vocation – as both the fulfillment of this most basic obligation to God and the most fundamental way of being just, useful, and charitable to one's fellow man. However, Luther also saw man as a fundamentally weak and sinful creature, and the energy and conscientiousness

---

[14] Davis, "Poor Relief, Humanism, and Heresy," in her *Society and Culture in Early Modern France* (Stanford University Press, 1975), 17–64; Pullan, *Rich and Poor in Renaissance Venice: The Social Institutions of a Catholic State to 1620* (Harvard University Press, 1971); and Pullan, "Catholics and the Poor in Early Modern Europe," *Transactions of the Royal Historical Society* 26 (1976), 15–34.

[15] Ingomar Bog, "Über Arme und Armenfürsorge in Oberdeutschland und in der Eidgenossenschaft im 15. und 16. Jahrhundert," *Jahrbuch für fränkische Landesforschung* 34/35 (1974/75), 983–1001. This argument has been reinforced by the recent wave of research on early modern *Polizei*.

[16] Geremek, *Poverty*, 73–141; Jütte, *Poverty and Deviance*, 21–61; and Lis and Soly, *Poverty and Capitalism in Pre-Industrial Europe*.

with which the individual labored to discharge these obligations represented not a means of achieving, or a sign of, spiritual perfection, as it later was for the Calvinists, but rather a means of mortifying the flesh that enabled the individual to submit more fully to God. The correlate of this work obligation was an equally universal condemnation of begging, and this imperative was reinforced by the fear that idleness and any interruption in the ceaseless struggle between the will and the flesh would deliver individuals over to all their innate sinful urges.

Work also played a central role in humanist thinking on poverty and poor relief, and Juan Luis Vives's *On Assistance to the Poor* (1526) was the classic statement of humanist ideas on the reform of poor relief.[17] Like Luther, Vives believed that all men had the obligation to labor for their bread, and he, too, called for a general prohibition of begging. The most important difference between the two is that, while Luther insisted that man was permanently subjected to the tyranny of original sin, Vives argued in a manner both Catholic and humanist that individuals could through their own labors contribute to their spiritual perfection. The theoretical cornerstone of his proposals for the reform of poor relief was the belief that poverty could be prevented and the social problems of idleness, vagrancy, and vice solved by properly educating the young (and reeducating the wayward) in religious, social, and civic virtues. Able-bodied vagrants were to be returned to their own countries; the local poor were to be taught a trade if they had not learned one; and pauper children were to be sent to a public school to learn letters and morals. This pedagogical obligation, like the general supervision of morals and manners, was one of the chief obligations of a Christian magistrate, and Vives considered it "much more important for magistrates to work on ways of producing good citizens than on punishing and restraining evil-doers. How much less need there would be of punishment if these matters were attended to in the first place!"[18] While Vives's specific proposals for the reorganization of municipal relief contained little that was new, the influence of his work derived from their subordination to this broader pedagogical program. It was this program that distinguished humanist thinking on the social question from that of the Lutherans, and it was, as we shall see in the next chapter, to be of great influence in the development of the house of correction.

There was no single model for the reform of poor relief and charity in either Protestant or Catholic regions. Although a reform in one city might have influenced reforms elsewhere, local circumstances are so important that

---

[17] Vives, *On Assistance to the Poor* (*De subventione pauperum*), tr. Alice Tobriner (University of Toronto Press, 1999). Hans Scherpner, *Theorie der Fürsorge* (Vandenhoeck & Ruprecht, 1962), 66–109; and Wilhelm Traphagen, *Die ersten Arbeitshäuser und ihre pädagogische Funktion* (Berlin, 1935), 24ff., both provide important interpretations of Vives's work, while Paul Bonenfant, "Les origins et le caractère de la réform de la bienfaisance publique aux Pay-Bas sous le règne de Charls-Quint," *Annales de la Société Belge d'Histoire des Hôpitaux* 2 (1965), 115–47, situates Vives's proposals in relation to the reform of relief in the Netherlands.

[18] Vives, *On Assistance to the Poor*, 36–7.

no one city can be said to be representative of others. Not every Lutheran city that reformed its poor relief impropriated endowments or other church properties and incomes and consolidated them in a common chest, though this was long taken to be the distinguishing feature of Lutheran charity. On the other hand, some Catholic cities ultimately attempted to prohibit begging, despite the apparent inconsistency of this step with Catholic doctrine. Moreover, not only was there a broad spectrum of opinion within each camp; reform was not a once-and-for-all action, but a process that aimed at a constantly shifting target. And even if a city arrived at a clearly defined system for assisting the deserving poor and combating vagrancy, there was no assurance that such a policy would ever be successfully enforced, much less enforced over a sustained period of time, or that the magistrates would not be forced to retreat from this position because of local opposition or the force of events. Logical issues notwithstanding, the only general statement that can be made concerning the reform of poor relief in the sixteenth century is that no generalization holds without qualification or exception.

The framework for the reform of poor relief within the Holy Roman Empire was established by the Reich police ordinances, whose relevant provisions were repeated without major modification across the sixteenth century. The 1497 ordinance, which reflected the social policies of the increasingly self-conscious urban magistracies as much as it authorized them, attempted to regulate begging along the lines marked out in Nuremberg, rather than to ban it. Only the infirm were to be permitted to beg. The children of beggars were to be taken from their parents and either taught a trade or placed in service in order to break the cycle of poverty. The 1530 ordinance codified the central principle that each community should be responsible for assisting its own poor, with the poor permitted to beg in other places only if their own town had more poor than it could care for, and in the following decades most every Reich territory issued laws putting these imperial regulations into practice in their domains.[19]

This attempt to devise a territorial solution to the problems of poverty and vagrancy helped codify the boundaries of existing communities and made membership therein – along with the ability to work and conformity to community morality, as discussed earlier – into the second basic criterion for determining eligibility for assistance.[20] But this mechanism of inclusion also served as a mechanism of exclusion as cities began to rely on settlement restrictions and

---

[19] Elisabeth Schepers, *Als der Bettel in Bayern abgeschafft werden sollte. Staatliche Armenfürsorge in Bayern im 16. und 17. Jahrhundert* (F. Pustet, 2000), 60ff.; and Friedrich Battenberg, "Obrigkeitliche Sozialpolitik und Gesetzgebung. Einige Gedanken zu mittelrheinischen Bettel- und Almosenordnungen des 16. Jahrhunderts," *Zeitschrift für historische Forschung* 18 (1991), 33–70. The relevant sections of the 1530 Reichsabschied (Kap. 34, §§1–2) are reprinted in Theodor Strohm and Michael Klein, eds., *Die Entstehung einer sozialen Ordnung Europas*, Bd. 2 (Universitätsverlag Winter, 2004), 154–8, which conveniently reprints many of the most influential municipal and territorial poor laws from the sixteenth century.

[20] Castel, from Manual Workers to Wage Laborers, Chapter 2.

residence requirements to limit the costs of poor relief,[21] and the generalized pursuit of a beggar-thy-neighbor policy – in the very literal sense – also forced many of the itinerant poor into a state of permanent marginality. These persons were then harassed from place to place in a sort of Brownian motion by local officials who, in the absence of a territorial mechanism capable of providing a collective good, relied on increasingly harsh, but ultimately ineffective, repressive measures to solve their local problems.

The centralization of existing charitable institutions – if not directly in the hands of municipal authorities, then at least under their indirect supervision – was the most basic precondition for rationalizing assistance to the poor. While hospitals had increasingly been coming under magisterial control since the 1300s (though without necessarily losing their religious character), most endowed foundations made no pretense of determining whether supplicants were deserving of assistance, and their distribution of the designated kinds of assistance (cash, various kinds of food and drink, articles of clothing, etc.) on holidays or other specified occasions hardly lent itself to the systematic support of the deserving poor. Centralization often entailed the creation of a specialized charity office (*Almosenamt*) or some other administrative authority – the most famous of these being the Lutheran common chest – to provide greater control over available resources and expenses. These important municipal offices were administered by prominent citizens (variously known as *Armenpfleger*, *Provisoren*, or *Kastenherren*) who were subject to the general authority of the magistrates. Bureaucratization also involved the establishment of written rules for organizing and administering relief, the creation of a clear hierarchy of offices, the adoption of uniform procedures, and the employment of a growing number of persons to perform all the distinct tasks required by this rationalizing project. And in many cities the reform of poor relief also led to efforts to centralize alms collection as well. Here, the poor (or a representative section thereof) would be paraded through the city on one or more days of the week and on holidays by citizens or municipal employees, who would be responsible for collecting the alms and then disbursing the proceeds to the deserving poor. Sometimes these *Bettelzüge* would be accompanied by city councilors as well in order to emphasize the solemnity of such charity and its importance to the civic community.

Obviously, the "poor" did not represent an undifferentiated mass whose individual members were treated in an identical manner. Men and women were treated differently, with varying forms of institutional and outdoor relief being offered according to a variety of factors, including age, health, marital status, family size and structure, reputation, work history, and social status, and there were foundling homes and apprenticeships for needy boys, while needy or orphaned girls could be placed in service. But the important thing here is that, no matter what the specific circumstances of a needy individual, the

---

[21] Fischer, *Städtische Armut*; and Parker, *The Reformation of Community*, 75ff.

rationalization of assistance required the development and application of a uniform definition of need and, at a minimum, rules of thumb prescribing the kind and amount of assistance that were to be offered in specific situations.

The most basic task here was to determine who was to be considered deserving of assistance. The 1370 Nuremberg ordinance had not bothered to define need because it was assumed that the upright citizens who were to support any application for a begging license would recognize need when they saw it, and the 1530 Reich Police Ordinance simply spoke of infirmity. The 1523 Leisnig poor relief ordinance, which was drawn up with Luther's direct involvement, excluded "nonresident, fictitious poor and idlers who are not really in need" and approved assistance to "those individuals in our parish and assembly who are impoverished by force of circumstance and left without assistance by their relatives... and those who are unable to work because of illness or old age and are so poor as to suffer real need." Such descriptions of the poor, both deserving and undeserving, tended to become more detailed and more restrictive as the century progressed, with fiscal pressures most often providing the stimulus for such definitional tightening. The Leisnig ordinance is interesting not because of its uniqueness, but because of its typicality, its assumption that public charity was subsidiary to both self-help and the mutual obligations among family members, and its limitation of charitable obligations to members of "our parish."[22]

The provisions for apprenticing or otherwise educating beggar children also reflected a new concern with preventing poverty. In fact, apprenticing out a child was often a backdoor way of assisting parents, whose household costs would thereby be diminished. Conversely, the offer of apprenticeship or other assistance could be predicated on improved conduct on the part of the parent and/or their consent to such an apprenticeship or other employment (which would place the child in a positive environment and prevent the parents from sending him or her out to beg). Such was the nature of social discipline and social assistance in everyday practice.[23]

The rationalization of charity on the basis of the work principle required a census of the city's poor in order to assay the relationship between needs and resources. But it also depended on the detailed, individualized inquiry into the character and circumstances of all applicants for assistance. But since family circumstances were constantly changing, a one-time inquiry was not by itself sufficient to establish need, and weekly or biweekly visits by relief officials to

---

[22] "Ordinance of a Common Chest," in Theodore Tappert, ed., *Selected Writings of Martin Luther, 1520–1523* (Fortress Press, 1967), 335–70, citations 361, 365. On the connection between sickness and poverty in early modern Europe, see Ole Peter Grell and Andrew Cunningham, eds., *Health Care and Poor Relief in Protestant Europe, 1500–1700* (Routledge, 1997); Grell, ed., *Health Care and Poor Relief in Counter-Reformation Europe* (Routledge, 1999); and Annemarie Kinzelbach, *Gesundbleiben, Krankwerden, Armsein in der frühneuzeitlichen Gesellschaft* (Steiner, 1995).

[23] Timothy Fehler, *Poor Relief and Protestantism. The Evolution of Social Welfare in Sixteenth-Century Emden* (Ashgate, 1999), 91–3, 169–70, 266–7.

distribute assistance to the residential poor (*Hausarmen*) also contributed to the more systematic, continuous surveillance of the poor. Everywhere, bailiffs (*Bettelknechte* or *-vögte*) were hired to enforce local laws concerning street begging, keep foreign beggars out of the city, and apprehend, appropriately punish, and expel those vagrants who managed to pass through the city gates. On the other hand, though, it should not be forgotten that the ultimate purpose of these measures was to ensure more adequate support for the deserving members of the community.

Confessional Differences and the Role of Religion in the New Poor Relief

Although the impetus for the rationalization and modernization of charity may well have come from the forces identified by the new social history, the impact of these socioeconomic changes was always mediated through religious beliefs, and the reform of poor relief took place in a set of increasingly distinct religious milieux whose beliefs positively influenced the local understanding of the aims of assistance and the strategies that could be deployed in support thereof.[24] It should, therefore, come as no surprise that scholars have again begun to inquire into the role of religion and confessional differences in the reform of poor relief.[25] But while the differing views on human nature and salvation espoused by the three major Christian confessions represent one obvious point of reference, we also need to focus on their respective understanding of both the relation between church and state and the role of relief in the maintenance of church discipline and communal solidarity.

In Lutheran areas, the reform of poor relief was more rapid and more radical because it was central to the broader Reformation of worship and religious governance.[26] Not only did the Reformation remove political and ecclesiastical obstacles to such measures; it also gave them a religious significance that distinguished the rationalization of assistance in Protestant areas from that undertaken in Catholic regions. For Lutheran reformers, the centralization of local charity under magisterial control represented a calculated attack on the

---

[24] Parker, *The Reformation of Community*, 12.
[25] Grell, "The Protestant Imperative of Christian Care and Neighbourly Love," in Grell and Cunningham, eds., *Health Care and Poor Relief*, 43–65; Philip Gorski, *The Disciplinary Revolution. Calvinism and the Rise of the State in Early Modern Europe* (University of Chicago Press, 2003); Sigrun Kahl, "The Religious Roots of Modern Poverty Policy: Catholic, Lutheran, and Reformed Protestant Traditions Compared," *European Journal of Sociology/Archives Européennes de Sociologie* 46:1 (2005), 89–124; and Philip Manow, "'The Good, the Bad, and the Ugly'. Esping-Andersens Sozialstaats-Typologie und die konfessionellen Wurzeln des westlichen Wohlfarhtsstaats," *Kölner Zeitschrift für Soziologie und Sozialpsychologie* 54:2 (2002), 203–25.
[26] Lutheran ideas on the organization of poor relief can be approached through Grell, "The Protestant Imperative"; Carter Lindberg, "'There Should Be No Beggars among Christians': Karlstadt, Luther, and the Origins of Protestant Poor Relief," *Church History* 46:3 (1977), 313–34; and Harold Grimm, "Luther's Contributions to Sixteenth-Century Organization of Poor Relief," *Archiv für Reformationsgeschichte* 61 (1970), 222–33.

Catholic doctrine of good works and the entire Catholic theory of justification. However, as we have already seen, Luther shared in the ecumenical belief in the presumed fraudulence of most begging, and his call for the complete prohibition of begging was the obverse of his belief that all men were condemned to labor for their daily bread.

But any plan to abolish begging had to ensure that the legitimate needs of the deserving poor were met, and Luther's own proposals – like those of Vives – were based on the optimistic expectation that the more careful management of revenues from endowments and regular donations by the congregation, combined with the more rigorous policing of begging by the undeserving, would together be sufficient to fund the community's charitable obligations toward its deserving poor. But the real question was not so much funding as the organization of assistance itself and, more specifically, whether the church or municipal authorities were to bear primary responsibility for assisting the poor. For the Lutherans, it was faith that made people just, not charitable good works, and charity toward one's neighbor was seen as the natural expression of gratitude to God for the grace he had so gratuitously bestowed. As such, it was a personal obligation owed by all members of the religious community. However, despite the religious value ascribed to personal charity, from the very beginning Lutherans viewed the organization of poor relief primarily as a matter for municipal authorities. This did not, however, mean that the Lutherans wanted to secularize poor relief. Both princes and urban authorities were regarded as Christian magistrates, who were responsible for both the spiritual and worldly well-being of their subjects, and the decision to delegate responsibility for this communal obligation to the magistrates was simply a matter of expediency. In Leisnig, for example, the laymen elected by the congregation as trustees of the common chest were also the persons responsible for distributing assistance to the parish poor.

This decision, though, was not without consequences. Although this Lutheran model appeared to assume that personal charity would sustain this magisterial assistance both morally and financially, this balance broke down once the initial enthusiasm for religious reform subsided and once the true magnitude of the task became evident. In addition, the Lutheran emphasis on both the gratuitousness of grace and the adiaphorous nature of social institutions combined with the desire of the territorial rulers to expand their direct authority over the social lives of their citizens to ensure that in Lutheran territories control over, and responsibility for, poor relief would steadily devolve onto public officials. Over the remainder of the early modern period, this initial modus vivendi between church and state would evolve into a more formal divorce that amounted to a de facto secularization of poor relief.

The organization of charity in Calvinist cities differed in several important respects from the Lutheran model. First, Calvin sought to abolish the Lutheran slippage between the personal religious motivation and the secular organization of charity by incorporating poor relief wholly into the church and elevating the diaconate – the church office responsible for assisting the needy – to the status of a formal church office in emulation of the institutions of the apostolic age. However, the actual organization and practice of Calvinist charity was shaped as much by political forces as by religious beliefs. On the one hand, the Calvinist movement was divided between those who wished to restrict communion (and poor relief) to those members of the "household of the faith," who met the rigorous moral and doctrinal standards laid down by the consistory (the college of pastors and lay elders who governed the Reformed church), and those who argued for the more "libertine" position, which maintained that communion and poor relief should be open to all members of the civic community. In those cities where the consistory prevailed in the struggle between church and state, the deacons were able to limit their assistance to members of the congregation and carry out their duties independent of magisterial supervision, though such a policy intentionally left space for the development of charity organizations by the other religious groups present in the city, a development that promoted both a degree of religious tolerance and the subsequent "pillarization" of welfare in the modern Netherlands. In those cities where the magistrates prevailed, the Calvinist churches were forced to collaborate with municipal poor relief in aiding all poor members of the local community, though in such cases they often attempted to privilege their own communicants in one way or another. However, even in cities such as Strassburg and Geneva, where the magistrates were friendly to the Reformed cause, it was difficult for the consistory to remain free of magisterial control. In the former city, Martin Bucer was unable to establish an independent diaconate because the magistrates already had authority over municipal poor relief, while in Geneva the magistrates still played an important, if publicly unacknowledged, role in church charity.[27]

There was also a second important difference between Lutheran and Calvinist charity. For the Calvinists, rigorous church discipline was the key to maintaining the purity of the Eucharistic community. In Lutheran areas, where the church was effectively incorporated into the state, and in those Calvinist regions where the consistory was not entirely independent of municipal or state authority, secular officials were always involved to some degree in church governance. However, the involvement of these officials in the disciplining of sinners meant that such discipline invariably assumed, at least in part, the character of a criminal punishment designed to exact retribution for past offenses and deter future ones. In contrast, in those areas where the consistory was able to govern the church without the involvement of secular officials, Calvinist church discipline had a very different character. Here, in its unalloyed form, the goal of church discipline was not to punish, but rather to effect a change of heart on the part of the wayward individual and persuade offenders to repent and make amends for their sins, thus opening the door to their reconciliation with, and eventual reentry into, the household of the faithful. Excommunication was a last step taken only in extremis, and this act of exclusion was not the primary function

---

[27] Parker, *The Reformation of Community*, 98ff.

of church discipline, but rather a recognition that such discipline had failed in its primary corrective and conciliatory function.[28]

This approach to church discipline obviously had important implications for the practice of poor relief in Calvinist cities. Calvinist deacons were constantly forced to decide whether the threat to withhold assistance or the offer of continued assistance would be the most effective way of encouraging these wayward members of the congregation to return to a more godly way of life. In practice, it seems that, despite the doctrinal harshness of ascetic Protestantism, the deacons and consistories of the Calvinist churches were reluctant to simply cut off assistance to church members who were under censure. No doubt they pursued such a policy because they recognized how material assistance could support their pastoral aims and because they feared that such a step would further weaken the ties binding these wayward congregants to the church. And where children or innocent spouses were involved, deacons were especially creative in seeking ways to assist the deserving poor without creating the appearance of rewarding the guilty.[29] This distinctly Calvinist approach to church discipline and poor relief is important to the larger narrative because it shows – in ways that the stronger version of the social discipline paradigm cannot – how such discipline, as a complex unity of pastoral solicitude and moral chastisement, could both integrate the poor into the community and exclude them from it.

Assistance to the poor was, almost by definition, more decentralized in Catholic cities, where monasteries, cathedrals, mendicant orders, confraternities, endowed masses, charitable foundations, parish relief, and personal charity survived relatively unscathed, than in cities that had followed the Lutheran path to a common chest.[30] Outdoor assistance to the resident poor was often organized around parochial "poor tables" (*Armenbretter*) or endowments that had been accumulated through bequests left to the respective parish churches, and religious brotherhoods were often responsible for distributing alms to the parish poor. However, this decentralization was offset in part by the authority of the magistrates, who enjoyed a general right to supervise the activity of these persons and institutions. More important, at the 1536 Council of Cologne, the

---

[28] Here I follow Heinz Schilling, "'History of Crime' or 'History of Sin'? – Some Reflections on the Social History of Early Modern Church Discipline," in E. I. Kouri and Tom Scott, eds., *Politics and Society in Reformation Europe* (St. Martin's Press, 1987), 289–310; and Schilling, "Reformierte Kirchenzucht als Sozialdisziplinierung? Die Tätigkeit des Emder Presbyteriums in den Jahren 1557–1562," in Wilfried Ehbrecht and Schilling, eds., *Niederlände und Nordwestdeutschland* (Böhlau, 1983), 261–327.

[29] Fehler, *Poor Relief and Protestantism*, 245ff.; and Parker, *The Reformation of Community*, 123ff.

[30] The following discussion draws on Jütte, *Poverty and Deviance*, 125ff.; Jütte, *Obrigkeitliche Armenfürsorge*, 218–330; Alwin Hanschmidt, "Armut und Bettelei, Armenpolizei und Armenfürsorge in der Stadt Münster im 17. Jahrhundert," in Franz-Josef Jakobi, et al., eds., *Strukturwandel der Armenfürsorge und Stiftungswirklichkeiten in Münster im Laufe der Jahrhunderte* (Aschendorff, 2002), 27–92; and Fischer, *Städtische Armut*.

German bishops – in an obvious reaction against the leading role ascribed to the magistracy in the reform of poor relief in Lutheran areas – affirmed that the care of the poor was a primary responsibility of the church, and episcopal influence over poor relief within the diocese was further strengthened by the Council of Trent.

Within Catholicism, there was a broad spectrum of opinion regarding the virtues of individualization and discrimination in the giving of alms, and it might be said that, although many Catholics shared modern ideas about the value of work, work did not displace good works as the organizing principle of Catholic assistance to the same degree as in Protestant territories.[31] Catholics also grappled with the problem of begging. Many Catholic cities employed the same strategies for rationalizing assistance and regulating begging that were discussed earlier. But Catholic efforts to eliminate begging were limited in several key respects. First, magistrates had only limited influence over alms that were distributed by religious institutions, which remained largely outside their authority and fiercely wedded to traditional forms of almsgiving and the rituals and forms of piety associated therewith. Second, canon lawyers insisted that municipal authorities could not "monopolize" charity; that is, they could not either require that all charity be routed to the poor through municipal hands or abridge the natural right to freely ask for alms outside the framework of municipal assistance in case of extreme need. But without a clear public commitment to meet the needs of the deserving poor and the resources to back up such a promise, these qualifications meant that most anyone could plausibly invoke the right to beg. Third, the exemption of a number of groups, including clergy, mendicants, pilgrims, and religious students, from restrictions on begging made it all the more difficult to enforce restrictions on others. And, fourth, there was often relatively little public support for antibegging measures because broad segments of the population continued to hold very traditional ideas on charity. Even when Catholic cities such as Münster went so far as to forbid begging, such efforts yielded little success, though they did show both the possibilities and the limitations of Catholic reform.

All these efforts to devise a comprehensive solution to the problems of poverty and vagrancy justifies us in speaking of a Catholic system of "poor relief," even if this system took the form of the supervision and coordination of the endowed charities, religious organizations, parish relief, hospitals, and the like, rather than a system of direct communal responsibility. The question, though, is what happened to Catholic poor relief once it began to come up against its theological and administrative limits, especially when it was forced to respond to the massive increase in poverty and need at the end of the 1500s? Did it simply decline into a state of disorder and ineffectiveness from which it would not emerge until the end of the 1800s? For some places, the answer

---

[31] For the spectrum of Catholic thinking here, see Pullan, "Catholics and the Poor in Early Modern Europe," especially 27–8.

Confessional Differences and the Role of Religion in the New Poor Relief 29

is an emphatic "yes."[32] However, we also need to look at the ways in which the Counter-Reformation and confessionalization drove the reform and modernization of Catholic charity.

Pullan has argued that at the end of the 1500s and in the first decades of the 1600s there were important innovations in Catholic relief in France and northern Italy that were closely linked to the Counter-Reformation.[33] The primary aim of this new charity, according to Pullan, was to save the souls of vagrants, endangered women, and all those unrespectable poor whose poverty and social marginality placed them in immediate danger of damnation. Here, material assistance was not an end in itself, but rather a means of influencing the beliefs and behavior of these outcasts, while service to the poor was itself understood as a means of mortifying the flesh. The primary agents of this new charity were new religious confraternities, which were founded as part of the Counter-Reformation renewal of Catholic piety, and religious orders such as the Jesuits and the Society of St. Vincent de Paul.

These new organizations insisted that they could only achieve their goal of reclaiming the souls of the fallen and the outcast by confining these persons in institutions such as Magdalene homes for fallen or endangered women and general hospitals, where they could be subjected to an all-encompassing ascetic regime modeled on monastic life. This new charity appears to have functioned as a mechanism for social disciplining and confessionalization in ways that more closely resemble the operation of church poor relief in Calvinist territories than the more traditional-looking Catholic attempts to regulate begging, and the internal regime of these seventeenth-century general hospitals bears an undeniable similarity to the German houses of correction, which have long been seen as a distinctly Protestant institution. It could well be that the Thirty Years' War retarded the development in the Germanies of the new and more modern forms of Counter-Reformation charity found in Italy and France. At a minimum, one can say that the systematic reform of poor relief was largely dependent on the confluence of Catholic religious renewal and absolutist state making, something that occurred later and less systematically, if at all, in the smaller states of southwestern Germany.[34]

In conclusion, we need to ask how successful were these sixteenth-century reforms? This is a difficult question that needs to be answered in four distinct ways. First, the many reforms introduced across the 1500s and their subsequent reforms and revisions betray a level of sustained attention by public officials at

---

[32] Konrad Dussel, "Katholisches Ethos statt Sozialdisziplinierung? Die Armenpolitik des Hochstifts Speyer im 18. Jahrhundert," *Zeitschrift für die Geschichte des Oberrheins* 143 (1995), 221–44.

[33] Pullan, "Catholics and the Poor in Early Modern Europe" and "Support and Redeem: Charity and Poor Relief in Italian Cities from the Fourteenth to the Seventeenth Century," *Continuity and Change* 3:2 (1988), 177–208.

[34] Marc R. Forster, *Catholic Renewal in the Age of the Baroque. Religious Identity in Southwest Germany, 1550–1750* (Cambridge University Press, 2001).

the municipal and territorial levels that could not have been without effect, at least in the short run, though one could also argue that the constant tinkering with poor relief ordinances and the repeated efforts to get a grip on begging show that this shift was not one of seismic proportions. There was clearly a change in mentality in Protestant areas and even among public officials in Catholic states, and whatever enduring improvements were made in assistance for the deserving poor were probably bought at the cost of the intensified marginalization of the itinerant poor.[35]

Second, not only did the institutions created by Protestant reformers not fully fill the gaps created by the dissolution of older Catholic charitable institutions. Nowhere did the sixteenth-century reforms succeed for a sustained period of time in either adequately supporting the deserving poor or effectively abolishing begging. The cities lacked the economic resources to achieve the former and the political and administrative capacity to achieve the latter. Even in Protestant areas, municipal officials were seldom willing to use tax revenue to compensate for the inadequate income flowing from the assets of the common chest. As a result, assistance was determined less by need than by available resources. In this situation, begging by the deserving poor regained some of the legitimacy that it had lost earlier in the century. However, once the door was opened to one group of beggars, other less deserving persons took advantage of this opportunity, and the entire war on vagrancy invariably collapsed.

Third, even if this had not been the case, it is unlikely that reformed poor relief could have survived the economic crises of the sixteenth century. Population increases and rising grain prices led to the steady impoverishment of the laboring classes; long-term trends in trade and commerce led to the deterioration of the economic position of many cities during the 1500s; and the real purchasing power of wage earners in urban and rural areas declined substantially during this period.[36] These trends were complicated by religious warfare and recurrent harvest failures. Thus, it is not so much that these reforms failed on their own terms as that not even the best organized poor relief system would have been able to offset the impact of economic and demographic trends of such magnitude.

Fourth, all these limitations and failures produced their own effects. To the extent that the moral right to relief was defined in terms of the (im)morality of the poor, the discourse on relief was permanently haunted by a blind spot: the inability to grasp the extent to which poverty was due to the inadequate wages and existential uncertainties of the laboring classes. This constitutive blindness doomed the modern assistantial project to a futile and contradictory logic that could only save the integrity of both the system and the community whose boundaries it defined by demonizing the poor and making them into the undeserving and incorrigible authors of their own misfortune. By the end

---

[35] Schubert, *Fahrendes Volk im Mittelalter*, 358ff.
[36] Jütte, "Poverty and Poor Relief," who takes his data on the decline in real wages from Abel, *Massenarmut*, 63.

of the century, at the very latest, it had become clear that, regardless of confession, the sixteenth-century reforms had failed to live up to their promise to abolish begging, or at least to abolish socially disruptive begging by the sturdy poor. When officials looked for an explanation, they tended to find it in the character of the undeserving poor, whose criminality and asociality had been confirmed – if not produced – by disciplinary poor relief. This interpretation of the limitations and failures of the sixteenth-century reforms would, in turn, influence the way the problem of vagrancy would be approached in coming years.

2

The Rise and Fall of the Workhouse
Poor Relief in the Age of Absolutism

Rethinking the Disciplinary Telos

The house of correction (*Zuchthaus*), or the workhouse (*Arbeitshaus*), as it is more commonly known, was the most important innovation in the organization of poor relief in the seventeenth and eighteenth centuries, and it was the cornerstone of public efforts to combat both poverty and vagrancy during these years.[1] Although the workhouse has gone down in the history of the poor laws as an institution for the exploitation, oppression, and degradation of the poor, it has in recent years become increasingly clear that the house of correction was originally envisioned as something very different.[2]

---

[1] The German word *Zucht* has a variety of related meanings, including discipline; punishment; chastisement, and correction; and cultivation in the sense of selective breeding to improve the quality of something. All these meanings were at play in the original houses of correction, which bore a variety of names, including workhouse, which reflects the centrality of work for this process of reeducation; *Besserungshaus*, or house of improvement; and *Spinnhaus* or, in the Netherlands, *raspbuis*, which refer to the main kinds of work performed in these institutions (i.e. spinning and the rasping of imported dyewoods).

[2] Over the past decade or so, a number of important studies have appeared that have collectively made possible a thorough reappraisal of the history of houses of correction in early modern Germany. These include Joel Harrington, "Escape from the Great Confinement: The Genealogy of a German Workhouse," *JMH*, 71 (June 1999), 308–45; Bernhard Stier, *Fürsorge und Disziplinierung im Zeitalter des Absolutismus. Das Pforzheimer Zucht- und Waisenhaus und die badische Sozialpolitik im 18. Jahrhundert* (Thorbecke, 1988); Dirk Brietzke, *Arbeitsdisziplin und Armut in der Frühen Neuzeit. Die Zucht- und Arbeitshäuser in den Hansestädten Bremen, Hamburg und Lübeck und die Durchsetzung bürgerlicher Arbeitsmoral im 17. und 18. Jahrhundert* (Verlag Verein für Hamburgische Geschichte, 2000); Ulrich Eisenbach, *Zuchthäuser, Armenanstalten und Waisenhäuser in Nassau. Fürsorgewesen und Arbeitserziehung vom 17. bis zum Beginn des 19. Jahrhunderts* (Historische Kommission für Nassau, 1994); Peter Spierenburg, *The Prison Experience. Disciplinary Institutions and their Inmates in Early Modern Europe* (Rutgers University Press, 1991); Norbert Finzsch, *Obrigkeit und Unterschichten. Zur Geschichte der rheinischen Unterschichten gegen Ende ds 18. und zu Beginn des 19. Jahrhunderts* (Franz Steiner, 1990); and Finzsch and Robert Jütte, eds., *Institutions of Confinement: Hospitals, Asylums, and Prisons in Western Europe & North America, 1500–1950* (Cambridge University

Rethinking the Disciplinary Telos

The first continental houses of correction were primarily founded as institutions of moral betterment and social reintegration, not as institutions of retribution.[3] They embodied a characteristically early modern form of paternalistic social governance in which Christian magistrates of all confessions regarded it as their right and duty to guide the private lives of their subjects in order to promote the spiritual and material well-being of both the individual and the community. This solicitude could assume many different forms, ranging from material assistance to the deserving via education, chastisement, and correction for the wayward all the way to the punishment and exclusion of the incorrigible. The threat of correction was always latent in the offer of assistance and education just as the most rigorous measures to repress and punish vice always contained within themselves, if only in a highly attenuated form, the promise of rehabilitation and social salvation. The originary coupling of conditional assistance and potential sanction could appear in an infinite number of gradations depending on context, and the institutions and programs that made up the "socio-corrective complex" – including poor houses, outdoor relief, orphanages, hospitals for the elderly and infirm, *Pesthäuser* for the isolation and care of persons suffering from contagious diseases, and insane asylums, as well as houses of correction – provided the magistrates with a broad spectrum of alternatives that they could draw on to provide the specific combination of assistance and discipline they believed to be most appropriate in any given case.[4]

A number of theories have been advanced to explain the origin and operation of the house of correction. Legal historians and penologists have argued that the house of correction represented the crucial institutional innovation that made it possible to substitute deprivation of freedom for capital and corporal punishment, a move that ultimately led to the birth of the modern penitentiary and the substitution of betterment for retribution as the primary purpose of confinement.[5] A second school has linked the genesis of the workhouse to the rise of manufacture capitalism by either emphasizing the role of the workhouse in accustoming the poor to the rhythms and forms of labor discipline associated with the new mode of production or portraying the workhouse as an institution

---

Press, 1996); as well as Hannes Stekl, *Österreichs Zucht- und Arbeitshäuser, 1671–1920. Institutionen zwischen Fürsorge und Strafvollzug* (Vienna, 1978); and Stekl, "'Labore et fame' – Sozialdisziplinierung in Zucht- und Arbeitshäusern des 17. und 18. Jahrhunderts," in Christoph Sachße and Florian Tennstedt, eds., *Soziale Sicherheit und soziale Disziplinierung* (Suhrkamp, 1986), 119–47.

[3] Harrington, "Escape from the Great Confinement" and Günther Lottes, "Disziplin und Emanzipation. Das Sozialdisziplinierungskonzept und die Interpretation der frühneuzeitlichen Geschichte," *Westfälische Forschungen* 42 (1992), 63–74.

[4] The notion of a socio-corrective complex is taken from Stier, *Fürsorge und Disziplinierung*, 15–32.

[5] The classic statement of this interpretation is Robert von Hippel, "Beiträge zur Geschichte der Freiheitsstrafe," *Zeitschrift für die gesamte Strafrechtswissenschaft* 18 (1898), 419–94, 608–66.

for the direct exploitation of unskilled labor.[6] The other major account of the workhouse comes from Michel Foucault. In *Madness & Civilization*, Foucault argued that, by the mid-1600s, idleness and sloth had supplanted leprosy as the most basic marker of otherness, and he portrayed the workhouse and the general hospital as the institutional cornerstones of a movement that he dubbed the "Great Confinement." The purpose of these institutions was to confine the idle and the deviant so as to better subject them to an all-encompassing, total regime of work and religious education that could end only when these persons had so completely internalized the value of work that the laws of the heart coincided without remainder with the laws of the state. It was at this point that – in theory, at least – the contradiction between education and discipline would be resolved and the use of disciplinary power justified.[7]

Although Foucault provides a masterful account of the political rationality of power within the workhouse and of the moral economy of confinement, he does not offer an explanation of the origin and end of this disciplinary process. Here, I would like to argue that the history of the workhouse was influenced in important ways by developments in penology and the rise of capitalism, but that neither of these theories alone provides an adequate account of the origins of the house of correction or its subsequent evolution into the repressive workhouse known to posterity. Rather, as we saw in Chapter 1, it was Calvinist theories of church discipline and the humanism of Juan Luis Vives that provided the decisive positive rationales for the use of public power to reeducate idlers, vagrants, the profligate, and the dissolute. This set their approaches to the treatment of the undeserving, able-bodied poor apart from that of the Lutherans, who eventually came to support the workhouse more for Cameralist reasons than out of a faith in the possibility of human betterment.

Since the great wave of sixteenth-century reforms embodied from the very beginning a complex mixture of assistance and discipline, we need to rethink the telos at work in those accounts that assume that the house of correction was from the very beginning primarily an institution of repression. The following sections will, therefore, focus instead on understanding how the rehabilitative aims of the house of correction were originally understood and then describe the combination of external and internal forces that, beginning in the second half of the 1600s, disrupted the balance between assistance and discipline in the early houses of correction and gradually transformed these rehabilitative institutions into the repressive workhouse. The concluding section

---

[6] For an overview of this literature, see Brietzke, *Arbeitsdiziplin und Armut*, 21–4 and Spierenburg, *The Prison Experience*, 123–34. Christoph Sachße and Florian Tennstedt portray the workhouse largely as a creature of mercantilism in *Geschichte der Armenfürsorge in Deutschland*, 3 vols. (Kohlhammer, 1980–92), I:113ff.

[7] Foucault, *Madness and Civilization* (Vintage, 1973), 38–64. Robert Jütte reads early modern poor relief through the lens of Foucault's *Discipline & Punish* (Vintage, 1979) in "Disziplinerungsmechanismen in der städtischen Armenfürsorge der Frühneuzeit," in Sachße/Tennstedt, eds., *Soziale Sicherheit und soziale Disziplinierung*, 101–18.

will analyze the impact of the Enlightenment on assistance to the poor in the Germanies.

The Formation of the Classical Workhouse

The first house of correction established in Europe was the London Bridewell, which opened in 1555, and it became the model for the workhouses established across the country in the latter part of the century. The first house of correction on the continent was established in Amsterdam in 1596 (with a separate house for women being opened in 1598). In contrast with the London Bridewell, which seems to have had little direct influence on developments on the other side of the channel, these Amsterdam institutions had a broad influence in both the Netherlands, where ten other cities had opened houses of correction by 1625, and the Germanies. The first houses of correction in the Germanies were established in the Hansa cities that enjoyed close commercial and social relations with Amsterdam, including Bremen (1608), Lübeck (1613), Hamburg (1622), and Danzig (1629), with the Kassel workhouse (1617) being something of an outlier. During these early years, houses of correction were also established in other European cities, including Copenhagen (1605), Bern (1614), Basel (1616), Lyon and Madrid (1622), and Stockholm and Brussels (1624). The Peace of Westphalia shifted the center of political gravity in the Germanies from the cities and the empire to the territorial states, which were concerned above all with repairing the damage wrought by three decades of warfare and developing the economic resources, bureaucratic infrastructure, and war-making capacity needed to make good on their new claims to sovereignty. While the first houses of correction had been established by the cities, the desire of the territorial states to use the workhouse as a means of simultaneously combating vagrancy and promoting economic development accelerated the spread of the institution. The first workhouses of the post-Westphalian era were not founded until the last third of the century, when institutions were established in a number of major German cities, including Breslau and Nuremberg (1670), Vienna (1671), Frankfurt (1679), Munich (1682), Spandau and Magdeburg (1687), and Berlin (1687, 1695/1702). By the end of the 1700s, approximately 110 workhouses had been established in the Germanies (excluding Austria).[8]

---

[8] These data are taken from Brietzke, *Arbeitsdisziplin und Armut*, 72ff.; Stier, *Fürsorge und Disziplinierung*, 218–22; and Helga Eichler, "Zucht- und Arbeitshäuser in den mittleren und östlichen Provinzen Brandenburg-Preussens," *Jahrbuch für Wirtschaftsgeschichte* (1970), 127–47. These totals are only approximations. Not all of these workhouses were in operation at any given moment; not all workhouses were necessarily coercive institutions; and subsequent research has identified some workhouses that are not included in these surveys. For the debates over the confinement of the poor that were taking place in France at this time, see Jean-Pierre Gutton, *La Société et les pauvres. L'Example de la généralité de Lyon 1534–1789* (Paris, 1971), 295ff.

The idea of confining the poor and putting them to work in order to impress on them the value of bourgeois virtues had already been formulated in the early 1500s. However, it was not possible to envision the widespread adoption of such an approach until the initial enthusiasm of religious reform had subsided and the limitations of the sixteenth-century reforms had become evident.

The reforms undertaken during the previous century had enjoyed only limited success because the cities could neither assist all the deserving poor, provide employment to all those who sought it, nor constrain the poor to comply with official definitions of deservingness. The policies adopted by the cities in the 1500s were bound to fail because simply declaring some of the local poor to be undeserving and thus ineligible for relief did not make these persons go away. The policy of banishing the foreign poor was no more effective. However, it was impossible to confine all the undeserving poor. No single city had the resources to do so, and, in any case, such a policy could not have been reconciled with the essentially local orientation of municipal social policy. Nor was there any central authority in the Germanies that could have directly undertaken such a policy on a territorial basis.[9]

The house of correction appeared to provide a way of squaring this circle, at least in part. The confinement and more effective policing of sturdy beggars and the undeserving poor offered the possibility of linking improved assistance to the deserving with the war on vagrancy in a more integral manner than before. But the houses of correction were not intended simply to warehouse the idle, but rather to remold their character, teach them to value work, discipline, and the other bourgeois virtues, and thus to abolish vagrancy *tout court* by attacking its inner, spiritual causes. This was the enabling myth of social happiness that Foucault espied at work in the Great Confinement. In this way the house of confinement became the keystone in the theoretical and organizational edifice of rationalized poor relief constructed since the 1520s, and the systematic prohibition of begging, which could not be enforced in any sustained manner in the 1500s, was finally introduced in the Hansa cities in conjunction with the establishment of the houses of correction.[10]

The original houses of correction were institutions of magisterial police, not criminal justice, and one indication of their social and rehabilitative function is the fact that they were often founded in part as an alternative to criminal punishment for rebellious apprentices and wayward children from upstanding citizen families.[11] In such cases, authorities were reluctant to impose criminal

---

[9] The later, 1662 decree of Louis XIV mandating the creation of a nationwide network of hôpitaux generales represented just such an attempt to escape from the contradictions of localism. Tim McHugh, *Hospital Politics in Seventeenth-Century France. The Crown, Urban Elites and the Poor* (Ashgate, 2007), 44–5. Abram de Swaan places the collectivizing process and the production of collective goods at the center of his account of the formation of the welfare state in *In Care of the State. Health Care, Education and Welfare in Europe and the USA in the Modern Era* (Oxford University Press, 1988).

[10] Brietzke, *Arbeitsdisziplin und Armut*, 106ff., 108ff., 149, 298ff., 320ff., 382f.

[11] See the case discussed in Spierenburg, *The Prison Experience*, 41ff.

sanctions because they felt that the character of these youths was still malleable and that they were capable of mending their ways. The house of correction provided a mechanism for chastising and correcting these youths without either lumping them together with older, confirmed criminals or imposing criminal penalties, whose defaming character would have prevented their eventual reintegration into society. Moreover, the primary occupants of the first institutions were not convicted offenders, whose presence would have undermined the honorable character of the institution in the eyes of the public, but rather local beggars and vagrants, whose sundry vices flowed from what contemporaries regarded as a fundamental aversion to work, discipline, and an orderly way of life.

Confinement and coerced labor in the house of correction could have a number of different meanings. In the sixteenth and seventeenth centuries, magistrates often sought to assist the deserving local poor by providing them with work, most often spinning. Sometimes this work would be performed by the poor in their own homes. At other times, these persons might work in a municipal spinning house (or similar institution) during the day and return to their homes at night. At yet other times, local beggars might be picked up by the bailiffs and given refuge and employment in the spinning house, or the spinning house might be used to keep a closer eye on those persons who could not be trusted to perform the work offered by the city.[12] And at the far end of the spectrum were the sturdy beggars, vagrants, and other dissolute and immoral persons for whom confinement and forced labor were conceived less as an offer of assistance than as a means of chastisement and punishment. This latter category included, in the words of the 1622 regulations of the Hamburg *Werk- and Zuchthaus*, "many sturdy, lazy, impertinent, desirous, godless, mischievous, disobedient, sottish drunkards, beer-bellies, both men and women, who grew up among vice, harlotry, theft, and every form of sin and shame and who diligently set themselves to begging every day at house doors and on the streets."[13] Here, the transition between outdoor assistance through work, the supervision of slackers, coerced corrective labor, and outright punishment was gradual and fluid, and the Janus-faced character of these institutions was reflected in the motto engraved over the door of the Hamburg house of correction: "Labore nutrior, labore plector," or "Through work I am nourished, and through work I am punished." The reintegrative intention of the house of correction was also evident in the fact that it was primarily – though the early houses were not entirely consistent in this matter – reserved for the local poor, whose wayward habits were to be corrected in an "honorable" manner, while

---

[12] On the connection between assistance through work and the workhouse, see Brietzke, *Arbeitsdisziplin und Armut*, 86–9, 111, 147; and Harrington, "Escape from the Great Confinement," 327, who argues that the former *Pesthaus*, where the local poor were housed and put to work, retained the connection between work and discipline, but that "it remained within a predominantly rehabilatory and supportive context."

[13] Cited in Brietzke, *Arbeitsdisziplin und Armut*, 146–7.

foreign vagrants were subjected to a variety of dishonorable punishments (such as street cleaning and heavy labor on fortifications) before being banished from the city.

In the middle decades of the seventeenth century, however, a number of forces came together to fundamentally alter the nature and function of the workhouse. First, the Thirty Years' War in the heart of the empire decimated the economy of the region and led to a 30% decline in the population. These economic problems were especially severe in the cities. Their economic position had already been weakened by the demographic and economic crises of the late 1500s even before the war disrupted their markets and led to their inundation by a seemingly endless flood of refugees whose homes, livelihoods, and communities had been destroyed by marauding armies. Reorganizing assistance to the poor was not a high priority during the war; the ruin of municipal finances brought a screeching halt to any reform plans whose goal was not an immediate reduction of relief costs; and, as a result, the middle decades of the seventeenth century are something of a blank spot in the history of the German poor laws.

Second, the war seems to have brought about a retreat from the paternalism of earlier years and a hardening of attitudes toward both the local and the foreign poor, whose poverty and homelessness were increasingly seen – all contemporary experience notwithstanding – as the product of vice and dissipation. Three factors contributed to this tendency to assimilate begging to sloth, sin, and crime. On the one hand, during the last years of the war beggars and soldiers had begun to coalesce into bands of semi-criminal *Gauner*, who wandered the countryside asking for alms, but who did so in an aggressive manner intended to make it clear that they were willing to take by force that which was not given to them voluntarily. These bands posed a major threat to public order and were a central concern of territorial authorities during these years. On the other hand, by the early 1600s both the propertied and the poor had begun to draw their own conclusions from the failure of the sixteenth-century reforms. Public officials increasingly adopted a more jaded attitude toward the itinerant poor as they came to blame the persistence of vagrancy and related forms of antisocial behavior on the willful disregard of Christian morality, rather than on ill-designed poor relief or economic forces. Conversely, as the official demonization and marginalization of the *fahrendes Volk* began to widen the social gap between them and the settled population, the former learned to become more aggressive in demanding the charity that was no longer given to them so willingly. The ensuing spiral of mistrust reinforced the belief in the underlying immorality of marginal groups and justified harsher policies toward them.[14] Lastly, these harsher attitudes were also legitimated by Lutheranism, which, as we have seen, equated begging with disobedience to God's will.[15] To the

---

[14] Norbert Schindler, "The Origins of Heartlessness: The Culture and Way of Life of Beggars in Late Seventeenth-Century Salzburg," in his *Rebellion, Community and Custom in Early Modern Germany* (Cambridge University Press, 2002), 236–92.

[15] Joachim Heinrich Peter, *Die Probleme der Armut in den Lehren der Kameralisten* (Berlin, 1934).

extent that such persons were seen not simply as wayward, but rather as deeply ingrained in their immoral and socially harmful ways, chastisement through hard labor was seen as more appropriate than the offer of assistance and rehabilitation, and this growing reliance on punitive labor inevitably began to alter the character of the house of correction.

This process was intensified by the rise of the territorial state and the emergence of Cameralism, the science of state resources and power that represented the German variant of west European mercantilism. The war had created a paradoxical situation in which a shortage of workers was coupled with a quantum increase in the poor. By linking the wealth and power of states to the size of their productive population, Cameralism provided an additional incentive for the nascent territorial states to put the unproductive poor to work, rather than to chase them away, and the workhouse with its new and harsher methods seemed to be the ideal mechanism for converting idle social ballast into a productive resource.[16] Once coerced labor within the workhouse had assumed a harsher, more punitive character and shed its original educative, rehabilitative pretensions, the workhouse became, so to speak, structurally available for the incarceration and punishment of persons convicted of serious crimes.

Collectively, these developments transformed the house of correction into the repressive institution that many people believe it to have been since the beginning, and in this form the classical workhouse remained the cornerstone of absolutist social policy from the late 1600s to the late 1700s. The cure for willful idleness was believed to lie if – not in converting idlers to the gospel of work – then at least in accustoming them to a life of regular work and social discipline. The architecture, routines, and rules of the institutions – especially ceaseless labor from morning until night with interruptions only for bodily nourishment and religious instruction – were all designed to further this end. The work was monotonous, physically demanding, and performed under unhealthy conditions, often intentionally so; every aspect of life within the institution was carefully regulated to leave no opportunity for idleness or disrespect; disciplinary techniques were perfected across the century; and infractions of these rules were punished harshly by a subaltern staff often composed of retired military officers.[17]

Workhouse officials were not unconcerned about the profitability of this work, and, as the success of the institution came to be measured in terms of the quantity of work extracted from the inmates, these fiscal interests were increasingly lashed to Cameralist strategies for economic development. State officials

---

[16] On the central role of a large, productive population in Cameralist thought, see Martin Fuhrmann, *Volksvermehrung als Staatsaufgabe? Bevölkerungs- und Ehepolitik in der deutschen politischen und ökonomischen Theorie des 18. und 19. Jahrhunderts* (Schöningh, 2002), 23ff.

[17] Workhouse conditions, routines, and regulations are discussed in Stekl, *Österreichs Zucht- und Arbeitshäuser*; Stekl, "'Labore et fame'"; Stier, *Fürsorge und Disziplinierung*, 42–182; Spierenburg, *The Prison Experience*, 171–219; and Sachße and Tennstedt, *Geschichte der Armenfürsorge*, I:118ff.

hoped that workhouse inmates would provide a pliable, captive workforce that could be parachuted into economic spaces that were otherwise regulated by guilds and custom and deployed there to introduce new products and manufacturing methods that Cameralist theorists believed would contribute to the power of the state and the welfare of the population.

However, the workhouse failed in virtually every respect to fulfill the hopes placed in it. Since the architects of the classical workhouse presumed that poverty was primarily the product of sloth and personal immorality, the workhouse was designed only to combat the need attributable to such causes, and the seductiveness of this vision blinded policy makers to the economic and demographic causes of need and thus prevented them from taking meaningful steps to remedy these problems. Nor is it likely that the workhouse succeeded in bettering more than a small proportion of the persons who passed through its gates. The risk of confinement was relatively small – in the 1770s, for example, only a couple of thousand persons out of a population of approximately 5 million were confined to workhouses in Prussia[18] – and sentences were generally short. However, the harsh regime of the classical workhouse was primarily intended to deter vagrancy, not to rehabilitate vagrants. Prison workhouses were expensive to maintain, and authorities would probably have not been willing to subsidize them at such great cost if they did not believe in their broader deterrent effect.

But the workhouse also failed to live up to the hopes of those who saw it as a promising vehicle for economic development. The age and/or infirmity of the inmates, their lack of skills, and their constant turnover limited the kind of work that could be performed to tasks that were mechanical, repetitive, quickly learned, and easily performed by unskilled workers with no intrinsic motivation. Therefore, rather than serving as a training ground of a new class of artisans who owed their loyalty to the state rather than the guild, workhouses were frequently forced to rely on unskilled tasks relating to textile manufacture. As a result, the original idea of "education through work (*Arbeitserziehung*)" was progressively attenuated as economic concerns came to dominate Cameralist policy, and the hope that coerced labor would transform inmates into useful members of the community was narrowed so that usefulness came to be understood almost exclusively in terms of extracted labor, rather than in terms of the development of individual capacities.[19]

Lastly, the expanded scope and altered function of the workhouse also contributed to its ultimate failure. Over time, the classical workhouse did not shed its original social functions, but simply accumulated new ones. In addition to its original function as an institution for correcting those who offended against community morality, the workhouse served as a combined poorhouse for the elderly and infirm, orphanage, penal institution for all those caught up

---

[18] Sachße/Tennstedt, *Geschichte der Armenfüsorge*, I:120ff.

[19] Heide Kallert, *Waisenhaus und Arbeitserziehung im 17. und 18. Jahrhundert* (Dissertation, Frankfurt, 1964).

in the never-ending war on vagrancy, asylum for the insane, and prison workhouse for those convicted of serious crimes. The problem was that the needs of these groups were often incompatible with each other and with the desire to minimize the burden of the workhouse on the public purse. This functional overburdening of the workhouse resulted in harsh and inadequate care for the deserving poor, the ineffectual application of the work regime to those for whom it was intended, a schizophrenic oscillation between laxity and brutal discipline, and a general decline into a state of disarray. In the words of one modern author, the workhouse was, for most of its history, less a Benthamite panopticon than a pandemonium.[20]

Although the workhouse was central to the war on vagrancy in the seventeenth and eighteenth centuries, it did not exhaust the field of state activity in the field of poor relief during these years. Even before the war, the territorial states had begun to play a more active and constructive role in the organization of poor relief, and one can speak of a halting effort at the state level in the 1600s and the first half of the 1700s to codify the principle of local responsibility that had been laid out by the imperial decrees of the early 1500s.[21]

But the war also drew local officials more deeply into the provision of poor relief by ruining the finances of endowed foundations, which were the pillar of municipal poor relief, while the general impoverishment of the population was reflected in a precipitous drop in charitable contributions. This created a gap that could only be filled – however inadequately – by local government. Although this increase in the relative importance of municipal contributions to local assistance costs was a universal phenomenon, it impacted the organization of relief in Lutheran areas in a specific way. If in earlier years one could have spoken of public officials as the organizing form that guided the charitable spirit of the local congregation, the war disrupted this equilibrium and definitively shifted the balance of initiative and responsibility from the church to the local state.[22] This withering away of Lutheran church charity, which was tantamount to its secularization, was intensified by Cameralist theorists, who called for the virtual absorption of individual almsgiving and church charity by public poor relief.[23]

To a certain extent, the poor law history of many German states in the century following the Peace of Westphalia consists of little more than the monotonous repetition of prohibitions on begging, edicts requiring the ablebodied to accept whatever work was offered to them, and increasingly draconian punishments – on paper, at least – for vagrancy and property crimes, and

---

[20] On this functional overburdening of the multifunctional workhouse, see Stekl, *Osterreichs Zucht- und Arbeitshäuser*, 66ff., and "'Labore et fame.'" For the juxtaposition of panopticon and pandemonium, see de Swaan, *In Care of the State*, 47.

[21] Elisabeth Schepers, *Als der Bettel in Bayern abgeschafft werden sollte. Staatliche Armenfürsorge in Bayern im 16. und 17. Jahrhundert* (Verlag Anton Pustet, 2000) is the best account of the poor laws of any German state in the first half of the seventeenth century.

[22] Gerhard Uhlhorn, *Die christliche Liebestätigkeit*, 2. Aufl. (Stuttgart, 1895), 633.

[23] Peter, *Die Probleme der Armut*, 198, 212, 217.

every account of poor relief during this time refers to the – literally – dozens of anti-vagrancy decrees issued in every territory.[24] But the most basic reason why every effort to combat vagrancy was doomed to fail is that such programs never grasped the root of the problem in rural overpopulation and underemployment, continuing instead to see vagrancy primarily as a problem of individual morality best met through repressive means. The problem of vagrancy, however, was unintentionally aggravated by public officials, whose instinctive response to the actual or potential cost of poor relief was to shove the indigent across the nearest border in the general direction of their ostensible places of birth.[25] The territorial fragmentation of old regime Germany, which was especially severe in the southwest and along the Rhine, meant that the itinerant poor often had to do little more than move on to the next village in order to escape the reach of whichever officials happened to be pursuing them. The war on vagrancy was also hindered by the persistence of traditional attitudes toward poverty and the poor; as long as such ideas prevailed, it was impossible to even think about abolishing begging, regardless of confession or state capacity.[26] Even those persons with jobs, homes, and a settled place in the community were well aware of the precariousness of their own existence, and they could mobilize both to support their neighbors and to defend their plebeian notions of justice against outside interventions. Every study of poor relief in this period recounts incidents where the populace acted collectively to liberate beggars whom they believed had been unjustly arrested for vagrancy by local bailiffs.[27]

During the last century of the old regime, public policy toward begging and vagrancy was shaped by both the "real" social and economic conditions of the lower classes and the discursive schemata through which vagabondage was constructed. Across the Germanies and, indeed, across all of Europe, the population, which over the previous century had slowly recovered from the decimation of the Thirty Years' War, began to increase at a much more rapid pace than heretofore. This was especially the case among the rural and urban underclasses, who were already living on the margins of subsistence. Those groups who lived wholly or in part from potentially unstable wage labor on the margins of the corporate world included apprentices whose advance in the

---

[24] Lotte Koch, *Wandlungen der Wohlfahrtspflege im Zeitalter der Aufklärung* (Erlangen, 1933), 66 refers to over 100 such decrees from the Mark Brandenburg, 50 of which date from the 1700s. Other examples can be found in Sachße/Tennstedt, *Geschichte der Armenfürsorge*, I:109.

[25] For a good description of these problems and the efforts to establish an effective, regional framework for the repression of vagrancy in the late 1700s, see Klein, *Armenfürsorge und Bettelbekämpfung*, 262–81.

[26] Jean-Pierre Gutton, *La Société et les pauvres en Europe (XVIe-XVIIIe siècles)* (PUF, 1974), 136–44, who cites the persistence of such ideas as one important qualification of Foucault's theory of the "great confinement." Gutton also emphasizes (145ff.) the survival of numerous other organization and institutions devoted more to assistance than to confinement.

[27] Jean-Pierre Gutton, *La Société et les pauvres... Lyon*, 351ff. is especially good on these factors. See also Eisenbach, *Zuchthäuser*, 33–5. Finzsch, *Obrigkeit und Unterschichten*, 26, 86, 163, repeatedly emphasizes how thoroughly the poor were integrated into the local community, even at the turn of the nineteenth century, and how little street beggars differed in their social composition from the residential poor.

Meisterstand was permanently blocked, people who illicitly practiced a trade protected by guild privileges, servants, persons who provided low-skill urban services (messengers, scribes, and shop assistants), day laborers and "teamsters" (to use a modern shorthand), farmers whose land shortage required them to hire themselves out to others as laborers, cottage workers, seasonal and migrant workers, and the "proto-proletariat" employed in shipyards, mines, forges, and early mills and manufactories. By the end of the 1700s the German states were facing the same pressures on resources and productive capacity that they had faced at the end of the 1500s. The result was a Malthusian crisis that was to drag on through the 1840s in the form of pauperism.[28] These secular trends were aggravated by the Seven Years' War (1756–63) and a series of poor harvests, including the severe hunger crisis of 1770/2, when harvest failure and high grain prices led to mass starvation across the continent.[29] For all those persons whose fates and fortunes were caught up in these pressures, the downward transition from everyday hardship within their community to destitution, homelessness, and social marginality was gradual, and their paths to penury were infinitely diverse. There was, as a result, little to distinguish the large majority of vagrants from the underclasses from whom they were recruited – except their misfortune – though the boundaries between this group and the residuum of confirmed beggars, idlers, drunks, and pickpockets were no doubt fluid. Yet, this vagabond class was perceived as a permanent danger to society and treated as such. Why? This demonization of the homeless and their consequent repression was, Robert Castel has argued (in a manner akin to Mary Douglas' definition of ritual pollution), the only way that contemporaries could make sense of people who were "out of place" in a society that lacked the capacity to improve the conditions of the social groups from which this class was continuously replenished. As a result, the vagabond question became the "manner in which the social question of pre-industrial society was simultaneously formulated and mystified."[30]

Beyond the Workhouse: Industriousness, Education, and the Prevention of Poverty in the Age of Enlightenment

The Enlightenment and enlightened or reform absolutism brought new ideas and new accents to the theory and practice of poor relief in the Germanies

---

[28] Robert Castel, *From Manual Workers to Wage Laborers. Transformation of the Social Question*, trans. Richard Boyd (Transaction Publishers, 2003), 128, 139–49 argues that the eighteenth century marked a fundamental change in the nature of poverty and the social question because social marginality was increasingly due to the generalization of unstable wage labor, while the socioeconomic forces that were driving this new social system simultaneously increased the resources available to society, which for the previous half millennium had been the primal cause of vagabondage.

[29] Wilhelm Abel, "Massenarmut und Hungerkrisen im vorindustriellen Deutschland," in Ulrich Herrmann, ed., *"Das pädagogische Jahrhundert". Volksaufklärung und Erziehung zur Armut im 18. Jahrhundert in Deutschland* (Beltz Verlag, 1981), 29–52.

[30] Castel, *From Manual Workers to Wage Laborers*, 79.

and Austria, but they did not mark a fundamental discontinuity. Rather, what happened was that the pendulum began to swing back from the monocular focus on repressing individual immorality that had dominated thinking on the social question since the mid-1600s toward a greater appreciation of both the social causes of poverty and the possibility of preventing it. The real break came not at the beginning of the Enlightenment, but at its end, when the rise of liberalism led to a broad retreat from the paternalist principles of early modern social governance.

Pietism and *Aufklärung* were two of the most important intellectual influences on eighteenth-century thinking on poor relief.[31] The Enlightenment, however, was not exclusively an affair of the mind, and the contours of Enlightenment social policy were shaped by the collision between the poor law reforms promoted by reform absolutism and traditional ideas and institutions. Especially in Catholic states, the only force that was powerful enough to challenge existing institutions and practices, sanctioned as they were by the authority of the church, were absolutist bureaucrats eager to extend the power of the ruler further into the interstices of social and religious life. However, even in the Austrian territories of southwestern Germany, the efforts of Joseph II to transform the Habsburg monarchy into an absolutist state could do no more than partially instrumentalize existing institutions for state ends. In other places, where state capacities were more limited and where absolutist rulers generally displayed less interest in reforming poor relief, the story is one of state inactivity, a lack of resources, and an inability to prevail over the combined resistance of the church, local authorities, and traditional attitudes.[32]

Enlightenment ideas on prevention had their most visible impact on the reform of institutional assistance. The accumulation of functions and dysfunctions by the classical workhouse did not go unnoticed by contemporaries, who increasingly saw these institutions as human dumping grounds. For example, Heinrich Balthasar Wagnitz, the chaplain of the Halle workhouse and a disciple of the English prison reformer John Howard, cataloged these failings in his *Historical Reports and Observations Concerning the Most Notable Houses of Correction in Germany* (1791/4).[33] Wagnitz's work was an accurate reflection of public opinion, which had come to the conclusion that the composite nature of the workhouse was making it impossible to accomplish any of its

---

[31] The precise nature of Pietist influence on poor relief remains a matter of debate. See Richard Gawthrop, *Pietism and the Making of Eighteenth-Century Prussia* (Cambridge University Press, 1993); Philip Gorski, *The Disciplinary Revolution. Calvinism and the Rise of the State in Early Modern Europe* (University of Chicago Press, 2003); Udo Sträter, "Pietismus und Sozialtätigkeit. Zur Frage nach der Wirkungsgeschichte des 'Waisenhauses' in Halle und des Frankfurter Armen-, Waisen- und Arbeitshauses," *Pietismus und Neuzeit* 7 (1981), 201–30; and Kurt Aland, "Der Pietismus und die soziale Frage," in Aland, ed., *Pietismus und moderne Welt* (Luther-Verlag, 1974), 99–137.

[32] Klein, *Armenfürsorge und Bettelbekämpfung*, 14ff., 73, 321.

[33] Wagnitz, *Historische Nachrichten und Bemerkungen über die merkwürdigsten Zuchthäuser in Deutschland...* (Halle, 1791–4), 29ff., 56ff.

original goals. Relying as it did on natural rights doctrine, the legitimacy of the absolutist state was based on its claim to promote the common weal. Although this was a highly malleable doctrine that tended to define the welfare of the individual in terms of the wealth and power of the state, it also included, if only in an implicit and attenuated form, the obligation to ensure that the individual members of the population had the opportunity to support themselves through productive labor. This posed no problems as long as idleness and vagrancy could be interpreted primarily as the product of individual vice best combated by the workhouse, the ebbing of these harsh seventeenth-century views raised the question of how the rights of the deserving jobless might be secured? This new perspective gave rise to a broad movement to break up the multifunctional workhouse and replace the costly and often counterproductive confinement of the poor either with outdoor assistance through work or with "voluntary" workhouses (*freiwillige Armenbeschäftigungs-* or *Armenarbeitsanstalten*). Both of these approaches provided the residential poor with the opportunity to support themselves – wholly or in part – through work provided by public officials. Such work – again, most often spinning – was often required of relief recipients, and the repressive workhouse continued to function as a necessary flanking mechanism. This trend was reinforced by developments in criminal law and penology, where the closer integration of the *Zuchthaus* into the penal system at the close of the century combined with Enlightenment ideas on correction and improvement of serious offenders to give birth to the modern penitentiary. But the converse of this explicit penalization of the *Zuchthaus* was a tendency to hive off, physically and/or administratively, that section of the institution that was devoted to work assistance and to rebaptize it as an *Arbeitshaus* in order to emphasize its social function and honorable quality, though this disentanglement was never realized in a fully consequent manner.[34]

There was a similar controversy – the so-called *Waisenhausstreit* – over the relative virtues of institutional and family care for orphans, one that ended in a clear victory for the latter. But this controversy also reflected changing ideas on education and the prevention of poverty, and it was the Swiss pedagogue Johann Heinrich Pestalozzi who translated Pietist ideas on the role of work and education in hardening children against the temptations of sin into the utilitarian language of the Enlightenment, where they provided the conceptual foundation of the new "industry schools," which became the primary form

---

[34] Thomas Nutz, *Strafanstalt als Besserungsmaschine. Reformdiskurs und Gefängniswissenschaft 1775–1848* (Oldenbourg, 2001); Stier, *Fürsorge und Disziplinierung*, 37ff.; Stekl, *Österreichs Zucht- und Arbeitshäuser*, 70ff.; and Finzsch, *Obrigkeit und Unterschichten*, 135, for one example (Cologne) of this late Enlightenment division of the workhouse into punitive and rehabilitative sections along the lines proposed by Wagnitz. Klaus Wohlrab, *Armut und Staatszweck. Die politische Theorie der Armut im deutschen Naturrecht des 18. und 19. Jahrhunderts* (Keip Verlag, 1997) nicely captures – at the level of political theory – the early liberal hollowing out of the positive state obligation to relieve the poor that had been formulated by natural law theories of the state. As he shows, this process was always tempered by the efforts of the liberals to develop their own approach to the problem of poverty and its social consequences.

of youth welfare in the late Enlightenment.[35] The mission of the Göttingen industry school, which was one of the best-known institutions of the age, was to promote a cluster of virtues (*Fleiß, Betriebsamkeit, Industrie*) that are all best translated into English as "industry," and its founders envisioned it as "a school for thrift, order, and cleanliness for the children.... This institution stimulates and nourishes... the proper desire for honor and that striving that has almost died out among the lower orders.... In this institution, we seek and hope to educate good servants, children who will be thankful towards old, helpless parents and benefactors... and patriotic subjects."[36] Here, children were instructed in a variety of semiskilled tasks in textile production, agriculture, and stonecutting, jobs for which there was local demand, and during pauses they were taught the basics of reading, writing, arithmetic, and religion. Without these Cameralist family values, it was all too easy for a child to descend the slippery slope from idleness to crime. In the words of Ludwig Gerhard Wagemann, the director of Göttingen poor relief in the 1780s and 1790s and an influential social reformer,

the usual consequence of accustoming children to begging is, when they reach adolescence, theft and disinclination towards work.... And even if a young boy who grew up in this manner decides when he is 15 or 16 to take up an occupation,... this seldom lasts very long. The unaccustomed constraint becomes burdensome to him, and he abandons his master and therewith discipline and order. Unacquainted with the religion that should guide him, he lives simply according to his senses. His heart is open to every vice. He becomes, out of necessity or simply because the occasion corresponds with his passions, a thief, a perjurer, a traitor, a murderer.... When we imagine the history of the education and early activities of the thieves and murders, which we perhaps know ourselves or which are related to us by others, we will find the root of all vice in the lack of instruction and a disorderly childhood way of life.[37]

During the eighteenth century, Josephine Austria was the only central state in the Holy Roman Empire to attempt a systematic reform of poor relief within its borders.[38] But far and away the most successful – and the most widely renowned – Enlightenment reform of poor relief was that carried out in Hamburg beginning in 1788.[39] Although the Hamburg reforms followed in well-worn tracks in aiming to reorganize their relief system on the basis of the work principle, their novelty lay in the scope of their commitment to prevention and

---

[35] On the industry school movement, see Kallert, *Waisenhaus und Arbeitserziehung*, 80ff., and Ulrich Herrmann, "Armut – Armenversorgung – Armenerziehung an der Wende zum 19. Jahrhundert," in Herrmann, ed., *'Das pädagogische Jahrhundert'*, 194–218.
[36] Cited in Herrmann, "Armut – Armenversorgung – Armenerziehung," 207.
[37] Cited in Herrmann, "Armut – Armenversorgung – Armenerziehung," 206.
[38] Klein, *Armenfürsorge und Bettelbekämpfung*, 66ff., 198ff.
[39] The following account is drawn from Mary Lindemann, *Patriots and Paupers. Hamburg, 1712–1830* (Oxford University Press, 1990); Detlev Duda, *Die Hamburger Armenfürsorge im 18. und 19. Jahrhundert. Eine soziologisch-historische Untersuchung* (Weinheim/Basel, 1982); Brietzke, *Arbeitsdisziplin und Armut*; and Koch, *Wandlungen der Wohlfahrtspflege*, 153–9.

in the sustained mobilization of the citizenry to monitor the poor in order to ensure the rigorous enforcement of this principle.

The 1788 reforms consolidated the many existing public, religious, and private programs for assisting the poor under a single organization, the General Poor Relief. The General Poor Relief was the brainchild of the Hamburg Patriotic Society. The involvement of the Patriotic Society and of similar associations in other cities in the reform of poor relief is an indicator of an important phenomenon: the emergence of what Jürgen Habermas described as the "bourgeois public sphere," that is, the gathering of private individuals to discuss and influence issues of shared concern, thereby giving these issues a public, political dimension.[40] The formation of patriotic, useful (*gemeinnützig*), and philanthropic societies for the diffusion of useful knowledge and the remediation of most every conceivable social ill are among the first examples of such private individuals coming together on the basis of shared convictions to challenge – if only implicitly – the monopoly on political knowledge claimed by the absolutist state. The causes of poverty and the best means of assisting the poor were one of the favorite topics of the journals published by these societies and of the "moral weeklies" that were so important in the constitution of the identity of the new middle classes. These questions were also the topic of numerous essay contests sponsored by learned societies across the continent.

For the actual distribution of outdoor assistance, the city of Hamburg was divided into five districts, each under the supervision of two directors. In turn, each of these districts was divided into twelve quarters, in which relief was administered by two supervisors who were responsible for overseeing the work of the three guardians elected from each quarter. Overall responsibility for the General Poor Relief lay in the hands of an executive council, the *Armen-Kollegium*, which was composed of the district directors; the five administrators of the parish poor chests; the directors of the charitable foundations of the city; the governors of the orphanage, the workhouse, and the *Pesthof*; and seven members appointed by the city's various governing bodies. The guardians were responsible for visiting applicants for relief in their homes and carefully investigating their character and circumstances through the use of a printed questionnaire that was to serve as a permanent case record for the family. On completing their inquiry, the poor guardians passed on their recommendations to the district supervisors, who then presented the particulars to the executive council, which formally decided on the petitions for relief and then returned the questionnaires to the poor guardians for their use and retention.

The General Poor Relief was based on the principles of self-help and subsidiarity. All citizens were expected to support themselves through their own labor as far as possible, and those deserving poor who were legitimately unable to satisfy their basic needs through their own exertions enjoyed a (moral) right

---

[40] Habermas, *The Structural Transformation of the Public Sphere* (MIT Press, 1989).

to assistance sufficient to ensure a minimum standard of living. As the directors explained in their first annual report,

> first, the Relief investigates how much each pauper requires for subsistence. Then the Relief ascertains how much he earns by his labor and is able to earn and how much he already receives in charity. Once those things have been determined, it becomes a simple matter to decide how much additional assistance he must receive in summer and in winter, in sickness and in health. As long as the Relief adheres to these elementary principles, it will never run the danger of neglecting the truly needy or of advancing alms to those who really do not require them or are not worthy of them or are wastrels.[41]

The active participation of so many citizens was crucial to the success of this new system. At a very basic level, in a city as large as Hamburg, any attempt to systematically discriminate between the deserving and the undeserving poor by investigating their individual circumstances and continuously monitoring their public and private lives required large numbers of warm bodies from the propertied classes. Although the principle of individualization had been articulated in the 1500s, the inability to apply this principle, along, of course, with the sheer inadequacy of resources, had been the major cause of the failure of so many previous reforms. Instead of placing the administration of the system in the hands of the police or some other public authority, the decentralized organization of the Hamburg system and the devolution of authority down to the district and quarter level proved to be an effective mechanism for mobilizing the middle-class manpower needed to make the system of individualized outdoor assistance work. In turn, service as a relief officer soon came to be viewed as both a school for civic virtue and the first rung on the ladder of municipal office.

The Hamburg reforms also embodied a systematic commitment to the prevention of poverty. The organizers of the Hamburg reforms, especially Johann Georg Büsch and Caspar Voght (who was later involved in the reorganization of poor relief in Vienna and Munich), recognized that much of the need in their city was due to economic factors that lay beyond the control of the poor, rather than sloth or profligacy, and they saw that a well-ordered poor relief system would have to depend as much on constructive policies for the able-bodied as on the repression of vagrancy. Their solution to this problem was to make large-scale use of assistance through work in order to support the able-bodied, encourage self-reliance among the poor, and test their willingness to work and thus their worthiness for assistance. Soon after its founding, the General Poor Relief employed some three thousand persons (at wages below the prevailing market rate), some of whom worked directly for the General Poor Relief, while others worked under contract for private employers.

This program was hugely expensive, and one of the most serious problems faced by poor relief officials was to find a way of employing the able-bodied

---

[41] Cited in Lindemann, *Patriots and Paupers*, 139.

without unduly burdening municipal finances. The General Poor Relief ultimately decided that the poor could be best set to work spinning flax in their own homes because such work dovetailed with the economic needs of the city and did not require special skill or strength. Although the Hamburg reformers understood how the new poverty was caused by the decline of manufacturing and the growing dependence of the lower classes on wage labor in commerce, they were by no means oblivious to the temptations of idleness, and the workhouse continued to serve as the sanction of last resort.

These work programs were coupled with two other preventive programs. There was an ambitious program of outdoor medical relief, which had been established independently, but whose activity was coordinated with that of, the General Poor Relief. This program was premised on the idea that there was an integral connection between illness and poverty that could not be completely reduced to a matter of individual character. Moreover, this medical relief was not limited to the registered poor, but rather was made generally available to the city's laboring classes because its sponsors recognized that health and ability to work were all that in many cases separated this class of potential poor from actual destitution. Despite the costs entailed by this program, the Hamburg reformers argued that these programs were economical in the long run because they helped sustain the productivity of the city's laboring classes while delaying disability, death, and the economic consequence they entailed.[42]

The last major component of the Hamburg reforms were programs for assisting the children of the poor. If the cardinal principle of poor relief was not to provide the poor with anything that they could earn themselves, here one can see the Hamburg reformers edging beyond poor relief and feeling their way toward something akin to modern child welfare. Like enlightened reformers everywhere, the Hamburg reformers regarded the education of pauper children as the key to preventing future poverty.[43] The original core of the Hamburg reforms in this area were industry schools to educate poor children and accustom them to the life of labor to which their social station had predestined them. Parents who were receiving public assistance were required – as a condition of continued support – to send their children to these schools; house visits aimed at ensuring that the good habits learned at school were not undone by an unhealthy home environment; and at school their work and well-being were monitored by teachers and medical officers.

Poor parents, however, relied on the income of their children, and they were sometimes reluctant to allow their children to attend industry schools rather than to take up better-paying work elsewhere. To overcome this resistance, children were paid a premium that made up the difference between what

---

[42] On the role of medical relief in the Hamburg reforms, see Lindemann, *Patriot and Paupers*, 102–9, and Lindemann, "Urban Growth and Medical Charity: Hamburg, 1788–1815," in Jonathan Barry and Colin Jones, eds., *Medicine and Charity before the Welfare State* (London, 1991), 113–32.
[43] Scherpner, *Geschichte der Jugendfürsorge*, 96ff.

they earned at the industry school and what they could have earned in other employment. These schools were open not only to the registered poor, but to all children of the poorer classes, who were also eligible for these premiums, and by 1800 such children made up more than 80% of the students enrolled in these schools. The changing mission of these programs was reflected in the fact that responsibility for these schools and the expanding network of preventive social services linked to them was transferred from poor relief authorities to the municipal school commission.

The Hamburg reforms did not survive the Napoleonic era. While the financial viability of the system and the commitment to the prevention of poverty depended on a favorable economic conjuncture, the war permanently dislocated the economy of the city-state and ruined its eighteenth-century prosperity. But there were also deeper forces at work, which were independent of the Napoleonic conjuncture. Although the General Poor Relief may have collapsed – like poor relief programs in many other cities – under the pressures of war, after 1815 a conscious decision was made not to resurrect it in its original form. The directors of the General Poor Relief rejected the previous policy of providing work for the poor, arguing that such programs actually caused poverty by weakening the self-reliance of the poor, and they sharply curtailed the scope of both medical relief and public education for poor and working-class children for the same reason.[44]

This reorientation was part of a broader retreat from the paternalistic forms of social intervention that had formed the core of early modern social policy. This rethinking of the role of the state resulted in part from a sense of exhaustion and frustration at the failure to make the paternalistic social project work.[45] However, this disillusionment would not by itself have led to such a far-reaching reorientation of social policy had it not been complemented by a compelling reason to limit the role of the state in the social domain. This rationale was provided by liberalism, and the withdrawal of the early modern police state from its expansive notion of paternalistic social governance did not so much create a vacuum as mark the transition to what Foucault called a liberal mode of governmentality. This liberal mode of social governance relied less on direct paternalistic intervention than on the combined disciplinary effects of the market and moral reform associations, which emerged in the nineteenth century as the most important noneconomic agents of social governance. These institutions served to "responsibilize" the poor – that is, to teach them to govern themselves by internalizing those norms and habits (such as industriousness, discipline, foresight, and procreative prudence) – and thus to create the forms of subjectivity on which the self-regulating character of civil society and market economy was believed to depend.[46]

---

[44] Lindemann, *Patriot and Paupers*, 202–13.
[45] Klein, *Armenfürsorge und Bettelbekämpfung in Vorderösterreich*, 74, 319ff.
[46] Foucault, "Governmentality," in Graham Burchell, Colin Gordon, and Peter Miller, eds., *The Foucault Effect. Studies in Governmentality* (University of Chicago Press, 1991), 87–104; Mitchell Dean, *The Constitution of Poverty. Toward a Genealogy of Liberal Governance*

In the economic discourse of the seventeenth and eighteenth centuries, the ruler was expected to take positive steps to increase the size of the population, promote the development of industry and trade, and ensure that the population engaged in productive labor. Such actions were basic duties of a Christian ruler and essential elements of state power. At the turn of the nineteenth century, however, this understanding of the relationship between individual and national prosperity was inverted, and the laboring poor replaced the idle as the pivot of the new political economy. From the perspective of thinkers such as Thomas Malthus, high birth rates were seen as a danger to the welfare of both the laboring classes and the nation, rather than as a source of state power, and these economists warned that public intervention to ensure the productive employment of the poor would ultimately lead to their impoverishment by weakening their self-reliance and discouraging procreative restraint.[47] The founding principle of this brave, new liberal world was the natural right to work, that is, the belief that the wealth of nations depended on the abolition of all restrictions on the freedom of the individual to apply his or her industry and skill in whatever domain appeared to promise the greatest return. In the new political economy, the natural, automatic forces of want and hunger obviated the need for any external mechanism to force the poor to seek out work (or to provide it for them), and the poverty of the laboring masses came to be seen as basic engine of economic growth and the ultimate source of the wealth of nations.

This optimism concerning the emancipatory force of the labor market was, however, soon belied by low wages, inadequate employment, the structural asymmetries of an ostensibly free labor contract between the owners of property and those who were driven by hunger to accept the price that was offered for their labor, and, more generally, the chasm that separated the abstract equality of citizenship and the concrete inequalities of bourgeois society. As a result, the history of nineteenth-century social reform is the history of successive efforts to manage this permanent slippage between the political and the economic domains – between capitalism and democracy.

This understanding of the relation between poverty, labor, and wealth gave a new dynamic to nineteenth-century poor relief, whose constitutive fiction was the belief that assistance to the poor was not only harmful, but also unnecessary, because unrestricted freedom to sell one's labor power in the market would ensure that any industrious and able-bodied person would be able to secure the necessities of life through his or her own labor. Only the impotent, the slothful, and the criminal would be without work, and the task of deterrent poor relief would be to police the distinctions between these groups and the independent laboring poor.

(Routledge, 1991); and Dean, *Governmentality. Power and Rule in Modern Society* (Sage, 1999).

[47] See Dean's discussion of the mercantilist "discourse on the poor" and its subsequent dissolution at the turn of the liberal era in *The Constitution of Poverty*.

The advent of these ideas marked the end of the early modern era in the domain of poor relief. The workhouse, which for two centuries had been the most visible embodiment of paternalist social governance, lost virtually all its social functions and survived across the nineteenth century primarily as a penal institution, housing only a small residuum of incorrigible vagrants and morals offenders while being singularly uninterested, and ineffective, in correcting them. It would be nearly a century before the preventive approach to poverty worked out in Hamburg would again influence the theory and practice of poor relief in Germany. The intervening years would be dominated by a much harsher attitude which, like that of the Cameralist moment before it, regarded poverty largely as a problem of character and morality to be solved through deterrence.

3

Pauperism, Moral Reform, and Visions of Civil Society, 1800–1870

Voluntary Associations and the Problem of Social Governance

Writing with measured hyperbole, Thomas Nipperdey began his history of Germany from 1800 to 1866 with the assertion that "in the beginning was Napoleon."[1] What followed from this Napoleonic big bang was a three-dimensional process that, according to Nipperdey, defined the course and dynamic of German history across the first two-thirds of the nineteenth century: the formation of territorial, bureaucratic states, and, within the political spaces created by this process, the evolution of a market economy and a modern bourgeois civil society. Poor relief and charity were deeply implicated in these processes both as their object and as their agent.

For its early theorists, civil society represented the optimistic potential of modernity. It was a sphere of individuation, self-fashioning, and social progress that was hollowing out the older corporate order and transforming it from within through the emergence of voluntary associations, the market economy, and a bourgeois public sphere, all of which embodied – or so the early liberals believed – the immanent capacity of civil society to organize and regulate itself without the need for traditional authorities.[2] If this picture captures the diverse ways in which the idea of civil society embodied the promise of modernity and the personality principle, we also need to bear in mind that individuation and decorporatization also set in motion an equally dynamic process of social disorganization whose direction was regarded by many in far less sanguine terms.[3] Equally important, all these developments interacted with the secular trends

---

[1] Thomas Nipperdey, *Deutsche Geschichte 1800–1866. Bürgerwelt und starker Staat* (C. H. Beck, 1983), 11.
[2] Nipperdey, "Verein als soziale Struktur in Deutschland im späten 18. und frühen 19. Jahrhundert," in his *Gesellschaft, Kultur, Theorie* (Vandenhoeck & Ruprecht, 1976), 174–205.
[3] Werner Conze, ed., "Das Spannungsfeld von Staat und Gesellschaft im Vormärz," in *Staat und Gesellschaft im deutschen Vormärz 1815–1848* (=Industrielle Welt, Bd. 1, Klett, 1962), 207–69, especially 248–61.

in population growth noted in the previous chapter, changes in landholding patterns, and early industrialization to precipitate a massive wave of social dislocation that came to be known as the crisis of pauperism. For the entire transitional period stretching from the end of the Napoleonic Wars through the revolution of 1848 and into the 1850s, it was not clear which of these two trends would prevail, and the ultimate outcome was an industrial society whose contours few had foreseen.

Revolutionaries such as Marx regarded these developments as the manifestation of an inner contradiction in the capitalist system that would eventually lead to the self-overcoming of the bourgeois order in an age of postpolitical abundance. However, those members of the middle classes – both liberal and conservative – whose sensitivity to the plight of the pauperized masses, and whose fear of the dangers that emanated from them, prevented them from fully subscribing to the rhetoric of utopian capitalism were forced to grapple with the contradiction between socioeconomic inequality and the notional claims to political equality on the part of the popular classes in the postrevolutionary world. To legitimate their privileged position in the bourgeois social order, the middle classes were constrained to seek the explanation for these inequalities in the disadvantaged classes themselves, and their efforts to solve the riddle of social inequality led them to explain poverty and material destitution as the product of that combination of immorality, cultural deprivation, and individual demoralization that came to be known as pauperism. Framing the issue in this manner meant that every expression by the poor of their sense of inequality and disadvantagement would be regarded as a manifestation of vice, sin, and character failing that could only be combated through pedagogical means, rather than as a legitimate demand for equal status within the community to be redressed through the political process. The solution to the problem of pauperism and the social disorganization that it entailed was, therefore, to inculcate in the poor the diverse virtues – providence, industriousness, discipline, responsibility, thrift, and respect for constituted authority – which they were believed to lack and thus to mold this rough human material into the normalized, self-governing subjects who could thrive in the new civil society taking shape in these decades. This strategy marked the birth of both the "social question," as it was understood across much of the nineteenth century, and the social domain as a sphere of pedagogical antipolitics.[4]

Although early liberals demanded that the scope of state activity be limited to an absolute minimum and be only negative in nature, this view of the state did not diminish the moral obligation of the community toward the needy, and

---

[4] My thinking here and in the following draws on Giovanna Procacci, *Gouverner la misère. La question sociale en France (1789–1848)* (Seuil, 1993); Robert Castel, *From Manual Workers to Wage Laborers. Transformation of the Social Question*, trans. Richard Boyd (Transaction Publishers, 2003), 139–246; and Klaus Mollenhauer, *Die Ursprünge der Sozialpädagogik in der industriellen Gesellschaft. Eine Untersuchung zur Struktur sozialpädagogischen Denkens und Handelns* (Julius Betz, 1959).

the conviction that individual citizens should be personally responsible for all the matters of public concern that lay outside the proper scope of state activity made voluntary social engagement the logical counterpart to the minimal state and a distinguishing characteristic of nineteenth-century notions of citizenship. But this displacement of the locus of social reform from the state to civil society raises two questions: What was the source and nature of the authority that reformers hoped to exercise over the poor, and how was such voluntary assistance to be organized?

Shaping the personality or subjectivity of the individual poor without resorting to direct coercion was a tricky issue. The only way to legitimate the authority of social reformers was through the voluntary consent of the individual poor, and the central concepts through which this displacement of political authority were conceptualized were "friendship" and "helping," which were institutionalized in a variety of ways that will be discussed in the following pages. The relations of personal deference that were to be established in this manner were meant to serve as the starting point for a long apprenticeship in social and civic virtues. This strategy, however, was predicated on the belief that poverty and the entire spectrum of immoral, illegal, improvident, disorderly, promiscuous, insubordinate, and asocial behaviors that were grouped under the rubric of pauperism were the result – if not of active choice by the individual – then at least of character weakness. Consequently, the goal of helping and friendly house visiting was to gain the confidence of the poor in order to convince them to defer to the judgment and guidance of their social superiors, who were to encourage them to resist temptation and adhere more firmly to prevailing norms of social respectability. I would like to characterize this program of individualized antipolitical uplift as "moral reform."[5] Moral reform was different from traditional charity in that it sought less to alleviate the immediate symptoms of distress than to prevent pauperism by attacking its roots in the individual personality, though these positive efforts to influence individual character were everywhere supported by disciplinary mechanisms, such as the workhouse and the police, which sought to reinforce social norms through punitive sanctions for deviant behavior.

The history of voluntary associations – especially moral reform associations – is, for a number of reasons, central to the history of nineteenth-century efforts to solve the social question. The very idea of civil society was based on the belief that this social formation could find its organizing principles within itself, and this principle was reflected in the exponential growth – beginning in the 1830s and 1840s – of voluntary organizations through which concerned individuals came together to imprint their own collective moral personality on the life of the nation. This new associationalism was made possible by the retreat of the state from the direct regulation of social life noted in the previous chapter; the insistence by these associations on the right to represent the

---

[5] I take the phrase from M. J. D. Roberts, *Making English Morals. Voluntary Associations and Moral Reform in England, 1787–1886* (Cambridge University Press, 2004).

nation in matters of general concern was both a sign of the expanding bourgeois public sphere and a challenge to the late absolutist state; and during these years, voluntary associations began to supplant traditional endowed charities as the primary form of social engagement by the middle classes. Not only did this proliferation of associations institutionalize the shift in the locus of social regulation from the state to society; the multiplication of agents of social governance made the exercise of social power more diffuse and, at least potentially, more pervasive and more effective.

The associations in which the middle classes united to pursue matters of common concern also served as an important vehicle for the consolidation and performance of the social identity of these classes.[6] During these decades, the figuration of paupers, proletarians, and the "dangerous classes" – along with nurturing and excessively sentimental women – as the constitutive Other of the autonomous, rational, disciplined male subject of public life was essential to the imaginative constitution of civil society. Such a construct, however, raises question about the role of such caring in the constitution of female subjectivity.[7] More important, it also obscures the fact that despite the general apprehension regarding the dangers posed by the pauperized masses, the propertied classes were sharply divided among themselves concerning the causes of pauperism and social disorganization and the best means of responding to these developments. These divisions were to be of crucial importance in the subsequent history of poor relief and welfare in Germany because they gave rise to a process of competitive association building as the different cultural and religious groups active in the social sector vied with one another to mobilize the public behind their respective reform programs. In the long run, the inability of the religiously divided and politically polarized country to resolve these nineteenth-century culture wars and unite behind a higher national purpose was one of the key factors behind the corporatist fragmentation of the social sector in the twentieth century.

---

[6] Marcus Gräser, *Wohlfahrtsgesellschaft und Wohlfahrtsstaat. Bürgerliche Sozialreform und welfare state building in den USA und in Deutschland 1880–1940* (Vandenhoeck & Ruprecht, 2008), and Stephen Pielhoff, *Paternalismus und Stadtarmut. Armutswahrnehmung und Privatwohltätigkeit im Hamburger Bürgertum 1830–1914* (Verein für Hamburgische Geschichte, 1999) both address this issue in greater detail. See also Manfred Hettling, "Bürgerliche Kultur – Bürgerlichkeit als kulturelles System," in Peter Lundgreen, ed., *Sozial- und Kulturgeschichte des Bürgertums* (Vandenhoeck & Ruprecht, 2000), 319–39; Jürgen Kocka, "The Middle Classes in Europe," *JMH* 67 (December 1995), 783–806; and Kocka, "Bürgertum und Bürgerlichkeit als Probleme der deutschen Geschichte vom späten 18. zum frühen 20. Jahrhundert," in Kocka, ed., *Bürgertum und Bürgerlichkeit im 19. Jahrhundert* (Vandenhoeck & Ruprecht, 1987), 21–63. Over the past fifteen years, *Bürgertum* research has been a minor growth industry. The Lundgreen volume summarizes the research of the Bielefeld school, and Jan Palmowski, "Mediating the Nation: Liberalism and the Polity in Nineteenth-Century Germany," *German History* 18:4 (2001), 573–98, provides an excellent review of the state of the field.

[7] On the former point, see Annemieke van Drenth and Francisca de Haan, *The Rise of Caring Power: Elizabeth Fry and Josephine Butler in Britain and the Netherlands* (Amsterdam University Press, 2000).

The history of voluntary associations can also serve as a barometer for measuring the changing relations between state and society. The parameters of political life in the *Vormärz* were defined by the "monarchical principle," which granted representative bodies the right to cooperate in certain narrowly defined areas of governmental activity, but placed legislative initiative and ultimate political authority in the hands of the monarch and his officials. While liberal ideas on the separation of state and society reflected their understanding of the role of representative institutions in policing a monarchical regime that excluded popular representatives from the policymaking process, German liberals also saw associations as a vehicle through which citizens could actively participate in matters of public concern and serve the common good, and they emphasized the role of associations in completing the state and mediating between state and society.[8] In the words of one anonymous contributor to the *Deutsche Vierteljahrs-Schrift*, the leading social affairs journal of the day, "a primary indicator of the widely perceived need for the reorganization of society lies without doubt in the eagerness to turn to associations of the different classes of society to fill those gaps which are in part too distant from the government and in part not yet serious enough to attract its attention. In this manner, associations form the mediating links between the government and the governed."[9] This statement also spells out what was to become one of the enduring rationales that would be repeatedly advanced in the coming decades to justify the existence of voluntary social associations: their ability to ferret out and respond to emergent social problems.

The first wave of recognizably modern philanthropic associations in Germany dates from the Napoleonic Wars. In 1810, Napoleon established the Imperial Society for Maternal Charity and required government officials and local notables to found local branches throughout the empire, including eventually the German lands then under French rule.[10] This kind of state-sponsored, semiofficial association was a clear reflection of the limited autonomy of civil society at that point. The General Charity Association (*Allgemeiner Wohltätigkeitsverein*), which was established in Württemberg in 1816, was a similar hybrid, and in part the history of voluntary associations is the history of their conflicts with the late absolutist police state.[11] But these struggles also had a very important gender dimension. During the wars of liberation, a large

---

[8] Friedrich Müller, *Korporation und Assoziation. Eine Problemgeschichte der Vereinigungsfreiheit im deutschen Vormärz* (Berlin, 1964).

[9] "Kurze Notizen," *Deutsche Vierteljahrs-Schrift*, 1845, Heft 2, 335f.

[10] Christine Adams, "Maternal Societies in France. Private Charity before the Welfare State," *Journal of Women's History* 17:1 (2005), 87–111.

[11] On the General Charity Association, see Lisgret Militzer-Schwenger, *Armenerziehung durch Arbeit. Eine Untersuchung am Beispiel des württemgergischen Schwarzwaldkreises 1806–1914* (Tübinger Vereinigung für Volkskunde, 1979), and Carola Lipp, "Verein als politisches Handlungsmuster. Das Beispiel des württembergischen Vereinswesens von 1800 bis zur Revolution 1848–1849," in Étienne François, ed., *Sociabilité et société bourgeoise en France, en Allemagne et en Suisse, 1750–1850* (Paris, 1986), 275–96, especially 276f.

number of women's associations were founded to outfit volunteers, care for the wounded, and support the families of these men.[12] The fact that the members of these associations were women enabled them to at least partly escape the reactionary downdraft after 1815 by redirecting their energies from explicitly patriotic goals to more maternal, and therefore less (overtly) political, tasks such as care for the sick, poor mothers, and children. However, many officials regarded these associations as a serious threat to both prevailing gender hierarchies and the structures of political authority, and they redoubled their efforts to dissolve these associations, or at least to limit the potential political implications of their work.

There were, in fact, many reasons for the state to be supportive of voluntary associations, especially philanthropic ones. In many states, modernizing bureaucrats had been instrumental in clearing away the older corporate constraints on individual activity, and public officials – especially at the local level – often played a prominent role in associational life, thereby mediating in their persons between state and society. This collaborative potential was further strengthened by ties of family, friendship, religion, and social class that bound together local notables both inside and outside government. There were, to be sure, strict limits on associational freedom, especially in the *Vormärz*. However, as we shall see in this and subsequent chapters, relations between state and association were far more complex than one might be led to believe by the liberal doctrine of the separation of state and society, and, depending on time and place, they could be as much collaborative as oppositional.

Pauperism, the Dangerous Classes, and the Social Question

There was no fundamental discontinuity in the organization of assistance to the poor across the Napoleonic divide in Germany, except perhaps in those areas along the Rhine that were under direct French rule for an extended period of time. Although poor relief was reformed in a number of German states and cities between the 1790s and the 1830s, these reforms followed in the well-worn tracks of the late absolutist reforms described in the previous chapter.[13]

The first important reform of poor relief in the Germanies during the revolutionary era was contained in the Prussian General Code (*Allgemeines Landrecht*), which was promulgated in 1791. The General Code was a thoroughly

---

[12] Dirk Alexander Reder, *Frauenbewegung und Nation. Patriotische Frauenvereine in Deutschland im frühen 19. Jahrhundert (1813–1830)* (SH-Verlag, 1998), and Rita Huber-Sperl, "Organized Women and the Strong State: The Beginnings of Female Associational Activity in Germany, 1810–1840," *Journal of Women's History* 13:4 (Winter 2002), 81–105. On the role of charitable-patriotic associations as a vehicle for the self-representation of aristocratic women in the nineteenth century, see Jean Quataert, *Staging Philanthropy. Patriotic Women and the National Imagination in Dynastic Germany, 1813–1916* (University of Michigan Press, 2001), Chapter 2.

[13] Klaus Wohlrab, *Armut und Staatszweck. Die politische Theorie der Armut im deutschen Naturrecht des 18. und 19. Jahrhunderts* (Keip Verlag, 1997), captures the coexistence of the old and the new in contemporary theorizing on the role of the state in the relief of the poor.

Pauperism, the Dangerous Classes, and the Social Question

ambiguous document standing on the watershed between the old regime and the modern world. Although its invocation of the authority of the sovereign territorial state was an unmistakable sign of its modernity, this authority was invoked in order to codify the basic institutions of a corporate order – an order which, however, was already being transformed from within by social changes that were being actively promoted by the modernizing state.[14] The Code proclaimed that the state was responsible for assisting the deserving poor, but only insofar as the family, the local community, or existing corporate bodies did not have a prior obligation to do so, and the state itself retained only the most attenuated, subsidiary responsibility.[15] The Rhenish cities of Cologne and Münster, which came under direct French rule before being annexed to Prussia after 1815, were much more directly affected by the French Revolution.[16] Under French rule, religious corporations were dissolved, the previous system of parish-based church charity was abolished, outdoor assistance was centralized in the hands of a public welfare bureau, and hospitals and endowed foundations were secularized and placed under the authority of a centralized hospital commission. In the south, the governmental centralization undertaken in conjunction with the territorial reorganization of Bavaria after the dissolution of the Holy Roman Empire led to the traumatic incorporation of former imperial cities such as Augsburg and Regensburg into the Bavarian state and to the temporary subordination of municipal relief to the central state.[17]

Nassau and Württemberg also reformed their poor laws at the end of the Napoleonic wars.[18] The problems of rural overpopulation and underemployment were particularly acute in these states; they both sought to make the

---

[14] On the General Code and its influence on German society and politics in the *Vormärz*, see Reinhart Koselleck, *Preußen zwischen Reform und Revolution. Allgemeines Landrecht, Verwaltung und soziale Bewegung von 1791 bis 1848*, 3. Aufl. (Klett-Cotta, 1981).

[15] The relevant provisions of the *Landrecht* are reprinted in Christoph Sachße and Florian Tennstedt, *Geschichte der Armenfürsorge*, 3. Bde. (Kohlhammer, 1980/92), I:275–6. See also Michael Doege, *Armut in Preußen und Bayern (1770–1840)* (Neue Schriftenreihe des Stadtarchivs München, 1991), 176ff.

[16] For Münster, see Thomas Küster, *Alte Armut und neues Bürgertum. Öffentliche und private Fürsorge in Münster von der Ära Fürstenberg bis zum Ersten Weltkrieg (1756–1914)* (Aschendorf, 1995), and, for Cologne, Norbert Finzsch, *Obrigkeit und Unterschichten: Zur Geschichte der rheinischen Unterschichten gegen Ende des 18. und zu Beginn des 19. Jahrhunderts* (Steiner, 1990), Ulrike Dorn, *Öffentliche Armenpflege in Köln von 1794–1871. Zugleich ein Beitrag zur Geschichte der öffentlichrechtlichen Anstalt* (Böhlau, 1990), and Christian Wißbach, "Das Kölner Armenwesen 1815–1830," *Jahrbuch des kölnischen Geschichtsvereins* 66 (1995), 85–126.

[17] Susanne Eser, *Verwaltet und verwahrt – Armenpolitik und Arme in Augsburg. Vom Ende der reichsstädtischen Zeit bis zum Ersten Weltkrieg* (Jan Thorbecke Verlag, 1996), 94ff., and Karl Kick, *Von der Armenpflege zur Sozialpolitik. Die Entwicklung des Fürsorgewesens im 19. Jahrhundert am Beispiel Regensburgs* (Universitätsverlag Regensburg, 1995). Munich had already begun to reform its poor relief system in the 1790s. See Angelika Baumann, "*Armuth ist hier wahrhaft zu Haus...*" *Vorindustrieller Pauperismus und Einrichtungen der Armenpflege in Bayern um 1800* (Neue Schriftenreihe des Stadtarchivs München, 1984).

[18] Peter Blum, *Staatliche Armenfürsorge im Herzogtum Nassau 1806–1866* (Veröffentlichungen der Historischen Kommission für Nassau, XLIV, 1987), and Militzer-Schwenger,

rigorous enforcement of the work obligation into the cornerstone of their reforms; and they both responded with the familiar combination of voluntary work programs, industry schools, and workhouses, as well as efforts to secure the more continuous and effective surveillance of the poor. However, the thrust of these reforms was contradictory and their impact uneven. They were progressive in their goal of preventing poverty, their understanding of the connection between illness and poverty, the establishment of a broad medical assistance program, and the attempt to create a centralized organization to coordinate assistance within the state and alleviate the worst failings of hopelessly underfunded local relief authorities. Although the precarious state of local finances forced authorities to set assistance rates below the subsistence level and limited the scope of work creation programs, officials continued to support these programs because they felt that they helped prevent the complete demoralization of the poor. Similarly, while officials hoped that industry schools would teach the poor new skills that would increase the productivity of local industry and expand employment opportunities, such policies made sense only as long as the work offered by these programs corresponded to the general level of technology employed by the putting-out system, and they became increasingly irrelevant with the spread of industry and the transition from extensive to intensive production. However, the belief that the poor could find work if they really tried gave relief in both states a repressive, moralizing streak, and the idea of eliminating poverty by promoting savings associations was well meaning but irrelevant to those who could barely afford to eat.

All these reforms were based on the assumption that the number of deserving poor would remain relatively stable at a level that was not incommensurate with available resources. However, this condition quickly ceased to hold after 1815, and in the coming years poor relief systems throughout the Germanies were simply overwhelmed by the rising tide of pauperism.

What concerned most contemporary observers was less the level of absolute material deprivation than the social consequences of economic change and what they perceived as the moral degeneration of the impoverished masses, whose alienation from and hostility toward society made them less an object of charity than one of fear. The culture of pauperism was regarded, if not as a contradiction in itself, then at least as the antithesis of civil society, and growing incivility and immorality, it was feared, was making the poor into criminals, sinners, and revolutionaries who would become the gravediggers of the bourgeois order.

Armenerziehung durch Arbeit. On developments in Hesse, see Susanne Grindel, *Armenpolitik und Staatlichkeit. Das öffentliche Armenwesen im Kurfürstentum Hessen (1803–1866)* (Hessische Historische Kommission, 2000), and Susanne Grindel and Winfried Speitkamp, eds., *Armenfürsorge in Hessen-Kassel. Dokumente zur Vorgeschichte der Sozialpolitik zwischen Aufklärung und Industrialisierung* (Hessische Historische Kommission, 1998).

Pauperism, the Dangerous Classes, and the Social Question

In the 1830s and 1840s, there was an extensive debate over the causes and meaning of pauperism.[19] Twentieth-century debate on the topic has pitted Marxists, who regarded the immiseration of the factory working classes as a distinguishing feature of early industrialization, against historical demographers, who have viewed pauperism as the last Malthusian crisis before industrialization broke through the resource limits that had so mercilessly checked population growth in earlier ages. The biggest problem with the Marxist approach is that pauperism antedated the beginnings of industrialization in the Germanies by several decades and was often most severe in those areas with little or no industry. The main weakness of the demographic approach is that it ignores the ways in which trends in population, productivity, and prices were themselves determined by power relations and the distribution of resources within the prevailing mode of production. More recently, the concept of proto-industrialization has facilitated a middle way between these two interpretations by showing how the expanded employment opportunities resulting from the spread of both agrarian capitalism and the putting-out system sustained a steadily rising rural population – if only at a minimal standard of living and thanks in part to the introduction of the potato – from the second half of the 1700s into the 1820s and 1830s, when a saturation point was reached at which neither agriculture nor manufacture was capable of absorbing additional population.[20] Between 1780 and 1850, the population of the Germanies increased from 21 to 35 million, or 67%, and it was precisely those groups who lacked property and a secure place in the social order that were multiplying most rapidly.[21]

These demographic developments, however, also coincided with structural crises in agriculture, the skilled trades, and proto-industrial manufacture, and the pauper "class" was composed of a number of distinct elements. First, in the south partible inheritance led to the continuous fragmentation of holdings that, as in Ireland, pointed toward a developmental cul-de-sac as available land was unable to either produce enough to support this population or yield the profits necessary to modernize production. People who did not own a critical mass of property were forced off the land, especially as a second factor diminished the primary alternative source of supplementary income. The collapse of manual

---

[19] This literature has been repeatedly anthologized and commented. See Martin Kukowski, *Pauperismus in Kurhessen. Ein Beitrag zur Entstehung und Entwicklung der Massenarmut in Deutschland 1815–1855* (Hessische Historische Kommission, 1995), 445–546, Martin Fuhrmann, *Volksvermehrung als Staatsaufgabe? Bevölkerungs- und Ehepolitik in der deutschen politischen und ökonomischen Theorie des 18. und 19. Jahrhunderts* (Schöningh, 2002), and Klaus-Jürgen Matz, *Pauperismus und Bevölkerung. Die gesetzlichen Ehebeschränkungen in den süddeutschen Staaten während des 19. Jahrhunderts* (Klett-Cotta, 1980), 51–93, all of which provide guides to the older literature.

[20] Hans-Ulrich Wehler, *Deutsche Gesellschaftsgeschichte, Bd. II: Von der Reformära bis zur industriellen und politischen "Deutschen Doppelrevolution" 1815–1845/9*, 2. Aufl. (Beck, 1989), 281–96.

[21] Blum, *Staatliche Armenfürsorge im Herzogtum Nassau*, 17.

textile production in the face of English exports and early domestic mechanization was one of the most important factors contributing to the pauperism crisis because it undermined the economic viability of precisely that sector that had heretofore sustained the proto-industrial population boom. The third major group that was drawn into the crisis of pauperism was the guild artisanate. The establishment of occupational freedom led to the overpopulation of many trades as journeymen set themselves up as independent producers in trades where the number of masters and apprentices had previously been restricted by the guilds. These factors, together with limited recourse to migration and the inability of early industrial manufacture to provide an alternative source of employment that would come anywhere near offsetting the number of livelihoods that it destroyed, were all condensed for a few decades in what proved to be a massive transitional crisis. The costs of such widespread destitution weighed heavily on the cities, with perhaps a quarter of the population in some places receiving public assistance at times in the 1830s and 1840s.[22] During these decades, therefore, stark, traumatic visions of the decay and disorganization of the older corporate order overlapped with more optimistic visions of the emancipatory potential of modern society without it being quite clear about how a new and more stable social formation might emerge out of this chaos.

In 1846, the Brockhaus *Conversations-Lexikon* defined pauperism as a neologism that had been coined to describe a new kind of mass poverty that was different from both the natural poverty resulting from physical infirmity or individual misfortune and the poverty of those who had always lived on the margins of corporate society. What distinguished modern pauperism was that it represented a condition "where a numerous class of people can secure through the most strenuous work at most the most minimal subsistence (and can not even be certain of this), a class whose members are – even before they are born – doomed for their entire lives to such a condition, a class that has no prospects of improvement and that, in fact, sinks deeper and deeper into lethargy and brutality, temptation, drink, and animalistic vices of all kinds, that supplies a constantly increasing number of recruits to the poorhouses, workhouses, and jails, and that yet still manages to replenish itself and increase its numbers with great rapidity."[23]

---

[22] For Cologne, see Gisela Mettele, *Bürgertum in Köln. Gemeinsinn und freie Association* (Oldenbourg, 1998), 133, and Petra Witting, "Die Situation der Armen im mittleren Drittel des 19. Jahrhunderts. Dargestellt am Beispiel Kölns," *Jahrbuch des kölnischen Geschichtsvereins* 57 (1986) 75–146, especially 136. Reinhart Koselleck, "Staat und Gesellschaft in Preussen," in Werner Conze, ed., *Staat und Gesellschaft im deutschen Vormärz 1815–1848* (=*Industrielle Welt*, Bd. 1, Klett, 1962), 101, reports that one-fourth of the Berlin population was receiving public assistance in the 1840s.

[23] "Pauperismus," *Brockhaus' Conversations-Lexikon der Gegenwart*, (Leipzig, 1840), IV:65, cited in Wolfram Fischer, *Armut in der Geschichte* (Vandenhoeck & Ruprecht, 1982), 62. See also Conze, "From 'Pöbel' to 'Proletariat'. The Socio-Historical Preconditions of Socialism in Germany," in Georg Iggers, ed., *The Social History of Politics* (Berg, 1985), 49–80.

What is interesting about this passage is the way that it moves imperceptibly from a recognition of the historical novelty of pauperism to an informed explanation of the economic causes of the uncertainties faced by these new underclasses to the conclusion that the utter hopelessness of their situation and the pressures of their hand-to-mouth existence had combined to render them susceptible to every conceivable vice. These were the dangerous classes, whose disrespect for work, authority, and property, the middle classes feared, was leading them headlong into perdition and poverty and making them into a palpable threat to a social order in which they had no stake. While some observers spoke of "demoralizing poverty" (*entsittlichende Armut*),[24] for most the equation ran in the other direction, with immorality being viewed as the cause of poverty. As one anonymous author wrote in the *Deutsche Vierteljahrs-Schrift*, "the causes of pauperism are without a doubt to be found more in the degeneration of morals than in the relative insufficiency of work.... We view pauperism as a moral disease of the people and consider barbarism and brutality, as they reveal themselves in vagrancy, idleness, drink and prostitution, as both signs of its presence and the conditions of its growth."[25] The list of moral failings ascribed to paupers can be expanded at will (irreligion, dissipation, profligacy, sloth, emancipation of the flesh, licentiousness, gambling, and drink), but all of these concepts can be described, in one way or another, as the antithesis of those norms of work, thrift, and family responsibility that were the foundation of social status and material well-being in bourgeois society.[26] Here, the rhetorical conflation of poverty with vice, crime, and revolution represented less an attempt to objectively describe a sequence of cause-and-effect relations between material destitution and individual character than to erect an extended chain of signifiers in which the pauper was constructed as the Other in which the bourgeois self could see its own virtues mirrored and affirmed. Although the inability to anchor this referential chain in any external reality rendered it intrinsically unstable, it nevertheless prevented destitution from being represented as anything other than self-incurred, and it authorized both the signifying structures of the discourse of moral reform and the assistantial practices in which this discourse was embodied.[27]

---

[24] C. G. Kries, "Betrachtungen über Armenpflege und Heimathsrecht," *Zeitschrift für die gesamte Staatswissenschaft* 9 (1853), 3–78, 311–70, citation 8.
[25] Anonymous, "Die Zwangsarbeitshäuser, ihre Zöglinge und die Vereine," *Deutsche Vierteljahrs-Schrift* (1844, Heft 1), 15–16.
[26] Sabine Lippuner, *Bessern und Verwahren. Die Praxis der administrativen Versorgung von "Liederlichen" und "Arbeitsscheuen" in der thurgauischen Zwangsarbeitsanstalt Kalchrain* (Historischer Verein des Kantons Thurgau, 2005), 35–41.
[27] Louis Chevalier, *The Laboring Classes and the Dangerous Classes in the First Half of the Nineteenth Century* (Howard Fertig, 1973), especially 93ff. Dietlinde Hüchtker, *"Elende Mütter" und "liederliche Weibspersonen". Geschlechterverhältnisse und Armenpolitik in Berlin (1770–1850)* (Westfälisches Dampfboot, 1999), 118ff., and Pielhoff, *Paternalismus und Stadtarmut*, both make a similar point.

Although a strong state was always a valued bulwark against crime and revolution, when defined in these terms the key to solving the social question was to be found less in the economic or political spheres than in the social domain, that is, in the remoralization of the pauperized poor, the restoration of their belief in the value of work, property, family, and authority, and, through this, the reintegration of these atomized and alienated masses into the community. However, the question was how best to achieve this goal, and the two most active reform groups in the *Vormärz* explained this crisis in very different ways and adopted strategies that reflected their divergent visions of both human nature and civil society.

Protestant Social Conservatism and the Founding of the Inner Mission

Beginning in March 1848, revolution rippled through the Germanies in the wake of the February uprising in Paris. In France, the key events were the founding of the Second Republic, the creation and subsequent dissolution of the national workshops, which embodied both the promise and the danger of a social republic, and the bloody street battles in June, where the meaning of citizenship was defined on the barricades. In the Germanies, too, the constitutional question and the social question were yoked together in the revolution, yet in a different way than was the case in France, where capitalism and industry were both far more advanced. In the Germanies, the antithesis of social order and the moderate constitutional reform envisioned by the liberals was less socialism and the organization of labor than the anarchy and depredations by the rabble that the propertied classes expected would invariably follow on the proclamation of a republic. Yet such diffuse fears could have little direct impact on the reform of relief and charity. National unification and constitutional reform dominated the deliberations of the Frankfurt parliament, and within its influential committee on economic affairs the social question was addressed primarily through the conflict over free trade, whose dynamic and social consequences could still only be dimly perceived.

Both conservatives and liberals saw moral reform as the antithesis of revolution. However, the events of 1848/9 were much more traumatic for Protestant social conservatives than for the liberal movement. The thinking of conservative Protestants on the social problem was indelibly marked by their opposition to the Enlightenment, religious rationalism, and revolution, which they regarded as the destructive apotheosis of the essentially atheistic belief that the individual could find a moral ground and purpose within him- or herself. They insisted that human existence was defined above all by original sin, and they argued that certain social institutions had been divinely instituted to protect individuals from their innate sinfulness, educate them in the cardinal virtues of religious and social life, and thus lead them toward salvation and well-being. The most basic of these institutions was the family, or the patriarchal household to be more precise. Within the family, the father was the concrete embodiment of the principle of personal authority, and it was within the private sphere of the family and through the learned and willing obedience to their fathers that children developed all the social virtues. As the most fundamental institution of human society, the family also had to be the fulcrum for all efforts to elevate public morality, renew the religious life of the community, and solve the social question, though it too was embedded in set of concentric institutions (community, guild, church, and state), which mirrored the structure and function of the family at higher levels of generality.

In the post-Napoleonic years, the most important vehicle through which this conservative vision of society and social reform was translated into practice was the "house of salvation" (*Rettungshaus*), sixty-four of which had been founded by 1848, mostly in southern Germany.[28] These institutions were organized as extended families under the guidance of a "house father," and they were deeply influenced by Pietism, with its emphasis on a personal consciousness of sin and redemption, rather than doctrinal purity. In the *Vormärz*, the master concept in the social imagination of these conservative reformers was *Verwahrlosung*, a term which they used to refer to a state of neglect, endangerment, or waywardness resulting from the failure of the family and other institutions to protect the individual from his or her innate sinful urges or to give the child the spiritual fortitude to resist temptation from without.[29] The ultimate cause of *Verwahrlosung* was the rejection of God, and without faith the entire fabric of society would unravel, starting from the family. In the words of Ludwig Völter, one of the leading figures in the house of salvation movement, "religion is, however, the foundation of families as of states. Where it is absent, so are domestic bliss and domestic discipline. Impurity, domestic strife, conjugal faithlessness, the search for diversion outside the home, dissipation, gambling, drink, poverty and need gain the upper hand. What is missing are the truly conserving spiritual forces, as is – lastly – the courage to subordinate oneself to the duties and burdens of an orderly household."[30] Ultimately, Völter argued, without some sense of higher purpose that could provide a moral center, the resulting sense of hopelessness would tempt the individual to seek salvation in vice, crime, and revolution:

How often does the poor man so lose courage and trust in God that he comes to believe that even with the greatest effort he can no longer sustain himself and his family. Desperation drives him into the arms of vice, and he hopes to drown his resentment in wine or brandy.... Or poverty makes him unloving towards and jealous of the propertied, who in his eyes are the more fortunate. He is filled with rage and hate

---

[28] On the houses of salvation, see Ludwig Völter, *Geschichte und Statistik der Rettungs-Anstalten für arme verwahrloste Kinder in Württemberg* (Stuttgart, 1845); Karl Ruth, *Die Pädagogik der süddeutschen Rettungshausbewegung. Chr. H. Zeller und der schwäbischen Pietismus* (Berlin, 1927); Hans Scherpner, *Geschichte der Jugendfürsorge* (Vandenhoeck & Ruprecht, 1966), 117ff.; and Edward Ross Dickinson, *The Politics of German Child Welfare from the Empire to the Federal Republic* (Harvard University Press, 1996), Chapter 1. The number of houses of salvation is cited from Dickinson, *The Politics of German Child Welfare*, 13.

[29] Völter, *Geschichte und Statistik der Rettungs-Anstalten*, 14.

[30] Völter, *Geschichte und Statistik der Rettungs-Anstalten*, 33–7, citation 37.

towards them, declares proper war against them, lays his hands on the property of others, and ultimately ends up in the courts and the workhouses.[31]

The houses of salvation were not the only form of conservative Protestant social engagement in the *Vormärz*. These decades also saw the creation – as a conservative alternative to the liberal kindergarten movement – of day-care centers (*Kleinkinderbewahranstalten*) for the young children from working-class families,[32] the establishment by Theodor Fliedner of an institution to train devout women as deaconesses to minister to the physical and spiritual needs of the sick in accordance with evangelical principles,[33] and the halting spread of traditionally minded women's friendly visiting associations modeled on the work of the Women's Association for the Care of the Poor and Sick, which was founded in 1832 in Hamburg by Amalie Sieveking.[34] But the most important Protestant moral reform association established during these decades was the Inner Mission, which was founded in 1848/9 by Johann Hinrich Wichern, who took up the program of the houses of salvation, which had originally been a movement for the reclamation of endangered children, and expanded it into a broader program for the religious renewal of the nation.[35]

---

[31] Völter, *Geschichte und Statistik der Rettungs-Anstalten*, 38–9.

[32] Ann Taylor Allen, "Gardens of Children, Gardens of God: Kindergartens and Day-Care Centers in Nineteenth-Century Germany," *Journal of Social History* 19 (Spring, 1986), 433–50, and Johann Baptist Ristelhueber, *Ueber die Nothwendigkeit der Errichtung von Arbeits- und Erziehungs-Anstalten für sittlich verwahrlosete Kinder, nebst Anleitung, wie dergleichen Institute zu errichten und zu verwalten sind* (Stuttgart, 1828).

[33] For an introduction to Fliedner's work, see Albin Gladen, "Theodor Fliedner," in Martin Greschat, ed., *Gestalten der Kirchengeschichte*, 9/1 (Kohlhammer, 1985), 293–307. Fliedner also founded the *Rheinisch-Westfälische Gefängnisgesellschaft*, which was one of the leading organizations in the field of penology into the twentieth century.

[34] On Sieveking and her charitable work, see Pielhoff, *Paternalismus und Stadtarmut*; Ursula Baumann, *Protestantismus und Frauenemanzipation in Deutschland 1850 bis 1920* (Campus Verlag, 1992), Chapter 2; and Catherine Prelinger, *Charity, Challenge, and Change. Religious Dimensions of the Mid-Nineteenth-Century Women's Movement in Germany* (Greenwood Press, 1987). Both Baumann and Prelinger emphasize the role of religious rivalries and intolerance in the early history of these women's associations.

[35] In 1975, the Inner Mission was consolidated with the Hilfswerk der Evangelischen Kirche in Deutschland, which had been founded after World War II, and the new organization, the Diakonisches Werk, became the official charity organization of the German Evangelical Church. As such, it remains one of the major social service providers in the Federal Republic. The literature on Wichern and the Inner Mission is extensive. The account here draws on William O. Shanahan, *German Protestants Face the Social Question*, (Notre Dame University Press, 1954), 208–23, 232–8, 290–301, 383–8; Martin Gerhardt, *Ein Jahrhundert Innere Mission. Die Geschichte des Central-Ausschusses für die Innere Mission der Deutschen Evangelischen Kirche*, 2 vols. (Bertelsmann, 1948); Günter Brakelmann, *Kirche und Sozialismus im 19. Jahrhundert. Die Analyse des Sozialismus und Kommunismus bei J.H. Wichern und Rudolf Todt* (Luther-Verlag, 1966); and Peter Meinhold, *Wichern und Ketteler. Evangelische und katholische Prinzipien kirchlichen Sozialhandelns* (Wiesbaden, 1978). Wichern's writings are collected in *Sämtliche Werke*, 10 vols., edited by Peter Meinhold (Lutherisches Verlagshaus, 1962–88).

Wichern grew up in an impoverished Hamburg household, and he owed his education to the patronage of Hamburg elites influenced by the Pietist awakening. After completing his theological studies, he taught Sunday school and made house visits in the lower-class districts of the city. In 1833, Wichern founded his own house of salvation, the *Rauhes Haus*, outside of Hamburg on land provided by the Sieveking family. Wichern saw the cities, where *wilde Ehen*, illegitimate children, and prostitution were openly accepted and where the impoverished and endangered masses lived outside of the church and beyond the reach of the gospel, as a reflection of the pervasive godlessness of the times, and he felt that institutions like the house of salvation were so urgently needed because the family life of the Hamburg proletariat was so deformed, defiled, and disorganized that it was impossible for the children of these classes, who were constantly exposed to all sorts of unnatural and immoral acts, to receive a proper upbringing.[36] By removing these children from this environment (with the permission of their parents), they would be protected from these corrupting influences and experience that combination of discipline and love that could flourish only within a Christian family.[37] Although Wichern recognized that the poverty of the lower classes weighed heavily on them and that their continuous struggle for existence rendered them susceptible to temptation and often undermined in advance any efforts at self-improvement, he nevertheless maintained that poverty was most often the product of immorality, irreligion, and the "impure" character of their family life.[38]

For Wichern, pauperism was the product of a crisis that was simultaneously one of religious faith, political authority, and social order. The ultimate origin of this crisis was the ignorance or rejection of God, and the practical expression of this state of unbelief was to be found in revolution and that totally sinful and degenerate state of social (dis)order that Wichern defined as communism. Revolution, he argued, could never be constructive because it invariably led to the inversion of the divine order of things, that is, "the overturning of the divinely established difference between above and below, rulers and ruled, parents and children, lords and servants, authorities and subjects," and he saw communism simply as "the systematization of the sinful appetites, which dares to justify itself before God with all of those consequences that are so flattering to the flesh and which then, with all the anger that comes from the lack of faith in God and the absence of morality, attempts to ruin mankind in order to create a new and presumably better world."[39]

Wichern believed that the 1848 revolution represented a turning point in world history, and he came to believe that the path to social regeneration was

---

[36] Wichern, "Ein Votum über das heutige Sodom und Gomorrha" (1851), *Sämtliche Werke*, II:214–25 and I:212–13.
[37] Wichern, "Die öffentliche Begründung des Rauhen Hauses," *Sämtliche Werke*, IV:96–114.
[38] Wichern, "Die öffentliche Begründung des Rauhen Hauses," *Sämtliche Werke*, IV:104, and "Über Armenpflege" (1855), III/1:38, and I:123, 180.
[39] Wichern, *Sämtliche Werke*, I:256.

to be found in what he called an "inner mission" to that growing section of the people whose poverty and immorality were signs of their inner godlessness. The Conference of German Protestants that was convoked in September 1848 to rally the churches against the revolution endorsed Wichern's program, and the following year saw the founding of the Central Committee for Inner Mission and the publication of Wichern's book-length "Protestant manifesto," which laid out the principles that were to guide the work of the organization.[40] The Central Committee was a loose association of highly placed conservative notables whose goal was to mobilize concerned Christians against liberalism and revolution, encourage the foundation of local associations and institutions, and serve as a national umbrella organization to concentrate and direct the energies of its member organizations. The Inner Mission expanded rapidly in the first decade of its existence. Between 1849 and 1852, some hundred new houses of salvation were established, as were a number of city, provincial (Prussia), and state associations, and by the end of the 1850s the Inner Mission already had a substantial presence across much of the nation.[41]

There was, however, broad resistance to the association on the part of the Lutheran establishment, which feared that the self-organization of the laity would diminish the sacerdotal dignity of the clerical office, submerge the sharp contours of doctrinal orthodoxy in a watered-down, interconfessional commitment to brotherly love, and possibly open the door to a new wave of Pietist sectarianism.[42] Wichern tried to dispel these concerns, emphasizing that the associational activity of the Inner Mission emanated from within the institutional church and ultimately worked back toward it.[43] However, like the relationship between secular associations and the state, the relation of the Inner Mission to the established churches remained a matter of contention until the disestablishment of the church after 1918.

Wichern's views on the nature and scope of church charity need to be seen in conjunction with the debate over the reform of public poor relief, which we will examine in Chapter 4.[44] While influential Protestant charity reformers such as Thomas Chalmers had questioned the very legitimacy of public poor relief, Wichern argued that problem was to properly delimit the respective spheres of church and public poor relief so that each could fulfill those tasks for

---

[40] Wichern, "Die innere Mission – eine Denkschrift an die deutsche Nation (1849)," *Sämtliche Werke*, I:175–439.

[41] Gerhardt, *Ein Jahrhundert Innere Mission*, 204–34.

[42] "Der Verein als Lebensform in der Kirche," in *Die Innere Mission* 50:8 (1960), 225–52; Gerhard Uhlhorn, *Die christliche Liebestätigkeit*, 2. Aufl. (Stuttgart, 1895), 718ff.; and Wilhelm Rothert, *Die innere Mission in Hannover*, 3. umgearbeitete Aufl. (Gütersloh, 1909), 1ff. Rothert and Walter Vogel, *Fünfzig Jahre Innere Mission im Kgr. Sachsen* (Leipzig, 1917), provide good overviews of the early activity of the Inner Mission in their respective states.

[43] Wichern, *Sämtliche Werke*, I:112, 170.

[44] The following paragraphs are drawn primarily from several essays and talks by Wichern, dating from 1855 to 1856, which were published under the title "Über Armenpflege," *Sämtliche Werke*, III/1:21–70.

which it was best suited. For Wichern, material destitution and immorality were simply the external expressions of an inner distress that could only be overcome through spiritual means, and he insisted that the church had to recognize its responsibility for finding new ways to bring the gospel to the unchurched. However, preaching alone was not sufficient. Since the pressures of poverty rendered the poor particularly susceptible to temptation and endangered any efforts to help these persons better themselves, Wichern insisted that material assistance was a vital element of church relief, though only insofar as it could be made into a mechanism for the inner spiritual elevation of the poor.

The privileged objects of church relief were the deserving but impoverished members of the congregation who, with the help of such assistance, would be able to maintain their own households, and assistance to these deserving residential poor provided the model for Wichern's idealized vision of church charity. Since the recognized uprightness of these persons obviated the need to investigate their personal circumstance or police their behavior, church relief could be represented as a form of charity in which visitors came as sympathetic friends and spiritual advisors, whose visits would bring comfort – both material and spiritual – and renew the bonds of community, rather than as representatives of local authorities, whose concern to ferret out dissimulation required them to parcel out material assistance in accordance with bureaucratic procedures on the basis of some abstract standard of need.

Wichern insisted that the monies required for church charity had to be raised through voluntary contributions because charity could touch the hearts of the poor only if it were unmistakably clear that the assistance offered to them was freely given by the congregation out of personal concern for the welfare of their less fortunate brethren. Wichern expected that this personal sacrifice would be repaid in the currency of gratitude, and he hoped that this would lead the poor to redouble their efforts to help themselves in order not to be an excessive burden on their benefactors. But Wichern also argued that pastoral care for the deserving poor had to focus on the maintenance of their family life. As he explained, church relief for the deserving members of the congregation "is not only care for the poor in their houses, but rather simultaneously the care of the house(hold) of the poor, which should be honored, edified, and hallowed as a divine institution and God's dwelling." However, this vision of church charity had decidedly conservative implications, and Wichern hoped it would teach the poor the value of humility and reconcile them with their worldly misfortune by revealing to them its greater religious significance: "Need now becomes the key to life, and the poor person learns to thank God for the poverty through which he has become rich in such experience."[45]

On the other hand, Wichern believed that the church could never do without the support of public authority because there were many cases where the personal help described earlier was neither possible nor appropriate. Since

[45] Wichern "Über Armenpflege," *Sämtliche Werke*, III/1:39–40.

Germany was a confessionally mixed country, the state had the obligation to assist those persons who resided in places where they could not fall back on congregational assistance. However, for Wichern the most important function of public authorities was to police and discipline the undeserving poor, and he took such a jaundiced attitude toward vagrancy because he equated it with crime, sin, and revolution. As he wrote in 1855,

> the poor person who has taken to begging does not want to help himself, will not let himself be helped, and conceals this not-wanting with inability in one form or another of idleness. He wants only to consume, but no longer to produce. He does not want to work any longer, but rather to let others work for him, in some form or another of deceit in word and deed, and as a cheat and loafer make poverty into an occupation and a source of gain. For this reason, professional begging is a dangerous first step towards theft. In fact, it is essentially already theft. It is a communist weed from whose roots sin, dishonor and crime of all sorts sprout. The professional beggar has already transgressed against the human and divine order. He is no longer simply a poor person, but rather one who uses his poverty to commit sin before God and punishable offenses before man.

Wichern encapsulated this antagonism between vagrancy and Christian civil society in the terse insistence that the idea of a beggar family "is a complete self-contradiction."[46]

In 1848, Wichern had characterized the work of the Inner Mission as a form of Christian socialism. However, in the following years, he became increasingly close to the high Protestant establishment, and their rigid conservatism deprived the Inner Mission of any serious need to understand the social changes taking place after 1848 and of the intellectual tools with which to do so. There were some conservatives, such as Victor Aimé Huber, who sought to help the Inner Mission understand the linkages between socioeconomic change and the culture of the emergent factory working classes, but they had little influence on the organization.[47] Wichern himself remained singularly blind to real social and economic forces. The only social reform that he could envision was a return to an earlier, corporatist organization of society; the cultivation of personal piety increasingly came to serve as an alternative to social reform, rather than preparation for it; and this reduction of the social question to one of personal morality ensured that the work of the Inner Mission would be of only marginal relevance to the great majority of independent, self-supporting working men and women, who saw the key to improving their conditions not in charity but in suffrage, social reform, and social revolution.

---

[46] Wichern, "Der Anteil des bürgerlichen Gemeinwesens an der Armenpflege" (1855), *Sämtliche Werke*, III/1:45–61, citation 46–7.

[47] On Protestant social thought at mid-century, see Hermann Beck, *The Origins of the Authoritarian Welfare State in Prussia. Conservatives, Bureaucracy, and the Social Question, 1815–1870* (University of Michigan Press, 1995), and, on Huber in particular, Shanahan, *German Protestants*, 282–96, and Ingwer Paulsen, *Viktor Aimé Huber als Sozialpolitiker* (Berlin, 1956).

Mobility, Modernity, and the Liberal Response to the Social Question

Protestant social conservatives believed, as we have seen, that the primary cause of the social problem was the decline of family life and religious faith, which they attributed to the spread of religious rationalism. In their eyes, the fatal flaw of this modernist doctrine was that it made man, rather than God, the measure of all things. As Völter explained, "if the human spirit was independent and its own ground, if it lived out of itself, then it would not need any God because it would be its own God."[48] However, the same conception of human freedom and self-determination that Völter condemned as folly and sacrilege was the cornerstone of the worldview of the liberal movement, and this understanding of human nature gave the liberals a very different view of civil society, the causes of pauperism, and the means for overcoming it.

In contrast to this Lutheran misanthropology, liberals, who were by no means antireligious, viewed natural man not so much as intrinsically sinful as deprived of education and culture; they attributed the poverty, immorality, and the social disorganization of the *Vormärz* to these disadvantages; and they responded to this crisis not by seeking to restore older forms of authority and personal dependence, but rather by helping the poor acquire the resources they needed to govern themselves and thus compete successfully within the nascent market society that was taking shape during these years. The foundation of the worldview of the early German liberals was the idea of independence, which encompassed both emancipation from all forms of tutelage and the capacity for self-governance, and liberals saw education and, especially, labor – that is, the permanent, agonistic struggle between individual industriousness and sloth, dependence, and dissipation – as the driving force behind the development of the individual and the progress of the species.[49]

In the *Vormärz*, German liberalism was rooted in a society that was post-"feudal" yet preindustrial, and Lothar Gall has described the social ideal of early German liberalism as that of a "classless society of state citizens of middling means," in which economic activity was dominated by artisanal production and independent farmers. The liberal movement drew its support from the entire spectrum of social groups that stood between the landed aristocracy and the poor, and they defined their own identity in opposition to these two groups. They saw the weakening of the old order as an opportunity for emancipation, civil (if not social or political) equality, the rule of reason and law, and careers

---

[48] Völter, *Geschichte und Statistik der Rettungs-Anstalten*, 19.
[49] The leading liberal proponent of the education of the lower classes in the 1830s and 1840s was the Rhenish industrialist and social reformer Friedrich Harkort. See Harkort, *Bemerkungen über die Hindernisse der Civilisation und Emancipation der unteren Klassen* (1844), reprinted in Harkort, *Schriften und Reden zu Volksschule und Volksbildung*, edited by Karl-Ernst Jeismann (Schöningh, 1969). On Harkort's work as a social reformer, see Wolfgang Köllmann, "Gesellschaftsanschauungen und sozialpolitisches Wollen Friedrich Harkorts," *Rheinische Vierteljahrsblätter* 25:1–2 (1960), 81–99.

open to talent and industry, and they hoped that education and economic development would gradually draw more and more of the population into this middling estate.[50]

This vision began to break down as industrialization took off at the end of the 1850s, and across the empire the liberal movement was continuously fragmented and reconstituted over constitutional, socioeconomic, religious, and foreign policy issues. In imperial Germany, the dominant fraction of the liberal movement was the National Liberals, who, broadly speaking, were the representatives of industry, commerce, and the dynamic forces of the new industrial world. Together with the various left liberal parties, the National Liberals dominated political life in the major cities, which served as their power base in the Reichstag, and during the heyday of industrialization and urbanization they were the moving force behind the professionalization of municipal government and the expansion and rationalization of municipal services, including poor relief.

The early liberal movement valued associations because, at the most basic level, they viewed the act of joining an association as something akin to an act of religious conversion. It was a way of turning one's back on the feckless and quasi-criminal proletariat and demonstrating that one was, or at least that one desired to become, a respectable, independent member of society. While associational life represented a way of reversing and overcoming that process of atomization and alienation that was making the proletariat into the enemy of the social order,[51] associations were also valuable in yet another sense because the moral benefits of associational activity were generally coupled with the tangible benefits of mutuality. In addition to the ubiquitous burial funds that were everywhere a sign of working-class respectability, the core of these social associations were savings associations, mutual assistance funds (*Unterstützungskassen*) for sickness, old age, disability, and death (widows' and orphans' benefits), associations for worker education and the dissemination of useful knowledge, reading clubs, and temperance associations.

Middle-class liberals tended to attribute poverty less to inadequate wages than to the failure of the wage-earning classes to plan for the future and set aside a portion of their earnings to tide them through the unavoidable periods

---

[50] Lothar Gall, ed., "Liberalismus und 'bürgerliche Gesellschaft'. Zu Charakter und Entwicklung der liberalen Bewegung in Deutschland," in *Liberalismus*, 3. Aufl. (Athenäum, 1985), 162–86; Gall "'...Ich wünschte ein Bürger zu sein'. Zum Selbstverständnis des deutschen Bürgertums im 19. Jahrhundert," HZ 245 (1987), 601–23; and James Sheehan, "Liberalism and Society in Germany, 1815–1848," JMH 45:4 (December 1973), 583–604. Mary Poovey provides an illuminating account of the *Bildung* of the bourgeois subject in *Uneven Developments. The Ideological Work of Gender in Mid-Victorian England* (University of Chicago Press, 1988), Chapter 4.

[51] See the arguments set out by Johannes Fallati, professor of history and statistics in Tübingen and later delegate to the Frankfurt National Assembly, in his often-cited essay "Das Vereinswesen als Mittel zur Sittigung der Fabrikarbeiter," *Zeitschrift für die gesamte Staatswissenschaft* 1 (1844), 737–91, especially 744–5.

of unemployment and sickness and to support themselves in their old age. They invoked savings associations in a disturbingly frequent and simplistic manner as a panacea for the social ills of the time because such associations promised to solve these problems by encouraging the cardinal virtue of thrift, by providing a practical means through which it might be practiced, and by socializing the risks associated with wage labor, though in a way that did not weaken personal responsibility. What distinguished these associations from traditional charities was that they were to be self-help associations *of* the laboring classes, not charitable associations *for* these classes, even though savings associations generally operated under the patronage of socially-minded middle-class reformers and depended on the financial subsidies they provided. One of the reasons why liberals favored savings accounts was that savings sustained the idea that even the humblest of persons were capable of moving upward into the property-owning class. They were also more consistent with the liberal ideal of a society of private property owners than were pensions and social insurance, which presumed the permanent division of society into property owners and wage earners.[52] However, while savings did provide some degree of protection against the risks of working-class life, in the absence of some mechanism for socializing these risks, the ability to save itself depended on avoiding those risks against which saving was intended to insure. In any case, the poor simply did not earn enough to enable them to provide for their own old age, and no amount of thrift could permit the laboring poor to save what they did not earn and thus leap over the shadow of their own poverty.[53]

Despite their continuity with older forms of social security, mutual assistance funds were a distinctly modern attempt to insure individuals whose emancipation from the constraints of family, church, guild, and community had also deprived them of the security offered by these institutions. The debate over mutual assistance funds was also one of the main avenues through which the social question was transformed from a debate over how best to dispauperize the demoralized poor into a question of how best to increase the economic security of the factory working classes, though liberal associational discourse often failed to distinguish clearly between the role of associations in elevating the morality of the former and the practical benefits that they offered to the latter.

The history of mutual associations in the 1840s and 1850s is the history of a complex, essentially local, and thus highly fragmented development, and

---

[52] Castel, *From Manual Workers to Wage Laborers*, 280ff.
[53] Karl Ditt, "'Soziale Frage', Sparkassen und Sparverhalten der Bevölkerung im Raum Bielefeld um die Mitte des 19. Jahrhunderts," in Werner Conze and Ulrich Engelhardt, eds., *Arbeiterexistenz im 19. Jahrhundert. Lebensstandard und Lebensgestaltung deutscher Arbeiter und Handwerker* (=Industrielle Welt, Bd. 33, Klett, 1981), 516–38. In contrast to mutual savings institutions, those savings associations that were sponsored by either middle-class associations or factory owners and that paid a premium to encourage savings by the lower classes could serve as a powerful vehicle for paternalistic tutelage and social disciplining of lower-class savers. See Pielhoff, *Paternalismus und Stadtarmut*, 251–3.

here we will focus more on the debates over associations as a vehicle of social policy than on their actual development.[54] Although some of these funds were established by workers themselves in the form of friendly societies that built on older, guild-based forms of mutual assistance, many were sponsored by employers out of a combination of Christian paternalism, local patriotism, and a forward-looking approach to industrial relations. Such corporate social institutions represent yet another of the voluntaristic roots of the welfare state.[55] Mutual assistance funds were also one of the early objects of state social legislation, especially in Prussia. Prussian social policy during these decades was characterized by a contradiction between liberal economic policies and the desire to combat the consequences of economic development through backward-looking, conservative social policies. The result was a social policy that was both ineffective in preserving the guild-based organization of production and neglectful of the needs of the new factory working classes.[56] Moreover, many people saw mutual assistance as the solution to the conflict among different fractions of the bourgeoisie, who were divided over the fact that tax-funded poor relief represented a means of socializing the cost of the social reproduction of the factory working classes, while the production and profits made possible by these expenditures accrued to factory owners alone.

The 1845 Commercial and Industrial Code sought to shore up the artisanate while bringing existing mutual assistance funds under state supervision to ensure that they did not become a vehicle for the political organization of their members. The 1849 amendment to this law, which was the first Prussian law to recognize factory workers as a distinct occupational group, went further than the original 1845 act and permitted local government to require employers to contribute to mutual assistance funds (up to 50% of worker contributions). Although this law was clearly meant to encourage local government to sponsor

---

[54] On the development of mutual assistance funds from the 1840s to the 1880s, see E. P. Hennock, *The Origin of the Welfare State in England and Germany, 1850–1914. Social Policies Compared* (Cambridge University Press, 2007), 151ff.; Eckart Reidegeld, *Staatliche Sozialpolitik in Deutschland. Historische Entwicklung und theoretische Analyse von den Ursprüngen bis 1918* (Westdeutscher Verlag, 1996), 157ff.; Ute Frevert, *Krankheit als politisches Problem 1770–1880* (Vandenhoeck & Ruprecht, 1984), 149ff.; and Heinrich Volkmann, *Die Arbeiterfrage im preußischen Abgeordnetenhaus 1848–1869* (Duncker & Humblot, 1968).

[55] On these factory-based social programs, see Günther Schulz, "Betriebliche Sozialpolitik in Deutschland seit 1850," in Hans Pohl, ed., *Staatliche, städtische, betriebliche und kirchliche Sozialpolitik vom Mittelalter bis zur Gegenwart*, VSWG Beiheft 95 (1991), 137–76, and Ludwig Puppke, *Sozialpolitik und soziale Anschauungen frühindustrieller Unternehmer in Rheinland-Westfalen* (Köln, 1966). Christiana von Hodenberg explores the nature of middle-class paternalism in "Der Fluch des Geldsacks. Der Aufstieg des Industriellen als Herausforderung bürgerlicher Werte," in Manfred Hettling and Stefan-Ludwig Hoffmann, eds., *Der bürgerliche Wertehimmel. Innenansichten des 19. Jahrhunderts* (Vandenhoeck & Ruprecht, 2000), 79–104. See also François Éwald, *Der Vorsorgestaat* (Suhrkamp, 1986), 150ff. Bavaria required all incorporated firms to provide such social programs for their employees.

[56] Wolfgang Köllmann, "Die Anfänge der staatlichen Sozialpolitik in Preußen bis 1869," in Ernst-Wolfgang Böckenförde, ed., *Moderne Deutsche Verfassungsgeschichte* (Kiepenheuer & Witsch, 1972), 410–29.

such funds for qualified workers, in the 1850s the manufacturing classes were often able to successfully resist, delay, and subvert the efforts of state officials in this direction.

The social policies of both Prussia and the southern states increasingly regarded the preservation of monarchical authority as more important than measures to combat pauperism and the social dislocation of early industrialization. The resulting absence of clear state leadership in responding to the problems of early industrialization left a broad space for voluntary initiative by liberal reformers – one that was filled in part by the Central Association for the Welfare of the Laboring Classes, the most prominent liberal reform association from the 1840s into the 1860s. The Central Association was founded in 1844 by a group of liberal industrialists and officials.[57] It was created against the background of both the successful trade exhibition of the *Zollverein* states, which confirmed the confidence of the middle classes, and the uprising of the Silesian weavers, which reinforced their apprehensions about the social consequences of economic change. The Central Association viewed itself as a combination think tank and coordinating committee, and its founders sought to establish a network of affiliate associations that would put into practice at the local level policies that were debated and refined within this central, nationwide body. The Central Association saw the key to solving the social question in the creation of a network of savings and mutual assistance funds, day-care centers to stem the *Verwahrlosung* of working-class children, and continuing education programs to elevate the laboring classes – all under the paternalistic guidance of the industrial and commercial middle classes who employed them.

These ambitious plans were upset by the Prussian government, and the subsequent history of the Central Association is emblematic of the troubled relation between state and society during the 1840s. Although the liberals tried to leverage the looming social crisis to obtain political concessions, the state refused to either undertake constructive policies on its own account or give societal organizations, such as the Central Association, the freedom to put their own ideas into practice. The Prussian government refused to certify the statutes of the Central Association and closed many of its local member associations because it feared that the internal organization of these bodies smacked too much of democracy and because their proposed reforms went beyond what the conservative state could countenance. This alienated the liberal middle classes, who increasingly came to believe that meaningful social reform could only be achieved by mobilizing against the state, rather than through cooperation with it. Many of the leading members of the Central Association were elected to the Frankfurt National Assembly, where they dominated the work of its committee on social and economic affairs. The Prussian government approved

---

[57] This and the following draw on Jürgen Reulecke, *Sozialer Frieden durch soziale Reform. Der Centralverein für das Wohl der arbeitenden Klassen in der Frühindustrialisierung* (Peter Hammer, 1983), and Toni Offermann, *Arbeiterbewegung und liberales Bürgertum in Deutschland 1850–1863* (Neue Gesellschaft, 1979), 158ff.

the statutes of the Central Association only after the moment for constructive social reforms had already passed.[58]

During the 1848 revolution, the Central Association sought to systematize the diverse reforms that had been initiated at the local level over the preceding decade. The leadership of the organization criticized the 1849 revision of the Commercial and Industrial Code for pandering to the protectionist fears of the guild artisanate while ignoring the needs of the growing number of factory workers, and Adolf Lette, the chairman of the Association, ventured so far as to call for the creation of factory committees to protect workers from the arbitrary decisions of their employers.[59] However, this proposal was stillborn, and in the early 1850s the Central Association shifted its energies back to mutual assistance. It tried to devise a workable plan for a national pension program to ensure that industrious workers would never have to depend on poor relief in their old age. In the reactionary 1850s there was no chance that such a proposal could have been implemented even if the Association's theoretical labors had been able to navigate successfully around the Gretchen question of the age: self-help or state help. Moreover, even though the members of the Association believed that such a plan would be a major step toward the integration of the working classes into the bourgeois order, it was by no means clear that the chief problem of the wage laboring classes was the lack of thrift or that even the best conceived plan could have succeeded without a substantial improvement in wages.

Beginning in 1857/8, there was an important reorientation in the thrust of liberal associational thought. Although this shift brought liberal ideas more closely into line with social and economic developments taking place during these years, it did so at the cost of revealing the growing ideological threadbareness of the liberal faith in self-help and association. At the political level, these years saw the revival of the liberal movement and the constitution of a nationwide liberal public sphere through such institutions as the National Association. Economically, the 1850s were the years of Germany's industrial takeoff, and the changing scale and organization of production posed new problems for liberal social thought, whose central problem was the future of the artisanate.[60] Since the 1840s, the defenders of the guild system had been fighting a rearguard battle against freedom of trade, the spread of the market, and the introduction of new forms of production. But the consolidation of a national market and the beginnings of self-sustaining industrialization in the Germanies deprived this strategy of any prospect of long-term success. This meant that, if artisans and small-scale producers hoped to survive, they would

---

[58] Reulecke, *Sozialer Frieden durch soziale Reform*, 109, 126–31; Koselleck, *Preußen zwischen Reform und Revolution*, 337ff.; and Christof Dipper, "Sozialreform. Geschichte eines umstrittenen Begriffs," *AfS* 32 (1992), 323–51.
[59] Reulecke, *Sozialer Frieden durch soziale Reform*, 214.
[60] Offermann, *Arbeiterbewegung und liberales Bürgertum*, makes this point, and the following paragraphs draw on this work.

have to adjust to the changing market conditions and make themselves the masters of mechanization, rather than its opponents. This entailed a far-reaching reorganization of both the mind-set and the workshops of artisanal producers, and the ideas of the free traders, who increasingly dominated German social and economic thought during these years, appealed to a considerable segment of the skilled working classes because they were able to make a convincing argument that economic development offered a real possibility for personal advancement and, at a broader level, that it represented the cure for, and not the cause of, pauperism.

At this point, it was by no means impossible for skilled workers to become capitalist employers of wage labor, even if the liberals tended to overestimate the likelihood of any individual making this transition, and the focus of liberal associational thought gradually shifted from helping wage earners insure themselves against the risks of wage labor to facilitating the social and economic modernization of the artisan classes. The obverse of this commitment to social integration through economic modernization was the denial of both the existence of a class of factory laborers whose interests were systematically different from, and perhaps antagonistic to, those of the employing classes and the need for social policies to meet the needs of the former group. It was precisely at this point – where the liberal ideal of a classless society of independent citizens of the middling estate was confronted by the reality of a factory working class – that it became impossible to overlook the limitations of liberal social thought.[61]

Liberal thinking on social policy, charity, and poor relief had always been shaped by the principle of self-help. As Johannes Fallati had written in the 1840s, the very existence of the liberal movement was predicated on the opposition to the principle of charity: "We do not want to help workers ourselves or to see that they are helped by others. We only want them to be helped to help themselves."[62] The conflict between those who sought to make charity more effective and those who sought to render it unnecessary reflected the divergent understanding of the social question held by the two groups and the different target audiences at which they directed their respective efforts. These differences came to the surface at the 1857 International Conference of Charities, which was held in Frankfurt. When the liberals failed to persuade the Conference to adopt their views, they founded their own organization, the Congress of German National Economists, to promote their program of economic and social reform.[63] The initiative for the founding of the Congress came from

---

[61] Geoffrey Finlayson, *Citizen, State, and Social Welfare in Britain 1830–1990* (Oxford University Press, 1994), 104, similarly argues that the ideology of individualism and self-help was best suited to the specific moment of the 1850s and 1860s.

[62] Fallati, "Das Vereinswesen als Mittel zur Sittigung der Fabrikarbeiter," 774.

[63] Reulecke, "Formen bürgerlich-sozialen Engagements in Deutschland und England im 19. Jahrhundert," in Jürgen Kocka, ed., *Arbeiter und Bürger im 19. Jahrhundert. Varianten ihres Verhältnisses im europäischen Vergleich* (Oldenbourg, 1986), 261–85; Volker Hentschel, *Die deutschen Freihändler und der volkswirtschaftliche Kongreß 1858 bis 1885* (=Industrielle Welt 16, Klett, 1975); Offerman, *Arbeiterbewegung und liberales Bürgertum*, 169ff.; and Ernst

Viktor Böhmert, a young economist who had made his reputation with a prize-winning tract that aimed at persuading skilled workers of the benefits to be derived from occupational freedom.[64] There was substantial overlap between the membership of the Congress and that of the Central Association, and for many years Böhmert edited the official organ of the Central Association, *The Worker's Friend*. In addition to Böhmert and Lette, the other founding members of the Congress included Hermann Schulze-Delitzsch (the leading figure in the liberal cooperative movement), the publicists Max Wirth, August Lammers, Arwed Emminghaus, and Heinrich Rickert (the editor of the *Danziger Zeitung* and the father of the neo-Kantian philosopher), all of whom were to be frequent interlocutors in the debate over the reform of poor relief from the 1860s through the 1880s.

The most systematic statement of the views of these liberals regarding the role of charity and the reform of poor relief came at the 1869 annual meeting of the Congress.[65] The immediate occasion for the debate was the introduction of the freedoms of occupation and movement in the North German Confederation and the need to bring the organization of poor relief into accordance with this legislation. But the liberals were also reacting to the introduction in Prussia and elsewhere of statutory poor relief (to be discussed in Chapter 4). Here it is important to note that both liberals and conservatives were concerned that the poor might mistakenly equate the communal obligation to provide assistance with a right to relief, and they feared that such legislation would undermine the work ethic of the poor, lead them to make unlimited claims on the property of others, and thus turn class against class.

At the conference, Böhmert argued that society had a moral obligation to assist the deserving poor, but that this obligation was one best discharged by voluntary associations, not public authorities, and he coupled this praise of voluntarism with the call for the revocation of the offending poor relief legislation.[66] Böhmert's reasoning here was inspired by a highly idealized view of individual self-help. Wherever people enjoyed the full freedom to dispose of their own property (including their own labor), state assistance was, Böhmert insisted, neither necessary nor legitimate, especially since most poverty was "self-incurred," the result of the failure of the poor to help themselves and "uncomprehending, uneconomical expenditure and consumption that is all

---

Engel, "Soziale Selbsthilfe," *Arbeiterfreund* 1 (1863), 131–48. These priorities were reflected in Lette's report to the Congress, which focused primarily on statutory and voluntary efforts to elevate the laboring classes and dealt with the organization of poor relief in a much more cursory manner and with charities not at all. See Lette, "Ueber den Zustand der Arbeiter- und der Armen-Bevölkerung im Preussischen Staate," *Congrès Internationale de Bienfaisance* (Frankfurt, 1858), II:80–151 and Wichern's response II:193–203.

[64] Böhmert, *Briefe zweier Handwerker. Ein Beitrag zur Lösung gewerblicher und socialer Fragen* (Dresden, 1854).

[65] The minutes of this session are reprinted in *Vierteljahrschrift für Volkswirthschaft und Kulturgeschichte* 27 (1870), 149–202. See also Hentschel, *Die deutsche Freihändler*, 174–8.

[66] Ibid., 149–51.

out of proportion to the income and other resources of the individual."[67] Since it was impossible to abolish personal weakness, insure against all possible risks, and eliminate general economic crises, some form of social assistance would always be necessary. However, Böhmert argued that the system of statutory poor relief that had evolved over the previous decades was positively dysfunctional in virtually every respect:

> Poor rates are levied that are only grudgingly paid. Salaried poor guardians give freely from the public purse, but without the investigation that would accompany the personal help of citizens concerned for the welfare of the community. The obligation to help the poor, which should have its natural source in pity for the suffering of one's neighbor, has become a burdensome, purely external duty. We no longer take joy in helping as the most beautiful wage for such labor, but only hear everywhere a hue and cry over the cost of assisting the poor.[68]

The obvious escape from these ills was to revert to a system of voluntary poor relief, where assistance would be given willingly by a public that had again learned to love their less fortunate brethren, who – once they were disabused of the idea that they had a legal claim to the property of others – would recognize that any assistance extended to them would be predicated on their demonstrated willingness to help themselves. But most important, Böhmert insisted that assistance had to be given in a way that exerted a positive influence on the character of the poor and prevented the abuse of charity by the undeserving.[69]

Although the other conference participants may have agreed, at least in principle, with Böhmert's philippic against statutory relief, the pragmatic critics of Böhmert's proposals had their ears closer to the ground and were unwilling to throw it over in favor of a purely voluntary system.[70] As we shall see in the following chapter, despite their common initial antipathy to statutory relief, both liberals and conservatives very soon made peace with the reformed system of poor relief being adopted during these years because it incorporated the ideas of self-help and individualization while providing a broad scope for voluntary personal engagement within this statutory framework.

[67] Ibid., 153.
[68] Ibid., 158.
[69] Ibid., 158–65.
[70] Ibid., 172ff.

4

The State, the Market, and the Organization of Poor Relief, 1830–1870

The reform legislation of the Napoleonic era abolished personal servitude and established the freedoms of occupation, movement, and marriage. In the medium run, though, this proved to be a mixed blessing for the lower classes because the socio-economic forces unleashed by these new freedoms deprived these persons of the social security provided by families, guilds, and lords at the same time that the crisis of pauperism was heightening their need for such protection. While the deepening social crisis provided the stimulus for the growth of moral reform associations, the sheer scope of material distress made it inevitable that poor relief would also have to be restructured in order to respond more effectively to the new forms of social insecurity associated with these personal freedoms. In this respect, the reform of poor relief in the Germanies from the 1830s to the founding of the empire represents the capstone of the reform legislation of the Napoleonic era.

Despite their common interest in consolidating control over newly acquired territories and forging a unified, territorial economic and political space, Prussia and the southern states ultimately adopted diametrically opposed approaches to poor law reform. While the right to determine the conditions under which an individual could become a local citizen, reside in the town, marry, exercise a trade, and receive public assistance had long been both symbol and substance of the corporate liberty of the cities, during these decades the newly consolidated territorial states were also trying to assert their internal sovereignty against the resistance of the remaining corporate bodies, and settlement and poor relief legislation were two of the key sites of conflict in this struggle between the local and territorial states.

This debate was complicated by the fact that the question of the location of sovereignty could not be separated from the question of how such power would be used. In Prussia, liberal officials educated in the spirit of Kant and Smith saw the creation of a more mobile labor force and a unified, territorial labor market as the solution to the problem of pauperism, and their aim was to design a poor relief system that would help achieve these goals.[1] In contrast, officials in central and southern Germany sought to gain a handle on the problems of overpopulation and underemployment through tighter restrictions on settlement, marriage, and eligibility for poor relief. However, this southern strategy tended to aggravate these problems, rather than solve them, and it was abandoned in the 1860s, thus paving the way for the Prussian system to become the model for poor relief throughout the nation after the founding of the empire in 1871.

Reform Strategies in Prussia and Southern Germany

In the post-1815 period, the most serious policy issue faced by every German state – aside from the sheer scope of poverty – was the fact that the reform legislation had expanded the freedom of the subject population to leave their homes and masters, marry and establish a family, and take up an occupation of their choice without guaranteeing that these persons would be able to settle in a new location, especially if local authorities suspected that the newcomer was likely to become a financial burden on the community. This problem was aggravated by the extreme parcelization of poor relief obligations. While each manor or village was in theory responsible for its own poor, the population of these dwarf entities was too small to effectively socialize the cost of supporting the needy. Consequently, local residents and local officials often sought to relieve themselves of the cost of supporting the poor by relieving themselves of the poor, that is, by picking up the sick and infirm and forcibly depositing them on the far side of the nearest border.[2] On the other hand, the lack of a state- or nationwide set of poor laws meant that both sides could have the law on their side in disputes over who was obligated to support an indigent individual. Such disputes often led to costly litigation among local authorities, each seeking to reduce its own poor relief burden at someone else's cost. No matter which community might ultimately be proved legally responsible, the poor themselves were certain to be the losers in this process.

As long as the right to poor relief was determined by residence in the community, the poor laws could not be reformed without at the same time reforming settlement laws, and in Prussia difficulties in achieving consensus on these

---

[1] George Steinmetz, *Regulating the Social. The Welfare State and Local Politics in Imperial Germany* (Princeton, 1993) has made a compelling argument for both the modernity of German poor relief in the nineteenth century and the relative autonomy of the state in using social policy to promote industrialization, even when such a policy appeared to run against the traditional interests of the agrarian nobility.

[2] For example, in 1849, of the 36,588 Prussian rural communities, 8,355 had a population of less than 100, and 32,296 had a population of less than 500. C. G. Kries, "Betrachtungen über Armenpflege und Heimathsrecht," *Zeitschrift für die gesamte Staatswissenschaft* 9 (1853), 3–78, 311–70, citation 22n.

issues delayed the drafting of a new poor law through the 1820s.[3] The official responsible for drafting new settlement and relief legislation, State Minister von Schuckmann, regarded settlement restrictions as a primary cause of poverty and as a "manifest infringement on the natural freedom of the individual... to gain a living."[4] He believed that the unrestricted freedom of movement would improve the situation of the poor and demonstrate that the conflict of interest between town and town, and between the towns and the state, in the domain of poor relief was illusory. As soon as each town realized that no other town could manipulate settlement and poor relief restrictions to its own advantage and that any additional relief costs that one town might be forced to bear as a result of this freedom of movement would be offset by the movement of its own indigent individuals to other locales, all citizens would, Schuckmann insisted, quickly identify their own best interest with the general interest of the state in reducing the total cost of supporting its indigent citizens, rather than with the narrow fiscal concerns of the particular locale in which they happened to reside.[5]

Most of the Prussian provincial assemblies endorsed the draft legislation that was circulated in 1831. It was supported by the eastern, agrarian provinces because it promised to accelerate migration and thus free them from the burden of assisting their surplus population, while more urban, industrialized regions put their collective finger on the neuralgic point of this vision by demanding that the cities be sheltered in various ways from the adverse effects of the anticipated movement of the poor from the countryside. However, the Rhenish assembly objected in principle to the very idea of statutory poor relief, and these reservations regarding the potentially baneful effects of statutory poor relief, as well as the implied superiority of voluntary and church charity, were to be central motifs in the mid-century debate over the reform of poor relief.[6]

It took another decade to reach a consensus on these issues, and at the turn of 1842/3 the Prussian government promulgated a quartet of laws regulating the related issues of settlement, communal responsibility for poor relief (both December 31, 1842), the punishment of vagrants, beggars, and the work-shy,

---

[3] On the Prussian poor laws during this period, see GStAPrK I. Hauptabteilung, Rep. 84a, Nr. 10954–7; Harald Schinkel, "Armenpflege und Freizügigkeit in der preußischen Gesetzgebung vom Jahre 1842," *VSWG* 50 (1963/4), 459–79; Michael Doege, *Armut in Preußen und Bayern (1770/1840)* (Neue Schriftenreihe des Stadtarchivs München, 1991), 193–226; and Hermann Beck, *The Origins of the Authoritarian Welfare State. Conservatives, Bureaucracy, and the Social Question, 1815–70* (University of Michigan Press, 1995).

[4] "Votum Sr. Excellenz des Herrn Geheimen Staatsministers von Schuckmann (22.5.1824) die Verpflegung der Armen und der Unterbringung der Vagabonden betr.," GStAPrK, Nr. 10954.

[5] The debates within the relevant ministries and the provincial assemblies during these years is recapitulated in the "Allerhöchste Kabinettsordre vom 18ten Februar 1838...," GStAPrK, Nr. 10955. The arguments concerning freedom of movement and state sovereignty are laid out on 10ff. and 35ff., citation 37.

[6] "Allerhöchste Kabinettsordre vom 18ten Februar 1838...." The Rhenish Landtag is cited on 101–2.

and the acquisition and loss of Prussian citizenship (both January 6, 1843).[7] This legislation was repeatedly revised, but not fundamentally altered until the poor laws themselves were virtually abolished in the 1920s.

The settlement law laid down the principle that all Prussian subjects who were either economically independent or physically capable of supporting themselves were free to reside in the place of their choice. The mere suspicion that an otherwise able-bodied person might at some point become a burden on the community was not to be considered an adequate ground for denying the right to settle, and the only persons who could be turned away were those who were already indigent and physically unable to support themselves.[8] This law played a major role in transforming the towns from fully self-governing bodies endowed with corporate privileges into administrative units of the sovereign state, though it did not by any means eliminate their significance in social politics, as we shall see.

The poor law was designed to facilitate the freedom of movement that was necessary if labor were to be transformed into a commodity that could be bought and sold within a national or territorial market, and the law sought to achieve this goal by laying down a uniform set of rules specifying who would be responsible for assisting which persons in case of need. What the law did was to infer from the act of settlement the intention of the individual to become a member of the community, and on this basis it designated that community – in the terminology of later legislation – as the person's "relief residence" (*Unterstützungswohnsitz*), which, instead of place of birth, would be responsible for supporting the person in case of need. Although the poor could settle wherever they chose, they had to maintain their usual residence in the new community for a period of three years before they could establish a claim to support from this new community. However, the law sought to diminish the risk involved in making use of the freedom of movement by stipulating that, if the poor had to be supported by public relief during this three-year period, the new community of residence was required to provide this assistance, but that they were entitled to seek reimbursement for such

---

[7] The first three of these laws are reprinted in Christoph Sachße et al., eds., *Armengesetzgebung und Freizügigkeit. Quellensammlung zur Geschichte der deutschen Sozialpolitik 1867 bis 1914*, 7. Band, (Wissenschaftliche Buchgesellschaft, 2000), 2. Halbband, 916ff. The citizenship law had its origin in the need to define precisely who was and was not obligated to perform military service, but it overlapped with the poor laws by virtue of the need to limit the scope of the poor laws to a clearly delimited segment – that is, Prussian citizens – of an increasingly mobile population. See Dieter Gosewinkel, *Einbürgern und Ausschließen. Die Nationalisierung der Staatsangehörigkeit vom Deutschen Bund bis zur Bundesrepublik Deutschland* (Vandenhoeck & Ruprecht, 2001), 67–101.

[8] Towns were, however, permitted to expel anyone who applied for poor relief within a year of his or her arrival if it could be shown that the person did not possess the basic qualifications (i.e., property or labor power) when he or she first arrived in the community. At the time, one of the most contested issues was whether towns should have the right to turn away criminals or offenders against public morality. The Prussian settlement law limited this power to individuals whose personal freedoms had been restricted for violations of the criminal code.

assistance from the community where the person had previously resided. The transitional character of Prussian society at this point between a traditional corporate order and a modern society was reflected in the article that stipulated that servants, apprentices, factory workers, and those who were engaged in the "service" of others could not establish a residence in the local where they were employed (or at least that they could not do so simply by virtue of this employment). But relief residences were not forever, and the individual's rights would lapse after an absence of three years. Since it was possible for a person to lose one relief residence without having gained a new one in the meantime, the law also established regional or provincial relief authorities (*Landarmenverbände*) to assist those persons who fell into the cracks of the system. But with the exception of a small number of provinces in the Prussian east, the number of these *Landarmen* remained insignificant.[9] The law on the punishment of vagrants, beggars, and the work-shy required that hard-core vagrants (*Landstreicher*) be sent to prison for between six weeks and six months, after which they were to be sent to a workhouse, while simple beggars could be confined for a maximum of six weeks. These provisions would later be taken over into the 1851 Prussian Criminal Code, where sentences for both *Landstreicher* and beggars were substantially reduced.

No one was satisfied with the 1842 law, and debate over its revision began almost immediately.[10] As noted earlier, contemporaries were concerned that the codification of the local obligation to assist the poor might be construed as constituting a right to such relief – with all the deleterious consequences that could be expected to follow therefrom. Proponents of statutory relief argued that these dangers were more imaginary than real, and they buttressed their position through casuistic reasoning that maintained that the obligation to assist the needy was one that the towns owed to the state, not the poor themselves. This casuistry was, however, given legal force by the fact that the only recourse open to individual applicants for assistance was to higher administrative authorities, not the courts. In the early 1850s, the Prussian legislature also seriously considered delegating to the churches this newly codified responsibility to assist the poor, but rejected the idea – though only by a narrow margin – because at that point the Lutheran church did not have a nationwide network of local organizations that would be required to carry this out.[11]

The other main source of dissatisfaction with the 1842 law was the claim by the cities that they had been treated unfairly by these laws, which extended the settlements rights of the poor while limiting the ability of urban officials

---

[9] Josef Mooser, "Gleichheit und Ungleichheit in der ländlichen Gemeinde. Sozialstruktur und Kommunalverfassung im östlichen Westfalen vom späten 18. bis in die Mitte des 19. Jahrhunderts," *AfS* 19 (1979), 231–62, especially 255ff., describes the impact of this legislation on rural communities.

[10] Heinrich Volkmann, *Die Arbeiterfrage im preußischen Agbeordnetenhaus 1848–1869* (Duncker & Humblot, 1968), 80–92.

[11] "Bericht der Zwanzigsten Kommission... (7. Mai 1853), GStAPrK, Nr. 10956, 2ff. and Bericht der Vierzehnten Kommission..., ibid., Bl. 127ff. and 165ff.

to ensure that these new residents did not become a burden on the public purse. The 1855 amendment of the poor law took account of this grievance by requiring persons to reside in a new community for a full year after having established residence there (i.e. three years plus one) before this new community became obligated to support them in case of indigence. The right to determine the length of this waiting period represented the most important mechanism for influencing the distribution of poor relief costs, and, as we shall see in later chapters, for the remainder of the century it remained a point of contention between the economic bourgeoisie, agrarian elites, and state officials.[12] The 1855 law also included a number of disciplinary provisions: homeless persons who did not make what the police considered to be a good faith effort to find a new place to live could be sent to a workhouse, as could both persons who accepted public assistance, but refused to perform the work assigned to them by relief officials, and husbands who abandoned their families and thus left them dependent on poor relief.

In contrast to Prussia, the states of Bavaria, Baden, Württemberg, and Hesse tended to look at pauperism from the other end of the telescope and to see it as a problem of too much freedom exercised in an unwise manner. In the south, eligibility for poor relief continued to be regulated by "home law" (*Heimatrecht*), which tied eligibility for assistance to a person's place of birth (or to some other place where the person had been explicitly admitted to the community). Although home law reduced confusion over who was responsible for assisting whom and ensured that no one could lose the rights to settlement and assistance without obtaining equivalent rights in another community, it tended to limit the mobility of the poorer classes because the only place where they were legally entitled to assistance was their place of birth. However, the reform of poor relief in the south was influenced as much by political externalities as by the need to adapt home law to the challenge of pauperism. The 1830 revolution in France and the deepening crisis of pauperism at home led to an alliance between increasingly conservative state governments and hometown communities based, in contrast to the Prussian approach, on the reaffirmation of local autonomy and the shift to more restrictive settlement, population, and relief policies.[13] However, these restrictive policies were never particularly effective in achieving their stated goals, and may well, as Mack Walker has argued, have actually played a bigger role than early mechanization in creating an "extra-communal, wage-earning class" in these regions.[14]

---

[12] Sachße et al., eds., *Armengesetzgebung und Freizügigkeit. Quellensammlung*, 7/II:935–8.

[13] Klaus-Jürgen Matz, *Pauperismus und Bevölkerung. Die gesetzlichen Ehebeschränkungen in den süddeutschen Staaten während des 19. Jahrhunderts* (Klett-Cotta, 1980), especially 175ff., 186–8; Martin Fuhrmann, *Volksvermehrung als Staatsaufgabe? Bevölkerungs- und Ehepolitik in der deutschen politischen und ökonomischen Theorie des 18. und 19. Jahrhunderts* (Schöningh, 2002); and Mack Walker, *German Home Towns. Community, State and General Estate 1648–1871* (Cornell University Press, 1971), 291ff., 336ff., 390–404.

[14] Matz, *Pauperismus und Bevölkerung*, 37, 192, 201–69 and Walker, *German Home Towns*, 334–7, 354ff.

By the 1860s, this south German strategy had largely been overtaken by events, in particular, the waning of the post-1848 reaction and the spread of mechanized production for a national market. With the founding of the North German Confederation in 1867, public debate on poor law reform became closely linked to the question of how to give real substance to the idea of national citizenship. The reform of the poor laws proved to be one of the most difficult problems faced by the new polity because some of the member states feared that allowing the confederation to legislate in this domain would amount to a de facto abrogation of their sovereignty, while the advocates of greater national integration welcomed such legislation for precisely this reason.[15]

In drafting a poor relief law for the confederation, lawmakers were guided by the principle that the community that benefited from the labor of an individual should also be responsible for supporting the person in time of need. On this basis, the law extended the waiting period for the acquisition of a local right to relief from one year to two after having established residence in the locale (with a relief residence being lost through a continuous absence of the same duration). Although the legal age of majority was 21, the Reichstag set 26 as the minimum age for acquiring a relief residence (or, to be more precise, the completion of the two-year qualifying period after having reached the age of 24). Lawmakers felt that many young men between the ages of 21 and 26 were either still completing their apprenticeship or serving in the army and thus had neither become self-supporting nor contributed enough to their new community to have earned a corresponding right to its support. These provisions worked to the disadvantage of agrarian regions, forcing them to assist more migrant poor for a longer period of time than had been required by earlier Prussian legislation. The Relief Residence Law that was adopted by the Bundestag of the North German Confederation on June 6, 1870 was the last major piece of social and economic legislation passed before the founding of the empire in 1871.[16] It extended the Prussian relief residence system to all of the states of the confederation. With the founding of the empire, this system was further extended to all the federal states except Baden, Württemberg, and Bavaria, which were permitted to retain their systems of home law, and the *Reichsland* Alsace-Lorraine, which retained its French system of poor relief until 1910. While Baden and Württemberg adopted the relief residence system in 1873, Bavaria retained its home law system until 1916.[17]

---

[15] Klaus Erich Pollmann, *Parlamentarismus im Norddeutschen Bund 1867–1870* (Droste, 1985), 484–8.

[16] *Stenographische Berichte*, I:85–94 (February 25, 1870), II:899–988 (May 14, 16 and 17, 1870), and II:1096–1108 (May 21 and 23, 1870), and *Bundesgesetzblatt* (June 6, 1870), 360–73. Two of the many commentaries on the Relief Residence Law are Friedrich Arnoldt, *Die Freizügigkeit und der Unterstützungswohnsitz* (Berlin, 1872), and C. Rocholl, *System des deutschen Armenpflegerechts* (Berlin, 1873).

[17] The Bavarian laws on *Heimat*, marriage, settlement, and poor relief passed in 1868/9 did, however, take a large step toward the modernization of these traditional institutions. Sachße et al.,

The problem was that, because of the federal structure of both the confederation and the empire, their legislative competence was limited to matters that bore directly on freedom of movement and settlement, and the Relief Residence Law – like its 1842 Prussian predecessor – simply required the member states to create a network of local relief authorities, but said nothing at all about who was to be considered needy or what kind of assistance was to be provided to such persons. Although the Relief Residence Law did create a special administrative court, the Federal Office of Relief Residence Affairs (*Bundesamt für das Heimatwesen*), to adjudicate disputes between poor relief authorities in the various federal states, it had not been originally conceived of as equivalent to the British Local Government Board and did not evolve into a central, national agency charged with rationalizing local relief practice. The impetus for the dynamic modernization of local poor relief, and for the later emergence of more modern forms of social welfare, came from other directions, and in the following section we will examine the theory and practice of poor relief at the local level and their role in the development of a market society across mid-century.[18]

The Elberfeld System and the Formation of a Market Society, 1850–1870

In most cities, poor relief was in a parlous condition in the early industrial era. The investigation of the personal circumstances of relief applicants remained cursory, assistance insufficient, and control inadequate. Looking backward in 1873, the Crefeld industrialist and social reformer Ludwig Friedrich Seyffardt described what he regarded as the vicious circle of public assistance and pauperism that had prevailed in mid-century:

The approval of alms would not take place according to the degree of need, but rather as a kind of compensation in order to be rid of the burdensome applicant. Once a person had received this assistance, he regarded this support as a personal right since it was seldom withdrawn and even then only under unusual circumstances. The distribution of assistance in money and bread took place weekly in the office of the poor relief administration and frequently led to tumultuous scenes among the idling crowd. The result of this system was that many of those whose need was only temporary were labeled permanent alms recipients, the sense of honor among the lower classes was alarmingly damaged, and the genuinely needy who were sick or unable to work were

---

eds., *Armengesetzgebung und Freizügigkeit*, 7/II, includes the parliamentary and ministerial debates leading up to these laws, which are reprinted on 821ff. and 876ff. See also Walker, *German Home Towns*, 414ff.

[18] E. P. Hennock, *The Origin of the Welfare State in England and Germany, 1850–1914. Social Politics Compared* (Cambridge University Press, 2007), 23–38, and Marcus Gräser, *Wohlfahrtsgesellschaft und Wohlfahrtsstaat. Bürgerliche Sozialreform und welfare state building in den USA und in Deutschland 1880–1940* (Vandenhoeck & Ruprecht, 2008), Chapter III.1. The development of its case law can be followed in *Entscheidungen des Bundesamts für das Heimatwesen* (1873ff.).

forced to beg because the alms they received did not suffice to meet their daily needs. Almost every family of the middle and upper bourgeoisie designated one day of the week when a small amount was given to every beggar, and in the more affluent districts a crowd of tattered figures gathered almost every day on the street corners to beg for charity two or three times at the same house, according to circumstances. Children were trained how to beg, and in many cases they had to bear the larger share of the burden of supporting their debauched parents.[19]

It was conditions such as these that gave rise to the widespread sense that the existing system of public assistance was bringing the cities to the brink of fiscal collapse as they were forced to cover out of general tax revenues an ever larger percentage of a total relief budget that was itself increasing in step with urbanization. It was this sense of crisis that in most instances provided the stimulus for the reform of municipal poor relief in the early industrial era.

The new paradigm of poor relief that was developed in response to these problems is most closely identified with the reformed system adopted in 1853 by the city of Elberfeld.[20] The Elberfeld system played the same pivotal role in the history of nineteenth-century German poor relief as the passage of the 1834 Poor Law did for Britain. However the two systems differed in important respects. The Elberfeld system aimed at perfecting the organization of outdoor relief, rather than abolishing it through reliance on the workhouse; it placed a premium on establishing close personal bonds between poor guardians and the poor and the careful investigation of the personal circumstances of the latter, rather than on the self-acting workhouse test, which the British preferred precisely because it would obviate the need for such investigation;[21] and it was

---

[19] Seyffardt, *Bericht der Städtische Armen-Deputation zu Crefeld über ihrer zehnjärige Wirksamkeit seit Einführung des Elberfelder Systems der Armenpflege* (Crefeld, 1873), 3.

[20] The most important modern accounts of the Elberfeld system are Bernd Weisbrod, "Wohltätigkeit und 'symbolische Gewalt' in der Frühindustrialisierung. Städtische Armut und Armenpolitik im Wuppertal," in Hans Mommsen and Winfried Schulze, eds., *Vom Elend der Handarbeit. Probleme historischer Unterschichtsforschung* (Klett-Cotta, 1981), 335–57; Steinmetz, *Regulating the Social*, 149ff.; Christoph Sachße and Florian Tennstedt, *Geschichte der Armenfürsorge* (Kohlhammer, 1980–92), I:214ff.; and Giovanna Berger, *Die ehrenamtliche Tätigkeit in der Sozialarbeit – Motive, Tendenzen, Probleme, dargestellt am Beispiel des 'Elberfelder Systems'* (Frankfurt, 1979). The most important older works are Victor Böhmert, *Das Armenwesen in 77 deutschen Städten* (Dresden, 1886), and Emil Münsterberg, *Das Elberfeld System. Festbericht aus Anlaß des fünfzigjährigen Bestehens der Elberfelder Armenordnung*, SDV, 63 (1903).

[21] Karel Williams, *From Pauperism to Poverty* (Routledge, 1981), 58, and Gertrude Himmelfarb, *The Idea of Poverty. England in the Early Industrial Age* (Knopf, 1984), 147ff. Unfortunately, there is no German equivalent to the revisionist economic history of the English poor laws, which has effectively criticized the wholesale condemnation of the ostensibly pauperizing effects of parish relief before 1834. For the English literature, the interested reader is referred to Anthony Brundage, *The English Poor Laws, 1700–1930* (Palgrave, 2002) and Fred Block and Margaret Somers, "In the Shadow of Speenhamland: Social Policy and the Old Poor Law," *Politics & Society* 31:2 (June 2003), 283–323.

The Elberfeld System and the Formation of a Market Society, 1850–1870

based on a very different understanding of the relation between voluntary action and the activity of the (local) state than its British counterpart.[22]

The Elberfeld system united within itself what Foucault has referred to as security and pastoral power, that is, the aspiration both to secure outward compliance with social norms and to bring about an inner change of heart. It was based on the principle that the able-bodied poor were to be encouraged in their independence by helping them find work, rather than pauperized by charity (*Arbeit statt Almosen*), in order to preserve the integrity of the labor market and the family, as well as the system of bourgeois individualism on which they rested. The realization of this goal depended on finding ways to simultaneously restrict relief to the deserving, limit the ability of the able-bodied to subsist outside the labor market, dispauperize the dependent poor through moral reform and personal helping, and, at the margin, criminalize incorrigible vagrancy and other socially transgressive behavior – with the workhouse and the police serving as the ultima ratio of these assistantial and rehabilitative institutions.[23] However, while coercion may have been acceptable at the margin or in time of emergency, the ultimate goal was, as we saw in the previous chapter, to win the working classes over to the gospel of work and individual achievement and thus transform them into self-governing subjects of bourgeois society.

The events leading up to the reform of poor relief in Elberfeld in the 1850s were fairly typical of the problems faced by the new industrial cities. In the first half of the nineteenth century, Elberfeld, which is now part of the city of Wuppertal in North Rhine-Westphalia, was one of the most industrially advanced cities in western Germany, and its economy was dominated by one of the leading industries of the early industrial era: textiles. Up to the end of the 1700s, poor relief had been the responsibility of local religious congregations. However, poor relief was centralized in municipal hands in 1800, and this centralized municipal relief system was itself reformed at the end of the Napoleonic period. The city's population exploded across the first half of the 1800s, rising from 12,000 in 1800 to more than 39,000 in 1841 and 50,000 in 1852 before leaping to 106,000 in 1885. During this period 10–20% of the population received poor relief on a regular basis. Expenses for

---

[22] Jürgen Reulecke, "Formen bürgerlich-sozialen Engagements in Deutschland und England im 19. Jahrhundert," in Jürgen Kocka, ed., *Arbeiter und Bürger im 19. Jahrhundert. Varianten ihres Verhältnisses im europäischen Vergleich* (Oldenbourg, 1986), 261–85.

[23] Mitchell Dean, *The Constitution of Poverty. Toward a Genealogy of Liberal Governance* (Routledge, 1991), 154, 218–19. Much of the impetus for the creation of modern urban police forces came from the conflation of poverty and crime in the notion of the dangerous classes, and a substantial proportion of police activity in the nineteenth century dealt with vagrancy and begging. However, the police also interacted with the poorer classes in ways that cannot be so directly equated with social discipline. See Paul Lawrence, "Policing the Poor in England and France, 1850–1900," in Clive Emsley et al., eds., *Social Control in Europe. Volume II: 1800–2000* (Ohio State University Press, 2004), 210–25.

poor relief regularly exceeded income from endowed foundations, voluntary contributions, and weekly donations to the churches, and local taxpayers were unhappy not only because they had to foot the bill for the difference, but also because they felt that the system was being abused by the undeserving. The poor relief system was again reorganized in 1841. However, when the reformed system failed to achieve its goal of pushing more of the poor into the labor market and more effectively monitoring relief recipients, the city swung to the opposite extreme and considered turning responsibility for municipal assistance back over to the churches. However, this proposal fell through in part because the churches were unable to raise the necessary resources and in part because the Reformed congregation – the largest in the city – felt that the conditions imposed by municipal authorities would not permit the church to adequately subject the recipients of relief to the kind of congregational discipline described in Chapter 1. In view of these obstacles, the city was left with no alternative but to again reorganize municipal assistance.[24]

The 1853 reform was the brainchild of a group of industrialists, merchants, and bankers, including Daniel von der Heydt, the primary author of the new poor relief law and the brother of the Prussian commerce minister. The key features of the Elberfeld system can be easily described. The new system divided the city into districts, which were further subdivided into quarters, each of which was the responsibility of a poor guardian who was expected to reside in this quarter. Applicants for assistance had to address their requests to the guardian for the quarter in which they resided. Decisions concerning the granting of assistance were made on a collegial basis by the guardians at their regular biweekly district meetings. If a guardian felt that immediate aid was justified, he could approve emergency relief, but only enough to tide the applicant over until the case could be considered at the next regular district meeting.[25]

The Elberfeld regulations insisted that work was the best form of assistance, and the primary duty of the poor guardians was to help their charges find employment. Although the Elberfeld system prohibited long-term support for the able-bodied, temporary assistance was allowed, but only if the applicant could prove to the satisfaction of the guardian that he or she had sought work in good faith. In practice, whatever assistance that was granted to the able-bodied was based on other kinds of need, such as age, illness, and/or family size, rather than the mere fact of joblessness. Even though the day rate for unskilled labor was regarded as the existence minimum, assistance rates were set below this level in order to uphold the principle of less eligibility, that is, the principle that those who received public assistance should always find themselves worse off than those who managed to support their families without the assistance of others, and relief was provided only on a subsidiary basis, that is, only if

---

[24] Weisbrod, "Wohltätigkeit und 'symbolische Gewalt'" and Tânia Ünlüdag, *Historische Texte aus dem Wupperthale. Quellen zur Sozialgeschichte des 19. Jahrhunderts* (Born, 1989), 383ff.
[25] Böhmert, *Das Armenwesen in 77 deutschen Städten*, Allgemeiner Teil, 49–96.

the individual or family were totally bereft of resources and if no one else was legally obligated (and able) to support them. However, since relief applicants were expected to take any kind of work, no matter what the pay or conditions, and since the willingness to accept such work was regarded as the best test of the applicant's work ethic and deservingness, applicants found themselves in the paradoxical situation where the best proof of their merit was the fact that they no longer needed assistance.

Although it was a linear descendant of the Hamburg reforms in its search for organizational mechanisms that would ensure close, constant, individualized supervision of poor, what was unique about the Elberfeld system was its mobilization of a broad segment of the urban middle classes behind this program. In this way not only did the Elberfeld system provide a mechanism through which the urban middle classes could participate in the public life of the city. It also facilitated the constitution of their social identity by mobilizing them around a common set of values and a common social program while endowing these shared convictions with the legitimacy and institutional power of the local state.

The priority that the Elberfeld system gave to work over assistance was one of the reasons why the involvement of middle-class men, who had the best knowledge of the local job market, was indispensable to the success of the system. The *grande bourgeoisie*, including bankers and industrialists such as von der Heydt, dominated citywide policymaking positions, while master artisans, merchants, homeowners, and other members of the middling and lesser bourgeoisie served as poor guardians. This division of labor remained unaltered until at least the end of the century.[26] The devolution of authority to approve or deny applications onto the guardians themselves meeting in the district committees helped bridge the gap between the public and the private because the people who decided how much assistance should be granted to whom were the same people who taxed themselves to fund municipal poor relief. At the same time, the fusion of public authority and private, voluntary initiative in the person of the guardian offered a way of resolving the conflicting imperatives of charity and fiscality.[27]

This decentralization of authority also helped sustain the interest and engagement of these middle-class men and ensured that they would maintain a lively personal interest in the welfare of those supplicants whose petitions they supported. Service as a poor guardian was a voluntary and honorary office open to local (male) citizens, though in the mid-1860s the Elberfeld Women's Association was established to complement the official work of these guardians. Service as a poor guardian was as much an obligation as an honor. In theory,

---

[26] Ludovica Scarpa, *Gemeinwohl und lokale Macht. Honoratioren und Armenwesen in der Berliner Louisenstadt im 19. Jahrhundert* (Historische Kommission zu Berlin, 1995), 9, 16, 38.

[27] Karl Kayser, *Die Stellung der ehrenamtlichen Organe in der Armenpflege*, SDV, 49, (1900), 8–9.

refusal to serve as a poor guardian entailed the temporary forfeiture of municipal suffrage and other civic rights, as well as the payment of higher taxes, though municipal officials were understandably reluctant to impress unwilling citizens into serving in an office whose success was so dependent on personal inclination and energy.

Regular house visiting was the basic mechanism for the individualization of assistance, that is, the systematic, intensive, and continuous investigation of the personal circumstances of each applicant for assistance and the calibration of assistance based on this knowledge, and such visiting quickly became recognized as the sine qua non of modern poor relief and scientific charity. The most important theorist of house visiting in the first half of the nineteenth century was the French philanthropist Joseph-Marie de Gérando, whose *Le Visiteur du pauvre* (1820) defined what quickly became the philanthropic common sense of the age.[28] Like his contemporaries, Gérando was concerned that any assistance that was given without detailed prior knowledge of the applicant would encourage sloth, immorality, and dependence, and in this work he called for the creation of a new form of enlightened or scientific charity that would avoid the moral hazards associated with indiscriminate almsgiving. Only the comprehensive investigation of both the circumstances of the poor and the moral causes of their distress, Gérando claimed, would make it possible to distinguish between the deserving and the undeserving poor, determine the precise nature, scope, and duration of the supplicant's need, and thus provide exactly the right kind of assistance and provide it in a way that would help the poor regain their independence.

Enlightened charity, Gérando maintained, had to be informed by equal measures of solicitude and skepticism. But if it was the former that moved the visitor to action, it was the latter that determined the character of his inquiries. Gérando was obsessed by the fear that the misery displayed so ostentatiously by the beggars who constantly accosted the wealthy was feigned, or at least substantially exaggerated, in hopes of more easily exciting the affections of the donor. Although poor mothers with their children were universally recognized as the most deserving of the deserving poor, Gérando insisted, for example, that, before providing for them, one had to make certain that these children were, in fact, this woman's own children and that she had not borrowed or stolen them from someone else in order to give greater credibility to a fictitious tale of woe. Gérando displayed the same fundamental skepticism toward all groups of the deserving poor. Did not, he felt compelled to ask, the elderly or the disabled have families who were able and obligated to care for them? How could one be certain that charity given to assuage genuine need would not be squandered to immoral ends? The only way to escape from these nagging uncertainties, Gérando insisted, and distinguish real need from that which was feigned was to visit the poor in their homes. Not only would the mere threat of

---

[28] Gérando, *Le Visiteur du pauvre* (Paris, 1820), translated as *The Visitor of the Poor*, intro. Joseph Tuckerman (London, 1833).

The Elberfeld System and the Formation of a Market Society, 1850–1870 93

a house visit make false need disappear in a puff of smoke; such visits would also provide the positive knowledge of the poor that was essential to the proper functioning of a system of outdoor relief.

The knowledge produced by house visits, though, was anything but simple and direct. For Gérando, the home, that is, both the physical living space and the character of family life, was an unerring reflection of the inner character of the poor, even if this truth was one that could only be teased out through the interpretive labors of a skilled observer. In *Le Visiteur du pauvre* Gérando illustrated how the close observation of the poor in their own homes and the systematic questioning of the poor, their neighbors, their employers, and so on could produce truthful knowledge of the poor – as much by the silences and prevarications through which they hoped to obscure their own faults and fabrications as by the actual information obtained through these inquiries. The primary function of house visits was, therefore, to ferret out the vice that almost invariably lay at the root of need and unmask the simulation through which the poor tried to hide the true causes of their misfortune.[29] The challenge for the visitor was to learn how to observe and how to interpret the "thousand looks and gestures, any one of which would have betrayed their secret."[30] But since the visitor had to be most on his or her guard in those cases where need appeared to be most real, genuine need tended to appear only as a provisional determination and as a residual category wherever immorality could not be readily established, and this obsession with abuse often consigned both the impotent poor and those whose poverty was due to factors beyond their control to a permanent blind spot in the minds of charity workers and relief officials. Whether one views this as the blindness of ideology or as a productive insight made possible by the blindness of a discourse to the conditions of its own constitution, the virtual unthinkability of poverty that was real but not self-incurred was one of the axioms of poor relief and charity across mid-century.

The poor guardian (*Armenpfleger*) was meant, quite literally, to care for and exercise tutelage over those persons whose dependence was a sign of their social incompetence. House visits gave the guardian the opportunity to console the poor in their misery and shepherd them back onto the path of working-class virtue. As the guidelines for the work of Elberfeld poor guardians explained, they were to use these house visits as an opportunity "to rebuke any disorder or bad habits that they encountered, admonish [the poor] to order, cleanliness and honesty, encourage parents to see to the proper education of their children

---

[29] Gérando, *The Visitor of the Poor*, 24. Peter Mandler, ed., *The Uses of Charity. The Poor on Relief in the Nineteenth-Century Metropolis* (University of Pennsylvania Press, 1990); Lynn Lees, *The Solidarities of Strangers. The English Poor Laws and the People, 1700–1948* (Cambridge University Press, 1998); and Dietlind Hüchtker, *"Elende Mütter" und "liederliche Weibspersonen". Geschlechterverhältnisse und Armenpolitik in Berlin (1770–1850)* (Westfälisches Dampfboot, 1999) all analyze the rhetorical strategies and power relations that structured charitable giving, as well as the inevitable slippages between the intent of donors and the uses of charity by the poor.

[30] Gérando, *The Visitor of the Poor*, 17.

and be attentive to their school attendance, encourage children to show respect for their parents and to support them, and – draped in the prestige of an organ of municipal authority – seek to exert a salutary influence on the moral sensibility of the poor."[31] Although this tutelage was to be informed by the knowledge derived from these house visits, the problem was, as we saw in Chapter 3, to establish the authority of the guardian and create a bond of trusting deference that would enable the guardian to influence the character of the poor, rather than simply demand external compliance. To ensure that guardians were able to cultivate these personal relations with their charges, the Elberfeld system limited the responsibility of each poor guardian to four individuals or families – in contrast to earlier in the century, when guardians were responsible for overseeing relief to as many as fifty households. Guardians were expected to visit their clients every two weeks to ascertain whether there had been any substantive changes in the family situation. In turn, visiting provided the guardians with the occasion to perform their social status within the smaller, more self-contained, and familiar community of the quarter.[32] Certainly, the prospect of assistance guaranteed the guardians a degree of leverage over the poor, as did their position as the representative of municipal authority. However, the Elberfeld system was premised on the assumption that it was possible to recreate those seemingly natural forms of deference and paternalistic solicitude that had supposedly prevailed in earlier times. This idealized, deferential relationship between the propertied and the poor flowed together with the individualized, scientific philanthropy theorized by Gérando to give rise to the idea of "individualized personal help" (*Hilfe von Mensch zu Mensch*), which, together with the decentralization of decision making through the quarter and district system, represented the distinguishing features of the Elberfeld system.

The most effective means of reconciling the contradiction between assistance and discipline – at least in the minds of the guardians themselves – and masking the nature of the authority that the propertied exercised over the poor was to assimilate their work to two ideologies of selfless service: Christian charity and civic patriotism, which in practice tended to blur into one another. As the guidelines for the Elberfeld poor guardians explained, their work demanded "a generous measure of active charity and an earnest sense of justice: love in order to take in the pleas of the poor with friendliness and a sympathetic heart; earnestness in order to reject unjustified claims, investigate carefully to determine the proper measure of assistance, and insure that the support that is granted does not promote idleness and immorality."[33] Although this ideal

---

[31] "Instruction für die Bezirks-Vorsteher und Armenpfleger vom 4. Januar 1861," §16, cited in Böhmert, *Das Armenwesen in 77 deutschen Städten*, 74, and Hartmut Dießenbacher, "Der Armenbesucher: Missionar im eigenen Land," in Christoph Sachße and Florian Tennstedt, eds., *Soziale Sicherheit und soziale Disziplinierung* (Suhrkamp, 1986), 209–44.

[32] Scarpa, *Gemeinwohl und lokale Macht*.

[33] "Instruction für die Bezirks-Vorsteher und Armenpfleger vom 4. Januar 1861," §6, cited in Böhmert, *Das Armenwesen in 77 deutschen Städten*, 73.

of selfless service captures important elements of the lived experience of the guardians, it is by no means clear how far this idea corresponded to either social "reality" or the self-perception of the poor themselves. As a result, helping was inevitably intertwined with various kinds of coercion, which neither contemporaries nor much of the subsequent literature on social work has been able to theorize.[34]

Despite these limitations, the ideology of helping played an absolutely crucial role in reconciling conservative and liberal critics of statutory relief with the expanded role of the local state in this area. As we have seen, many contemporaries were highly critical of both the principle and the practice of statutory poor relief.[35] The operative assumption underlying these criticisms was that municipal poor relief could be nothing other than the schematic distribution of material assistance, which could have no edifying effect on the poor and which, in fact, often further demoralized them. While this may have been true in the past, when the distribution of assistance had been relegated to the police or low-level municipal employees, the task, as Elberfeld Oberbürgermeister Lischke explained in 1858, was "to fill the dead forms [of municipal regulations] with energetic love and the spirit of personal sacrifice," and he felt that Elberfeld system, with its principled reliance on the voluntary service of its middle-class citizens as poor guardians, made this possible.[36] The reliance on voluntary and honorary poor guardians – many of whom belonged to local charitable associations – allowed municipal government to extend a hand to churches and charity associations while permitting Protestants, Catholics, and liberals to see their own visions of helping and service reflected in public poor relief system.[37] In the long run, German relief officials came to portray the Elberfeld system as the golden mean between the British statutory system, which guaranteed relief to the needy poor, but only in the form of the cold, unfeeling workhouse, and the French system of voluntary assistance, which preserved the best features of personal charity, but which could not guarantee that such succor was made available to all the deserving poor.

---

[34] Weisbrod, "Wohltätigkeit und 'symbolische Gewalt'." On the perception of poverty by the laboring classes, and the conclusions that they drew from these views, see Lees, *The Solidarities of Strangers*, chapter 5.

[35] In France this opposition was strong enough to delay the creation of a public system of social assistance until the end of the nineteenth century. See Timothy Smith, "The Ideology of Charity, the Image of the English Poor Law, and Debates Over the Right to Assistance in France, 1830–1905," *The Historical Journal* 40:4 (1997), 997–1032.

[36] Beilage zu Nr. 264 der *Neuen Preußischen Zeitung* in LAB A Rep 003-01, Nr. 348.

[37] By the end of the century, Catholics were particularly eager to claim the Elberfeld system as their own in order to better refute charges that their own charity was backward and indiscriminate. On this Catholic genealogy of the Elberfeld system, see Ewald Frie, "Da nun die städtische Armenpflege der Armenpflege des St. Vincenz-Josefs-Vereins gleichen soll...." Offene Armenfürsorge der Stadt Münster um die Jahrhundertwende," in Franz-Josef Jakobi, ed., *Stadtgesellschaft im Wandel. Untersuchungen zur Sozialgeschichte Münsters im 19. und 20. Jahrhundert* (Münster 1995), 13–59. The other reformer whose work was often seen as the inspiration of the Elberfeld system was Thomas Chalmers.

By all contemporary estimates, the Elberfeld system was a great success. In the decade following the 1853 reorganization, the proportion of the city's population receiving public assistance dropped to approximately 2%.[38] At the same time, it was reported that street begging virtually disappeared as residents – now reassured that the deserving poor would be adequately assisted by public officials – ceased to give alms indiscriminately to unknown persons who knocked on their doors.

Unification brought about a substantial increase in the pace of industrialization, urbanization, and migration. When Germany's industrial take-off began with a vengeance in the 1870s and 1880s, more and more cities found themselves subjected to the same forces that had motivated the precocious Elberfeld reforms several decades before, and the Elberfeld system spread rapidly as it rode the wave of industrialization that swept across the country during these decades, as can be seen in Table 1. In fact, the Elberfeld system was so successful that relief officials and social reformers came to see it as the embodiment of the very idea of rational, yet compassionate, assistance, and reformers would often debate whether the reorganization of relief in a specific city truly embodied the principles of the Elberfeld system with the same fervor with which theologians once debated the doctrine of real presence.

The reform of public poor relief also had important implications for the scope and organization of charity. Meaningful data on charitable spending are impossible to come by. However, nineteenth-century commentators were unanimous in their belief that charitable giving substantially exceeded public spending for poor relief, though this probably says as much about the level of charitable generosity as it does about the miserliness of poor relief, and the relation between the two was probably not altered fundamentally until World War I.

The 1860s and 1870s saw the first tentative steps toward the rationalization of voluntary charity. Here, all of the challenges facing relief officials and philanthropists from the 1860s into the 1880s were condensed in the twin problems of indiscriminate almsgiving and pauperism. There was a pervasive fear that the inability of the charity associations to apply the principles of scientific charity, the lack of coordination among these associations and between them and municipal relief, and the susceptibility of well-meaning but weak-willed donors to the importuning of the poor was actually encouraging the abuse of such charity by "professional beggars." As Böhmert told the 1869 Congress of German National Economists, "every penny that is wasted in putting the poor in a better position than the independent worker is a direct premium for idleness and vice.... Everyone who gives charity to a person whom he does not know without the careful investigation of this case commits a dual wrong against the beggar, who is thereby confirmed in his vagabondage, and against bourgeois society, whose efforts to combat poverty are thereby thwarted."[39]

---

[38] Böhmert, *Das Armenwesen in 77 deutschen Städten*, 62.
[39] "Verhandlungen des elften Kongresses deutscher Volkswirthe," *Vierteljahrschrift für Volkswirthschaft und Kulturgeschichte* 27 (1870), 160.

TABLE 1. *Adoption of the Elberfeld System, 1853–1900*

1853	Elberfeld
1863	Barmen, Duisburg, Krefeld, Halberstadt
1864	Essen
1865	Altona
1867	Ruhrort
1868	Hagen
1870	Neuwied
1871	Kiel
1874	Dortmund
1875	Elbing, Stuttgart, Bremen
1876	Darmstadt
1877	Düsseldorf, Oldenburg, Naumburg, Siegen
1878	Königsberg, Landsberg, Hanau
1880	Dresden, Mühlheim
1881	Kassel, Leipzig, Rostock, Bremerhaven
1882	Magdeburg, Potsdam, Stralsund, Dessau
1883	Frankfurt, Zwickau, Fulda
1884	Gotha, Halle
1885	Posen, Greifswald
1888	Cologne
1889	Aachen, Bielefeld
1893	Hamburg, Salzburg, Erfurth
1895	Breslau, Mainz, Stoppenberg, Münster, Mühlhausen
1896	Graz
1898	Mannheim, Danzig

Note: Sachße and Tennstedt, *Geschichte der Armenfürsorge*, I:218, supplemented by Steinmetz, *Regulating the Social*, 159. This table generally reflects the date when the reforms were completed. Münsterberg, *Das Elberfelder System*, 44, reports that, of some 200 major German cities, only 30 had not adopted the Elberfeld system in some form or degree.

These dangers could only be avoided by the modernization of both poor relief and charity and their closer integration with each other, and the driving force behind reforms in both these domains was the German Association for Poor Relief and Charity (*Deutscher Verein für Armenpflege und Wohltätigkeit*), which was founded in 1880/1.[40] The association became an effective vehicle for the representation in national debates on poor relief and social policy of the views of the liberal municipal politicians who dominated its membership, though its deliberations were often marked by differences between National Liberals, who were willing to support the more statist, conservative policies of the government in the 1880s and 1890s, and left liberals, who were more skeptical of such measures.

[40] On the founding and later role of the association, see the minutes of its first meetings in LAB A Rep 003, Nr. 634, Gräser, *Wohlfahrtsgesellschaft und Wohlfahrtsstaat*, chapters II.2 and III.1, and Florian Tennstedt, "Fürsorgegeschichte und Vereinsgeschichte. 100 Jahre Deutscher Verein in der Geschichte der deutschen Fürsorge," *ZfS* 27 (1981), 72–100.

While the Elberfeld system provided the model for the modernization of poor relief, the starting point for the organization of charity in Germany were the associations for the "prevention of poverty and begging" that were established in many cities between the 1860s and 1880s.[41] The goal of these associations was to enlighten the propertied classes concerning the dangers of indiscriminate charity and coordinate and rationalize the work of their member groups. These associations often established central information bureaus, which maintained card files on all applicants for charity for public assistance; they obligated their members to refer anyone seeking assistance to these central offices; and in many cases the coordination of public poor relief and voluntary charity was secured through a sort of personal union in which the city councilor responsible for poor relief also served as chair of the anti-begging association.[42] Since charitable assistance did not prevent individuals from acquiring a relief residence, local officials insisted that these charity associations let them know the names of the persons they assisted to ensure that migrants who could not support themselves did not rely on private charity to acquire a relief residence and thus become a permanent burden on the community. Although many cities insisted that local charities refer all such applicants to municipal poor relief authorities, many charities – especially religious groups – were very sensitive regarding their independence, and their efforts to protect their prerogatives from municipal oversight often led to an embarrassing shell game between themselves and poor relief officials.[43]

All the reform strategies charted in this and the previous chapter were based on a characteristically nineteenth-century view of the individual as a rational, autonomous subject who could be held responsible for his or her actions, and they all sought to combat pauperism by altering the equation through which the rational subject calculated the potential costs and benefits of public assistance. However, beginning in the 1890s this understanding of the social question would be challenged by the emergence of a social perspective on poverty. As we shall see in later chapters, this new understanding of the social problem as a problem of the social order, rather than one of the poor themselves, would have far-reaching consequences for the organization of social assistance.

---

[41] Virtually nothing has been written about these associations. On the Berlin association, see Wolfgang Straßmann, *Geschichte, Verfassung und Wirksamkeit des Vereins gegen Verarmung in Berlin* (Berlin, 1873), and Scarpa, *Gemeinwohl und lokale Macht*, 200ff.

[42] Böhmert, "Die Organisation und Verbindung der amtlichen und nichtamtlichen Armenpflege in Dresden," *Arbeiterfreund* 19 (1881), 134–49, and Böhmert, "Die Verbindung der amtlichen und nichtamtlichen Armenpflege," *Arbeiterfreund* 32 (1894), 1–20.

[43] Paul Aschrott in *Stenographischer Bericht, SDV*, 20 (1894), 77.

5

The Assistantial Double Helix

Poor Relief, Social Insurance, and the Political Economy of Poor Law Reform

The liberal architects of the freedoms of movement, trade, marriage, and settlement had hoped that these measures would smooth the transition to a market society, help resolve the social question, and accelerate the inner consolidation of the new state. The relief residence system played a pivotal role in this strategy.[1] However, the relentless pace of industrialization, urbanization, and migration during the empire simply transformed the social problem, rather than resolving it, and it was during the 1860s and 1870s that the question of pauperism was definitively supplanted by the "worker question" (*Arbeiterfrage*), that is, the problem of ensuring the economic security, cultural elevation, social integration, and political loyalty of the new class of wage-earning factory workers.[2]

In 1866/7, much of Germany was unified with the founding – under Prussian leadership – of the North German Confederation, and the remaining German states were brought into this political union (and Austria definitively excluded) with the founding of the German Empire in 1871. Universal male suffrage was instituted in the confederation, and then in the empire, by Bismarck, who expected that the peasantry and urban workers would serve as a political counterweight to urban liberalism. However, the May 1869 suffrage law of the North German Confederation, which was taken over by the Empire, also stated that persons who had received public assistance during the preceding

---

[1] Christoph Sachße et al., eds., *Armengesetzgebung und Freizügigkeit. Quellensammlung zur Geschichte der deutschen Sozialpolitik 1867–1914*. I. Abt.: *Von der Reichsgründungszeit bis zur Kaiserlichen Sozialbotschaft (1867–1881)*, Bd.7, (Darmstadt: Wissenschaftliche Buchgesellschaft, 2000), xxviii–xxxii. The 1867 Passport Law of the North German Confederation was also part of this process. See John Torpey, *The Invention of the Passport. Surveillance, Citizenship and the State* (Cambridge University Press, 2000), Chapter 3.

[2] See Ralf Stremmel et al., eds., *Grundfragen der Sozialpolitik in der öffentlichen Diskussion: Kirchen, Parteien, Vereine und Verbände. Quellensammlung zur Geschichte der deutschen Sozialpolitik 1867–1914*. I. Abt.: *Von der Reichsgründungszeit bis zur Kaiserlichen Sozialbotschaft (1867–1881)*, Bd.8, (Darmstadt: Wissenschaftliche Buchgesellschaft, 2006).

year were not eligible to participate in national elections. This combination of universal suffrage and political disenfranchisement politicized the worker question in new ways, and poor law reform was rendered increasingly urgent by both rising poor relief costs and the growing political self-consciousness of skilled workers, who saw deterrent poor relief as a symbol of their economic exploitation and social degradation.

By the end of the 1870s, social reformers and government officials were coming to see social insurance as the key to solving both the fiscal and the political crises of the existing poor relief system. On the one hand, they hoped that social insurance would help the laboring classes protect themselves against the insecurities associated with wage labor while reinforcing the basic principles of work and self-reliance. On the other hand, they anticipated that, at the price of a limited right to benefits and a degree of working-class control over the administration of these programs, social insurance would relieve the cities of a substantial proportion of their rising poor relief costs while muting the resentment of the newly enfranchised working classes. Poor law reform and the development of social insurance were, therefore, intertwined in imperial Germany like two strands of DNA, and this chapter will reconstruct the social policy strategies guiding their dual evolution and then analyze the impact of social insurance and socioeconomic change on relief practice from the 1870s to the eve of World War I.

Poor Law Reform by Another Name

Since its passage in 1870, Prussian conservatives had raised a steady drumbeat against the Relief Residence Law, and in 1877 the Prussian government agreed, in principle, to push for a reform of the Relief Residence Law along the lines advocated by the agrarians by (1) reducing the age at which a person could acquire a relief residence from 26 to 21 while reducing the waiting period from two years to one, (2) expanding the responsibility of factory owners for assisting sick workers who resided in a different locale, (3) making it easier to shift from local to regional relief authorities responsibility for assisting individuals who had no relief residence, and (4) permitting relief officials to administratively sentence able-bodied vagrants to the workhouse, rather than having to rely on the courts.[3] Although these Prussian proposals were soon tabled because of the resistance of other states, the wheels of legislative action were again set in motion by an 1881 Reichstag motion by the conservative Karl Gottlob von Varnbüler, who blamed the relief residence system for all of the moral and material ills of the age – real and imagined – and called for its wholesale replacement with a new system of home law.[4]

---

[3] Sachße et al., eds., *Armengesetzgebung und Freizügigkeit*, 442ff.
[4] Sachße et al., eds., *Armengesetzgebung und Freizügigkeit*, 603–5. For the ensuing Reichstag discussion, see *Stenographische Berichte der Verhandlungen des Reichstages*, 4. Periode, 49. Sitzung, 1291–1310.

Poor Law Reform by Another Name

The defenders of the relief residence system pointed out that this system was nothing more than a set of rules for regulating the assistance obligations of the communities toward the mobile workers who made up the national labor force, and they argued – a bit disingenuously – that the system was not the cause of increased mobility but rather was itself a response to the problems created by autonomous social processes. Although conservatives such as Varnbüler might extol the moral virtues of *Heimat*, these modernizers argued that it was impossible to turn back the clock in an attempt to recapture a golden age of doubtful historicity, and they insisted that the task was rather to bring the poor laws into conformity with the needs of the new social and economic order. The strategy proposed by Reich officials was to use the existing network of sickness funds as the foundation for a system of state-sponsored social insurance programs whose development they regarded as the precondition for any meaningful reform of the poor laws.

The details of this strategy were spelled out in a policy paper written in October 1881, a month before the issuance of the imperial proclamation on social affairs (November 17, 1881) in which the Kaiser announced his commitment to the creation of a system of social insurance programs.[5] This memorandum argued that the root of the problem was that each local relief authority had a powerful financial incentive to manipulate the rules in order to shift the cost of supporting the poor onto other shoulders. This resulted in skyrocketing administrative costs and many hardships for the poor themselves. The government's strategy was to make the entire system more humane and less costly by reducing these incentives. While the proposed social insurance programs would help free the working classes from their dependence on poor relief, a substantial portion of the benefits paid by the social insurance programs would offset municipal poor relief expenditures, which, along with municipal taxes, were expected to decline with the creation of a social insurance system. The government then hoped to reduce this local burden even further by shifting to state and provincial authorities responsibility for the expensive institutional care of the insane, the mentally retarded, deaf-mutes, and other persons who were not the appropriate objects of individualizing assistance. Once local poor relief costs had been reduced to a minimum by an expanded social insurance system and a new method for financing institutional care, and once relief officials had been equipped with more effective means for dealing with vagrants and the workshy, it would then be possible to abandon the relief residence system in favor of a current residence system in which each relief authority would be responsible for assisting all needy persons living within its boundaries, irrespective of their place of origin.

Such policies were part of a broader desire to make the administrative parameters of the highly fragmented poor relief system correspond more closely to

---

[5] This and the following paragraph draw on Sachße et al., eds., *Armengesetzgebung und Freizügigkeit*, 606ff. The authoritative survey of the German poor laws during these years is Emil Münsterberg, *Die deutsche Armengesetzgebung und das Material zu ihrer Reform* (Leipzig, 1887).

the actual contours of economic and communal life, which generally embraced larger regions, and to shift the cost of relief onto geographically larger, fiscally stronger, and administratively more professional bodies akin to English poor law unions.[6] The success of this strategy depended on creating a more robust and extensive mutual insurance system. The problem with existing funds was that only a minority of workers could afford to pay the premiums required to secure adequate benefits in time of need. Workers without regular jobs or adequate earnings could not afford to join such associations; the sick and those past their working prime were generally excluded as bad risks; and women and children were often excluded because they were not employed in skilled trades or because their support was regarded as the responsibility of the family breadwinner. In other words, mutual assistance was least accessible to those who needed it most. At the most basic level, the social insurance programs established in the 1880s were so successful because their organizational principles – their national scope, compulsory membership for clearly defined groups of workers, uniform minimum benefits, the portability of coverage from one employer to another, and the permanence and the actuarial soundness provided by the state – solved many of the problems that had plagued earlier mutual insurance schemes. However, these technical reasons by no means provide an adequate explanation of the adoption of social insurance in the 1880s.

The historiography of the German social insurance system has long focused on Bismarck's political strategies and the problem of explaining what led the conservative chancellor to promote such an innovative and apparently progressive solution to the social security of the working classes. Virtually every study has argued in one way or another that social insurance represented the carrot which Bismarck held out to the working classes to soften the impact of the repressive Anti-Socialist Law (1878/90) and convince them that the state was genuinely concerned with their well-being. However, it has never been entirely clear why industry, agriculture, the state bureaucracy, and Bismarck himself were willing to support these ideas, especially when these programs were opposed by both the liberals – many of whom were wary of state intervention in such matters and doubted the value of compulsory virtue – and the organized working classes, who saw – correctly – the proposed social insurance funds as an attempt to diminish the political role of their own funds, which were used both to support strikes and to provide various benefits to union members. Part of the solution to this riddle may be that social insurance was not intended primarily to benefit the working classes, or at least not to benefit them in ways in which they themselves would have liked to have been helped.[7]

---

[6] Similar ideas were advanced at the same time from a municipal perspective by Franz Adickes in "Die Vertheilung der Armenlasten in Deutschland und ihre Reform," *Zeitschrift für die gesamte Staatswissenschaft* 27 (1881), 237–91, 419–31, 727–822.

[7] E. P. Hennock, *The Origin of the Welfare State in England and Germany, 1850–1914. Social Policies Compared* (Cambridge University Press, 2007) provides an excellent account of the evolution of German social policy during these decades.

Poor Law Reform by Another Name

Bismarck was consistently concerned with the international competitiveness of German manufactures, and his attitudes toward social insurance depended on the possibility of using these programs to secure two goals that could not easily be combined: lowering the costs of production (especially by reducing the level of tax-financed municipal poor relief) and containing the political influence of the working classes. Like most conservatives, Bismarck believed that the spread of socialism was due in large part to outside agitators stirring up a basically patriotic common folk, whose loyalty could be regained by arresting the agitators while satisfying legitimate demands for modest material security. However, before 1880 Bismarck did not view social insurance as a particularly promising way of achieving this goal. It only became an important weapon in his social policy arsenal as part of a broader effort to forge a conservative consensus on domestic policy after his break with the liberals in 1878, and Bismarck's state paternalist intentions can be discerned most clearly in the funding mechanisms and administrative structure of the insurance systems, at least in the form in which they were originally proposed.[8]

The point of departure for Bismarck's legislative efforts was the reform of industrial accident insurance.[9] The main stimuli here were the problems resulting from the 1871 Accident Liability Law. This law gave workers employed in mines, quarries, and factories the right to sue their employers in case of accident-related disability. Since injured workers could obtain compensation for their injuries only if they could prove employer negligence, this law led to a surge in civil court cases that multiplied uncertainty without resolving the monetary issues to the satisfaction of either side. The 1884 Accident Insurance Law, in contrast, was based on the principle that, since industrial work was inherently risky, the task was less to assign blame than to develop a mechanism for fairly compensating those who were affected by this risk, and compensation – in the form of both rehabilitative services and pensions – depended on the establishment not of liability, but of disability, a concept that was constituted through the interaction of medical, actuarial, social, scientific, fiscal, bureaucratic, and legal discourses.[10]

---

[8] One of the other main issues is the German preference for insurance (i.e., compensating individuals for damages suffered) over the principle of prevention. On all of these questions, see Hennock, *The Origin of the Welfare State in England and Germany*, and Florian Tennstedt, "Der deutsche Weg zum Wohlfahrtsstaat 1871–1881," in Andreas Wollasch, ed., *Wohlfahrtspflege in der Region. Westfalen-Lippe während des 19. und 20. Jahrhunderts im historischen Vergleich* (Paderborn 1997), 255–67. See also Tennstedt, "Vorgeschichte und Entstehung der Kaiserlichen Botschaft vom 17. November 1881," *ZfS* 27 (1981), 633–729; Tennstedt and Heidi Winter, "'Der Staat hat wenig Liebe – activ wie passiv'. Die Anfänge des Sozialstaats im Deutschen Reich von 1871," *ZfS* 29 (1993), 362–92; and Tennstedt and Winter, "'Jeder Tag hat seine eigenen Sorgen, und es ist nicht weise, die Sorgen der Zukunft freiwillig auf die Gegenwart zu übernehmen' (Bismarck). Die Anfänge des Sozialstaats im Deutschen Reich von 1871," *ZfS* 41 (1995), 671–706.

[9] Eckart Reidegeld, *Staatliche Sozialpolitik in Deutschland. Historische Entwicklung und theoretische Analyse von den Ursrpüngen bis 1918* (Westdeutscher Verlag, 1996), 220ff.

[10] Greg Eghigian, *Making Security Social. Disability, Insurance, and the Birth of the Social Entitlement State in Germany* (University of Michigan Press, 2000) argues that the law led to the

Since the Accident Insurance Law had specified that injured workers were to be supported by sickness insurance for the first thirteen weeks of their disability, this latter program had to be in place before the former one could go into effect. The Sickness Insurance Law, which was the program with the greatest continuities with previous mutual associations, was the first program approved by the Reichstag (1883). The law compensated insured workers for wages lost to serious illness and helped them afford – and encouraged them to seek out in a timely manner – medical treatment that might prevent such illness from permanently impairing their health and earning power. In this way, the workers and their families would be better protected against the social consequences of serious illness, while municipal budgets would be shielded against its financial impact. The sickness insurance program generated less controversy than the debate over industrial accident insurance because it simply codified the basic principles of state-regulated sickness funds since the 1840s: obligatory employer contributions equal to one-half of those made by workers, a decentralized network of funds (organized on the basis of occupation or locale), a unified system of minimal benefits, and both employer and public influence over the administration of the funds.

The Disability and Old Age Insurance Law proved to be the most controversial of the three original social insurance programs.[11] It was unclear how many people would be affected by the law, and many employers feared that the prospect of such a pension would undermine the thrift of their workers, though these reservations about the proposed program were eased by the fact that the program graduated pensions according to earnings. Nevertheless, the law passed the Reichstag only by a slim majority. It covered all workers earning less than 2,000 marks, including servants and agricultural workers, who had been excluded from the other insurance programs. Insured workers were eligible for disability pensions based on medical determination after contributing to the system for at least five years, and they were eligible for old-age pensions when they reached the age of 70, regardless of their ability to work, if they had paid into the system for thirty years. Disability pensions did not, however, have as much impact as they might have otherwise had because few workers lived to the age of 70 without having qualified for a disability pension at an earlier

---

politicization of these discourses and to the creation of a new form of social politics – the politics of social entitlement – which replaced political economy as the dominant language through which the rights and duties of individuals in the welfare state were defined. See also Julia Moses' forthcoming comparative study of accident insurance in Britain, Germany, and Italy.

[11] Monika Breger, "Der Anteil der deutschen Großindustriellen an der Konzeptualisierung der Bismarckschen Sozialgesetzgebung," in Lothar Machtan, ed., *Bismarcks Sozialstaat* (Frankfurt/New York, 1994), 25–60; Reideigeld, *Staatliche Sozialpolitik in Deutschland*, 242ff. Lothar Machtan, "Der Arbeiterschutz als sozialpolitisches Problem im Zeitalter der Industrialisierung," in Hans Pohl, ed., *Staatliche, städtische, betriebliche und kirchliche Sozialpolitik*, VSWG Beiheft 95 (1991), 111–36; and Machtan and Hans-Jörg von Berlepsch, "Vorsorge oder Ausgleich – oder beides? Prinzipienfragen staatlicher Sozialpolitik im Deutschen Kaiserreich," *ZfS* 32 (1986), 257–75, 343–58.

Poor Law Reform by Another Name

age, and by the immediate prewar years the number of old-age pensioners was dwarfed by the growing number of disability pensioners.[12] Moreover, disability pensions were hardly a panacea for the problem of old-age poverty. To keep costs down and uphold the work ethic, benefits were set at such a minimal level that they never exceeded what the elderly would have received from poor relief and private charity, and the architects of the system recognized that to make ends meet pensioners would still have to rely on such assistance, along with casual work and help from family and neighbors. As a result, the program was initially more successful in improving the health of municipal finances than in enhancing the social security of its ostensible beneficiaries.[13]

The decisive advantage of these programs was, however, that they established a legal right to benefits under specified conditions that did not require the recipient to submit to a means test and that did not entail the loss of political rights. These programs collectively played an important role in constructing the male breadwinner family, and the security and independence that they guaranteed was one of the factors that respectable workers pointed to in order to distinguish themselves from the rougher members of the working classes. Although the sphere of persons covered under these insurance programs had originally been carefully circumscribed, eligibility was extended steadily to include both dependent family members and workers in many occupations that had originally been excluded, and the scope of benefits also expanded at the same time that benefit levels rose. With the creation of a separate insurance system for white-collar workers in 1911, virtually all workers and their dependents were at least minimally insured, either directly or indirectly, against the major risks associated with wage labor and the life cycle – except for unemployment.

In contrast to England, Germany had no central agency for collecting relief statistics and thus lacked a baseline against which to measure the anticipated impact of social insurance. To remedy this problem, in 1885 separate surveys were conducted by the Imperial Statistical Office and by Viktor Böhmert for the German Association for Poor Relief and Charity (Table 2). These were the only national poor relief statistics collected before 1918. The results of these inquiries are shown below.

There are a number of things that should be noted about these statistics. The first is that they counted only those persons who were supported by public

---

[12] For example, in Frankfurt fewer than fifty workers were receiving old-age pensions in 1909 as compared with approximately six hundred disability pensioners. Ralf Roth, *Gewerkschaftskartell und Sozialpolitik in Frankfurt am Main* (Studien zur Frankfurter Geschichte, Bd. 31, 1991), 190.

[13] Lujo Brentano, "Die beabsichtigte Alters- und Invaliden-Versicherung für Arbeiter und ihre Bedeutung," *Jahrbücher für Nationalökonomie und Statistik* N.F., 16 (1888), 1–46; and Gerhard A. Ritter, *Social Welfare in Germany and Britain* (Berg, 1986), 41ff. Hennock, *The Origin of the Welfare State in England and Germany*, argues that Bismarck saw social insurance primarily as a means of winning the loyalty of the working classes, rather than as a mechanism of poor law reform, which he believes was the case in England, but he recognizes that it impacted poor law finances in the manner described by Brentano.

TABLE 2. *Causes of Public Assistance Cases (in percent)*

Imperial Statistical Office[14]		Böhmert/German Association for Poor Relief and Charity[15]	
Accident-related poverty		Illness	44.89
Personal injury	2.1	Old Age	15.75
Injury of breadwinner	0.2	Unemployment or inadequate earnings	10.33
Death of breadwinner	0.9	Death of parent(s)	5.57
		Large number of children	4.94
Non-accident-related		Insanity, mental retardation	3.37
Death of breadwinner	17.5	Abandonment by breadwinner	2.53
Illness of relief recipient or family member	28.4	Imprisonment of breadwinner	1.69
Physical or mental disability	12.3	Accident/Injury	1.09
		Blindness	1.08
Other		Physical defect	1.01
Old-age infirmity	14.9	Drink	0.96
Large number of children	7.1	Work-shy	0.75
Unemployment	5.4	Delinquency	0.64
Drink	2.1	Other	0.59
Work-shy	1.2	Pauper burial	0.22
Miscellaneous	7.8	Physical or mental infirmity of breadwinner	0.21
Not given	0.1	Death of breadwinner caused by accident	0.03

poor relief, not the number of persons in need, and they made no pretension to discover the actual extent of poverty, however this may have been defined.[16] According to the official statistics, in those parts of the country that had adopted the relief residence system (i.e., everywhere but Bavaria and Alsace-Lorraine), 5.3% of the urban population and 2.1% of the rural population (793,000 and 412,000 persons, respectively) were supported by public assistance at the time of the survey. These numbers reflected the well-known fact that assistance rates were much higher in cities, where resources were greater, than in rural areas,

---

[14] Kaiserliches Statistisches Amt, ed., *Statistik des Deutschen Reiches*, N.F. Bd. 29: *Statistik der öffentlichen Armenpflege im Jahre 1885* (Berlin, 1887), 40. In 1880/1 the government had made a survey of the impact of industrial accidents on poor relief, but the results had not been considered reliable enough to publish.

[15] Böhmert, *Das Armenwesen in 77 deutschen Städten* (Dresden, 1886), Allgemeiner Teil, 114. Böhmert's figures to not add to 100%. On Böhmert's work as a social reformer, see Sebastian Kranich, "Victor Böhmert (1829–1918)," in Klaus Tanner, ed., *Gotteshilfe – Selbsthilfe – Staatshilfe – Bruderhilfe* (Evangelische Verlagsanstalt, 2000), 71–88, and Andrew Lees, *Cities, Sin and Social Reform in Imperial Germany* (University of Michigan Press, 2002), 191–221.

[16] Ernst Mischler, "Die Methode der Armenstatistik," *Bulletin de l'Institut International de Statistique* 14:2 (1904), 108–42.

where the lower standard of living narrowed both the span of relative deprivation, which was essential for determining need, and the resources available to help those deemed deserving of assistance.[17]

The second thing that should be noted is the differences in the way the two surveys attempted to define the different dimensions of need. On the one hand, the official statistics sought to group the causes of need according to the degree of personal fault – with poverty due to accident being distinguished from both life-cycle risks and those forms of dependence that were more properly ascribed to individual moral failings. On the other hand, both surveys concluded that the lion's share of dependence could be attributed to the interrelated but not identical factors of illness, old-age disability, and the death of the family breadwinner, precisely the risks that the social insurance system was intended to insure against. The social insurance laws set in motion a process by which this complex was disaggregated into its constituent parts, thus making possible the emergence of old age as a distinct social problem in modern society and the development of an assurantial mechanism for meeting the needs of the "pensioner."[18] Much the same could be said regarding sickness, disability, invalidity, and maternity – all of which were the assurantial correlates of the gendered familial subjects to be discussed in Chapter 7. However, it is also possible to state the issue in slightly different and more general terms. The proliferation of individual causes reflected the extent to which contemporary thinking continued to view need primarily in terms of individual character, choice, and circumstance, rather than as instantiations of risks inherent in and specific to the structure and dynamics of the industrial economy and bourgeois society.[19]

Lastly, these statistics shed some interesting light on the role of vice as a cause of poverty. Although drink, idleness, and immorality figured prominently in middle-class discourse on the social question, these factors were virtually absent from the 1885 statistics, though they were often reintroduced through the back door by regarding them either as contributory factors or as the effect, rather than the cause, of destitution. Officials in the Prussian East had long complained that they were being overburdened by the cost of supporting young people who had imprudently left their homes and succumbed to the temptations

---

[17] *Statistik der öffentlichen Armenpflege*, 29. For an illustration of this point, see M. Schumann, "Die Armenlast im Deutschen Reich," *Jahrbücher für Nationalökonomie und Statistik*, N.F. 17 (1888), 594–630, especially 617. Hennock, *The Origin of the Welfare State in England and Germany*, 41–5, extends this observation to account for the fact that relief spending was substantially higher in England than in Germany, which at that point still had a lower standard of living than did the English.

[18] Christoph Conrad, *Vom Greis zum Rentner. Der Strukturwandel des Alters in Deutschland zwischen 1830 und 1930* (Vandenhoeck & Ruprecht, 1994); Gerd Göckenjan, ed., *Recht auf ein gesichertes Alter? Studien zur Geschichte der Alterssicherung in der Frühzeit der Sozialpolitik* (Augsburg, 1990); and Pat Thane, *Old Age in English History. Past Experiences, Present Issues* (Oxford University Press, 2000).

[19] Christian Topalov, *Naissance du chômeur 1880–1910* (Albin Michel, 1994), 358ff., 375ff.

of the city, while urban officials insisted that freedom of settlement was, in fact, unfairly burdening their taxpayers. In fact, however, Böhmert's statistics showed that neither of these scenarios was correct. According to his figures, the overwhelming majority of relief recipients had resided in their new community for a decade or more before and were well into – if not beyond beyond – their most productive years when they first applied for public assistance.[20]

Liberal municipal politicians initially saw the proposed social insurance programs as an attempt by the state to limit the scope of municipal self-government in the all-important field of social politics, though they soon made their peace with the new system, whose advantages they recognized.[21] Serious illness often started the family down the slippery slope to destitution. However, medical care was prohibitively expensive for the poor; relief officials could not provide medical care until the family had completely exhausted its savings; and the receipt of public medical assistance entailed the loss of voting rights. Therefore, workers often delayed seeking treatment until they were completely debilitated, rather than seeking care in the initial stages when an illness could be treated more effectively.[22] But the sickness insurance program still suffered from several important shortcomings.[23] Since benefits alone seldom sufficed to meet the actual needs of working-class families, relief authorities often had to provide additional assistance if there were a large number of young children or if the wife was unable to work, and many of those workers who formed the traditional clientele of municipal poor relief, including servants, casual laborers, agricultural workers, migrant workers, and home workers, were at first excluded from the system.

Although the direct effects of social insurance were, to a certain degree, easy to measure, at least in theory, it proved to be unexpectedly difficult to quantify the impact of social insurance on municipal poor relief.[24] One could count the number of people receiving pensions from the accident and disability insurance systems or the number of hospital days paid for by sickness insurance and make a strong counterfactual argument that these costs would have otherwise

---

[20] Böhmert, *Das Armenwesen in 77 deutschen Städten*, 124.
[21] See *SDV*, 14 (1891), 21 (1895), 23 (1895), 29 (1897), 34 (1897), as well as Friedrich Zahn, "Arbeiterversicherung und Armenwesen in Deutschland," *Archiv für Sozialwissenschaft und Sozialpolitik* 35 (1912), 418–86.
[22] Gerhard A. Ritter and Klaus Tenfelde, *Arbeiter im Deutschen Kaiserreich* (Dietz Nachf., 1992), 651ff.
[23] Richard Freund, *Prüfung der Frage, in welcher Weise die neuere sociale Gesetzgebung auf die Aufgaben der Armengesetzgebung und Armenpflege einwirkt*, *SDV*, 21 (1895), the discussion in *SDV*, 23 (1895), 21–48, "Die Einwirkung der Versicherungs-Gesetzgebung auf die Armenpflege," *Vierteljahresheft zu Statistik des Deutschen Reiches* 6:2 (1897), 1–54, and David Grünspecht, *Die Entlastung der öffentlichen Armenpflege durch die Arbeiterversicherung* (dissertation, Halle, 1906).
[24] Heinrich Silbergleit, *Finanzstatistik der Armenverwaltungen in 108 deutschen Städten*, *SDV*, 61 (1902). In accordance with the reform strategy described earlier, in 1891 Prussia approved a law transferring responsibility for the institutional care of physically and mentally handicapped persons to provincial relief authorities.

Old Conflicts and New Departures

been borne by municipal poor relief.[25] However, the establishment of the social insurance system did not lead to the anticipated decline in poor relief costs. In fact, the primary effect of these programs was less to reduce the absolute level of public spending on poor relief, which continued to rise 1890/1910, than to restructure spending patterns. Sickness and accident insurance reduced the amount that public authorities had to spend on short-term relief and medical assistance for the otherwise able-bodied. Conversely, a growing percentage of public relief spending went to the long-term support for the elderly and infirm (especially women), who constituted an increasingly large proportion of the clientele of poor relief.

Relief officials likewise began to develop a new understanding of the benefits of prevention, and their willingness to invest in prevention (at least to the minimal degree that this was permitted within the narrow scope of the poor laws) reflected their recognition that it was cheaper to prevent poverty (especially that caused by chronic, disabling diseases) than to provide long-term support to the poor. Political pressures, especially the growing influence of organized labor, also helped keep relief expenses from declining in proportion to the expansion of social insurance, as did increases in the level of assistance provided to elderly relief recipients, which may have been growing less inadequate.[26] Moreover, it is extremely difficult to isolate any of these effects from broader demographic and economic trends, such as the creeping inflation of the period, especially when rising poor relief costs could lead to a political backlash, as was the case in Augsburg in the 1890s.[27] Lastly, it must be recognized that every analysis of changes in public spending on poor relief is of limited value in the absence of comparable data on the level and patterns of assistance provided by voluntary organizations.

Old Conflicts and New Departures

The passage of the social insurance legislation of the 1880s did not, however, eliminate pressures to reform the poor laws. In 1893 the Reich government again began to push for the reform of the Relief Residence Law, and the law was revised in 1894 and again in 1908.[28] The 1870 law had specified that a person could acquire a relief residence by residing in a locale for two years after reaching the age of 24. These revisions lowered the age at which a person could begin to acquire a relief residence from 24 to 18 and then from 18 to 16,

---

[25] Susanne Eser, *Verwaltet und Vewahrt. Armenpolitik und Arme in Augsburg vom Ende der reichsstädtischen Zeit bis zum Ersten Weltkrieg* (Jan Thorbecke Verlag, 1996), 194–6, 207ff., and Thomas Küster, *Alte Armut und neues Bürgertum. Öffentliche und private Fürsorge in Münster von der Ära Fürstenberg bis zum Ersten Weltkrieg (1756–1914)* (Aschendorff Verlag, 1995), 265ff.
[26] Küster, *Alte Armut*, 266ff., makes this argument for Münster.
[27] Eser, *Verwaltet und Vewahrt*, 200–6.
[28] The following account draws primarily on the Reichstag debates, materials in BA RAdI Rep. 1276–80, and *Die Novelle zum Gesetz über den Unterstützungswohnsitz*, SDV, 76 (1906).

and the 1908 law shortened the term for acquiring (or losing) a relief residence from two years to one. These laws also took an important step away from the relief residence system toward a current residence system by increasing from six to thirteen weeks, and again from thirteen to twenty-six weeks, the length of time that local poor relief authorities had to bear the cost of supporting sick workers before they could begin to seek reimbursement from the person's relief residence.

Prussian agrarians were deeply ambivalent about this legislation. On the one hand, they favored lowering the age at which individuals could acquire a relief residence because it reduced their financial liability for the support of needy out-migrants. On the other hand, though, they also wanted to stem the flow of young migrants from the countryside because they felt that this was depriving them of much-needed agricultural labor and depriving the army of its most politically reliable recruits. Conservative proposals to restrict the freedom of movement drew predictable responses from those to their political left. The left liberal Theodor Barth, for example, characterized these proposals as a crass manifestation of agrarian special interest politics. He and other liberals argued that, since young people were leaving the countryside both to seek a better quality of life in the cities and to get out from under the thumb of the *Junkers*, the best way to retain these young workers was to improve social and economic conditions in the countryside.[29] And when these conservative proposals were finally brought up for a vote, the Social Democrats opposed them because they regarded these measures as part of a broader government effort to shift the costs of its *Weltpolitik* onto the cities and the urban working classes.[30]

More important than these marginal revisions to the relief residence system was a 1909 law that represented an important step toward the codification of the principle of prevention. By the turn of the century, the provisions of state and national electoral laws that deprived relief recipients of their suffrage rights were being criticized from two directions.[31] While the Social Democrats regarded these suffrage restrictions as simply another form of legal discrimination against the working classes, relief officials and social reformers argued that these laws were discouraging the needy from taking advantage of preventive social welfare programs, especially in the areas of medical relief and youth welfare that will be discussed in the following chapters, and thus negatively impacting the health and productivity of the nation. Already in 1896 the German Association for Poor Relief and Charity had called on the Reichstag to exempt preventive services that were provided to further specific public

---

[29] Barth in Reichstag 43. Sitzung (February 14, 1893) 1029, and Heinrich Rickert in ibid., 1022.
[30] BA RAdI Rep. 1275, vol. 4, Bl. 257ff. (November 3, 1900), and 30. Sitzung (January 29, 1906), 854.
[31] Paul Hirsch and Hugo Lindemann, *Das kommunale Wahlrecht* (Berlin, 1905), *Handhabung der Bestimmungen, betreffend den Verlust des Wahlrechts bei Empfang öffentlicher Armenunterstützungen*, SDV, 26 (1896), *Stenographischer Bericht über die Verhandlungen*, SDV, 28 (1896), 120–39, and "Der Verlust des Wahlrechts durch Armenunterstützung," *Zeitschrift für das Heimatwesen* 13:6 (March 15, 1908), 81ff.

interests, rather than to compensate for the irresponsibility or improvidence of the family head, from the discriminatory provisions of national suffrage legislation.[32] Although Reich officials did not take up the issue for another decade (apparently because they feared that such a step would benefit the Social Democrats), in 1909 the Reichstag finally passed a law that removed the suffrage disabilities associated with the receipt of several broad categories of preventive social welfare. However, this law did not alter the restrictive suffrage system that prevailed in most cities, and the political disqualification of relief recipients was not abolished until the 1918 revolution.[33]

The 1894 and 1908 amendments to the Relief Residence Law appeared to represent a victory for the agrarians because they would make the cities bear a greater proportion of the cost of supporting the nation's poor. However, municipal officials did not seem particularly threatened by these measures,[34] and this nominal victory of the conservatives came at a cost because the mechanisms that they relied on to shift poor relief costs toward the cities also facilitated out-migration (or at least that sanctioned a process that was following its own dynamic) and thus undermined the goal of preserving the patriarchal social relationships that conservatives imagined still prevailed in the Prussian East. The conservative project was also a failure in yet a larger sense. Despite the ingrained antimodernism of the conservatives and their jaundiced view of modern, urban life, the basic principles of the relief residence system – and the commitment to labor mobility, industrial development, and the creation of a market society which they implied – remained unaltered.[35]

[32] *Handhabung der Bestimmungen...*, SDV, 26 (1896), 33.
[33] Hansjoachim Henning, "Sozialpolitik und politische Partizipation. Die Diskussion um Armenunterstützung und Wahlrecht zwischen 1890 und 1909," VSWG Beiheft 120b (1995), 596–617, especially 607–11. Relief officials, however, feared that the law had interpreted the principle of prevention so broadly that public assistance would lose too much of its intended deterrent effect. Otto Lohse, "Die Einwirkung von Armenunterstützung auf öffentliche Rechte," ZfA 9:12 (December 1908), 353–61, and Lohse, "Die Einwirkung von Armenunterstützung auf öffentliche Rechte," ZfA 10:3 (March 1909), 65–7. For examples of similar trends in England, Sidney, and Beatrice Webb, *English Poor Law History. Part II: The Last Hundred Years*, vol. 2 (Frank Cass, 1963), 480ff.
[34] "Die Novelle zum Gesetz über den Unterstützungswohnsitz," ZfA 7:1 (January 1906), 2–8.
[35] George Steinmetz, *Regulating the Social. The Welfare State and Local Politics in Imperial Germany* (Princeton University Press, 1993), Chapter 4.

6

New Voices

Citizenship, Social Reform, and the Origins of Modern Social Work in Imperial Germany

Near the beginning of *The Promise of American Life*, which remains the classic statement of the ideals and aspirations of American Progressivism, Herbert Croly wrote that "when the Promise of American life is conceived as a national ideal, whose fulfillment is a matter of artful and laborious work, the effect hereof is substantially to identify the national purpose with the social problem." For Croly, the heart of the matter was that the absence of efficient state regulation of the economy had permitted competitive individualism to congeal into a system of political abuses and social inequalities, and this problem – in which the national was inextricable intertwined with the social and with the promise of human perfectibility – could simply not be avoided by an American national democracy without losing its soul and its promise.[1] Much the same could be said of imperial, and especially Wilhelmine (1890–1918), Germany.

Like the United States, Germany was also engaged in a furious search for both national efficiency and that elusive object of desire, social peace, and it pursued this end in the context of intensifying national rivalries and expanding mass democracy. In the decades following the founding of the empire, a distinct historical constellation took shape: the torrid pace of industrialization telescoped the first and second industrial revolutions into a single convulsive process with all of the usual urban, social, and demographic processes trailing in its wake; the religious question remained a latent threat to the unity of the nation, while the class question became an overt one; and the inner unity of the nation-state remained a matter of contestation at the same time that the

---

[1] Herbert Croly, *The Promise of American Life* (1909), 23–4, 399ff. Croly viewed Germany (246ff.) as a paragon of national efficiency, though he feared that militarism and foreign policy entanglements would distract Germany and the other European nations from this task. For the German debate on national efficiency and population policy, see Matthias Weipert, "Mehrung der Volkskraft". Die Debatte über Bevölkerung, Modernisierung und Nation 1890–1933 (Schöningh, 2006), and Rainer Mackensen and Jürgen Reulecke, eds., *Das Konstrukt "Bevölkerung" vor, im und nach dem Dritten Reich* (Verlag für Sozialwissenschaften, 2005).

solution to this question was becoming the key to defining the position of the new state in a constellation of international forces that was itself altered by this act of national unification. Here, the nation-state was more vision and anticipation than reality, and, as any good Freudian would note, the ritual invocation of Bismarck and the founding of the empire served as much to exorcize the demons of national weakness as to demonstrate the strength and unity of the nation. Although the precise direction of German political life may have been up for grabs, no one could avoid being drawn into the game.

Solutions to these national questions may well have required changes in the industrial and political organization of the nation, but such reforms would have been sterile, oppressive, and fragile were they not accompanied by corresponding changes in the domain of culture, values, and habits, those of both the working classes and the bourgeoisie. In the ceaseless dialectic of individual character and social institutions, the theorists of social welfare and social work increasingly recognized the influence of the latter on the former, as well as the importance of the social domain in mediating between them, and during these decades the family and its welfare stood at the focus of a modernist discourse on social reform that ran oblique to existing political parties and institutions.[2] The centrality of the social to the national question allowed social reform groups to harness social policy to an anticipated future of the nation and, on this basis, to stake out their claims to play a role in shaping this future. The parameters of citizenship were then expanded and redefined as these groups elbowed their way into the public sphere, thus challenging existing linkages between the national and the social and forcing older, established organizations to modernize their ideas and bring them into accord with the demands of the age.[3] This chapter will focus on three new groups that came to play an important role in the development of social assistance in the empire: the bourgeois women's movement, Catholic charities, and, to a lesser degree, Social Democracy.

This competitive proliferation of voluntary associations each seeking to shape the values and habits of the laboring classes in accordance with their own worldviews fragmented the social domain, multiplied the agents, institutions and discourses of social discipline, and redefined the state as the effect of

---

[2] Geoff Eley and James Retallack, eds., *Wilhelminism and Its Legacies. German Modernities, Imperialism, and the Meanings of Reform, 1890–1930* (Berghahn Books, 2003); Kevin Repp, *Reformers, Critics, and the Paths of German Modernity. Anti-Politics and the Search for Alternatives, 1890–1914* (Harvard University Press, 2000); James Kloppenberg, *Uncertain Victory. Social Democracy and Progressivism in European and American Thought, 1870–1920* (Oxford University Press, 1986); Jennifer Jenkins, *Provincial Modernity: Local Culture & Liberal Politics in Fin-de-Siècle Hamburg* (Cornell University Press, 2003); and Andrew Lees, *Cities, Sin and Social Reform in Imperial Germany* (University of Michigan Press, 2002).

[3] Eley, "Making a Place in the Nation: Meanings of 'Citizenship' in Wilhelmine Germany," in Eley and Retallack, eds., *Wilhelminism and Its Legacies*, 16–33. Rüdiger vom Bruch charts the growing population density of the social reform field in "Bürgerliche Sozialreform im deutschen Kaiserreich," in vom Bruch, ed., *Weder Kommunismus noch Kapitalismus. Bürgerliche Sozialreform in Deutschland vom Vormärz bis zur Ära Adenauer* (Beck, 1985), 61–179.

these reformist discourses and practices, rather than as their agent,[4] and the cities, rather than the Reich, emerged as the most important arena for social politics and as the most important providers of social services.[5] These conflicts were given an even sharper edge by the confessional tensions of the age. While religious pluralism represented an existential threat to churches that regarded doctrinal purity as a matter of paramount importance, the competition between the two Christian confessions was complicated by their need to define their relations not only to each other, but also to the sovereign state, liberalism, and the other new groups active in the social reform field. The politics of social reform must, therefore, be understood in relation to the ongoing formation of social, religious, and political milieus that was one of the distinguishing characteristics of imperial society.[6]

The question, though, is whether state toleration of these societal initiatives (if not their actual encouragement) enhanced the legitimacy of the state in the eyes of these groups or whether it simply encouraged these groups in their mutual hostility and their respective efforts to colonize the state. The German state could ride the tiger of politico-religious pluralism only as long as the organization of social reproduction remained a private matter for voluntary organizations. But the cleavages of German society ran too deep. In the long run, as we shall see in this and later chapters, the politicization of social services between 1910 and 1920 transformed limited mutual tolerance into a systematic antagonism that undermined the state's claims to represent the nation and thus delegitimated both the Wilhelmine state and its Weimar successor in the eyes of its ostensible citizens.[7] Although it is difficult in a nationally oriented study to capture the density of local associational life, the concreteness of local

---

[4] Dennis Sweeney, "Reconsidering the Modernity Paradigm: Reform Movements, the Social, and the State in Wilhelmine Germany," *SH* 31:4 (November 2006), 405–34.

[5] As Michael Willrich argues with regard to the United States, "to find the state in the Progressive Era, we need to go to the local level." Willrich, *City of Courts. Socializing Justice in Progressive Era Chicago* (Cambridge University Press, 2003), xxvi.

[6] For the religious dimensions of this process, see Olaf Blaschke and Frank-Michael Kuhlemann, eds., *Religion im Kaiserreich. Milieux – Mentalitäten – Krisen* (Chr. Kaiser, 1996). Jews occupy a specific place in the story being told here. Although many influential welfare reformers were of Jewish ancestry, Jewish organizations did not play an important role in welfare reform debates during these years and will not be dealt with in this chapter. On the development of Jewish charity during these decades, see Rainer Liedtke, *Jewish Welfare in Hamburg and Manchester, c. 1850–1914* (Oxford University Press, 1998), and Marion Kaplan, *The Making of the Jewish Middle Class. Women, Family, and Identity in Imperial Germany* (Oxford University Press, 1991). Forthcoming studies by Tobias Brinkmann and Christiane Reinecke will examine the role of Jewish welfare organizations in facilitating the migration of Jews from Eastern Europe and the development of state social hygiene programs to combat the perceived dangers emanating from these migrants.

[7] Tara Zahra characterizes this movement as the invasion of the public sphere by the private while showing how this very rhetoric depended on a normative construction of the family as a "private" institution that represented the natural and most appropriate environment for child rearing. "'Each Nation Only Cares for Its Own': Empire, Nation, and Child Welfare Activism in the Bohemian Lands, 1900–1918," *AHR* 111:5 (December 2006), 1378–1402.

The Inner Mission, 1870–1914

circumstance, and the myriad relationships between local state and association, these things should not be forgotten in the following discussion.

The Inner Mission, 1870–1914

In the early years of the empire, the social reform field was dominated by the same two groups that had dominated it in previous years: liberals and conservative Protestants. The liberals dominated urban politics through the empire. During these decades, the German Association for Poor Relief and Charity was the organizational home for liberal politicians interested in the modernization of poor relief, and these men saw many of their initial goals realized with the spread of the Elberfeld system and scientific charity – as described in Chapter 4. Protestant social conservatives, however, were much harder pressed than their liberal opponents to engage critically with the social consequences of industrialization and democracy, and the erratic participation of the Inner Mission in the Christian Social movement did little to overcome this handicap.[8] Despite these limitations, the Inner Mission continued to grow across the last third of the century. Socially minded conservative Protestants continued to give priority to the rescue of endangered children and delinquent youth. They founded railroad missions along with clubs and charitable associations for women workers in various trades to protect these women from the dangers of urban life. The Protestant "morality movement" (*Sittlichkeitsbewegung*) engaged in an ongoing struggle against prostitution, pornography, and "trashy" popular culture and tried valiantly to hold back the tide of changing sexual moeurs. And where such measures failed, these conservative social activists established homes for unwed mothers, where these young women were made to feel the shame of their transgressions. These people were also involved in temperance campaigns, the promotion of Sabbath observance, and pastoral care for seamen and prisoners, as well as urban missionary work.[9] In addition to his labors on behalf of the welfare of migrant workers (Chapter 8), during these years Friedrich von Bodelschwingh began to construct a network of institutions (Bethel bei Bielefeld) to care for the sick and mentally handicapped and train deacons and deaconesses to minister to the physical and spiritual needs of these persons. These were to become a mainstay of Protestant charity in Germany up to the present day.

---

[8] Theodor Strohm and Jörg Thierfelder, eds., *Diakonie im Deutschen Kaiserreich (1871–1918)* (C. Winter, 1995); Jochen-Christoph Kaiser and Martin Greschat, eds., *Sozialer Protestantismus und Sozialstaat. Diakonie und Wohlfahrtspflege in Deutschland 1890 bis 1938* (Kohlhammer, 1996); Wilfried Loth and Jochen-Christoph Kaiser, eds., *Sozialer Reform im Kaiserreich. Protestantismus, Katholizismus und Sozialpolitik* (Kohlhammer, 1997); and E. I. Kouri, *Der deutsche Protestantismus und die soziale Frage 1870–1919* (De Gruyter, 1984).

[9] Martin Gerhardt, *Ein Jahrhundert Innere Mission. Die Geschichte des Centralausschusses für die Innere Mission der deutschen evangelischen Kirche* (Bertelsmann, 1948), 167–280, and Bettina Hitzer, *Im Netz der Liebe. Die protestantische Kirche und ihre Zuwanderer in der Metropole Berlin (1849–1914)* (Böhlau, 2006).

Protestant women's associational life also developed rapidly during the Wilhelmine years. The spread of these associations brought about a broad feminization of Protestant charity, which under Wichern had been a male undertaking modeled on the role of the family patriarch.[10] Across most of the nineteenth century, the charitable activity of Protestant women tended to confirm, rather than challenge, traditional gender roles. At the turn of the century, though, the Association of German Evangelical Women (*Deutsch-Evangelischer Frauenbund*), the most important organization of conservative Protestant women, found itself in the uncomfortable position of trying – though with only a limited degree of success – to defend a more autonomous public role for women in the life of the church and its charities against its critics within the church, who wished to restrict women to unpolitical, subordinate caring work in the diaconical tradition, without itself being drawn into the tow of religious liberalism.[11]

During the last decades of the century, there was one last important change taking place in Protestant charitable culture, where there was growing support for establishing a formal system of parish charity within the institutional framework of the Lutheran church (as had long been the case in the Calvinist church). The proponents of this idea hoped to energize a church hierarchy that was notoriously indifferent toward social affairs and lend the local associations for Inner Mission that had grown up since the 1840s the authority of the church, with the local pastor providing support and overall direction for the charitable labors of the congregation. By the 1890s well over one thousand deaconesses trained at the institutions founded by Fliedner and Bodelschwingh were employed in the service of congregational charity in cities across the country.[12]

The Bourgeois Women's Movement, the Spiritualization of Motherhood, and Social Work as Social Reconciliation

By the end of the nineteenth century, social work had become one of the most important fields of engagement for the bourgeois women's movement, and the history of the former cannot be told without understanding how it grew out of the latter. In its emphasis on the development of the personality, the bourgeois women's movement was much closer to the liberal movement than to Protestant conservatives. However, the ideas on sexual difference held by

---

[10] Strohm, "Die Diakonie in den Umbrüchen des Deutschen Kaiserreichs," in Strohm and Thierfelder (eds), *Diakonie im Deutschen Kaiserreich*, 18–55, and Ursula Baumann, *Protestantismus und Frauenemanzipation in Deutschland 1850 bis 1920* (Campus, 1992).

[11] Baumann, *Protestantismus und Frauenemanzipation*, and Ute Planert, *Antifeminismus im Kaiserreich. Diskurs, soziale Formation und politische Mentalität* (Vandenhoeck & Ruprecht, 1998).

[12] Gerhard Uhlhorn, *Die kirchliche Armenpflege in ihrer Bedeutung für die Gegenwart* (Göttingen, 1892); Uhlhorn, *Die christliche Liebestätigkeit*, 2. Aufl. (Stuttgart, 1895), 755–6; and Walther Vogel, *Fünfzig Jahre Innere Mission im Kgr. Sachsen* (Leipzig, 1917), 57–9. Since the 1850s, these associations, as well as Lutheran clergy, had been trying to forge closer connections with municipal poor relief. See, for example, LAB A Rep. 003–01, Nr. 348, passim.

most members of the movement gave female *Bildung* a very different thrust than that normally associated with liberal Idealism, and these differences, in turn, shaped in decisive ways the development of the social work profession from the 1890s through World War I.[13]

This understanding of sexual difference emerged at the end of the 1700s in conjunction with the formation of a new social institution, the bourgeois family, and it served to naturalize the new sexual division of labor within the family and legitimate the hierarchies that it embodied. This sexual division of labor and the resulting separation of work and home among the social strata that came to make up the bourgeoisie brought about what has been called the polarization of sexual characteristics.[14] As part of this process, all of those characteristics that are associated with the world of work, high culture, and political life were identified as essentially masculine characteristics: instrumental reason and calculation, abstract reasoning, active striving, competitiveness, acquisitiveness, and strength of character. As bourgeois women were freed from the constraints of domestic production, their nature was recast as the antithesis of and complement to this emergent masculinity, and women were defined by emotionality, the capacity for love, self-denial, and empathetic identification with others, sexual modesty, and the ability to find fulfillment in the care and nurturing of others. These socially constructed sexual differences were then made the basis of an ostensibly natural separation between the public and the private spheres in which men and women, respectively, could most fully express their distinct sexual characteristics. The husband's right to govern the household and represent it in the political sphere was complemented by the natural dependence of women and their right to that support that would enable them to realize their domestic calling.

It was only by exiting the home and negating the immediacy of its pleasures that the man could undergo a process of personal growth and cultivation (*Bildung*) through labor that would reveal to him the universal significance of the experiences he had originally enjoyed in a natural, prereflective manner within the home. But this alienating sojourn in the public domain gave rise to an intense emotional investment in the home, which was increasingly viewed as a private domain of unalienated, purely affective relations between man and woman, who was idealized as the angel by the hearth. It was the full and

---

[13] In a recent essay, Marilyn Boxer has described the polemical construction of the concept "bourgeois feminism" by socialist women concerned about reinforcing the primacy of class over sexual struggle, and she warns against assuming that the ideas of bourgeois feminists were in any direct way an expression of their ostensible class interests. Boxer, "Rethinking the Socialist Construction and International Career of the Concept 'Bourgeois Feminism,'" *AHR* 112:1 (February 2007), 131–58.

[14] Karin Hausen, "Family and Role-Division: The Polarization of Sexual Stereotypes in the Nineteenth Century – An Aspect of the Dissociation of Work and Family Life," in Richard Evans and W. R. Lee, eds., *The German Family* (Barnes & Noble, 1981), 51–83; Barbara Greven-Aschoff, *Die bürgerliche Frauenbewegung in Deutschland 1894–1933* (Vandenhoeck & Ruprecht, 1981), 31ff.; and Ute Frevert, *Women in German History* (Berg, 1989), 11ff.

complete subordination of her individuality to that of her husband – which was portrayed as the highest calling of the female sex – that enabled the husband to overcome his alienation. The difference, though, was that, at least in this initial formulation of the dialectic of the sexes, women were destined to immediately complement their husbands and their children, an immediacy that was reflected in their limitation to their activity as wife, mother, and housekeeper within the private home.

The ethical impulses that inspired the German women's movement came from the critique of this last proposition.[15] The problem was that this idyllic notion of the complementary nature of sexual characteristics and their mutual completion in marriage was self-contradictory to the extent that women lacked the reflexivity needed to make them into intellectually equal companions for their husbands and ensure that they had the cultivation necessary to guide the development of their children. Drawing on Rousseau, this problem was first theorized by the leaders of the kindergarten movement, Johann Heinrich Pestalozzi and Friedrich Fröbel, whose sentimentalization of childhood and idealization of maternal guidance made them into advocates of formal education for motherhood.[16] This was the constitutive insight of the women's movement, and the solution to this problem was to "ennoble" these innate female characteristics, that is, to make these feminine virtues – which were grounded in biological difference and the capacity for motherhood – into the object of systematic reflection and self-conscious application and thus to render them more organized, more universal, and more spiritual. In the words of Louise Otto-Peters, the most prominent advocate of women's rights during the 1848 revolution and the spiritual grandmother of the German women's movement,

the task on which we labor is that of bringing to consciousness the Eternal Feminine in women and gaining recognition for it among mankind. Development is impossible without freedom. Therefore, the same freedom to develop one's individual characteristics that is given to men must also be given to women so that they can develop their own.... The Eternal Feminine, which draws forward the man who loves to higher nobility, but only in the love of specific individuals, in the true love of man for woman – this

---

[15] On the history of the bourgeois women's movement, see, in addition to Greven-Aschoff, Monika Simmel, *Erziehung zum Weibe. Mädchenbildung im 19. Jahrhundert* (Campus, 1980); Ann Taylor Allen, *Feminism and Motherhood in Germany, 1800–1914* (Rutgers University Press, 1991); Susanna Dammer, *Mütterlichkeit und Frauendienstpflicht. Versuche der Vergesellschaftung 'weiblicher Fähigkeiten' durch eine Dienstverpflichtung (Deutschland 1890–1918)* (Deutscher Studien Verlag, 1988); Dietlinde Peters, *Mütterlichkeit im Kaiserreich. Die bürgerliche Frauenbewegung und der soziale Beruf der Frau* (B. Kleine Verlag, 1984); and Irene Stoehr, *Emanzipation zum Staat?* (Centaurus, 1990).

[16] In addition to the works by Allen and Simmel, the connections between the kindergarten movement and the bourgeois women's project have also been analyzed in Katja Münchow, "The Relationship between the Kindergarten Movement, the Movement for Democracy and the Early Women's Movement in the Historical Context of the Revolution of 1848-49, as reflected in Die Frauen-Zeitung," *History of Education* 35:2 (March 2006), 283–92.

Eternal Feminine must influence all of human society so that it does not draw only the individual, but all humankind, to a higher plane, to greater perfection.[17]

The same point was made nearly fifty years later by Helene Lange, the dominant figure in the bourgeois women's movement at the turn of the century, who argued that the reliance on instinct and the aversion to the education of women was making motherhood into a caricature of itself: "On the basis of their instincts alone, they are not even capable of successfully discharging their maternal tasks. Only the feelings that have been controlled by reason and clarified by spiritual culture, together with good, practical schooling, makes her capable of meeting both challenges."[18]

By raising female sexual characteristics to a higher level of self-consciousness, this phenomenology of the female spirit and the resulting spiritualization of femininity broke the ties between women's self-realization and both the private household and biological motherhood.[19] This process could only be completed in the creation of a social and cultural world in which the female spirit could recognize itself – and in which it could serve as a corrective to the intrinsic limitations of a masculine public culture. As Lange wrote, "women can and must make out of the masculine world a world that bears the stamp of both sexes. She must bring her own values into the world and thereby help in the centuries-long labor of establishing a new social and ethical view of the world in which her own measures would have the same value as those of men. But she can only do all of this on the basis of an independent spiritual education under the direction of her own sex."[20]

This vision of the marriage of masculine and feminine cultures, which recapitulated at a higher level of universality the unmediated love of man and woman in marriage, provided the program for the first nationwide women's association, the General German Women's Association (*Allgemeiner Deutscher Frauenverein*, ADF), which was founded in 1865. While some German women insisted on the equality of men and women and on this basis demanded the right to vote, the moderates who made up the mainstream of the German women's movement subscribed to the understanding of sexual difference described earlier and saw the path to emancipation not in equality and sameness with men, but in the recognition of the equality in value of masculinity and femininity and in the conquest of a public space that would permit the full development of this feminine culture.[21]

---

[17] *Die deutsche Frauenbewegung. Ihre Anfänge und erste Entwicklung. Quellen 1843–1889*, edited by Margrit Twellmann (Anton Hain, 1972), II:38.
[18] Helene Lange, "Intellektuelle Grenzlinien zwischen Mann und Frau (1897)," in Lange, *Kampfzeiten. Aufsätze und Reden aus vier Jahrzehnten* (Berlin, 1928), 197–216, citation 215.
[19] Lange, Ibid., 207–9, regarded the traditional confinement of women to the private sphere of the home as the product of a false, mechanical sexual division of labor.
[20] Lange, *Lebenserinnerungen* (Berlin, 1921), in Twellmann, ed., *Die deutsche Frauenbewegung*, II:266.
[21] Bärbel Clemens, "'Der Staat als Familie' – oder – 'Menschenrechte haben kein Geschlecht,'" in Beatrix Bechtel and Eva Blimlinger, eds., *Die ungeschriebene Geschichte. Historische*

The ADF combined this broader vision of female culture with the class-specific concerns of bourgeois women, who saw education as a means of expanding the scope of suitable employment for unmarried women of their class, and they sought to justify this demand by coupling it with ideas on gender solidarity and the moral obligation of these well-situated women to better the conditions of their less fortunate sisters. The expansion of educational and occupational opportunities for women remained a central concern for the League of German Women's Associations (*Bund Deutscher Frauenvereine*, BDF), which was founded in 1894 as an umbrella organization to bring together all of the existing bourgeois women's organizations, both moderate and radical. What these women sought was a specifically feminine form of education that would not make them more like men, but rather one that would cultivate their femininity and render it more universal and more socially valuable. However, their efforts to define what they meant by female *Bildung* and to spell out precisely which fields of professional and occupational engagement were particularly well suited for women, and why this was so, made it uncomfortably clear that their rhetoric of sexual difference cut both ways.

It was in the early 1890s that social helping, and the education of bourgeois girls and women for such work, emerged as an important area of engagement for the bourgeois women's movement.[22] The precondition for this interest in social helping was the existence of a class of bourgeois girls and young women constrained by the conventions of their class to a life of enforced otioseness as they awaited the appearance of a suitable marriage partner, and the idea of social service in which they could find a sense of personal satisfaction while fulfilling the obligations of their class and their sex resonated powerfully with these women. In this project, the emancipation of women into the public sphere was always coupled with and conditioned by their duty to assist the needy. The engagement of bourgeois women in philanthropic activity on behalf of working-class women since the 1860s had led them to see the social problem primarily as a women's problem, that is, as a problem of unequal and inadequate wages combined with the inability to realize middle-class ideals of domestic life. These experiences had given rise to both a sense of gender solidarity that they felt transcended all considerations of class and a desire to

---

Frauenforschung (Wiener Frauenverlag, 1984), 53–69. The debate over the political implications of this conception of difference has been the focal point of the historiography of the German women's movement.

[22] Iris Schröder, *Arbeiten für eine bessere Welt. Frauenbewegung und Sozialreform 1890–1914* (Campus, 2001), Christoph Sachße, *Mütterlichkeit als Beruf. Sozialarbeit, Sozialereform und Frauenbewegung 1870–1929* (Suhrkamp, 1986), Elisabeth Meyer-Renschhausen, *Weibliche Kultur und soziale Arbeit. Eine Geschichte der Frauenbewegung am Beispiel Bremens 1810–1927* (Böhlau, 1989), Peters, *Mütterlichkeit im Kaiserreich*, and Nancy Reagin, *A German Women's Movement. Class & Gender in Hanover, 1880–1933* (University of North Carolina Press, 1995) all chart the connections between the women's movement and the social work profession. See also Seth Koven and Sonya Michel, eds., *Mothers of a New World. Maternalist Politics and the Origins of Welfare States* (Routledge, 1993).

combat this peculiarly gendered form of need in the name of "women's welfare" (*Frauenwohl*).[23] There was a natural affinity between this desire to perfect their own domestic skills and their obligation to assist those working-class women whose need was defined, to a large degree, in terms of an underdeveloped domestic culture.[24] Moreover, their Idealist conception of spiritualized motherhood pointed toward a novel conception of social helping that aimed at preventing need by helping the needy acquire the skills they were lacking in the areas of home economics, parenting, and hygiene. This was very different from the aims of traditional poor relief and charity, and this new pedagogical approach to social helping played an important role in legitimating both the broader public aspirations of the women's movement in the social sector and the new preventive social welfare.

By the 1890s the spirit of charity organization was in the air. Attacks on the dilettantism of ladies bountiful were becoming more frequent, and there was a growing sense that the social problem was too earnest a matter to be left to the fashions of high society. The Girls' and Women's Group for Social Assistance, which was founded in 1893 by Minna Cauer and Jeanette Schwerin, represented an attempt to modernize women's philanthropy so as to bring the theoretical foundations of such work into accord with the gravity and nature of the social problem. The founding of the group represents the origin of social work training in Germany.[25]

In their original call for members, the founders of the group explained that girls and women of the leisured classes were deeply implicated in the class hatreds of the time by their ignorance of the misery of the laboring masses, their lack of interest in the fortunes of this class, and the absence of any personal intercourse that might acquaint them with their needs and make them more sensitive to their plight. The mission of the group was to undertake a gigantic labor of social reconciliation for which its members had first to be educated.[26]

---

[23] Schröder, *Arbeiten für eine bessere Welt*, 40ff., 109ff.
[24] Simmel, *Erziehung zum Weibe*, 142ff., makes explicit this connection between the pedagogical expression of spiritualized femininity, bourgeois paternalism, and working-class domesticity in relation to the Fröbel-Pestalozzi-Haus and the Berlin Verein Frauenwohl. There are also important connections – in the persons of Progressive Reichstag deputy Karl Schrader, his wife Henriette Schrader-Breymann (who was one of the founders of the Fröbel-Pestalozzi-Haus), Minna Cauer (below), Lange, and Gertrude Bäumer (below) – between these new forms of preventive, pedagogical social work and the broader Progressive rethinking of the political rationality of public assistance that will be a key theme in the following chapters.
[25] On the group, see Schröder, *Arbeiten für eine bessere Welt*, 82ff.; Anja Schüler, *Frauenbewegung und soziale Reform. Jane Addams und Alice Salomon in transatlantischen Dialog, 1889–1933* (Steiner, 2004), 190ff.; Alice Salomon, *Zwanzig Jahre soziale Hilfsarbeit* (Karlsruhe, 1913); and *Mädchen- und Frauengruppen für soziale Hilfsarbeit. Denkschrift anläßlich des 10jährigen Bestehens, 1893–1903* (Berlin, 1903).
[26] Alice Salomon, "Die Frau in der sozialen Hilfsthätigkeit," in Helene Lange and Gertrud Bäumer, eds., *Handbuch der Frauenbewegung* (Berlin, 1901), II:1–122, reference 37. One could also read the enthusiasm of these young for social work as an attempt to sublimate romantic disappointment.

The founders of the group felt compelled to dispel in advance any suggestions that the group might be a vehicle for women's emancipation by portraying their work as the fulfillment of a duty to the community.[27] This was, of course, more than a bit disingenuous because the activity of the group was very much inspired by the bourgeois women's movement. What this disclaimer meant was that the group would not promote the emancipation of women in order to make them more like men. What it left unsaid, but clearly implied, was that the group would serve as a means of spiritualizing the natural sexual characteristics of its members and thus legitimating a greater public role for them.[28] After Schwerin's early death in 1899, the leadership of the group, and eventually Schwerin's leadership position in the BDF, passed to Alice Salomon, who was to be the dominant figure in the new profession until she was driven from Germany by the Nazis.[29]

The social education offered by the Berlin group, which had consisted of a loose series of lectures and supervised voluntary work in the various associations and institutions of the city, was made more systematic in 1899 with the establishment of a full-year course directed by Emil Münsterberg, a prominent social reformer and the director of the Berlin poor relief administration. In 1906/7 this course was expanded to two years, and this course of study provided the foundation for the "social women's school" (*soziale Frauenschule*) that was established in 1908 under Salomon's leadership.[30] The creation of this course and then the founding of the school need to be seen as part of a broader movement to find a way of providing more formal and systematic training for women involved in voluntary social work, though it also represented a response to both the growing demand by associations and local government for trained workers, especially in the fields of hygiene and child welfare, and the 1908 reform of girls' schooling. The League of German Evangelical Women had already established a Christian-Social Women's Seminar in 1905, and other schools were founded in the following years.[31] By the outbreak of World War I, there were nine social work schools across the country, and by 1919 the number had risen to twenty-six. The schools were sponsored not only by the bourgeois women's movement, but also in roughly equal measures by groups

---

[27] Reprinted in Salomon, *Zwanzig Jahre soziale Hilfsarbeit*, 8–9.

[28] This was made explicit in Salomon, *Zwanzig Jahre soziale Hilfsarbeit*, 99–101. The withdrawal of Cauer, who belonged to the radical wing of the women's movement, from the group should be seen as evidence of the group's commitment to the principle of sexual difference and the politics that flowed from it.

[29] Salomon's voluminous occasional pieces have been reprinted in Alice Salomon, *Frauenbewegung und soziale Verantwortung. Ausgewählte Schriften*, 3 vols., edited by Adriane Feustel (Luchterhand, 1997–2004), and her autobiography has recently appeared in English: *Character Is Destiny. The Autobiography of Alice Salomon*, edited by Andrew Lees (University of Michigan Press, 2004).

[30] A number of associations modeled on the Berlin Group were formed in other cities, and in 1912 they joined together to form their own organization. Schüler, *Frauenbewegung und soziale Reform*, describes this as a virtual youth movement within the broader women's movement.

[31] On the Christian-Social Women's Seminar, see Reagin, *A German Women's Movement*, 112ff.

associated with the two Christian confessions and by the cities themselves.[32] The war, as we shall see, dramatically expanded the scope of public social services and accelerated the integration of women into the municipal social bureaucracy, so that by the end of the war one can speak at least notionally of the professionalization of social work (leaving aside here the question of whether it is possible for social helping to evolve into a full-fledged profession, whatever that might mean).

The social women's schools crystallized many of the discrete impulses that flowed from the spiritualization of motherhood, and they became a center for the practical activities of the women's movement. But these schools were, as their representatives like to put it, schools of a "particular kind." They were schools not for the communication of knowledge as an end in itself, but rather schools for the formation of female character. This is not to say that theoretical knowledge of the social sciences was unimportant to the social women's schools.[33] But theoretical knowledge was valued and incorporated only to the extent that it fostered a greater sense of social obligation. This approach was reflected in the eclecticism of a curriculum that was designed to give students the knowledge they needed to serve immediate practical ends, rather than to explore these disciplines in depth for their own sake. This is why Salomon later argued that social work training should not be integrated into the university.[34]

The molding of female character and the spiritualization of female sexual characteristics in order to stimulate an immediate concern for needy persons outside the limited sphere of the private house was, however, a peculiarly daunting task in view of the protected life led by these leisured girls of the propertied classes. But the problem was less one of convincing prospective students, and the broader public, of the natural affinity between mothering and social work than one of giving the latter a viable ethical foundation. Much of the writing about the profession in its early years consisted of attempts to articulate a new "social" worldview that would motivate women for social helping while explaining how such engagement would remedy all the ills of the modern world. For example, Salomon began the address that she delivered to celebrate the opening of her school by proclaiming that the woman who had found her life's work was blessed, but she warned that work was valuable only as a calling in which one could invest one's entire personality.[35] The

---

[32] Alice Salomon, *Die Ausbildung zum sozialen Beruf* (Berlin, 1927), 8–9. A list of the existing social work schools, the year they were established, and the groups that sponsored them can be found on 57–60 of this work.

[33] Salomon, *Zur Eröffnung der sozialen Frauenschule. Ansprache gehalten bei der Eröffnungsfeier im Pestalozzi-Fröblhaus am 15. Oktober 1908* (Berlin, 1908), 3 (reprinted in Salomon, *Frauenemanzipation und soziale Verantwortung*, I:480–5) and Salomon, *Soziale Frauenbildung und soziale Berufsarbeit* (Berlin, 1917), 9. Selections from the first edition of this book, which appeared in 1908, are reprinted in Salomon, *Ausgewählte Schriften*, I:373–92.

[34] Salomon, *Soziale Frauenbildung und soziale Berufsarbeit*, 60–1.

[35] Salomon, *Zur Eröffnung der sozialen Frauenschule*, 2.

only way to keep this search for self-realization from degenerating into an avenue for subjective self-gratification, Salomon argued, was to view it as an obligation undertaken in the name of some higher ideal, and the writings of the founding generation of social workers are littered with references to love, duty, service, and selflessness. It was, as Gertrude Bäumer wrote, a sense of service, responsibility, and awe before some higher value that transformed instinctual female emotional warmth and empathy into a more spiritualized social consciousness.[36] While the confessional organizations had no trouble in arguing that these ideals could only be justified in terms of the subordination of the individual to a personal God, the transcendent ideal that Salomon and the other leading figures of the bourgeois women's movement ultimately held up as an alternative foundation for women's social work was a synthesis of a quasi-secularized, liberal Protestant ethic of brotherly love and the model of sexual complementarity that we have studied in the preceding pages.[37]

Salomon regarded social work – as the practical embodiment of this ideal of solidarity – as a means of expiating class guilt and promoting class reconciliation. Since, she argued, the ills of the modern world and the antagonisms to which they gave rise were due largely to the one-sided influence of masculine culture, the solution to the social problem was to be found not in socialism, but rather in the compensating influence of female culture. As Salomon explained in 1908, the propertied classes owed the laboring classes something more than an all-too-meager wage. Since it was the manual labor of these persons that gave the propertied the opportunity to engage in intellectual labor and higher cultural pursuits, the propertied owed to the laboring classes a debt that could only be repaid by ensuring that they benefited from those cultural achievements that had been made possible by their labor.[38] It was this dynamic of social solidarity that underlay the new understanding of social work as a pedagogical undertaking designed to elevate the culture of the laboring classes.[39] This experience of solidarity found its highest expression in an act of self-abnegation, sacrifice, and "unselfing" (*Entselbstung*): "One must be able to lose oneself in order to win others." This was the only way to touch the soul of the needy and dispel all suspicion that the help and advice offered by the social worker was intended to serve any ulterior end. It was also the only way to expiate class guilt.[40]

---

[36] Bäumer, "Die Ziele der sozialen Frauenschule und des sozial-pädagogischen Instituts in Hamburg," *Die Frau* 24:6 (March 1917), 338–48.

[37] According to Salomon, *Soziale Frauenbildung und soziale Berufsarbeit*, 3, this social disposition could be cultivated on either a religious (i.e., positive or confessional), a social-ethical, or a civic-political (*staatsbürgerlich*) basis. This second domain drew on both the Christian, but nonconfessional ethic of brotherly love, and secularized versions of this ethic such as that practiced by the Society for Ethical Culture, whose members were closely involved in the development of professional social work in Germany. Salomon herself was a nonpracticing Jew who converted to Christianity in 1914.

[38] Salomon, *Soziale Frauenbildung*, 10.

[39] Salomon, *Soziale Frauenbildung und soziale Berufsarbeit*, 34.

[40] Salomon, *Soziale Frauenbildung und soziale Berufsarbeit*, 85; *Zwanzig Jahre soziale Hilfsarbeit*, 63, and "Über die inneren Voraussetzungen der Wohlfahrtspflege," in *Vom Wesen der*

But this vision of solidarity was constructed in gendered terms that made women the privileged agents of social redemption. Salomon argued that the bitterness toward the propertied classes that drove so many people into the arms of Social Democracy and its program of class struggle was caused by the organization of society in accordance with essentially masculine principles: instrumental reason, unbridled acquisitiveness and competitiveness, and the division of labor, all of which were leading to the atomization of society. She also feared that the triumph of the industrial order and the material benefits that it had brought were making it easy for those who benefited from this process to forget that all the individual members of the community were bound together in an indissoluble whole and that anything that harmed one individual also affected the whole community.[41]

But if alienation were caused by this one-sided development of masculine culture, then society could only be made whole again by recapitulating at the social and institutional level the union of masculine and feminine sexual characteristics that was achieved at the immediate, personal level in marriage. Or, in Salomon's own words,

in an age of brilliant economic development and technical achievements, in which all of one's thought and efforts are focused on the product, on performance, on the domination of nature, the task of women is to counteract the dissipation and destruction of human life, to give new value in social life to the personal and the individual, which are schematized and extinguished by economic forces. For it is the essential peculiarity of women to attach great value to human life.[42]

This proposal made sense in terms of the historical self-understanding of the bourgeois women's movement and its belief that distress was primarily caused by the disruption of family life and the inability of the poor to participate in the benefits of modern culture. However, it is much less clear that this idea had much purchase among the socialist working classes themselves, who attributed alienation under capitalism to very different factors.

In an essay published shortly after the 1918 revolution, Salomon tried to define the position of social work in the postrevolutionary world.[43] She chided the socialists for believing that need was rooted only in economic forces and for thinking that personal helping had been rendered superfluous by the revolution. Nevertheless, Salomon argued that socialism and social work shared certain common principles, and on this basis she tried to rally to the profession and the republic those middle-class circles who had been the backbone of poor relief and voluntarism before the revolution, but who had been disaffected by it. What was common to both the social worker and the revolutionary, she

---

Wohlfahrtspflege. Festgabe für Albert Levy zum 25 jährigen Bestehen der Zentrale für private Fürsorge (Berlin, 1918), 11–14.
[41] Salomon, *Soziale Frauenbildung*, 5.
[42] Salomon, *Soziale Frauenbildung und soziale Berufsarbeit*, 11. Salomon repeated this passage almost verbatim ten years later in *Die Ausbildung zum sozialen Beruf*, 2.
[43] Salomon, "Soziale Arbeit und Sozialismus," *Die Frau* 26:9 (June 1919), 263–70.

argued, was their "social worldview." It was impossible, she continued, for someone who believed in economic individualism, unlimited acquisitiveness, and the right of the strong to exploit the weak to be a social worker just as no thinking and feeling person could see the misery caused by poor housing, the joyless lives of proletarian children, the bleak and soulless existence of workers, and the deadening burdens of proletarian women without longing for a new social order: "One can not experience all of that without becoming conscious of the social debt that must be paid off. In this social worldview, social workers are united among themselves and united with Social Democracy." Social workers could, she argued, make their peace with the revolution to the extent that it bent property relations in order to bring about a more just world, and the task was to overcome the idea of class struggle on the basis of the principle of human solidarity.

This was an ambitious ideal, and it is safe to say that it was not realized during the Weimar years, though it did continue to inspire the efforts of the bourgeois women's movement. But while the articulation of a rationale for an expanded public role for women was one thing, the actual institutionalization of female culture in the social sector was something else. This process was slow and uneven, and the ultimate breakthrough during the war years brought with it a number of problems that altered in important ways the original vision of professional social work as a female calling for women of the leisured classes.

The success of these women was determined not only – and not primarily – by the logic of their cultural project, but by the political-institutional framework within which they had to operate. Here, the key variable in determining the scope and nature of women's influence on the formation of the welfare state was not so much state "strength" (as measured by the existence of a centralized state and a bureaucratic apparatus capable of intervening in society) as the ability to influence those programs in which the specific kind of activity advocated by and for women – personal help directed toward the preservation of the family and the mobilization of its resources – was valued particularly highly. As Jane Lewis has argued for Britain, "not only were the voluntary sector and local government considered appropriate places for women to work, but contemporary social thought highlighted the importance of particular kind of work – personal social work – that women did at the local level. As the balance of the mixed economy shifted in favour of a centralized welfare state and the philosophy of welfare changed, so women's influence decreased. There is little evidence that women were able to cross the crucial boundary that lay not between the voluntary and the statutory sectors, but between local provision, both voluntary and statutory, and welfare provided by central government," which was primarily the site of rights-based programs designed to insure against those causes of poverty that could not be attributed to personal factors.[44] And,

---

[44] Lewis, "Gender, the Family and Women's Agency in the Building of 'Welfare States': the British Case," *SH* 19:1 (January 1994), 37–55, citation 40. The argument relating women's influence to state strength was stated most famously in Seth Koven and Sonya Michel, "Womanly Duties:

if we follow Marcus Gräser, women's influence was further limited in Germany by the fact that visiting, which was the primary avenue of women's influence in both Britain and the United States, had, at least in part, been preemptively captured as a masculine domain by both the Elberfeld system of official visiting by male guardians and the existence of vibrant local poor relief authorities staffed by men whose judicial training remained the primary qualification for managerial positions in this branch of municipal administration.[45] Together, these two arguments – the one relating women's influence to the diminishing importance ascribed to visiting in solving a social problem that was coming to be understood in different ways, the other explaining the particularly German limitations on both the social space open to women's activism and the degree to which such activity as was permitted could be professionalized – provide a compelling account of the obstacles to the institutionalization of women's social work.

It needs to be noted that the very idea of professionalizing an act so ostensibly intimate, individual, and personal as "helping" was intrinsically problematic and, in many ways, self-contradictory. Social workers had to find a way to bridge the gap between their role in resolving the great issues of the day and a daily routine whose individual tasks bore little obvious relation to the significance – both personal and social – that they attributed to their work. Professionalization also meant, as we shall see, a greater emphasis on paid work, and these women found themselves forced to decide whether they could reconcile helping with salaried work, what value they should place on their work, and what steps they should take to ensure that their wages, working conditions, and responsibilities corresponded to the value which they placed on their vocation. The integration of women social workers into larger organizations – local voluntary associations, nationwide *Verbände*, and municipal poor relief – suspended them between their allegiance to these organizations, their role as advocates for the needs of their clients, and their own personal beliefs and values. This problem was magnified by the cultural distance often separating the poor from those who sought to help them, and this points perhaps the thorniest problem faced by these women: resolving the apparent contradiction between helping and social discipline and finding ways to assist persons whom they regarded as needy, but who did not want their "help," or at least did not want it on the terms that it was offered. All these problems reflected in one way or another a slippage between the environment within which these women had to work and the exaggerated expectations held by the founders of

---

Maternalist Politics and the Origins of Welfare States in France, Germany, Great Britain, and the United States, 1880–1920," *AHR* 95:4 (October 1990), 1076–1108. Peter Baldwin has systematically deconstructed the traditional notion of state strength in "Beyond Weak and Strong: Rethinking the State in Comparative Policy History," *Journal of Policy History* 17:1 (2005), 12–33.

[45] Marcus Gräser, *Wohlfahrtsgesellschaft und Wohlfahrtsstaat. Bürgerliche Sozialreform und welfare state building in den USA und in Deutschland 1880–1940* (Vandenhoeck & Ruprecht, 2008), chapters II:1–3.

the profession. However, unable to recognize these contradictions, the theorists of the new profession tended to oscillate between projecting the problems they encountered back into the psyche of the social worker as motivational deficits and blaming them on an ungrateful, covetous clientele. These problems were only beginning to become visible at the end of World War I, and they were to get much worse during the Weimar years.[46]

The spiritualization of femininity could be real to the women's movement only if it led to the transformation of social life along the lines envisioned by Lange, and the efforts of the women's movement to expand the educational and employment opportunities open to them, their maternalist advocacy of suffrage rights, and their efforts to secure a foothold in municipal poor relief must be seen as three sides of the same coin. All these initiatives depended on the claim that women were peculiarly well suited for certain types of public social activity and that the failure to systematically cultivate these innate capacities and permit their full practical application was somehow depriving the nation of the vital contributions to be made by these women.

As early as 1868/70, the leaders of the ADF had begun to demand that women be permitted to hold those honorary municipal offices – including service as a poor guardian – that were appropriate to their sex, and one of the earliest examples of the integration of women into public poor relief was in the city of Kassel.[47] But the issue of women's service as poor guardians did not move to the front burner until the 1890s, and it was one of the topics on the agenda of the 1896 conference of the German Association for Poor Relief and Charity. Although most of the speakers at that conference favored women's participation in one form or another, they qualified this support in a variety of ways that reveal a deep-seated unease about the implications of allowing women to take this step into public life. There were two important arguments that were advanced in favor of expanded participation for women: (1) most need was related in one way or another to a disorganized domestic life (or at least regarded as such) and thus represented more a problem of domestic culture and home economics than one of work and income, and (2) most relief recipients were women and children. In both instances, it was believed that women's influence would be more appropriate and more beneficial. On the other hand, men feared that women guardians would be too softhearted in assessing applications for assistance, and they worried that the presence of women would disrupt the smooth functioning of their regular meetings. Not only would men not be able to smoke or drink in front of members of the opposite sex. Considerations of propriety would prevent them from discussing cases of vice and immorality in the presence of women, much less assigning

---

[46] On the contradictions of professionalization, see Richard Münchmeier, *Zugänge zur Geschichte der Sozialarbeit* (Juventa, 1981), Chapter 6, and Young-sun Hong, *Welfare, Modernity and the Weimar State, 1919–1933* (Princeton University Press, 1998), Chapter 5.

[47] Schröder, *Arbeiten für eine bessere Welt*, 115ff.

such cases to women guardians, and their reservations about giving women responsibility for all of the applications from a given geographical area were reinforced by the belief that a man's firm hand was necessary in dealing with rough men and rebellious boys. Lastly, they pointed out that there simply were not enough women who had the interest and training needed to serve as poor guardians. The leaders of the social work movement were especially indignant at this last suggestion, and they pointedly asked why the special training that was being demanded of women was not also required of men?[48]

Despite these reservations, in 1896 the German Association for Poor Relief and Charity came out in favor of the integration of women into municipal relief with the same rights as men, and in 1901 the Prussian Conference of Cities also endorsed the idea. However, the actual advancement of women into these communal offices was very much determined by local circumstances, and at the turn of the century there were a number of high-profile cases of male resistance to the idea of female guardians. In 1896, for example, the Berlin poor guardians threatened to resign collectively if women were forced on them, and in 1902, when city officials in Leipzig surveyed the city's guardians in response to a petition from the local women's association, the city's district relief commissions spoke out nearly unanimously against the idea. In most cities new guardians were co-opted by current office holders, and city officials could not force their preferences on guardians without running the risk of alienating the men on whose cooperation the smooth functioning of the city's relief system depended. However, in other cities, such as Frankfurt and Strassburg, the integration of women took place much more smoothly. By and large the integration of women guardians progressed slowly through World War I, as can be seen in Table 3. With the few notable exceptions that are included in this table, women made up fewer than 5% of poor guardians in virtually every city even as late as 1916 – and the table also gives an idea of the sheer number of bodies that it took to make a voluntary system work in the nation's largest cities.

The years between 1905 and 1914 were the take-off period for preventive social hygiene programs. Although traditionally minded guardians may have been able to limit the role of women within the poor relief administration, they had no such influence over voluntary programs that in the following years gradually displaced poor relief as the primary form of social assistance. Moreover, these new programs also opened up some of the first opportunities for full-time paid work for trained women social workers, and many of these first salaried social workers were charged with supervising the care of foster

---

[48] Rudolf Osius and Paul Chuchul, *Die Heranziehung der Frauen zur öffentlichen Armenpflege*, SDV, 25 (1896); *Stenographischer Bericht über die Verhandlungen*, SDV, 28 (1896); Münsterberg, *Weibliche Hülfskräfte in der Wohlfahrtspflege* (=*Schriften der Centralstelle für Arbeiterwohlfahrts-Einrichtungen*, 10, 1896); and Salomon, *Soziale Frauenpflichten. Vorträge gehalten in deutschen Frauenvereinen* (Berlin, 1902), 44ff. The most useful contemporary account is Hildegard Radomski, *Die Frau in der öffentlichen Armenfürsorge* (Berlin, 1916), and Schröder, *Arbeiten für eine bessere Welt*, 136ff., treats these struggles in detail.

TABLE 3. Women's Participation in Municipal Poor Relief, 1907–16

	1907		1909		1911		1913		1914		1915		1916	
	Total	Women	Total	Women	Total	Women	Total	Women	Total	Women	Total	Women	Total	Women
Berlin	4,984	28	5,498	129	5,530	157	5,530	157	5,707	141	5,857	157	6,028	159
Breslau	1,928	63	1,896	65	2,007	74	1,961	81	1,943	79	1,961	81	1,961	81
Elberfeld	420	7	611	7	611	7	560	8	560	8	628	17	628	17
Frankfurt	865	85	1,005	100	997	92	1,090	120	1,100	132	1,151	146	1,159	142
Hamburg	1,540	13	1,702	12	1,695	12	1,588	8	1,588	8	1,893	20	1,893	20
Leipzig	1,106	–	1,134	11	1,253	30	1,280	30	1,326	30	1,508	39	1,628	43
Munich	–	–	–	–	–	–	381	87	381	87	498	130	498	130
Strassburg	820	340	807	335	859	387	859	387	859	387	461	254	461	254

Source: Excerpted from Hildegard Radomski, Die Frau in der öffentlichen Armenfürsorge (Berlin, 1916), 42–44.

and illegitimate children, while others were employed in the tuberculosis and infant welfare centers that sprouted up during these years.[49]

The scale and scope of women's social work, both paid and voluntary, was altered fundamentally after 1914, and by 1917 or so all of the long-standing prewar casuistics about the appropriateness of such work were quickly coming to seem like quaint relics from the past. However, this unexpected opportunity proved, in certain respects, to be the undoing of the original vision of the profession. Wartime welfare programs and the deprivations and hardships of the war years forced women social workers to play by bureaucratic rules that were at best indifferent to the ideals of feminine culture and at worst hostile to them. Moreover, the early leaders of the profession feared that the quantum expansion in the scope of need during the war, the opening of more social women's schools, and the entry of so many untrained women into the field was depressing the status of the profession and the remuneration of trained workers. This gave the existing schools a greater interest in regulating the new profession, and at the end of 1916 the existing schools reacted to these developments by banding together to form the Conference of Social Women's Schools, whose initial goal was to establish curricular and admissions standards in order to protect their own status and that of their graduates. But the Prussian government was also interested in regulating social work training, and officials there had a very different vision of the role of women social workers. The story of this conflict, and of the closely related issue of the movement of women into "responsible" positions within the social bureaucracy, is part of the broader story of the gendering of the nascent welfare state.[50]

The social women's schools wanted their graduates to have not only practical skills in home economics, health care, and child care, but also the broad social scientific knowledge required to diagnose the needs of their clients and

---

[49] Radomski, *Die Frau in der öffentlichen Armenfürsorge*, 72ff., charts the growing role of women in infant and tuberculosis welfare, as well as labor exchanges and social programs for drinkers. Steven King, "'We Might be Trusted': Female Poor Law Guardians and the Development of the New Poor Law: The Case of Bolton, England, 1880–1906," *IRSH* 49 (2004), 27–46, makes a similar argument for England. In 1910, the League of German Women's Associations founded the Zentralstelle für die Gemeindeämter der Frau to provide information on the employment of women in municipal social services and, within a few years, to agitate for the expansion of such work. Schröder, *Arbeiten für eine bessere Welt*, 285ff. Jenny Apolant's survey *Stellung und Mitarbeit der Frau in der Gemeinde* (Leipzig, 1910) was initially quite cautious about the prospects for women's employment, but this assessment of the job market had already changed substantially even before the war. On the growth of women's work, both voluntary and salaried, in communal positions, see Apolant, "Die Mitwirkung der Frau in der kommunalen Wohlfahrtspflege," *Die Frau* 23:6 (March 1916), 330–8.

[50] On the following, see Young-sun Hong, "Femininity as a Vocation: Gender and Class Conflict in the Professionalization of German Social Work," in Geoffrey Cocks and Konrad Jarausch, eds., *German Professions, 1800–1950* (Oxford University Press, 1990), 232–51. For an analysis of the factors influencing wages and employment conditions, see Hedwig Wachenheim, "Die Lage der Groß-Berliner Sozialbeamtinnen," *Die Frau* 26:3–4 (December 1918 and January 1919), 82–5, 116–20.

the knowledge of pedagogy and psychology that they would have to have in order to put their social diagnoses into action. In contrast, Prussian Interior Ministry officials were somewhat skeptical of the extensive, but eclectic, curricula that they found in the schools; they envisioned women social workers playing a more subordinate role as faithful assistants to their better-educated male superiors; and the licensing regulations that were issued in September 1918 clearly reflected the wishes of these officials.[51] They required students to have trained as both health care workers and kindergarten teachers before beginning their social work studies, while the actual course of study in the social women's schools was shortened from two years to one and a half; most of the subjects in which students would be examined dealt in one way or another with hygiene; and the center of gravity of the curriculum was to be shifted correspondingly, with instruction in the social sciences being eliminated. The members of the Conference were extremely dismayed with these regulations, and in this sense the revolution proved to be a stroke of luck for them as the revised regulations issued in 1920 reflected their desires much more closely. These new regulations retained the broader focus of the curriculum (including pedagogy, psychology, and popular education) and a two-year course of study, and they permitted the students to concentrate in one of three fields – social hygiene, youth welfare, and assistance in economic and occupational matters – with admission requirements being tailored to the area of concentration. These skirmishes over the extent to which women social workers were to be permitted to put their vision of spiritualized motherhood into practice continued through the 1920s.

While the social women's schools had formed the Conference to protect their professional interests from the influx of untrained women, individual social workers were faced with the challenge of securing the material foundations for the pursuit of their calling without at the same time denaturing the purity of their commitment to helping. From the very beginning, Salomon had argued that the distinguishing characteristics of professional social work were training and a personal commitment to the vocation, rather than the receipt of a salary. It was easy for a woman of independent means to assume such a position, but the influx of so many new women – not all of whom came from the leisured classes – into the profession and the inescapable fact that even many of the women who had engaged in voluntary social work before the war now had to help support themselves raised a whole set of issues relating to remuneration and unionization.

Salomon deployed a variety of arguments to defend the ramparts of voluntarism against the forces that were besieging it. But her most basic point was that the value of voluntarism lay in the very act of volunteering and making a sacrifice for the sake of someone else. Voluntarism was the royal – and the only – road to social reconciliation, and the labors undertaken by volunteers

---

[51] Salomon, *Die Ausbildung zum sozialen Beruf*, 26ff.

could never be completely supplanted by salaried workers, she argued, because paid voluntarism was an absurdity.[52] The question of voluntarism versus paid work was closely related to the issue of unionization. What if social workers were constrained to take aggressive measures to defend the interests of their occupation because wages and working conditions were not adequate to permit committed persons to pursue their social calling? In 1916, these questions led to the formation of two occupational interest groups: the German Association of Women Social Work Professionals (*Deutscher Verband der Sozialbeamtinnen*) and the Association of German Catholic Social Workers (*Verein der deutschen katholischen Sozialbeamtinnen*).[53] These organizations had to grapple with the question of whether an ethos of service and sacrifice could be reconciled with occupational self-help and unionization and the problem of whether an occupational association that eschewed class struggle could effectively represent the interests of its members. The latter war years were a transitional period in this respect, and these issues were broached, but by no means resolved, during the war.[54] But their mere existence does serve as a measure both of how far the women's movement had come since the founding of the empire and of the problems they faced in making the social work profession into a vehicle for women's emancipation and for reshaping a divided world in accordance with the principles of female culture.

The Caritas Association and the Reluctant Modernization of Catholic Charity

Turning to Catholic charities, one thing that they had in abundance was a long and complicated prehistory. Aside from the Reformation, perhaps most important caesura in this story was the secularization of ecclesiastical power during the Napoleonic era. Secularization deprived the church of many of its charitable functions and much of the property that had supported this activity and thus forced it back on its original pastoral function. However, Catholic charities thrived across the first two-thirds of the century in the social space open to them, giving rise to a dense thicket of charitable orders and lay associations, including the Sisters of Mercy, St. Vincent de Paul associations (and their female counterpart, the Elisabeth associations), nursing orders, Catholic women's associations, and a multitude of charitable associations and foundations devoted to meeting the material and spiritual needs of a wide variety of occupational groups.[55] But the one thing that united all these disparate

---

[52] Salomon, *Die Ausbildung zum sozialen Beruf*, 40ff.
[53] Hedwig Wachenheim, "Die Berufsorganisation der sozialen Hilfsarbeiterin," *BfSA* 8:4 (April 1, 1916), 21–2, was the first public call for the creation of such an organization.
[54] The unresolved tensions of this transitional moment are reflected clearly in Gertrud Israel, "Die Sozialbeamtin als Glied der Volksgemeinschaft," *Die Frau* 25:3 (December 1917), 83–8. On these issues in the 1920s, see Hong, *Welfare, Modernity and the Weimar State*, 145ff.
[55] The history of Catholic charity in the nineteenth century can be approached through Erwin Gatz, *Kirche und Krankenpflege im 19. Jahrhundert. Katholische Bewegung und karitativer*

undertakings was their traditionalism and their faith in the power of personal charity to solve the social question.[56] The model of Catholic charity organization that emerged at the turn of the twentieth century represented a break with, though not a rejection of, the work of these earlier groups, and its history can only be understood in relation to both the modernization of Catholic social thought during the empire and the need to respond to the challenges posed by the expansion of both public poor relief and the number of other voluntary organizations active in the social sector.[57]

In the 1860s and 1870s, Catholic social thought first began to move away from its integralist opposition to the modern world. These developments paralleled the political strategy of Center Party, which, in the aftermath of the *Kulturkampf*, recognized that it would have to come to terms with the Protestant state and the capitalist world. The two key figures in this reorientation of Catholic social thought were Mainz archbishop Wilhelm Emmanuel Ketteler and Franz Hitze.[58] But while Ketteler invoked Thomist natural law to criticize the concept of bourgeois property and limit the scope of state activity, in the 1880s and early 1890s Freiherr Georg von Hertling turned to the Catholic natural law tradition to find a justification for those state social policy measures that he felt were necessary to preserve the natural rights of individuals and families in modern society.[59] Hertling, who became the Center Party spokesman on social policy after his election to the Reichstag in 1876, defended private property, which he saw as the foundation for all other rights. But he also argued

---

Aufbruch in den preussischen Provinzen Rheinland und Westfalen (Schöningh, 1971); Gatz, *Geschichte des kirchlichen Lebens in den deutschsprachigen Ländern seit dem Ende des 18. Jahrhunderts*, Bd.5: *Caritas und soziale Dienste* (Herder, 1997); Manfred Eder, "Helfen macht nicht ärmer". *Von der kirchlichen Armenfürsorge zur modernen Caritas in Bayern* (Altötting, 1997); and Catherine Mauerer, *Le modèle allemande de la charité. La Caritas de Guillaume II à Hitler* (Strasbourg, 1999).

[56] Gatz, *Kirche und Krankenpflege*, 3.
[57] On the history of Catholic social thought during the empire, see Franz Josef Stegmann, "Geschichte der sozialen Ideen im deutschen Katholizismus," in Helga Grebing, ed., *Deutsches Handbuch der Politik*, Bd. 5: *Geschichte der sozialen Ideen in Deutschland* (Isar Verlag, 1969), 325–482, and Clemens Bauer, "Wandlungen der sozialpolitischen Ideenwelt im deutschen Katholizismus des 19. Jahrhunderts," in Görres-Gesellschaft, ed., *Die soziale Frage und der Katholizismus. Festschrift zum 40jährigen Jubiläum der Enzyklika 'Rerum Novarum'* (Schöningh, 1931), 11–46.
[58] Ketteler, "The Labor Problem and Christianity" (1864) and "The Labor Movement and Its Goals in Terms of Religion and Morality" (1869) in *The Social Teachings of Wilhelm Emmanuel von Ketteler, Bishop of Mainz (1811–1877)*, edited by Rupert J. Ederer (University Press of America, 1981), and Hitze, *Kapital und Arbeit und die Reorganisation der Gesellschaft* (Paderborn, 1880).
[59] Hertling, "Einige Bemerkungen zu Franz Hitzes Kapital und Arbeit," in *Aufsätze und Reden sozialpolitischen Inhalts* (Freiburg, 1884), 27–74, especially 38–9. Wilfried Loth argues that Hitze, Hertling, and August Pieper played a key role in the "breakthrough to modernity" in the domain of Catholic social thought. Loth, "Die deutschen Sozialkatholiken in der Krise des Fin de Siècle," in Wilfried Loth and Jochen-Christoph Kaiser, eds., *Soziale Reform in Kaiserreich. Protestantismus, Katholizismus und Sozialpolitik* (Kohlhammer, 1997), 128–41.

in favor of social insurance and a minimum wage because he believed that workers enjoyed an equally fundamental right to the protection of their life, person, and health from the risks of industrial production. The family occupied a central position in Hertling's work. He argued that the state had a duty to protect the natural rights of the family, and he coupled his critique of child labor with a call for the breadwinner wage and the return of married women to the home.[60] In 1880 Hitze and the Rhenish textile manufacturer Franz Brandts founded Workers' Welfare (*Arbeiterwohl*, not to be confused with the postwar Social Democratic *Arbeiterwohlfahrt*) to encourage factory owners to establish social programs for their own workers and agitate on behalf of Catholic workers' associations, which they hoped would help deproletarianize the working classes by creating a sense of corporate identity. These efforts to bring Catholic social thought into line with the realities of industrial society were echoed in the 1891 encyclical "On the Condition of Labor" (*Rerum novarum*), which charted a path of moderate state industrial legislation and sanctioned such innovations as workers associations.[61]

The articulation of this new Catholic social doctrine depended on rethinking the idea that charity alone could solve the social problems of the industrial era.[62] However, if charity alone could not solve these problems, then what was its role, and in what ways would it, too, have to change in order to meet these challenges? In an 1890 memorandum to the archbishop of Cologne, Max Brandts, who was responsible for rural poor relief and correctional education for the Rhineland, argued that the influence of the Catholic church was being endangered by the steady expansion of municipal poor relief and by the fact that many of the new areas of social engagement were dominated by either Protestant or humanitarian associations. The Catholic community had to form a united front, he argued, to combat the worrisome tendency to separate charity "from its natural and fruitful foundation in religiosity." While Protestant associations and municipal government had taken the initiative in many of these areas, Brandts pointed out that Catholics had no comparable organizations and, worse, that they had no central organization to lead the way.[63] In this memorandum, Brandts remarked that contemporary political, economic, and social life reflected a pronounced tendency toward "organization," that is, the formation of centralized umbrella organizations (*Verbände*) to coordinate the work of groups that had up until then operated independently of one another. What he envisioned was a centralized coordinating body that would help instill a sense of common purpose among the many local Catholic charities

---

[60] Hertling, *Naturrecht und Sozialpolitik* (Köln, 1893), 26–7 and 42ff.
[61] "The Condition of Labor," *Five Great Encyclicals* (Paulist Press, 1939), 1–30.
[62] Erwin Iserloh, *Die soziale Aktivität der Katholiken im Übergang von caritativer Fürsorge zu Sozialreform und Sozialpolitik, dargestellt an den Schriften Wilhelm Emmanuel v. Kettelers* (Akademie der Wissenschaften und der Literatur, Mainz. Abhandlungen der geistes- und sozialwissenschaftlichen Klasse, 1975, Nr. 3).
[63] Brandts, *Denkschrift betr. die Stellung der katholischen Kirche zur sozialpolitischen Liebestätigkeit...*," copy in the library of the Deutscher Caritasverband, Freiburg.

and encourage the adoption of more modern forms of social work. Brandts's initiative ultimately led to the founding in 1897 of the Caritas Association for Catholic Germany.[64]

During the 1890s and early 1900s, the counterpart to this obsession with organization was a thirst for publicity. This meant, on the one hand, the exchange of ideas among Catholic charities. On the other hand, though, it also meant venturing beyond the comfortable confines of the Catholic milieu to demonstrate to the broader public the power of Catholic faith and the achievements of Catholic charity.[65] However, this required the development a systematic theory of Catholic charity, the modernization of Catholic social work in accordance with these ideas, and the creation of a centralized organization to ensure the most effective translation of these ideas into practice. In the words of one Catholic, it was necessary to modernize (*zeitgemäß umgestalten*) Catholic charity and, "in a certain sense and degree, become capitalist."[66] Many Catholics, especially the lower clergy, regarded this search for publicity as an unseemly display of egoism, and this dissonance between old and new charitable sensibilities proved to be a serious obstacle to the growth of the organization. However, the founders of the Caritas Association argued that a higher public profile would redound to the honor of the church, and they expected that a greater degree of publicity and centralization would put Catholic charities in a better position to represent their collective interests.[67] Despite their initial hostility, most Catholic charities gradually came to terms with statutory poor relief, an accommodation that was facilitated by the identification of the Elberfeld system with the system of friendly visiting long practiced by the Vincent associations.

For this new generation of Catholic reformers, charity and social policy stood in a complementary relationship. As Lorenz Werthmann, the first president of the Caritas Association, told the 1899 Conference of German Catholics, "caritas is the steam in the social machine.... It is the soothing oil that can smooth the towering waves of social discontent. Laws can sate the hunger of a worker, but can not reconcile his heart with his existence. There is the great mission of caritas: to be the agent of social reconciliation."[68] Or, as another

---

[64] Mauerer, *Le modèle allemande*, 35ff., 57ff., and Eder, "Helfen macht nicht ärmer", 309ff. The official publication of the association was *Caritas*, and many important early articles that appeared in the journal are reprinted, along with other relevant documents, in Deutscher Caritasverband, ed., *Denkschriften und Standpunkte der Caritas in Deutschland*, Bd. I: *Die Zeit von 1897 bis 1949* (Lambertus, 1997).

[65] *Caritas* (Programm-Nummer, October 1895), iv.

[66] Franz Schaub, *Die katholische Caritas und ihre Gegner* (Volksvereins-Verlag, 1909), 10.

[67] Lorenz Werthmann, "Die Ziele des Charitasverbandes," *Caritas* 3:11–12 (1898), 237–40, 261–5, citation 264, and Schaub, *Die katholische Caritas*, 11.

[68] Werthmann, "Die soziale Bedeutung der Charitas und die Ziele des Charitasverbandes," *Caritas* 4 (1899), 210–17, citation 211; see also Schaub, *Die katholische Caritas*, 34–5. Mauerer, *Le modèle allemande*, highlights the process through which the architects of modern Catholic social policy became aware of the distinction between social policy and charity and the respective roles they attributed to each.

ecclesiastical dignitary explained, charity must prepare the way for justice by making those hearts that have been hardened by egoism, hatred, and alienation from God receptive to healthy social reforms while making natural differences in wealth and status more bearable.[69]

Although the Caritas Association was a lay organization (though one with many clerical members), it had a decidedly less problematic relationship with the institutional church than did the Inner Mission.[70] In 1906, the Caritas Association sponsored its first social work training courses, and at the same time it established standing committees to discuss the specific problems of the different fields of social work (such as infant welfare and care for the handicapped) so as to be able to present a clear Catholic position on these issues.[71] However, although the Caritas Association hoped to establish bureaus in all major cities, by 1903 bureaus had only been established in five cities: Berlin, Essen, Frankfurt, Munich, and Strassburg.[72]

Like its Protestant counterpart, the Caritas Association saw its primary goal in the regeneration of the Christian family,[73] and the Catholics were determined to make sure that their vision of Christian family life prevailed. As Cyprian Fröhlich told the 1896 Conference of German Catholics, the family "is the battlefield on which all great questions – including the social question – will be decided. Therefore, if we restore Christian family life, the social question will be solved."[74] This is one reason why Catholic charities devoted such a large proportion of their energy to the creation of associations for female domestics and factory workers, the reclamation of prostitutes and "fallen" women and girls, and the protection of endangered, delinquent, and neglected children.[75]

---

[69] Hubert Theophil Simar, "Ein bischöfliches Wort über die christliche Caritas," *Caritas* 1:10 (1896), 205.

[70] See, for example, Bernhard Würmerling, "Oertliche Organisation der freiwilligen Armenpflege für sich und in ihrem Verhältnisse zur Zwangsarmenpflege," *Caritas* 2 (1897), 139–43, 155–8, 176–80, especially 158.

[71] Johannes Horion, "Abhaltung von Charitaskursen," *Caritas* 11 (1906), 47–51, and "Die Ausschüsse, die beratenden Versammlungen und die Beschlüsse des zehnten Charitastages," Ibid., 51–3.

[72] Würmerling, "Oertliche Organisation der freiwilligen Armenpflege," 180, Werthmann, "Der Caritasverband und die örtliche Organisation der katholischen Charitas," *Caritas* 6 (1901), 1–7, 25–9, 49–54, and Werthmann, "Das Wirken des Charitasverbandes im Jahre 1902/03," *Caritas* 8 (1903), 247–52.

[73] Werthmann, "Die soziale Bedeutung der Charitas," 212.

[74] Fröhlich, "Die socialen Aufgaben der christlichen Charitas," *Caritas* 1 (1896), 205–10, 229–31, citation 206, and Clara de Lamotte, "Vorsorge und Fürsorge für junge Arbeiterinnen," *Caritas* 7 (1902), 204–7.

[75] The leading Catholic organization in the field of *Mädchenschutz* was the Katholischer Fürsorgeverein für Mädchen, Frauen und Kinder (officially founded in 1900). See Agnes Neuhaus, "Die Aufgaben der Fürsorgevereine," *Caritas* 11 (1906), 129–40; Andreas Wollasch, *Der Katholische Fürsorgeverein für Mädchen, Frauen und Kinder (1899–1945). Ein Beitrag zur Geschichte der Jugend- und Gefährdetenfürsorge in Deutschland* (Lambertus, 1991); and Wilhelm Liese *Handbuch des Mädchenschutzes* (Freiburg, 1904). On the associations for servants and workers, see Alfred Kall, *Katholische Frauenbewegung in Deutschland* (Schöningh, 1983).

From its founding in 1897 until the eve of World War I, however, the Caritas Association enjoyed only mixed success. Brandts's program gave Catholic charities a coherent discourse with which to defend their traditional values. Yet the new central association received only a lukewarm reception from its intended audience. The local clergy who led many Catholic charities were suspicious of initiatives proposed by the social and ecclesiastical elites who led the Caritas Association, and from their provincial perspective the perceived benefits of organization were apparently not strong enough to offset the force of tradition.[76]

Social Democracy: The Demonization of the Capitalist System and Pragmatic Cooperation at the Local Level

It is much more difficult to write about the role of the organized working classes in the development of poor relief and welfare. Before the war, the socialist working classes were overwhelmingly the object of social assistance, not its subject, and poor relief figures only tangentially, if at all, in most histories of the working classes and working-class political organizations in imperial Germany. In the 1880s and 1890s, Social Democratic pronouncements on the topic tended to take the form of rhetorical grenades lobbed at a bourgeois institution that they detested and that they felt they had little chance of altering for the better. However, the evolution of Social Democratic views on poor relief and charity in the prewar years reflected both their growing involvement in municipal politics and the growing influence of reformist voices within the party.

The Marxist principles of the 1891 Erfurt Program taught German Social Democrats to see class poverty as the obverse of the colossal wealth accumulated by the capitalist class and to believe that the former could only be eliminated through the revolutionary overthrow of the latter. The Social Democrats insisted that poor relief and private charity were deeply implicated in the existing social order. Not only did they help sustain the industrial reserve army and enforce the exploitative discipline of the labor market. All forms of charity, both public and private, Social Democrats argued, simply mystified the prevailing unequal relations of property and power, whose true character was most clearly reflected in the workhouse. Although the overthrow of capitalism and the elimination of class poverty remained the ultimate goal, the Social Democrats insisted that, until the advent of a new social order, capitalist society had to guarantee the unpropertied either the right to work or a level of social assistance that would enable them to lead a dignified existence within that society.[77]

---

[76] Mauerer, *Le modèle allemande*, 58ff.
[77] These ideas were laid out by Karl Kautsky in *The Class Struggle* (Norton, 1971), his extended commentary on the Erfurt Program. See also Margarete Jacobsohn, *Die Arbeiter in der öffentlichen Armenpflege* (Leipzig, 1911), and Anneliese Monat, *Sozialdemokratie und Wohlfahrtspflege. Ein Beitrag zur Entstehungsgeschichte der Arbeiterwohlfahrt* (Stuttgart, 1961).

While poor relief and charity absolved society of the need to inquire into the causes of need by attributing it to personal factors, the Social Democrats regarded the poor primarily as victims of economic conditions. The Social Democrats traced all the practical problems that plagued the existing poor relief system back to the contradiction between the social causes of poverty and the invasive and humiliating efforts of poor guardians and charity workers to correct nonexistent character faults, and they harbored a special loathing for the confessional charities, whom they accused of unctuously instrumentalizing charity for religious and political ends. But the Social Democrats also labored to establish a distinction between the politically conscious, skilled laboring classes, whose resentment of the social degradation and political disabilities that accompanied the receipt of public assistance were a sign of their respectability and independence, and the residual "poor," who presumably did not share these values. In the words of one contemporary writer, "the higher that a worker has risen through skilled work and education, the more his disinclination has developed.... He thus summons up all of his powers of resistance to avoid applying for poor relief."[78]

The character of these debates began to change as the growth of Social Democracy opened the way to greater working-class participation in municipal government, and the development of Social Democratic municipal policies, and of socialist attitudes toward poor relief more specifically, tended to parallel the growth of reformism within the party. For example, the 1910 communal program of the Prussian Social Democrats insisted that the democratization of local government depended on the overthrow of class rule, but at the same time it praised at great length the Elberfeld system and its principle of individualization.[79] Between the turn of the century and 1914, Social Democratic municipal politicians began to call for the democratization of municipal poor relief, by which they meant the greater involvement of workers as poor guardians. Workers, they argued, would be better able to understand the culture and circumstances of the needy, and assistance received from them would be less degrading and more akin to mutual assistance than to charity.

Before 1914 workers never made up more than a small percentage the total number of poor guardians.[80] However, during the war the Social Democrats moved into all levels of government in unprecedented numbers; Social Democratic women began to buy into the notion of spiritual motherhood that had been propagated by the middle-class women's movement; and by the end of the

---

[78] Cited in Jacobsohn, *Die Arbeiter*, 1, and Eduard Bernstein, *Evolutionary Socialism* (Schocken, 1961), 169.

[79] *Das Kommunal-Programm der Sozialdemokratie Preußens*, edited by Paul Hirsch (Berlin, 1911), 3, 193–4. For the debate over the reformism of Social Democratic municipal policy, see Ursula Reuter, *Paul Singer (1844–1911). Eine politische Biographie* (Droste, 2004), 549ff., and Sweeney, "Reconsidering the Modernity Paradigm."

[80] One of the aims of Jacobsohn's book was to convince both the working classes and the middle classes of the benefits to be gained from such participation. See also Henriette Fürth, "Arbeiter und Arbeiterin in der Armenpflege," *Sozialistische Monatshefte* (1913), 618ff.

war moderate Social Democrats seem to have made their peace with municipal poor relief. The founding of the Social Democratic welfare organization Workers' Welfare (*Arbeiterwohlfahrt*) in 1919 to compete with the existing religious and humanitarian associations marked both the culmination of this ideological shift and a recognition of the political realities of the postrevolutionary republic.[81]

[81] Sachße, *Mütterlichkeit als Beruf*, 173–86. There was a world of difference in tone and content between the Erfurt Program and Lindemann, "Arbeit und Armenpflege," *Kommunale Praxis* 17:1–2 (1917), cols. 1–7, 17–23, which most relief officials could have subscribed to with few reservations.

7

The Social Perspective on Poverty and the Origins of Modern Social Welfare

The Social Perspective on Poverty and the Logic of Social Citizenship

The middle decades of the nineteenth century witnessed the creation of a system of poor relief and charity that was designed to consolidate the new bourgeois social order by molding the lower classes into those industrious, disciplined, and providential workers on whom this social formation was believed to depend. This assistantial regime was based on the combination of moral reform and the repressive promotion of self-reliance. However, beginning in the 1890s this regime was challenged by a new paradigm whose primary strategies were prevention and treatment, rather than deterrence. The basic form of social assistance provided under this new regime was known as "social relief" or "social welfare" (*soziale Fürsorge*), and both the political rationality that drove the development of these programs between 1900 and 1914 and the mechanisms of social intervention that they pioneered in order to achieve their preventive and therapeutic aims were soon to become defining features of the welfare state.

The history of the German welfare state in this period is an extraordinarily complex one that sprawls across the entire social landscape of imperial Germany, and it cannot easily be captured in a limited space. It developed at a number of different levels, each with its own logic and temporality, and it is important not to lose sight of the complexity, contradictoriness, and asynchronicity of the process even as we try to give the story a degree of conceptual and narrative unity. The Bismarckian social insurance programs have long been regarded as the *fons et origio* of the German welfare state, and this historiographical tradition, which has viewed social insurance as the creation of the strong central state and its officials, if not as the product of Bismarck's unique political genius, has consistently marginalized all forms of social assistance that cannot be neatly fitted into the narrative prehistory or subsequent development of these programs. This perspective is, at best, one sided. As we have seen in the preceding chapters, and as we will further see in the chapters to follow, many of those programs that are normally associated with central state initiative, such as health insurance, labor exchanges, and unemployment insurance, had deep roots in both the voluntary domain and local government initiative. This is even more true for the broad spectrum of preventive social welfare programs created from the turn of the century onward. Virtually all of the programs that later formed the core of the Weimar welfare system owed their origins to the voluntary initiative of individuals, philanthropic associations, and municipal government acting at the local level as they sought to find new ways of responding to a social problem that from the 1890s was coming to be understood in very different ways than had been the case in the heyday of the Elberfeld system. Any narrative that tends to reduce the welfare state to social insurance or to ascribe its growth primarily to the agency of the central state will produce a foreshortened, distorted account.

The central role of the local state was due in part to a federal political system, which gave the Reich only limited legislative competence in regulating many areas of social life; in part to the increasing density of urban life, the need to master the problems to which this gave rise, the growing professionalization of municipal administration after 1870, and the willingness of urban elites to take up these challenges in their capacity as both public officials and concerned citizens; and in part to the reluctance of the Reich to become directly involved in the provision of social assistance – at least until such a step became unavoidable during World War I. All of these factors made the imperial state into an enabling state of sorts, though this decision to leave the social field open to voluntary initiative was due as much to the principled belief in the superiority of voluntary social engagement as to the malign neglect of the social problem on the part of the Reich.[1]

Briefly stated, this and the following chapters will argue that modern forms of preventive social welfare developed out of the interplay between a social conception of poverty, which emphasized the structural and environmental determinants of need, rather than individual moral failings, and new notions of social citizenship, which provided the rationale for the development of preventive social welfare programs to combat this socially determined need. Although preventive social welfare was born out of the spirit of poor law reform, it followed a very different logic, and the history of social assistance in imperial Germany has to be understood as the history of the successive attempts to resolve the irresolvable conflict between the logic of deterrence and the logic of prevention. Preventive social welfare threatened to hollow out – and eventually overturn – nineteenth-century deterrent poor relief. However, neither the public nor the reform community was willing to simply jettison the poor

---

[1] Neil Gilbert, *Transformation of the Welfare* State (Oxford University Press, 2002), Chapter 2 – which should, however, be read against Peter Baldwin's reflections on the problems involved in conceptualizing the state in "Beyond Weak and Strong: Rethinking the State in Comparative Policy History," *Journal of Policy History* 17:1 (2005), 12–33.

laws or the social and moral distinctions which they embodied, and, as we shall see in Chapter 10, the German debate over the "social evolution" of poor relief simultaneously reflected the new commitment to prevention and social citizenship, the continued faith in deterrence, and the dead weight of tradition and fiscality.

From the 1890s onward, the evolution of social assistance in imperial Germany was driven by the emergence of a social or environmental understanding of the nature of dependence, delinquency, and other forms of need. What is meant by this? In the mid-nineteenth century, the individual was generally regarded as a rights-bearing free moral agent, who could be held responsible for his actions because he possessed the intellectual capacity to distinguish between right and wrong and the freedom of will to act on this knowledge in accordance with either the dictates of conscience or, in a more utilitarian frame, the calculus of pain and pleasure. The possession of all those character traits associated with self-governance – independence, responsibility, prudence, thrift, discipline, and industriousness – defined what it meant to be an individual in the strong sense of the term. In their absence, there could be neither rights, responsibility, nor accountability. Those who were presumed to lack these traits – notably women, children, lunatics, and the dependent poor – could not be the subject of rights and duties in the full sense of the term and had to be placed under the protection and guidance of others. In this individualist, voluntarist view, character trumped circumstance (in the words of Bernard Bosanquet, a leading thinker for the British Charity Organisation Society, "character is the condition of conditions"[2]), and people became dependent, delinquent, and criminal because they lacked the capacity to govern themselves – hence, the liberal tendency to conflate indigence, crime, and sin and to closely police all three.[3]

The social perspective on poverty inverted many of these assumptions in ways that would radically affect both the nature of citizenship and the practice of public assistance. The basic principle of this social perspective was the belief that the individual's character was shaped in essential ways by the social and material environment. This was a vision not of a disembodied, self-governing subject, but rather of an embodied subject who was embedded in a web of material social relations whose unremitting pressure conditioned the individual to think, believe, and act in certain ways. From this perspective, the character, culture, and morality of the individual could be no better and no other than what the environment permitted and encouraged him to be. Children neglected by working mothers and left to fend for themselves in the street could hardly be expected to become paragons of virtue, industrious workers, patriotic citizens, brave soldiers, or caring parents. The inescapable presence of dirt in the

---

[2] Cited in Nikolas Rose, *Powers of Freedom* (Cambridge University Press, 1999), 105.
[3] Patrick Joyce, *The Rule of Freedom. Liberalism and the Modern City* (Verso, 2003) and Rose, *Powers of Freedom*.

working-class home made it unreasonable for the working classes to accept the common sense of the middle-class habitus with regard to personal and household hygiene. Nor could unskilled or irregularly employed workers, who were forever at the mercy of volatile labor markets and subsistence wages, be expected to develop middle-class habits of thrift and self-discipline, which presupposed the availability of a very different set of economic choices than those open to these persons. These social factors did not absolve individuals of responsibility for making the most of the opportunities available to them, but they narrowed the horizons of individuals enmeshed in these forces and made character appear as an effect of circumstance, as well as its cause. The new sciences of social work, sociology, and criminology crystallized in part around the need for a more precise understanding of the ways in which social forces had deflected the development of the individual character away from the norm of individual autonomy, and it was this new social knowledge that provided the leverage for both individualized social work and broader social reform measures.[4]

The influence of heredity also played an important role in this retreat from the mid-century understanding of the rational, self-determining subject.[5] At first blush, the idea that poverty, crime, and other forms of social deviance could be the product of inherited mental inferiority might appear to call into question the very possibility of social work and social reform, if not to damn them as counter-selective programs that actively contributed to the degeneration of the race. However, to reason in this manner would be to overstate the case. First, even if one believed in the genetic determination of intelligence and character, the limits of eugenic explanation still left substantial room for the influence of constitution, disposition, and environment, to say the least. Second, the social work profession gradually availed itself of medical, especially psychiatric, expertise and sought to make use of whatever leverage was supplied by this knowledge. Lastly, despite the occasional intervention of eugenicists into concrete social policy debates and the broad currency of the rhetoric of degeneracy, the sciences of psychiatry and criminal biology were most influential among those social experts and administrators who dealt primarily with such marginal groups as recidivist vagrants and prostitutes, and the concepts of psychopathy, asociality, and incorrigibility were coined during these years to explain encounter of these social modernists with the limits of their pedagogical influence. However, hard eugenics had much less purchase in the broader social reform community, whose members were committed to the idea that the vast majority of the needy population could – through personal help and scientific

---

[4] On the emergence of this social perspective, see David Garland, *Punishment & Welfare. A History of Penal Strategies* (Gower, 1985), and Michael Willrich, *City of Courts. Socializing Justice in Progressive Era Chicago* (Cambridge University Press, 2003).
[5] On the medicalization of mid-century moral reform discourse, especially in the field of criminology, see, in addition to Garland, Richard Wetzell, *Inventing the Criminal. A History of German Criminology 1880–1945* (University of South Carolina Press, 2000).

The Social Perspective on Poverty and the Logic of Social Citizenship

social work – be bettered and taught to live in accordance with the norms of bourgeois social life.[6]

The key elements of the social interpretation of need can be illustrated by a 1904 essay on "the problem of poverty" published by Münsterberg, a student of Gustav Schmoller and the leading welfare reformer in Germany from the early 1890s until his death in 1911. In this essay, Münsterberg sought to illuminate the ways in which character and environment were mutually implicated by showing that it was no longer possible to sustain the traditional distinction between poverty that was self-incurred and that which was due to causes beyond the control of the individual. "A bad course of life," Münsterberg argued, "for which a vicious upbringing is to blame, is something for which, in a higher sense, the individual is not responsible." Juvenile delinquency, he argued, was similarly "bound up with social conditions," while he linked sickness in a recursive manner first to poor housing and diet and then to "wage and labor conditions which do not allow a sufficient expenditure for food and dwelling" and, beyond this, to the social and economic constitution of society, with the origin and precise nature of this infinitely complex chain of social causality invariably remaining "hidden in an almost impenetrable obscurity."[7]

If the causes of dependence were to be found more in the laws of industrial society than in the depths of the individual character, conceived as the locus of self-determining, uncaused moral action, then the best way to eliminate poverty was less the rationalization of relief and charity than the study – empirical, statistical, and theoretical – of society and the use of this knowledge to engineer a better world.[8] As Münsterberg explained, progress in this domain

> begins at the moment when poverty is no longer reckoned with as a condition established by the will of God, or as a necessary fact of human existence; and the question is thus raised whether poor relief itself cannot be absolutely banished from the world by the complete abolition of poverty itself and, without prejudice to the physical and mental inequalities in natural gifts which divide men, by the removal of that monstrous inequality which exists in the things of this world. From this point of view the problem of poverty is a problem of economics and sociology which investigates the whole relationship of man to man and to nature about him, and whose final aim must be

---

[6] Willrich, *City of Courts*, 85, 124, and 241ff., has much to say on the compatibility and permeability of environmental and eugenic explanation, and Rose, *Powers of Freedom*, 114ff., notes a tension or dualism between biological/racial and sociological theorizations of the "social."

[7] Münsterberg, "The Problem of Poverty," *The American Journal of Sociology* 10 (1904), 335–53. This essay, which was originally delivered at the International Scientific Congress in St. Louis, appeared in German as "Das Problem der Armut," *Jahrbücher für Nationalökonomie und Statistik*, 3. Folge, Bd. XXVII (1904), 577–91.

[8] For one account of the problems involved in the statistical constitution of such social knowledge, see Bénédicte Zimmermann, "Statisticiens des villes allemandes et action réformatrice (1871–194)," *Genèses* 15 (March 1994), 4–27. See Marcus Gräser's comments on the relationship between social knowledge, social politics, and professionalization in *Wohlfahrtsgesellschaft und Wohlfahrtsstaat. Bürgerliche Sozialreform und welfare state building in den USA und in Deutschland 1880–1940* (Vandenhoeck & Ruprecht, 2008), Chapter II.3.

to render to all an equitable share in the treasures that are to be wrung from nature through work, and also, by the creation of universal prosperity, to banish poverty from the world as the very contradiction of such prosperity.[9]

Such arguments entailed the definitive desacralization of poverty, and they marked the abandonment of the biblical injunction that the poor would always be among us. These modernist aspirations to make fate and fortune a matter of rational, human control were supported by the social survey and early sociological speculation, which sought to develop more abstract, synthetic concepts – such as unemployment, delinquency, sickness, disability, illegitimacy, and old age – to theorize the complex relationship between environment and individual need.

These studies informed the new social understanding of need, which was increasingly defined in functional terms as the environmentally conditioned deviance from presumed norms of social fitness. For example, in his 1905 study of the social conditions and differential life chances of illegitimate children in Frankfurt, Othmar Spann proposed that illegitimacy be understood as an "abnormal" form of reproduction in which children were considered to be needy to the extent that the conditions necessary for their physical, intellectual, and moral development were lacking in some degree because of the absence of the father. He contrasted this to the "normal" family, which he defined as one that was able to secure for its offspring conditions that would permit them to maintain the cultural level and social position of their parents, if not to rise above them. In this study, Spann documented the diverse facets of the social problem of illegitimacy with regard to the impaired physical development, weak constitution, limited occupational success, weak academic performance, and high criminality rates of the illegitimate population. But this investigation also led Spann conclude that children who were born to single mothers, but who were fully integrated into stepfamilies at an early age, should not be considered illegitimate in any functional sense, and his work left open the possibility that the children of married parents could be considered functionally illegitimate, that is, needy, if the preceding conditions were not satisfied. This knowledge of the specific ways in which illegitimate children were disadvantaged by the lack of a "normal" family, Spann argued, could be directly translated into social policy measures to compensate for these dangers, and he insisted that society had an obligation to engage in such action, not simply on humanitarian grounds, but wherever society had an interest in ensuring that needy persons acquired the capacity to perform the social functions expected of them.[10]

This functional understanding of need gave prevention a dynamic quality because the consciousness of a slippage between norm and reality gave rise

---

[9] Münsterberg, "The Problem of Poverty," 338.
[10] Othmar Spann, *Untersuchungen über die uneheliche Bevölkerung in Frankfurt am Main* (=*Probleme der Fürsorge*, 2, 1905), especially 7–11, and "Die Erweiterung der Sozialpolitik durch die Berufsvormundschaft," *Archiv für Sozialwissenschaft und Sozialpolitik* 34 (1912), 505–61.

to an imperative to close this gap through preventive or curative action, an imperative that could not arise so long as such deviance was seen as the result of character failing that would be further aggravated by such assistance. This reasoning also underlay the work of a second figure who played a central role in the development of social work and social welfare after the turn of the century: Christian Jasper Klumker. Klumker began as a follower of Friedrich Naumann; like Spann, he was also associated with the Institute for the Common Welfare (*Institut für Gemeinwohl*), a Progressive think tank founded in 1890 by the Frankfurt industrialist Wilhelm Merton, and the Central Bureau for Private Welfare (*Centrale für private Fürsorge*), which was a spin-off of the Institute; and he later became the first German professor of poor relief and social welfare (at the University of Frankfurt).[11] In his influential *Elements of Social Welfare* (1918), Klumker tried to interpret need and the process of impoverishment in terms of what he called uneconomicalness (*Unwirtschaftlichkeit*), that is, the inability to realize the social norms of self-support and economic independence through participation in the labor market. Klumker argued that, up to a point, the specter of poverty could indeed serve as a spur to individual industry and responsibility, but that, beyond this point, risk and uncertainty could have the opposite effect and lead individuals – as a form of psychological self-defense – to contract their economic horizons and cease to worry about how present actions might impact a future over which they had little direct control. This contraction, he suggested, set in motion a downward spiral of impoverishment in which discipline was progressively displaced by indiscipline, providence by improvidence, industry by sloth, and economic fitness (*Wirtschaftlichkeit*, i.e., the ensemble of personal characteristics and abilities that enable the individual to remain economically independent) by uneconomicalness.

Klumker believed that Malthusian tradition of deterrent poor relief was misguided on three accounts: first, in its insistence that less eligibility and deterrence were always the best way to promote self-reliance; second, in its equation of dependence with sin and immorality; and third, in its belief that charity and the "relief" of the poor diminished the resources of the nation. The poor, Klumker suggested, were recruited from all social classes, rather than exclusively from a self-perpetuating, procreatively imprudent underclass, because poverty was caused by the inevitable mismatch between individual dispositions and the constantly changing demands of the labor market. The community, he argued, had the obligation to lead the needy as far as possible along the road back to economic independence, to ensure that they contributed to the productive life of the nation in proportion to their abilities, and to provide for them to the extent that they proved to be permanently incapable of securing

---

[11] Unfortunately, there is no satisfactory study of the Institut für Gemeinwohl (established 1890). There are a number of suggestive comments in Kevin Repp, *Reformers, Critics, and the Paths of German Modernity. Anti-Politics and the Search for Alternatives, 1890–1914* (Harvard University Press, 2000), and the Institute is also treated in Christoph Sachße, *Mütterlichkeit als Beruf. Sozialarbeit, Sozialreform, und Frauenbewegung 1871–1929* (Suhrkamp, 1986), 79–95.

their basic needs through such labor. His ideas paralleled contemporary British thought in insisting that the basic criterion for determining the scope and nature of the assistance to be offered should be the receptiveness of the person to individualized rehabilitative measures, rather than the degree of ostensible moral fault.[12]

This new definition of need in terms of the historically conditioned deviance from presumed norms of social fitness also drove the development of other domains of social inquiry and action, such as social hygiene and nutrition,[13] and it had complex and far-reaching effects on the rationale for social services and the nature of citizenship. The last decades of the nineteenth century were an age of expanding democracy, growing tensions between the socialist working class and the propertied classes, and intensified military and economic competition between nations caught up in imperialist rivalries. In this context, the ability of the nation to prevail in these great struggles was believed to depend on the size and quality of the population, that is, on the health, productivity, cultural level, and social integration of the laboring classes.[14] While deterrent relief had regarded the poor as a burden on society and thus left them to their own devices, and their own fates, the emergent discourse on welfare increasingly regarded the laboring classes as a precious national resource that had to be carefully husbanded and cultivated, and dependence, sickness, delinquency, and criminality were seen to entail costs to the entire nation, which could no longer be tolerated in the age of imperialism. The social perspective on poverty thus led to the recognition of new forms of interdependence and solidarity, which provided a compelling rationale for the expansion of preventive social welfare programs. On the one hand, to the extent that the diverse forms of need could be attributed to environmental factors, that is, the social and economic relations that structured the life-world of the laboring classes and determined their opportunities in life, the democratic spirit of the age made it increasingly difficult to deny the claim that those classes that benefited from the unequal distribution of wealth, power, and culture had an obligation to elevate the conditions of those classes whose need was the counterpart to their own privilege. On the other hand, the recognition that individual need diminished the person's ability to discharge those citizenship duties on which the strength of

---

[12] Klumker, *Fürsorgewesen. Einführung in das Verständnis der Armut und der Armenpflege* (Leipzig, 1918). Klumker's ideas here clearly echo debates in criminology from the 1890s. See Wetzell, *Inventing the Criminal*, Chapter 2.

[13] Corinna Treitel, "Max Rubner and the Biopolitics of Rational Nutrition," CEH 41 (2008), 1–25.

[14] Matthias Weipert, *"Mehrung der Volkskraft." Die Debatte über Bevölkerung, Modernisierung und Nation, 1890–1933* (Schöningh, 2006). Michael Geyer, "Deutschland und Japan im Zeitalter der Globalisierung," in Sebastian Conrad und Jürgen Osterhammel, eds., *Das Kaiserreich transnational. Deutschland in der Welt 1871–1914* (Vandenhoeck & Ruprecht, 2004), 68–86, especially 79ff., and Thomas Bender, *A Nation Among Nations. America's Place in World History* (Hill and Wang, 2006), 134, both situate this new concern with biopolitics in relation to the mutually mediating processes of internal nation-state formation and national self-assertion in the global system.

the nation depended (and thus had a direct, negative impact on the welfare of the entire community) made the social problem into a matter of overriding national concern. Social hygiene – and especially the dangers posed by the *Volkskrankheit* tuberculosis – provides the best illustration of how the recognition of these solidarities gave rise to a new conception of social citizenship. Since any individual could become a victim of infection and a source of contagion, the fortunes of this individual could not be a matter of indifference to the community, which found itself potentially obligated – in ways which were unimaginable for classical liberalism – both to take positive steps to promote the health of the individual and to implement measures to compel the individual to act in certain ways (or to refrain therefrom). This same reasoning also held for all other forms of need, which similarly impacted the quality of the population and the strength of the nation. It was in relation to this perceived national interest in the quantity and quality of the population that poverty, disease, delinquency, and illegitimacy were constructed as distinctly social problems and a corresponding set of social rights (to work, health, and education), which could only be secured through the expansion of preventive, therapeutic social welfare programs, was inferred. In this way the social perspective on poverty inverted the logic of deterrence, insisting that, to the extent that need was socially determined, assistance was the precondition for the cultivation of those habits of mind required by a market society and citizenship in the modern state, not a danger to them, and that the purpose of social welfare was to put individuals in a position where they could fulfill the obligations of social citizenship – and where they could first be held responsible for failing to do so. This dynamic relation between assistance and personal responsibility was the heart of the new social contract that was being forged during these decades.[15]

The transformation of the welfare of the private individual into a matter of public, political concern gave rise to a new kind of social politics and set in motion a fundamental reconsideration of the distinction between the public and the private, and the history of preventive social welfare provides a perfect opportunity for studying the micropractices through which the nascent welfare state refigured the boundaries between the public and the private that had evolved across the nineteenth century.[16] The new social welfare was based on the principle that need could be prevented – and existing need cured – through

---

[15] T. H. Marshall defined social rights as "an absolute right to a certain standard of civilization which is conditional only on the discharge of the general duties of citizenship," and he linked the recognition of these rights to the need for educated citizens and workers. See Marshall, "Citizenship and Social Class," in *Class, Citizenship, and Social Development* (Doubleday, 1964), 71–134, citation 103. For one of the many critiques of the Whiggish underpinnings of Marshall's arguments, see Eric Gorham, "Social Citizenship and Its Fetters," *Polity* 28:1 (Autumn 1995), 25–47.

[16] Michael Katz and Christoph Sachße, *The Mixed Economy of Social Welfare. Public/Private Relations in England, Germany and the United States, the 1870's to the 1930's* (Nomos Verlag, 1996).

a combination of material assistance, enlightenment concerning the principles of modern hygiene and child raising, and so on, and advice on how to properly apply this knowledge. The problem, though, is that prevention, treatment, and enlightenment all appeared to require a much greater latitude for intervening into the private sphere than could be sanctioned by classical liberalism. While preventive social welfare could empower the needy by leveling out some of the concrete social inequalities they faced and expanding their opportunities to realize their full potential, it inevitably entangled them in networks of surveillance and control and thus threatened to diminish the very personal freedoms that they had been brought into existence to secure. It is impossible, however, to determine in advance precisely how the conflicting possibilities latent in the preventive project would be resolved in any specific instance. This is a question that can only be answered through historical analysis, not theoretical deduction, and the answer need not be the same for all of the individual programs created during these years.

The new interventionist strategies associated with preventive social welfare were predicated on a rethinking of the liberal social contract in terms of a complex web of social rights and social obligations that was the distinguishing characteristic of the Progressive movement, whose intellectual contours and social imaginary can be delineated much more clearly in the domain of welfare reform than in that of parliamentary politics. What appears in the recent literature as the distinguishing feature of the broad pan-Atlantic Progressive movement was the belief that liberty had to be understood less in terms of the freedom of the isolated individual to pursue his or her particular urges and interests than as the progressive perfection of the higher self. This was then combined with a strong conception of the interdependency of all individuals within the social body to arrive at an organic view of the relation between the individual and society whose corollary was that the pursuit of one's own freedom necessarily entailed a positive collective obligation to create the social and environmental conditions for the self-perfection of the other members of the community.[17] The issue on which this ecumenical reform movement irreparably fractured was that of the best way of achieving these goals, and the scholarly literature has adopted a chiasmic approach in order to show how different elements of this transatlantic reform movement – which embraced not only those who explicitly identified themselves as Progressives, but also Fabians, British New Liberals, French solidarists, and reformist Social Democrats – could draw antithetical conclusions from a shared commitment to these ideas.

[17] This and the following draw freely on James T. Kloppenberg, *Uncertain Victory. Social Democracy and Progressivism in European and American Thought, 1870–1920* (Oxford University Press, 1986); Marc Stears, *Progressives, Pluralists, and the Problems of the State. Ideologies of Reform in the United States and Britain, 1909–1926* (Oxford University Press, 2002); A.M. McBriar, *An Edwardian Mixed Doubles. The Bosanquets versus the Webbs. A Study in British Social Policy 1890–1929* (Oxford University Press, 1987); Stefan Collini, *Liberalism and Sociology. L.T. Hobhouse and Political Argument in England 1880–1914* (Cambridge University Press, 1979); and Michael Freeden, *The New Liberalism. An Ideology of Social Reform* (Oxford University Press, 1978).

Until recently, Progressivism has been largely absent from the historiographical landscape of imperial Germany.[18] Since the 1860s, the left wing of the liberal movement had gone through a series of secessions and mergers, and at the turn of the century Progressive cultural and social reformers found their political home in Friedrich Naumann's National Social Association (to which Klumker and Bäumer, among many others, belonged), the Radical Association (*Freisinnige Vereinigung*), and the Progressive People's Party (*Fortschrittliche Volkspartei*), which collectively filled the space on the political spectrum between the more conservative National Liberals and the Social Democrats. These left liberal parties, however, did not represent neat socioeconomic groups.[19] As Kevin Repp has shown, the Progressive reform community of the Wilhelmine years was unified not by common economic interests or loyalty to a particular party, but rather by a shared habitus that was reproduced through a set of networks, institutions, and discursive practices that he traces across the entire social landscape of the period. It included not only a broad swath of the bourgeois women's movement, but also many male reformers and municipal politicians. One of the many foci of the movement was the Institute for the Common Welfare (and the Central Bureau for Private Welfare), which combined theorizing about the reform of poor relief and charity with the coordination of voluntary agencies in the city. But the influence of these reformers was broadly diffused and multiplied by their membership in many of the leading social and cultural reform associations of the day, including the Social Policy Association, Social Reform Association, the German Association for Poor Relief and Charity, the Society for Ethical Culture, and the League for the Protection of Mothers, as well as other abstinence, popular education, and life reform organizations.[20]

The social question formed the center of gravity of this intellectual habitus, which was structured through a matrix of beliefs and attitudes that should be

---

[18] In addition to Kloppenberg, *Uncertain Victory*, the most important studies of German Progressivism are Detlev Peukert, *Grenzen der Sozialdisziplinierung. Aufstieg und Krise der deutschen Jugendfürsorge 1878 bis 1932* (Bund Verlag, 1986), Repp, *Reformers, Critics, and the Paths of German Modernity*, and Edward Ross Dickinson, *The Politics of German Child Welfare from the Empire to the Federal Republic* (Harvard University Press, 1996). On left liberalism, see Alastair Thompson, *Left Liberals, the State, and Popular Politics in Wilhelmine Germany* (Oxford University Press, 2000) and Holger Tober, *Deutscher Liberalismus und Sozialpolitik in der Ära des Wilhlehlminismus* (Matthieson, 1999).

[19] Thompson, *Left Liberals, the State, and Popular Politics*, 27ff., and James Sheehan, *German Liberalism in the Nineteenth Century* (University of Chicago Press, 1978), 241–3, 265–71.

[20] Repp, *Reformers*, 215ff., and Repp, "'More Corporeal, More Concrete': Liberal Humanism, Eugenics, and German Progressives at the Last Fin de Siècle," *JMH* 72 (September 2000), 683–730. The question, though, is how much impact these antipolitical alternative modernities could have had so long as they did not break through to challenge, or perhaps colonize, the domain of party politics. In a sense, Repp's book represents the photographic negative image of Christoph Dipper, "Sozialreform. Geschichte eines umstrittenen Begriffs," *AfS* 32 (1992), 323–51, who shows how the belief that Social Democracy could be integrated into the imperial state through the combination of paternalism and science without descending into the domain of political struggles ultimately rendered the social reform community irrelevant to these struggles.

familiar to students of any of the national varieties of Progressivism. While Detlev Peukert's seminal *Limits of Social Discipline* emphasized how the negative disciplinary potential latent within the Progressive project was increasingly radicalized by the encounter with the limits of social pedagogy, Repp argues that Progressive social politics, which was sustained by organicist theories of social progress and social integration, was moderate, evolutionary, and optimistically committed to humanist values. The novel dimension of Repp's work lies in his suggestion that the members of this Progressive reform milieu also shared a specific political style: an "antipolitics" that to a large degree eschewed party political engagement in favor of social and cultural reform. This strategy, Repp suggests, has rendered invisible to subsequent historiography the broad array of initiatives undertaken by these reformers and thus facilitated the oft-repeated, yet fundamentally false, pessimistic assessment of the achievements of Progressive social reformers from the 1890s onward.

The literature on American Progressivism has emphasized how the rise of big business led to the colonization of political life by social issues, the dissolution of traditional party loyalties, and the subsequent emergence of a number of extraparliamentary, single-issue movements.[21] One can make much the same argument for Wilhelmine Germany, where the Progressive antipolitics of social reform took the form of a steadily widening spiral of pragmatically experimental social programs and reform movements designed to combat the infinitely diverse manifestations of the social question. Although each of these initiatives was resolutely modern in its own individual way, they could not be integrated into a single vision of modernity or reduced to a fixed, static set of doctrines and positions. It is this incommensurability between the aims of Progressive reform and the infinity of practical means through which these ends were pursued that accounts for the contradictoriness and volatility – or, to express this idea in more positive terms, the openness and pragmatism – of Progressivism as a sociopolitical movement.

Familial Subjects – The Archimedean Point of Social Reform

The history of poor relief, charity, and social welfare during these decades cannot be separated from the history of social insurance, and the real question is how their relationship is to be understood. There are perhaps two main approaches to the history of this broader welfare complex. The first approach views the development of social insurance as a response to the decline of older, primarily familial and communal forms of social security and as an attempt to develop mechanisms that would better protect the new and more mobile industrial labor force against the risks associated with the spread of wage labor, as well as those linked to the life cycle and family structure (old age,

---

[21] Daniel Rodgers, "In Search of Progressivism," *Reviews in American History* 10:4 (December 1982), 113–32, and Rodgers, *Atlantic Crossings. Social Politics in a Progressive Age* (Harvard University Press, 1998), 52ff.

family size, and death of breadwinner).[22] But while social insurance gradually expanded to provide higher benefits and a greater degree of security against a broader spectrum of risks for a growing proportion of the laboring population, individualized social assistance remained as an inferior, residual safety net for that segment of the population that had not yet been brought under the umbrella of social insurance or whose need was attributed to personal factors and the failure of private reproduction.[23]

Feminist scholars have long been aware that this two-track system disadvantaged women, whose exclusion from the kinds of skilled, well-paid factory employment that would have put them in a position to enjoy the benefits of social insurance made them into the primary clientele of an inferior, discriminatory social assistance track. In response, they have sought to complicate this work-based view of the welfare state through the use of such concepts as caring regimes to theorize the centrality of unpaid domestic labor, and especially caring work, in the political economy of the welfare state.[24] The problem with both this modernization-theoretical account of the spread of social insurance and the feminist account of its role in perpetuating gender inequality is not so much that they are inaccurate as that they are incomplete. Both of these accounts presume that individuals, both male and female, already possessed those economic and social virtues that would enable them to thrive in a market society, and the exclusive focus on insurance and social assistance as mechanisms for regulating the labor market leads them to overlook the role of the both social insurance and social welfare in creating the subjects, and the specific forms of subjectivity, on which the functioning of the market, the family, and the other institutions of bourgeois society depended.[25]

All the fundamental norms of bourgeois society were condensed in the idea of the breadwinner family, whose reinforcement constituted the Archimedean point for social reform in imperial Germany. Since the significance of the

---

[22] Gerhard A. Ritter and Klaus Tenfelde, *Arbeiter im Deutschen Kaiserreich 1871 bis 1914* (Dietz, 1992), 549ff., provide an overview of these risks.

[23] Christoph Sachße, "Wohlfahrtsstaat in Deutschland: Strukturen, Paradoxien, Perspektiven," in Andreas Wollasch, ed., *Wohlfahrtspflege in der Region. Westfalen-Lippe während des 19. und 20. Jahrhunderts im historischen Vergleich* (Schöningh, 1997), 269–82, provides an excellent account of this expansionary dynamic and its contradictions.

[24] Barbara Nelson, "The Origins of the Two-Channel Welfare State: Workmen's Compensation and Mothers' Aid," in Linda Gordon, ed., *Women, the State, and Welfare* (University of Wisconsin Press, 1990), 123–51.

[25] Dorith Geva, "From Family Preservation to Nuclear Family Governance: Regulating Families through American Welfare Policy," presented at the September 2005 RC 19 conference on Re-theorizing Welfare States: Restructuring States, Restructuring Analysis" and Ann Shola Orloff, "'Markets Not States' The Weakness of State Social Provision for Breadwinning Men in the United States," in Lynne Haney and Lisa Pollard, eds., *Families of a New World. Gender, Politics, and State Development in a Global Context* (Routledge, 2003), 217–43. The same limitation holds for feminist accounts of caring regimes that recognize the role of unpaid domestic labor in social reproduction, but fail to interrogate the process through which caring and breadwinning were constituted as meaningful forms of social activity.

welfare complex is to be found as much, if not more, in its role in the formation and regulation of these familial subjects as in the direct provision of material assistance (which itself needs to be seen as a mechanism of social normalization), we need to focus on its role in constructing and reproducing the gendered subjects on which market and society depended and the linkages – which run in all directions – between the individual, the family, the market, and the social domain.

The new preventive social welfare programs stood at an oblique and contradictory relationship to the central institutions of bourgeois society. As we shall see in our account of youth welfare (Chapter 9), the wedge through which public social intervention first gained entry into the private sphere of the family was through the assumption that the family was failing to adequately perform those ostensibly "natural" duties on which the welfare of the nation was believed to depend. This failing justified the provision of material assistance and pedagogical support (or tutelage), practices that had the potential to expand the material security of the family while diminishing its autonomy. The primary aim of the various programs that constituted this welfare complex was to produce responsible, industrious, disciplined individuals who lived up to their obligations as familial subjects, and both insurance and welfare relied on specific strategies of responsibilization, which were embodied in specific social technologies that we will examine in the following chapters, to inculcate the desired forms of strategic rationality in their target populations.[26]

Wage earning and breadwinning were essential to, if not constitutive of, the identity of the male worker as husband and family head, and this individual gender norm was the point at which the economic, the familial, and the social domains all converged.[27] In fact, it was the concern for the social consequences of nonsupport that gave the problem of failed or neglectful breadwinners a resonance that extended beyond the question of its direct impact on relief costs, and it was in this context that desertion and slacking were first constituted as social problems.[28] The contribution of the welfare complex to the construction of masculinity and the male breadwinner family was complemented by its role in the construction of women as dependent persons who were deserving of "protection" because their natural maternal calling could only be realized in the domestic sphere. The positive content of this domestic calling was defined not only by the act of childbearing, but also by women's role in both ennobling those baser instincts that made men peculiarly well suited for public life and

---

[26] Peter Squires, *Anti-Social Policy. Welfare, Ideology and the Disciplinary State* (Harvester Wheatsheaf, 1990) and William Walters, *Unemployment and Government. Genealogies of the Social* (Cambridge University Press, 2000).

[27] Rose, *Powers of Freedom*, 123–4.

[28] On the regulation of slacking, the discovery of desertion as a social problem in the 1890s, and the interplay of gender and state-formation in the construction of the breadwinner family in the United States, see Willrich, *City of Courts*, and Anna Igra, *Wives without Husbands. Marriage, Desertion, and Welfare in New York, 1900–1935* (University of North Carolina Press, 2006).

nurturing their children, not to mention their unpaid domestic labor. A proper home was unimaginable without a central female presence, and the promise of such a home provided men with a constant reminder both of their obligations as breadwinner and family head and of the privileges and rewards associated with these duties. In this way, the social question came to be framed as a "woman question."[29] Of course, for the working classes the economic dependence of women, their protection, and their confinement to the domestic sphere was always only notional, and the definition of femininity in terms of dependence and domesticity left German social policy discourse with no conceptual space for female workers, whose existence could be tolerated, but whose needs could never be addressed in a systematic manner. As a result, state social policies oscillated between efforts to exclude (married) women from the industrial workforce and measures to make it easier for these women to balance paid employment with domestic duties, which were always seen as natural and primary.

The family was continually invoked as the most elemental, and therefore the most important, unit of social organization and as the basic mechanism for the biological and social reproduction of the nation. It should, therefore, come as no surprise that its failings – both real and imagined – were universally regarded as the root cause of virtually every dimension of the social problem or that it should be regarded as both the primary object and the primary agent of social intervention. In the 1880s, the problem of working-class housing emerged as a central element of the social question. Reformers were so concerned about the housing question because they saw the perceived disorder of the working-class home and the open families that inhabited it as symbols of the general disorder of contemporary society. Although social reformers were keenly focused on the intractable economics of the housing market, they could exert only limited influence in this area, and they downplayed this limitation by arguing that the real root of the social problem was to be found in the lack of proper domestic skills, which prevented working-class women from making the most out of the resources available to them and turning their dwellings into homes that would elevate the sentiments of their husbands and children. In the eyes of many reformers, the most basic task was to teach working-class women and girls how to run their households in an economical, hygienic manner. "Social work for the home" (*Wohnungsfürsorge*, *Wohnungspflege*, and *Wohnungsinspektion*, as well as *Hauspflege* for women who were recovering from childbirth or otherwise unable to perform their domestic obligations) became one of the main vehicles through which middle-class women sought to rationalize the

---

[29] Kathleen Canning, *Languages of Labor and Gender. Female Factory Work in Germany, 1850–1914* (Cornell University Press, 1996); Teresa Kulawik, *Wohlfahrtsstaat und Mutterschaft. Schweden und Deutschland 1870–1912* (Campus Verlag, 1999); and Sabine Schmitt, *Der Arbeiterinnenschutz im deutschen Kaiserreich. Zur Konstruktion der schutzbedürftigen Arbeiterin* (Metzler, 1995).

working-class household and teach working-class women "the grand art of living" – and in so doing to justify an expanded role for themselves in public life.[30]

Many middle-class social reformers warned in the direst terms that the lack of these skills and dispositions could have ruinous effects on the family and society.[31] As Darmstadt mayor Albrecht Ohly explained at a meeting of the German Association for Poor Relief and Charity, even the most diligent husband could not earn enough to offset what would be wasted by a wife who was ignorant of the domestic arts or who neglected her domestic duties. A dirty and disorderly household, miserable personal and domestic hygiene, and meals that were late, expensive, and lacking in both taste and nutrition would, Ohly claimed, poison the atmosphere of the home. Instead of good-natured conversation around the family dinner table, all that the husband would hear after a hard day's work would be bickering among ill-bred children and reproaches from his wife about wages that did not suffice for household needs. With a home like this, it was entirely understandable that the husband would seek respite in the local pub, even though this solution would only complicate the household disorder that had driven him there in the first place. This process of familial breakup and moral decline invariably gave rise, Ohly concluded, to the entire spectrum of social problems that exercised contemporary reformers: "the moral and material ruin of the man, the dissolution of the bonds of the family, the neglect of the children, the necessity of poor relief, and not seldom the

---

[30] Ulla Terlinden and Susanna von Oertzen, *Die Wohnungsfrage ist Frauensache! Frauenbewegung und Wohnreform 1870 bis 1933* (Dietrich Reimer Verlag, 2006); Dietlinde Peters, *Mütterlichkeit im Kaiserreich. Die bürgerliche Frauenbewegung und der soziale Beruf der Frau* (B. Kleine Verlag, 1984), 144ff., 295–329; Iris Schröder, *Arbeiten für eine bessere Welt. Frauenbewegung und Soziale Reform 1890–1914* (Campus Verlag, 2001), 125ff., 291ff.; Ursula Baumann, *Protestantismus und Frauenemanzipation in Deutschland 1850 bis 1920* (Campus Verlag, 1992), 169–74; and Nancy Reagin, *A German Women's Movement. Class & Gender in Hanover, 1880–1933* (University of North Carolina Press, 1995), 71ff. As Reagin notes, girls from the more respectable sections of the working class responded favorably to domestic science courses because they already shared the underlying notion of domesticity, while the skills taught there were less relevant to, and found less resonance among, girls from poorer families, who did not have the leisure to attend such courses.

[31] On the continuation schools and girls' education, see Derek Linton, *"Who Has the Youth Has the Future". The Campaign to Save Young Workers in Imperial Germany* (Cambridge University Press, 1991), chapters 4 and 8, and *Hauswirtschaftliche Unterweisung für die gesamte weibliche Jugend* (Flugschriften der Zentralstelle für Volkswohlfahrt, 2, 1909). For a discussion of these schools and their associational supporters in Bremen, see Elisabeth Meyer-Renschhausen, *Weibliche Kultur und soziale Arbeit. Eine Geschichte der Frauenbewegung am Beispiel Bremens 1810–1927* (Böhlau, 1989), 126–35. Nancy Reagin, *Sweeping the German Nation. Domesticity and National Identity in Germany, 1870–1945* (Cambridge University Press, 2007) connects domestic activity to the broader process of nation making. Such reasoning could easily cross the line from praising women for their accomplishments to blaming them for their failures. For a particularly crass example of the latter, see Albert Kern, "Hauswirtschaftliche Unterweisung schulentlassener Mädchen aus dem Arbeiterstande," *Caritas* 6 (1901), 181–7.

poorhouse or the workhouse."[32] While this understanding of family failure or breakup as the primal origin of the social problem could lead to the demonization of women, it also provided a powerful rationale for welfarist intervention both to assist the family in performing its natural functions and to compensate for its failings. The challenge was to devise "mechanisms that would support the family in its 'normal' functioning and enable it to fulfill its social obligations most effectively without destroying its identity and responsibility."[33]

In Wilhelmine Germany, the three most important fields of preventive social welfare were (1) social hygiene, especially programs to combat tuberculosis and infant mortality; (2) programs to assist the jobless; and (3) youth welfare and juvenile justice programs. I have written elsewhere about social hygiene programs and the right to health,[34] and in the next two chapters I will focus on the latter two sets of programs before returning in Chapter 10 to the efforts of reformers to think systematically about what these programs might mean and how their spread would impact deterrent poor relief.

---

[32] Albrecht Ohly, "Die hauswirtschaftliche Ausbildung der Mädchen aus den ärmeren Volksklassen," *SDV*, 6 (1888), 19–59, cited in Meyer-Renschhausen, *Weibliche Kultur und soziale Arbeit*, 128. See also the subsequent discussion of the problem in Fritz Kalle, "Die hauswirtschaftliche Unterricht armer Mädchen in Deutschland," *SDV*, 12 (1890).

[33] Rose, *Powers of Freedom*, 128. In *The Policing of Families*, tr. Robert Hurley (Pantheon, 1979), Jacques Donzelot argued that the whipsawing of the private family through the interplay of advice and control was leading to its notional dissolution into the social.

[34] Larry Frohman, "Prevention, Welfare, and Citizenship: The War on Tuberculosis and Infant Mortality in Germany, 1900–1930," *CEH* 39:3 (September 2006), 431–81, and "The Right to Health and Social Citizenship in Imperial Germany," in Anne Hardy, Frank Huisman, and Harry Oosterhuis, eds., *Health and Citizenship. Political Cultures of Health in Britain, the Netherlands, and Germany* (Pickering and Chatto, forthcoming).

8

From Fault to Risk

Changing Strategies of Assistance to the Jobless in Imperial Germany

Unquestionably, the greatest risk faced by the wage-earning classes was – and remains – to be without work. The threat of joblessness was a source of intense existential anxiety for the working classes, and both workers and their employers were acutely conscious of the disciplinary power that flowed from the power of dismissal.[1]

The history of assistance to the jobless in imperial Germany can best be understood in terms of the shift – slow, uneven, and ultimately only partial – from an individualist approach, which saw joblessness primarily as the result of sloth and regarded deterrence as the best means for promoting self-reliance and family responsibility, to a social approach to the problem. The social approach was based on the assumption that joblessness represented a risk inherent in the structure of the industrial labor market, and this new understanding of the problem made it possible to view the nation as a solidaristic community of wage laborers. It also pointed toward new social technologies that could be used to manage a risk that might randomly befall any individual member of this community: labor exchanges (i.e., employment offices) to diminish this risk and minimize its consequences, insurance programs to socialize that element of risk that could not be eliminated through such measures, and, at a chronological and theoretical distance, the management of aggregate demand for labor through what would later become Keynesian fiscal policy. The concept of "unemployment" was coined to describe joblessness among those workers who normally supported themselves and their families through regular wage labor, who were able to work, who were willing to do so, but who could not find work because of the shortage of jobs. Determining willingness to work, which was the cornerstone of the deterrent promotion of self-reliance, appeared to require an impossible knowledge of individual character. However, this Gordian know was

---

[1] Karl-Christian Führer, *Arbeitslosigkeit und die Entstehung der Arbeitslosenversicherung in Deutschland 1902–1927* (Colloquium Verlag, 1990), 20ff.

cut – though not without a moralistic remainder – by the automatism of contributory insurance, which, in conjunction with de facto work test made possible by the organizational linkage between labor exchanges and the unemployment insurance system, rendered it unnecessary to mix morals and mathematics, to borrow Churchill's phrase.[2]

This shift from character to socioeconomic structure as the basic level of social analysis and public intervention had far-reaching implications for the practice of social assistance and social reform. Since the risk of unemployment was not one that could be reduced to individual morality or effectively combated through deterrence, social policy measures to influence the structure and operation of the labor market gradually began to supplant deterrent poor relief as the primary means of preventing the social consequences of involuntary joblessness.[3] This new perspective, which presumed the responsibility and industriousness of the individual worker, rather than his sloth and improvidence, also provided a rationale for such action and made it possible to engage in constructive policies without being paralyzed in advance by the fear of the moral hazards traditionally associated with such measures.

The story, however, did not unfold in as smooth a manner as the preceding account might imply, and we need to guard against the presumption that the development of a state-sponsored system of labor exchanges and unemployment insurance was the logical or inevitable outcome of prewar initiatives. Ultimately, the absence of the requisite political conditions blocked the development of a nationwide system of labor exchanges, labor market statistics, and unemployment insurance in the immediate prewar years. This deadlock, which unintentionally enhanced the importance of local initiative in the field, was broken only by the realignment of political forces resulting from war and revolution.[4]

In the following pages, we will examine the history of assistance to the jobless in imperial Germany by looking first at those programs that diagnosed the problem in terms of moral failing and consequently saw their task as that of policing the marginal, itinerant, and potentially criminal poor. In the second part of the chapter, we will then turn to those programs that, on the basis of a more social understanding of joblessness, shifted their focus to enhancing the economic and social security of the much larger number of independent, but potentially unemployed, workers who made up the productive body of the nation.

---

[2] William Walters, *Unemployment and Government. Genealogies of the Social* (Cambridge University Press, 2000); Christian Topalov, *Naissance du chômeur 1880–1910* (Albin Michel, 1994); Bénédicte Zimmermann, *Arbeitslosigkeit in Deutschland. Zur Entstehung einer sozialen Kategorie* (Campus Verlag, 2006); and Peter Squires, *Anti-Social Policy. Welfare Ideology and the Disciplinary State* (Harvester Wheatsheaf, 1990).
[3] Character did, however, continue to influence the debate over unemployment in terms of the question of which specific workers would be affected by an overall scarcity of jobs.
[4] Zimmermann, *Arbeitslosigkeit in Deutschland*.

Migrant Relief, Workhouses, and the Policing of the Residuum

To understand the development of assistance to the jobless, it is necessary to begin with the restructuring of the labor market in imperial Germany. Even though the German population grew by 12% in the 1870s alone, the economic boom that stretched from the 1850s through the mid-1870s created enough new jobs to resolve the *Vormärz* crisis of overpopulation and underemployment, and over the course of the empire the expanding economy provided employment for virtually every job seeker in a population that itself expanded by 70% between 1870 and 1914, though this long-term trend was punctuated by spikes of conjunctural unemployment in 1892/4 and again in 1901/2.[5] These labor market trends were reflected in the development of real wages, which rose into the early 1870s, fell through the remainder of the decade, and began a more or less continuous upward trend in the 1880s. Overall, real wages increased by somewhere between 40 and 64% in the period 1880–1913.[6]

Industrialization was also leading to a complex restructuring of the labor market along sectoral and geographic lines. The keywords here are urbanization and migration.[7] The expansion of industry created an insatiable demand for labor and led to the continuous movement of workers from the countryside to the city. Between 1866 and 1914, the proportion of the population living in cities of more than five thousand jumped from 23.7 to 48.8%; the number of cities with more than 100,000 residents rose from eight to forty-eight during the same period; and the number of people living in these cities increased in absolute terms from 9.7 to 31.7 million. More than half of this growth was due to in-migration from rural areas. By 1907, only one in two Germans still lived in the same locality where they had been born. One-third had moved to another place within the state or province (Prussia) where they had been born, while 15% had migrated to a different state.[8] These trends were amplified by the fact that many people moved frequently both between towns and within the same city. The city of Duisburg provides a good example of this transience. Although the population grew from 13,000 in 1853 to 107,000 in 1904, more than 710,000 people officially resided in the town at one point or another during this period.[9] The size of these new metropolises, the complexity of the labor market, the geographical distance between rich and poor, and the

---

[5] Thomas Nipperdey, *Deutsche Geschichte, 1866–1918* (Beck, 1990), I:10.
[6] Gerhard A. Ritter and Klaus Tenfelde, *Arbeiter im Deutschen Kaiserreich, 1871 bis 1914* (Dietz, 1992), 492.
[7] On the timing and complex causes of both overseas emigration and long-distance domestic migration from the Prussian East, see Klaus Bade, "Massenwanderung und Arbeitsmarkt im deutschen Nordosten von 1880 bis zum Ersten Weltkrieg," *AfS* 20 (1980), 265–323, and Ritter and Tenfelde, *Arbeiter im Deutschen Kaiserreich*, 175–97.
[8] Nipperdey, *Deutsche Geschichte, 1866–1918*, I:9–42, and Stephan Bleek, "Mobilität und Sesshaftigkeit in deutschen Großstädten während der Urbanisierung," *GuG* 15 (1989), 5–33.
[9] Hans-Walter Schmuhl, *Arbeitsmarktpolitik und Arbeitsverwaltung in Deutschland 1871–2002. Zwischen Fürsorge, Hoheit und Markt* (Bundesanstalt für Arbeit, 2003), 3.

constant movement of the working classes made it far more difficult for relief officials to maintain that knowledge of and contact with the poor on which their vision of individualized personal help was predicated.[10]

It should not be surprising, therefore, that in the 1870s and 1880s the problem of assistance for the jobless was defined as much by their mobility as by their material need. But while increased geographical mobility may have been a social reality, the construction of vagrancy and homelessness as distinct social problems was a product of the social imagination of the middle classes.[11] Railroads, compulsory schooling, and universal conscription were powerful engines of social modernization and national unification. But they also had a darker side, and the absence of a fixed abode was regarded as a reflection of the absence of all those character traits that held society together.[12] The problems of joblessness and homelessness were, however, seen in distinctly gendered terms. Women who lacked a place to live and a regular income from a respectable source were invariably suspected of "sexual immorality" and prostitution. Although this was an important field for the church-based morality movement, to the extent that prostitution and the war on venereal disease were regarded as matters for the police and health officials, this question lies beyond the scope of this study.[13] By contrast, vagrancy was primarily regarded as the negation of breadwinning, labor and familial responsibility, which collectively represented the core of masculine identity. The combined problem of male joblessness and homelessness remained one of the central

---

[10] At least this is how the problem was seen by contemporaries. For an alternative reading that emphasizes the homogeneity of urban neighborhoods and the diverse mechanisms of social control prevailing therein, see Jean-Paul Burdy, "Social Control and Forms of Working-Class Sociability in French Industrial Towns between the Mid-Nineteenth and the Mid-Twentieth Centuries," in Clive Emsley et al., eds., *Social Control in Europe, 1800–2000* (Ohio State University Press, 2004), 25–69, especially 43ff.

[11] Eugene Weber, *Peasants into Frenchmen. The Modernization of Rural France* (Stanford University Press, 1979); Matthew Matsuda, *The Memory of the Modern* (Oxford University Press, 1996), 121–41; Bettina Hitzer, *Im Netz der Liebe. Die protestantische Kirche und ihre Zuwanderer in der Metropole Berlin (1849–1914)* (Böhlau, 2006); and Jürgen Scheffler, "'Weltstadt' und 'Unterwelt': Urbanisierung, Armenpolitik und Obdachlosigkeit in Berlin 1871–1914," *Internationale Wissenschaftliche Korrespondenz zur Geschichte der deutschen Arbeiterbewegung* 26 (1990), 158–81. Zimmermann, *Arbeitslosigkeit in Deutschland*, warns against seeing the development of new policies for the jobless as a direct response to socioeconomic change, while Jean-François Wagniart, *Le vagabond à la fin due XIXe siècle* (Paris, 1999), tries to close this gap between representation and reality by linking the intensification of the nineteenth-century war on vagrancy in France to the consolidation of power by the republicans.

[12] Matsuda, *The Memory of the Modern*, 125–6.

[13] On this movement and their institutions for the reclamation of fallen or endangered girls and women, see Isabell Lisberg-Haag, "Die Unzucht – das Grab der Völker". *Die evangelische Sittlichkeitsbewegung und die "sexuelle Moderne" 1870–1918* (Hamburg, 2002); Hitzer, *Im Netz der Liebe*, 355ff.; and Edward Ross Dickinson, "The Men's Christian Morality Movement in Germany, 1880–1914: Some Reflections on Politics, Sex, and Sexual Politics," *JMH* 75 (2003), 59–110. For the public health dimension of the issue, see Lutz Sauerteig, *Krankheit, Sexualität, Gesellschaft. Geschlechtskrankheiten und Gesundheitspolitik in Deutschland im 19. und frühen 20. Jahrhundert* (Steiner, 1999).

concerns of relief officials until World War I, while Protestant and Catholic charities created a network of railroad missions, shelters, and urban missions to compensate for the absence of those close-knit communities and paternalistic social institutions that they saw as the bulwark of traditional morality in the countryside.

This ambivalence toward mobility and the modernization of the countryside surfaced in every debate over the relief residence system, whose opponents argued that only a permanent *Heimat* could provide a moral anchor and serve as an effective agency of social control in an increasingly mobile and impersonal world. The debate over "migrant relief" (*Wandererfürsorge*) – the name given to those programs intended to assist and police the migrant poor in their quest for work and respectability – was also shaped by a culturally inflected view of vagrancy that was projected onto this segment of the population with an urgency that undoubtedly reveals as much about the anxieties of middle-class observers as the real criminality and immorality of this population. As one commentator wondered out loud in 1879, would effective measures to combat vagrancy have to wait "until the troops of idlers on the nation's roads take up with the army of socialist workers when these put down their work in order to fall upon proper citizens and plunder them?"[14]

At the end of the 1870s, it was estimated that some 400,000 persons, or 1% of the population, were living on the road. For relief officials the problem was to devise mechanisms for helping those who were willing to work find employment, while sheltering the impotent poor and disciplining the professional beggars, vagrants (*Landstreicher*), idlers, and criminals who were believed to make up about half of this mobile population. At least part of the blame had to be placed on the organization of assistance itself. The Relief Residence Law required local authorities to assist the migrant poor in the locale where they first became needy and permitted them to then demand reimbursement from the relief residence of the individual. In the best of cases, it was time consuming to determine a person's relief residence and seek reimbursement, and it was well-nigh impossible if the person did not have the necessary identification papers or wished to conceal parts of his past, such as a long record of public assistance or convictions for vagrancy or other offenses. As a result, local relief officials had a powerful financial incentive simply to shelter these people for the night and then send them on their way as quickly as possible.[15]

But what may have been rational for individual towns was irrational at the national level. Forced back onto the roads without any means of subsistence, the migrant poor had no alternative but to beg, and there was a widespread concern that relief policies were unintentionally promoting vagrancy. Gotha senator Albert Doell, who played an important role in founding the German Association for Poor Relief and Charity, likened this growing stream of

---

[14] Cited in Lisgret Militzer-Schwenger, *Armenerziehung durch Arbeit* (Tübingen, 1979), 38.
[15] For one account of this "public gift" (*Stadtgeschenk*) in the 1880s, see Hans-Peter Jans, *Sozialpolitik und Wohlfahrtspflege in Ulm 1870–1930* (Stadtarchiv Ulm, 1994), 81ff.

migrants to rising floodwaters that were lapping at the foundations of society. Continual begging, he argued, made people forget how degrading it was to depend on others, while the rootlessness of life on the road ate away at all of the social virtues. The migrant poor had to learn, he insisted, that "every legal occupation is more honorable than begging."[16] This policy of malign neglect was also creating both security problems and moral quandaries for the home-owning classes. In the absence of a donor of last resort, it was difficult to turn beggars away. But this was precisely what current poor law practice, obsessed as it was with the fear of pauperizing the able-bodied, was not providing, and so these problems continued to feed off one another.

This war on vagrancy was the main topic at the first meetings of the German Association for Poor Relief and Charity. The members of the association proposed a wide variety of measures designed to combat the epiphenomena of this restructuring of production and the labor market, including the formation of a nationwide network of anti-begging associations, the founding of labor exchanges, and repressive measures (the introduction of labor books and the revocation of freedom of movement) to be directed against hard-core vagrants.[17] The problem was that it was difficult enough for relief authorities to determine the worthiness of local poor, and it was impossible to do so for workers on the move in search of work.[18] The obvious solution was to institute some kind of work test, and contemporary thinking quickly coalesced around the idea of establishing voluntary associations to provide the migrant poor with assistance through work as they moved from city to city. The advocates of this approach hoped that such programs would inoculate respectable workers against the demoralizing effects of begging while enabling authorities to identify professional beggars and treat them accordingly.[19]

This was the rationale underlying the itinerant work stations (*Wanderarbeitsstätten*), which were the most important means of assisting the migrant poor from the early 1880s through the early 1900s. Although the first stations had been founded in Württemberg in the 1870s, they spread rapidly from the early 1880s through the end of the decade as they took root in western Prussia. The leading figure in the field of migrant relief was the Westphalian noble

---

[16] Albert Doell, *Die Reform der Armenpflege. Untersuchungen über die Handhabung der Unterstützungsgesetze und Vorschläge zu einer Organisation der amtlichen und der freiwilligen Armenpflege. Eine Denkschrift* (Bremen, 1880), 6–7, 29f. and 40f. in LAB A Rep 003, Nr. 634.

[17] *Stenographischer Bericht über die Verhandlungen am 7. und 8. Oktober 1882* and the printed reports in LAB A Rep 003, Nr. 634, as well as the published accounts of the conference in Franz Adickes, "Der erste deutsche Armenpfleger-Kongreß und die brennenden Fragen des Armenwesens," *Schmollers Jahrbuch für Gesetzgebung, Verwaltung und Volkswirtschaft* 6 (1882), 211–67, especially 261ff., and Adickes, "Die Verhandlungen von 1882 und die ferneren Aufgaben des deutschen Vereins für Armenpflege und Wohltätigkeit," *Schmollers Jahrbuch* 7 (1883), 141–87.

[18] Friedrich von Reitzenstein, *Ueber Beschäftigung arbeitsloser Armer und Arbeitsnachweis als Mittel vorbeugender Armenpflege*, SDV, 4 (1887), 45ff.

[19] Reitzenstein, *Ueber Beschäftigung arbeitsloser Armer*, SDV, 4 (1887), 1ff.

Friedrich von Bodelschwingh, and through Bodelschwingh the work of the stations, as well as that of the wayfarers' inns and labor colonies that came to be closely associated with them, was deeply influenced by the Lutheran social conservatism described in Chapter 3. The catch was that this conservative worldview limited the ability of the station advocates to understand either the changing nature of joblessness or the changing position of the working classes in the social order. As a result, although the stations were able to palliate some of the worst problems faced by the migrant poor, the very beliefs that accounted for their original popularity also led to their eventual marginalization.[20]

Bodelschwingh was sensitive to the contradictions of a poor relief system that denied assistance to the able-bodied jobless but then arrested them for vagrancy, and he regarded the offer of work in exchange for assistance as the only way to help the poor without pauperizing them.[21] However, he was primarily concerned with the spiritual and material needs of this itinerant population and the dangers that they posed to society, rather than with their integration into the labor market. Despite his frequent invocation of the "dear brothers of the highway" as the occasion for and object of Christian charity, Bodelschwingh tended to see homeless migrants as morally damaged individuals who were the authors of their own misfortune. As he wrote in 1887, "it should also be noted that only in the most seldom cases does it happen that someone finds himself in a situation where he is without means and work without himself being responsible for this state of affairs. Here in Germany, every young person, almost without exception, is placed in a proper job when he leaves school, and if he does as he is supposed to do in this job, then he gets along and does not need to suffer need."[22] In turn, life on the road bred dissipation because it separated the individual from those institutions of authority that were necessary to protect man from his own worst instincts, and the purpose of the work stations was not to provide succor to vagabonds in the manner of traditional Christian charity,

---

[20] Ewald Frie, "Fürsorgepolitik zwischen Kirche und Staat. Wanderarmenhilfe in Preussen," in Wilfried Loth and Jochen-Christoph Kaiser, eds., *Soziale Reform im Kaiserreich. Protestantismus, Katholizismus und Sozialpolitik* (Kohlhammer, 1997), 114–27; Frie, *Wohlfahrtsstaat und Provinz. Fürsorgepolitik des Provinzialverbandes Westfalen und des Landes Sachsen, 1880–1930* (Schöningh, 1993), 26ff.; Jürgen Scheffler, "Die Gründungsjahre 1883–1913," in Zentralverband Deutscher Arbeiterkolonien, ed., *"Arbeit statt Almosen". 100 Jahre Hilfe für obdachlose Wanderarme 1884–1984* (Verlag Soziale Hilfe, 1984), 23–35; Scheffler, ed., *Bürger und Bettler. Materialien und Dokumente zur Geschichte der Nichtseßhaftenhilfe in der Diakonie, Bd. I: 1854–1954. Vom Herbergswesen für wandernde Handwerksgesellen zur Nichtseßhaftenhilfe* (Bielefeld, 1987); Karl Heinrich Pohl, *Zwischen Protestantischer Ethik, Unternehmerinteresse und organisierter Arbeiterbewegung. Zur Geschichte der Arbeitsvermittlung in Bielefeld vom 1887 bis 1914* (Stadtarchiv Bielefeld, 1991); and Emil Münsterberg and Alexander Elster, "Wanderarbeiterstätten," in Elster, ed., *Handwörterbuch der Staatswissenschaften*, 3. Aufl. (1909/11), VIII:561–71.

[21] Friedrich von Bodelschwingh, *Vorschläge zur Vereinigung aller deutsche Arbeiter-Kolonien* (Bielefeld, 1883), 7, 5, 22–3, 16, 45, 53, 60, 65.

[22] Bodelschwingh, "Natural-Verpflegungsstationen," *Die Arbeiter-Kolonie* 4 (1887), 238–42, cited in Pohl, *Zwischen protestantischer Ethik*, 59.

FIGURE 1. Von Bodelschwingh at the Bethel bei Bielefeld workstation.

but rather – in a more modern, but still conservative, manner – to keep the migrant poor from losing their moral center and falling irreparably into a life of vagrancy, idleness, vice, and crime.

These stations were most often established by voluntary associations (primarily Protestant) in conjunction with municipal, provincial, and state government along the routes most frequently used by workers traveling in search of employment, and they enjoyed substantial popularity, at least in government circles and among relief officials and charity workers. By 1890, 1,957 stations had been founded, and in 1892 the existing stations came together to found a national association, the Gesamt-Verband Deutscher Verpflegungsstationen.[23]

The movement of the migrant poor between these stations, which were generally located two to three hours apart by foot, was regulated by a system of passes. These passes were issued by the stations to attest – to both the police and the next station along the road – that the bearer was in fact an orderly wanderer. Migrant workers had to break stones, chop wood, or perform some other kind of labor (see Figure 1) in the morning to pay for the previous night's food and lodging (hence the alternative denomination of these stations as "in-kind relief stations" [*Natural-Verpflegungsstationen*]), and they were then expected to tramp on to the next station in the afternoon. Their departure time and the next station along their route were stamped in their passes, and they had to arrive in a timely manner. While the stations provided lodging only to the completely destitute, they were closely associated with a network of

---

[23] "Vergleichende Statistik der Verpflegungsstationen in Deutschland 1890 und 1896," BA R1501, Nr. 101331.

wayfarers' inns (*Herberge zur Heimat*) that were also sponsored by charitably minded Protestant notables. But to ensure that the search for work did not become an excuse for malingering, station patrons were allowed to look for work only at the station itself or at labor exchanges that were associated with the stations. They could look for work only in the town with a special "looking around pass." And there could not be any unexplained gaps in their itinerary – as verified by the stamps that had to be placed in their passes at every station as evidence that they had satisfactorily performed the required work and otherwise complied with the station rules.[24]

The station associations regarded authority and discipline as the essence of charity toward their clientele, and they hoped that this continuous surveillance and discipline would keep these men (for the clientele of these stations was predominantly male) on the straight and narrow road, both literally and figuratively. People who failed to follow the prescribed routes or the station rules were subject to arrest since the permanent offer of work at the stations meant that idlers could no longer get off the hook by telling the police that they had tried to find work, but had not been successful. Moreover, anyone who applied to the stations for assistance, but who refused to accept the work they offered, could automatically be branded as a vagrant. As Bodelschwingh explained, "whoever registers at the station, but does not take a job that is offered to him, this person belongs to the police. He is without means; otherwise he is not allowed to avail himself of the stations. But nor will he take a job in order to earn money. Consequently, he is a vagrant (*Landstreicher*), and vagrants belong in a penal workhouse (*Korrektionshaus*)."[25]

The stations and lodges were flanked by another innovative social technology that is indelibly linked with Bodelschwingh's name: labor colonies.[26] The first labor colony in Germany was Wilhelmsdorf, which was founded by Bodelschwingh in 1882. By 1885, thirteen labor colonies had been founded, and by 1914 the number had grown to thirty-six with space for approximately 5,000 persons. Although there were a few Catholic colonies, this was by and large a Protestant undertaking.[27] Labor colonies were originally intended to serve able-bodied workers who had lost their jobs through no fault of their

---

[24] See the map of the Hanover stations and wander routes and the *Wanderordnung* of the Deutscher Herbergsverein, as well as the house rules for the Herberge zur Heimat, in ADW, BP 1907.

[25] Bodelschwingh, "Natural-Verpflegungsstationen," cited in Pohl, *Zwischen protestantischer Ethik*, 62.

[26] On German labor colonies, see Warren Rosenblum, *Beyond Prison Gates: Punishment and Welfare in Germany 1850–1933* (University of North Carolina Press, 2008). For contemporary accounts, see Georg Berthold, *Die Entwicklung der deutschen Arbeiterkolonien*, SDV, 3 (1887); Berthold, "Die Verhandlungen des deutschen Vereins," *Schmollers Jahrbuch* 8 (1884), 497–522; and Wilson and Victor W. Carlile, *The Continental Outcast. Land Colonies and Poor Law Relief* (London, 1906).

[27] Jürgen Scheffler, "Die Gründungsjahre 1883–1913," esp. 26, 28. In 1884 the Centralvorstand Deutscher Arbeiterkolonien was founded, and there was a personal union among the Centralvorstand, the Gesamt-Verband Deutscher Verpflegungstationen, and the Deutscher Herbergsverein, which had been founded in 1886 by the lodges, in the person of Karl Mörchen, a long-time

own. However, as the labor market improved across the 1880s and 1890s, they became a refuge for the unemployable. This group included the long-term unemployed, who had grown unaccustomed to regular work; persons who were too weak, sick, old, or psychologically unstable to completely support themselves, but who were not so incapable of work that they qualified for poor relief; habitual drinkers and others who had led a dissipated life, but who were hoping to change their ways; and former convicts and workhouse inmates, who hoped to prove that they were capable of performing an honest day's work.[28] The worker colonies represented a last opportunity for the unemployable to reestablish their membership in the community before being banished to the jail or the workhouse, and for many quasi-voluntary entry into a labor colony was a way of avoiding involuntary confinement in the latter, where the conditions were somewhat harsher.[29] At the end of the century this desire to distinguish those who could be reclaimed for society from the hopelessly incorrigible and protect society from the latter provided the inspiration for imperialist schemes to expand Germany's world power by deporting asocials to the overseas colonies.[30]

People often arrived at the colonies wearing little more than vermin-infested rags, and such persons often despaired of finding work because, after all, who would want to hire such a person? Entry into the labor colonies was strictly voluntary because voluntary submission to the strict house rules and the rigorous regime of outdoor work was regarded as the precondition for their reeducation. But the colony associations expected colonists to remain for at least three months because they felt that this was the minimum amount of time necessary to effect any enduring change in their character and work habits. During their stay, colonists performed hard agricultural labor, often reclaiming land that could then be planted to help offset the cost of the colony, and a goodly portion of their earnings during their stay frequently went to paying for presentable clothing that symbolized both the spiritual renewal of the colonists and their social reintegration.[31]

Opinion was divided concerning the effectiveness of the stations, inns, and colonies in combating vagrancy and its associated ills.[32] However, by the

---

follower of Bodelschwingh, who served as secretary of all three organizations. Mörchen was also editor of their common publication *Die Arbeiter-Kolonie* (from 1897 *Der Wanderer*).

[28] See the letter from the Central-Vorstand deutscher Arbeiter-Kolonien (February 29, 1904), BA R1501, Nr. 101332.

[29] Hitzer, *Im Netze der Liebe*, 344–53.

[30] Sebastian Conrad, "'Eingeborenenpolitik' in Kolonie und Metropole. 'Erziehung zur Arbeit' in Ostafrika und Ostwestfalen," in Sebastian Conrad and Jürgen Osterhammel, eds., *Das Kaiserreich transnational* (Vandenhoeck & Ruprecht, 2004), 107–28, and Rosenblum, *Beyond Prison Gates*.

[31] The masthead of *Die Arbeiter-Kolonie* showed an unkempt man in tattered clothing entering on one side and exiting on the other with a much more respectable appearance. See Scheffler, "Die Gründungsjahre 1883–1913."

[32] For a testimonial to their effectiveness, see Bodelschwingh, *Vorschläge*, 23ff. The stations tried to rebut the charge that they were actually promoting vagrancy by showing how many migrants they were saving from unjust punishment and how much money they were saving

mid-1890s the station movement found itself in a serious crisis. During the economic downturn of the early 1890s, there had been a huge increase in the number of people using the stations. While most stations were operated by voluntary associations with subsidies from municipal government, these remained voluntary expenditures, and, as the number of station visitors continued to rise, many communities decided that they could not afford the cost of maintaining their stations. This decision forced neighboring communities to either shoulder a disproportionate share of the total regional cost of supporting the migrant poor or close their own stations. The result was a downward spiral that by 1898 had led to the closure of over eight hundred stations, or more than 40% of the number that had been in operation at the beginning of the decade.[33]

The solution to this dilemma seemed to lie in the creation of a statewide network of publicly funded stations, and in 1895 the three major migrant relief associations tried to persuade the Prussian legislature to adopt such legislation. However, the proposed law failed to garner the necessary support for a number of reasons. In the agrarian provinces of the Prussian East, landowners feared that the spread of the stations would only further aggravate the shortage of agricultural workers; there was a diffuse but widespread suspicion that, like the relief residence system, the stations actually encouraged vagrancy; and the Landtag complained that the proposed legislation did not ensure close collaboration between the stations and labor exchanges. The timing of this legislative push was also inauspicious. The law came up for consideration at the same time that the Reich government was retreating from the social policy activism of the New Course, and, after the resignation of Interior Minister Eulenberg, who had been chair of the station association, there was little official support for such legislation.[34]

The 1895 proposal marked the beginning, rather than the end, of the legislative history of migrant relief. In 1905, Bodelschwingh was elected to the Prussian Landtag, where he campaigned for migrant relief legislation, and in 1907 the body passed a law that permitted provincial governments to establish station networks. However, this proved to be a problematic victory as only two provinces actually created work stations along the lines envisioned by the

---

the nation in comparison with the cost of confining vagrants. See, for example, the *Protokoll der Versammlung des Gesamtverbandes deutscher Verpflegungsstationen zu Berlin am 13. November 1907*, BA R1501, Nr. 10133, 14. On the other hand, the influential criminologist Robert von Hippel argued that only one-fourth of the colonists went directly to either a job or their families, and he suggested that the colonies produced no demonstrable benefit for the remainder. See Hippel, *Zur Vagabundenfrage* (Berlin, 1902), 22–4, and *Vierzehnten Bericht des Vereins für die Berliner Arbeiter-Kolonie für das Jahre 1899*, 3f., BA R1501 Nr. 101332. However, Hippel also noted that the large increase in the number of people using the stations from year to year reflected a real increase in need, rather than an increase in immorality, and he concluded that, for these people, the stations served a real need. *Zur Vagabundenfrage*, 18–19.

[33] "Vergleichende Statistik der Verpflegungsstationen in Deutschland 1890 und 1896," BA R1501, Nr. 101331, and Hippel, *Zur Vagabundenfrage*, 16–17, which reports figures for 1898.

[34] Frie, "Fürsorgepolitik zwischen Kirche und Staat."

law. By 1913, though, the Reich government had decided that the time was ripe for the national regulation of migrant relief. What had undermined the 1907 Prussian station law was the lack of a consensus as to whether the primary purpose of migrant relief programs should be to sustain the work ethic of the jobless or to help them find work.[35] The 1913 draft law clearly gave labor market integration priority over moral reclamation, and it paralleled broader social reform trends in stipulating that migrant relief for those persons who were deemed to be legitimately in search of work represented a field of positive social policy that was to be entirely separate from the deterrent, disciplinary poor relief system (as long as the assistance provided by the stations and colonies did not exceed the value of the labor performed).[36]

Consideration of this draft was cut short by the war, which also obviated, at least temporarily, the need for migrant relief, and by the time the dust had settled after the war migrant relief had become a much more marginal undertaking. The stations insisted that the provision of any kind of assistance without a work test simply encouraged idleness and dependency. However, the understanding of joblessness and homelessness that underlay their reasoning could not easily be reconciled with either the concept of involuntary unemployment or the principles of unemployment insurance, which considered benefits to be a form of collective self-insurance by thrifty, providential, and industrious workers. The effect was to sever the connection between the stations and the labor market and narrow their target population to the unemployable homeless, who could be safely left to the ministrations of the church charities. And if migrant relief had been called into question from the left by the expansion of the Weimar welfare state, after 1933 the stations were blindsided from the right by the Nazis, who took a much harsher line toward this particular manifestation of asociality.[37]

Relief officials and police also had to deal with those persons who were unable or unwilling to adapt to the routine of the stations, much less that of the labor market and the other institutions of bourgeois society. These were people who begged not out of need, but rather out of a positive aversion to work (*Arbeitsscheu*) or the burdens of family life. They were also the obvious candidates for the workhouse and the prison.

Workhouses played a very different role in Germany than they did in England. In England, workhouses were, at least in theory, the primary means of assisting the poor. In Germany, by contrast, workhouses had ceased in the early 1800s to serve as institutions of paternalistic social governance or as

---

[35] Frie, "Fürsorgepolitik zwischen Kirche und Staat."
[36] See the May 1913 draft and the attached Erläuterungsbericht in BA R1501 101335, Bl. 321ff.
[37] For the legislative history of migrant relief in the 1920s, see BA R1501 101337. On Nazi policies toward migrants and the homeless, see Wolfgang Ayaß, "Vagrants and Beggars in Hitler's Reich," in Richard J. Evans, ed., *The German Underworld. Deviants and Outcasts in German History* (London, 1988), 210–37, and Ayaß, *"Asoziale" im Nationalsozialismus* (Stuttgart, 1995).

mechanisms for providing voluntary work to the needy and had instead been transformed into penal institutions. The 1871 Imperial Criminal Code stipulated that persons who had been convicted of a number of socially harmful misdemeanors, such as vagrancy, prostitution, or the failure to provide because of gambling, drink, or aversion to work, could be jailed for between one day and six weeks. However, at the time of sentencing, judges were also permitted to order that, once these persons had completed their sentences, they be transferred to the police, who had the discretionary authority to detain the person for "supplemental corrective detention" (korrektionelle Nachhaft) in a workhouse for up to two years.[38] The number of persons convicted of vagrancy and begging spiked at the end of the 1870s as the economic downturn deepened before returning to its previous level in the mid-1880s, and it was unemployed artisans, rather than agricultural laborers or factory workers, who made up the majority of those convicted of begging and vagrancy.[39]

Public officials, however, were as concerned about the large number of people whom they feared were slipping through cracks in the system as they were about the number of persons actually convicted of vagrancy.[40] The inconsistent application of vagrancy laws and the ineffectiveness of their administration was regarded as such an urgent problem because they undermined the deterrent effect of this legislation and nullified the potential rehabilitative function of the workhouse. There were no firm rules concerning when vagrants were to be turned over to the police or the circumstances under which supplemental correctional custody was to be imposed, and local judges often lacked accurate information on the personal history and circumstances of the people brought before them by the police. These problems fueled the assumption, which was widely shared among relief officials, that many persons who had been forced to beg out of genuine need were being unfairly sentenced to extended periods in the workhouse, while an equally large number of incorrigible vagrants were escaping with relatively short jail sentences of questionable efficacy. Two-thirds of the 11–12,000 persons who were sentenced annually to these institutions had already served three or more workhouse sentences,[41] and officials readily

---

[38] The authoritative contemporary account is Robert von Hippel, *Die strafrechtliche Bekämpfung von Bettel, Landstreicherei und Arbeitsscheu* (Berlin, 1895), and the most useful modern work is Wolfgang Ayaß, *Das Arbeitshaus Breitenau. Bettler, Landstreicher, Prostituierte, Zuhälter und Fürsorgeempfänger in der Korrektions- und Landarmenanstalt Breitenau (1874–1949)* (Kassel, 1992). There was no clear criterion for distinguishing between misdemeanor vagrancy (*Landstreichen*) and begging (*Betteln*); legally, the only difference was that, in contrast to vagrants, beggars could be transferred to the police for possible workhouse detention only if they had already been convicted of begging during the previous three years.

[39] Hippel, *Die strafrechtliche Bekämpfung*, 189. The original data for these published numbers can be found in BA R1501 Nr. 101314. See Jans, *Sozialpolitik und Wohlfahrtspflege in Ulm*, 88–90, for the occupational makeup of those convicted of vagrancy.

[40] Hippel, *Die strafrechtliche Bekämpfung*, 207, 254, 130n.

[41] Hippel, *Die strafrechtliche Bekämpfung*, 132–3, 270–5.

admitted that the workhouses were much more effective in persuading potential inmates to mend their ways than they were in bettering the persons actually confined there.[42]

But workhouse administrators and poor relief officials nevertheless complained that, because of the imperfect information available to them, judges were unwilling to transfer convicted vagrants to the police or to impose workhouse sentences until the persons who came before them had become hardened and irreclaimable vagrants. Even in those cases where such persons were sent to the workhouse, the sentences imposed on people with long histories of vagrancy and jail time would often be too short to bring about any sustained improvement in their character. Although the government sought at the end of the 1880s to make the workhouse into a more effective deterrent by tightening up on sentencing guidelines, the first years of the twentieth century saw new departures in this domain that pointed beyond classical liberalism and toward more socialized forms of jurisprudence and the preventive social welfare programs that they made possible.[43]

Relief officials, criminologists, and social workers were all looking for ways to solve two related problems. On the one hand, they had no effective way to get hold of vagrants and endangered girls before they became confirmed in their gender-specific antisocial proclivities. On the other hand, they felt that their work was undermined by the short sentences imposed by procedurally-minded judges, and they needed to find a way to ensure that sentences were long enough to effect some positive change in the character of the persons confined in the workhouse. In their eyes, the solution was for them to be given the authority to administratively detain individuals who may not have (yet) committed a punishable offense, but whose behavior made them into a chronic danger to themselves and to society, rather than having to rely on the more uncertain recourse to the courts to convict them for violating §§361/362 of the Criminal Code. Confirmed vagrants were one obvious target for such measures, as were the work-shy and "neglectful breadwinners" (*säumige Nährpflichtige*), that is, men who deserted their families or squandered their earnings on drink.[44] The same arguments were deployed by the advocates of the new field of preventive welfare known as *Gefährdetenfürsorge* (i.e., welfare for the "endangered"), which represented a more modern approach to the problem of juvenile female

---

[42] Sabine Lippuner, *Bessern und Verwahren. Die Praxis der administrativen Versorgung von "Liederlichen" und "Arbeitsscheuen" in der thurgauischen Zwangsarbeitsanstalt Kalchrain* (Historischer Verein des Kantons Thurgau, 2005).

[43] Puttkamer to Bötticher (March 10, 1886), BA R1501, Nr. 101320, and Hippel, *Die strafrechtliche Bekämpfung*, 70ff.

[44] Otto Lohse and Hans Samter, *Zwangsmaßregeln gegen Arbeitsscheue und gegen säumige Nährpflichtige*, SDV, 88 (1909); *Stenographischer Bericht über die Verhandlungen*, SDV, 90 (1909), 8–61; Hermann Luppe, "Arbeitshaus," in Ludwig Elster et al., eds., *Handwörterbuch der Staatswissenschaften* (1923), I:742–6; and the materials on the 1912 Prussian *Arbeitsscheuengesetz* in LAB A Rep. 003–01, Nr. 206.

sexual immorality.⁴⁵ Such an approach was obviously incompatible with liberal procedural safeguards of individual liberty. However, the proponents of these new preventive strategies sought to justify their proposals by arguing that such "preventive detention" (*Verwahrung* or *Bewahrung*) could not be considered a violation of individual freedom because such persons were already so enslaved to their impulses that they could not, in the strict sense of the term, be considered free and responsible subjects endowed with such rights.⁴⁶ It proved to be much easier to justify such policies with regard to delinquent children (who will be the focus of Chapter 9) than asocial adults, and the debate over the legitimacy of preventive detention for these two marginal groups continued through the Weimar Republic.⁴⁷

From the Margins to the Center: The War on Labor Market Risk

The shift from the deterrence of pauperism and idleness to the management of risk was predicated on several developments, including (1) the generalization of wage labor; (2) the popular acceptance of the conceptual distinction between the regularly employed, responsible "worker" and those casual workers, slackers, and unemployables who deviated from this norm; and (3) the formulation – based on the representation of the economy and the labor market as collective social facts – of an alternative explanatory schema that located the causes of joblessness in the structure and rhythms of the industrial economy, rather than in the character of the individual.⁴⁸ In Germany the economic downturn of 1892/4 seems to have marked a turning point in this process. As Seyffardt, the chair of the German Association for Poor Relief and Charity, later wrote with reference to the downturn of the early 1890s, "poor relief has never witnessed a period in which moral influence through reference to assiduousness, industriousness and self-help had so little impact as this time."⁴⁹ The first major scientific gathering in Germany devoted to unemployment and labor exchanges was held in 1893.⁵⁰ In contrast to the figure of the pauper,

---

⁴⁵ For early developments in the field of *Gefährdetenfürsorge*, see Andreas Wollasch, *Der Katholische Fürsorgeverein für Mädchen, Frauen und Kinder (1899–1945)* (Lambertus, 1991), and Heike Schmidt, *Gefährliche und gefährdete Mädchen. Weibliche Devianz und die Anfänge der Zwangs- und Fürsorgeerziehung* (Leske & Budrich, 2002).

⁴⁶ As Hippel explained, the transgressions of the women to be targeted by such measures were attributable to their "craving for pleasure and above all their unrestrainable propensity toward sexual excesses," *Die strafrechtliche Bekämpfung*, 266. See the account of this turn in Lippuner, *Bessern und Verwahren*, 263ff.

⁴⁷ Matthias Willing, *Das Bewahrungsgesetz (1918–1967). Eine rechtshistorische Studie zur Geschichte der deutschen Fürsorge* (Tübingen, 2003), and Young-sun Hong, *Welfare, Modernity and the Weimar State, 1919–1933* (Princeton University Press, 1998), 243ff.

⁴⁸ See the works of Zimmermann and Topalev cited earlier.

⁴⁹ Seyffardt, *Erinnerungen* (Leipzig, 1900), 440–1.

⁵⁰ *Arbeitslosigkeit und Arbeitsvermittlung in Industrie- und Handelsstädten. Bericht über den am 8. und 9. Oktober 1893 vom Freien Deutschen Hochstift in Frankfurt a.M. veranstalteten sozialen Kongreß* (Berlin, 1894).

which had dominated social discourse in the 1840s, in the 1890s it was much more difficult to morally disqualify skilled workers with regular work histories who were suffering from industry-wide joblessness and whose political voice had strengthened substantially since the lapsing of the Anti-Socialist law in 1890. By the first years of the new century, public perception of the nature of the problem had already changed to such an extent that during the 1901/2 downturn joblessness was widely theorized as a problem of "unemployment," and the economic causes of unemployment, social policies to combat it, and the possibility of insuring against it were the topic of the annual conference of every major social reform and economic interest group held in 1902.

The history of labor exchanges and unemployment insurance has already been told by others, and there is little to be gained by repeating these stories in any detail, especially since developments in these areas before 1914 represent the prelude to a story that really belongs to the Weimar years. Therefore, I would like to limit myself to a few brief comments on how exchanges and insurance fit into the story being told here.

First, the idea of social insurance was predicated on the belief that industry, thrift, discipline, and family responsibility on the part of the respectable male worker – all of the key attributes of the liberal individual – could be stimulated as much by the promise of social security as by the threat of destitution, hunger, and dishonor. Unemployment insurance, which promised to reward industrious and thrifty behavior with security against the risk of involuntary joblessness through the horizontal redistribution of the wealth created by these very behaviors, seemed to many to hold the key to mitigating the social consequences of joblessness in a way that would strengthen personal responsibility and avoid divisive redistributive schemes. However, such incentives were always only conditional. They were invariably coupled with disincentives and the threat of disciplinary sanctions that were designed to elicit from the more uneconomical segments of the population (casual laborers, idlers, etc.) those desired behaviors that could not be produced through positive incentives alone. In other words, the expansion of social rights through social insurance and preventive social welfare had to be coupled with both the threat of sanctions and appropriate technologies (deterrent poor relief, confinement in labor colonies, etc.) for controlling, reeducating, and, at the extreme, excluding those individuals who engaged in asocial or antisocial activities.[51]

Labor exchanges, which began to emerge in the early 1890s as the most important tool for assisting able-bodied workers who found themselves without work, and the first experiments with unemployment insurance were as much an evolution out of traditional poor relief and charity as they were a rejection of their underlying principles. Their purpose was less to rationalize the relief of the poor than to prevent poverty. As such, they were predicated on the assumption that the root of the problem was to be found less in individual character than in

---

[51] See especially Squires, *Anti-Social Policy*.

the condition of the labor market. Although the first labor exchanges date back to mid-century, these early exchanges were associated with either municipal poor relief or charity organizations; employers were reluctant to hire persons referred by these exchanges because they suspected that anyone who had to rely on the assistance of municipal officials had to be of limited fitness; and workers were correspondingly reluctant to avail themselves of these services. Ultimately, the expanding scope of labor exchanges and rising cost of operating them overtaxed the capacities of exchanges operated by voluntary associations, and most of them were either dissolved or transformed into municipal labor exchanges, which were themselves increasingly separated from municipal poor relief and represented as social policy programs designed to assist respectable, independent workers.[52]

The later 1890s and early 1900s were a period of intensified industrial conflict, and labor exchanges were quickly drawn into this vortex because employers and unions both saw them as a vital means of controlling the labor supply and thus gaining (or losing) advantage in their struggle, depending on which end of the stick they were left holding. Ultimately, a compromise solution would be found in the form of municipal parity exchanges in which workers and employers were equally represented, and in some cities these municipal labor exchanges were combined with labor arbitration courts to form the first municipal labor offices.[53] However, this model of parity labor exchanges gained acceptance much more rapidly in southern Germany than it did in the industrial areas of Prussia and Saxony, where economic structures and the balance of political forces often conspired to block such initiatives,[54] and their success in the south depended both on the political support of the relevant parties and on their ability to attack at least some of the roots of unemployment.[55]

---

[52] On the history of labor exchanges in Germany, see Schmuhl, *Arbeitsmarktpolitik*, and Anselm Faust, *Arbeitsmarktpolitik im Deutschen Kaiserreich. Arbeitsvermittlung, Arbeitsbeschaffung und Arbeitslosenunterstützung 1890–1918* (VSWG Beiheft 79, 1986).

[53] For the early years of the labor arbitration courts, see Hans-Jörg von Berlepsch, *"Neuer Kurs" im Kaiserreich? Die Arbeiterpolitik des Freiherrn von Berlepsch 1890 bis 1896* (Bonn, 1987), 84ff., and, on the Frankfurt industrial court, Hans Kilian Weitensteiner, *Karl Flesch. Kommunale Sozialpolitik in Frankfurt am Main* (Frankfurt, 1976), 109ff., and Ralf Roth, *Gewerkschaftskartell und Sozialpolitik in Frankfurt am Main* (Studien zur Frankfurter Geschichte, Bd. 31, 1991). The other municipal social institution that eventually flowed into the labor offices were the legal advice centers. See Beatrix Geisel, *Klasse, Geschlecht und Recht. Vergleichende sozialhistorische Untersuchung der Rechtsberatungspraxis von Frauen- und Arbeiterbewegung (1894–1933)* (Nomos, 1997), and Holger Boettcher, *Fürsorge in Lübeck vor und nach dem Ersten Weltkrieg* (Schmidt-Römhild, 1988), 58–65.

[54] Pohl, *Zwischen protestantischer Ethik*, Paul Brandmann, *Leipzig zwischen Klassenkampf und Sozialreform. Kommunale Wohlfahrtspolitik zwischen 1890 und 1929* (Böhlau, 1995), Boettcher, *Fürsorge in Lübeck*, and Roth, *Gewerkschaftskartell und Sozialpolitik* all show how public parity exchanges were blocked, subverted, or at least challenged due to employer influence at the municipal level.

[55] Noel Whiteside, "Unemployment Revisited in Comparative Perspective: Labour Market Policy in Strasbourg and Liverpool, 1890–1914," *IRSH* 51:2 (April 2007), 45–56.

Already in the 1890s, these public parity labor exchanges began to form regional associations in order to gain a more comprehensive view of the labor market and thus facilitate the matching of labor supply and demand across broader geographical areas, and in 1898 most of the existing public labor exchanges came together to found the League of German Labor Exchanges (*Verband Deutscher Arbeitsnachweise*).[56] Unfortunately, this seemingly logical ascent from the local to the state to the national level was blocked by differences over precisely who was to be considered jobless, a question that could not be cleanly separated from the question of the policy goals of the agency that was to administer the system, and the Reich government, which had declared a halt to social policy legislation on all fronts for fear of further encouraging socialist agitation, was opposed to such a development.

The first programs that sought to provide a measure of security against the social consequences of involuntary joblessness were emergency work programs (*Notstandsarbeiten*). Since the 1880s, relief officials had experimented with emergency works to assist seasonally unemployed workers or to respond to particularly acute sectoral or conjunctural unemployment, and a number of larger cities adopted such programs in 1893/5 and again in 1900/3 and 1908/9.[57] During this period, these projects lost some of their ad hoc quality as municipal officials began to anticipate the possible need for such emergency employment and left themselves the budgetary leeway to carry out major construction projects, which were the main source of such employment, at a time and in such a way that the money spent supporting the unemployed could also serve as a productive investment in local infrastructure. And as these programs were recognized as a legitimate dimension of municipal social policy for the involuntarily jobless, they were also progressively separated from poor relief.

The decision to expand these programs reflected a variety of considerations, including a new appreciation of the structural causes of joblessness and the political advance of the Social Democrats at both the national and local levels, and George Steinmetz has argued that emergency works should be seen as a progressive measure in those cities where the Social Democrats were integrated into municipal political life on a reformist basis, but that in cities where they were excluded from local politics these programs should be viewed as a form of social control designed to diffuse the potential for popular unrest.[58] The problem was that these programs sought to tackle the problem by applying

---

[56] The official publication of the league was *Der Arbeitsmarkt*.

[57] On emergency works programs, see Paul Hartmann and Rudolf Schwander, *Die Einrichtung von Notstandsarbeiten und ihre Erfolge*, SDV, 58 (1902); Ernst Bernhard, *Die Vergebung der öffentlichen Arbeiten in Deutschland im Kampf gegen die Arbeitslosigkeit* (Berlin, 1913); Faust, *Arbeitsmarktpolitik im Deutschen Kaiserreich*, 114ff.; and Schmuhl, *Arbeitsmarktpolitik*, 41–5. Measures for combating unemployment were a main topic at the first meeting of the Städtetag in 1903. See Franz Adickes and Otto Beutler, *Die sozialen Aufgaben der deutschen Städte* (Leipzig, 1903).

[58] George Steinmetz, *Regulating the Social. The Welfare State and Local Politics in Imperial Germany* (Princeton University Press, 1993), 176–87.

pressure on the short end of the lever, that is, by combating a structural, economic problem through individualizing measures. As a result, these programs were, from the very beginning, hopelessly overburdened by contradictions and constraints. For businessmen, such programs manifested the entire panoply of evils associated with state interference in the labor market. They feared that emergency jobs programs would weaken the incentive for the unemployed to find private-sector employment and that they might be mistaken as implying the existence of a right to work. Moreover, it was extremely difficult to find work that could be carried out with few or no special skills, that could be made politically palatable by producing something of lasting value for the community, but that also did not involve illegitimate competition for private-sector workers and employers. While municipal officials generally opted for hard manual labor on road and other construction projects precisely to avoid this problem, skilled workers complained that such work was both degrading and detrimental to their skills. Although the wages paid by these programs had to be higher than relief rates if they were to provide a qualitatively better form of support for a more deserving population, they still had to be lower than the prevailing wage for unskilled labor in order to minimize the burden on local taxpayers, avoid distorting the local labor market, and keep from attracting larger numbers of unemployed from more distant areas. But despite these limitations, these programs were still expensive, and the potential sources of dissatisfaction were magnified by the fact that such jobs were offered only to a limited number of persons, primarily married men with families.

These emergency works programs, which remained a foreign element in the labor market, were at best stopgaps that can hardly be seen as precursors to later Keynesian countercyclical public spending policies. But the adoption of an unemployment insurance system required the resolution of a host of practical and political issues. Most fundamentally, in the absence of national labor market statistics, no one knew how many people were without work for which reasons, in which trades, and for how long. Moreover, the impact of any such system, and thus its political acceptability, would be influenced in important ways according to whether it would be administered by the Reich, the states, cities, unions, employers, one of the existing insurance funds, or some other agency. Seasonal and conjunctural unemployment each presented formidable actuarial problems. And then there was the challenge of designing a system that would provide appropriate benefits (however that might be defined) without making the entire system prohibitively expensive. There were also continuing concerns about the moral hazard involved in insuring against an injury that could be so easily self-incurred, and the most serious practical problem was the need to find a way to test the genuineness of an unemployed person's desire for work without subjecting the unemployed to the same kind of intrusive and degrading means testing employed by municipal poor relief. Labor exchanges, and the access to the labor market which they guaranteed, were an ideal means of keeping costs down and ferreting out malingerers. However, they did not have any direct impact on the overall number of jobs available, though their supporters hoped that the establishment of a network of exchanges would make it possible to gather reliable labor market statistics and thus generate pressure for more active labor market policies. Consequently, slow progress in the development of unemployment statistics became a major obstacle to the development of unemployment insurance.[59]

The earliest forms of insurance against the risk of joblessness were the funds established by the trade unions, and the first municipal unemployment insurance program established in Germany was set up in Cologne in 1896.[60] However, German experiments with unemployment insurance centered on the system that had been introduced in the Belgian city of Ghent in 1900, where the municipality provided subsidies to top off benefits paid by union funds, with the unions assuming responsibility for policing their own members. Moreover, while the socialist unions came to support the Ghent system because it combined the advantage of union funds with the recognition – in the form of public subsidies – of the public obligation to compensate persons disadvantaged through the operation of the economic system, many reformers who otherwise favored the idea of unemployment insurance objected that the Ghent system strengthened the socialist unions in an unfair and politically dangerous manner. And many people were simply flat-out opposed to any form of unemployment insurance. By 1914, sixteen German cities had instituted some form of unemployment insurance, while another thirty-five had considered, and rejected, the idea.[61] The 1927 Labor Exchange and Unemployment Insurance Law approached the problem in a different way and placed responsibility for assisting the jobless in the hands of parity labor offices in the hope that this arrangement would depoliticize these programs and encourage social self-government on the part of the labor market parties. Many people favored such an arrangement because they felt that a more integral connection between labor exchanges and unemployment insurance would make it possible to square the circle of deterrence and prevention.[62]

This, however, is getting ahead of the story and anticipating a development that in August 1914 would have seemed, if not exactly utopian, then certainly not one that would arrive in the near future. But the theoretical debates and municipal experiments of the prewar years do permit us to see the extent that attitudes and policies toward those without work had changed since the founding of the empire, and the progressive separation of programs to assist the jobless from the realm of poor relief and philanthropy was an accurate

---

[59] Faust, *Arbeitslosigkeit*, 46, and Schmuhl, *Arbeitsmarktpolitik*, 50–1.
[60] Faust, *Arbeitslosigkeit*, 134ff., and Klaus Schönhoven, "Selbsthilfe als Form der Solidarität. Das gewerkschaftliche Unterstützungswesen im Deutschen Kaiserreich bis 1914," *AfS* 20 (1980), 147–93.
[61] Führer, *Arbeitslosigkeit*, 57, 114–18, and Faust, *Arbeitslosigkeit*, 144–7. Of the sixteen cities that had taken the plunge, none were located in the industrial regions where class antagonisms were sharpest.
[62] Führer, Arbeitslosigkeit, and Peter Lewek, *Arbeitslosigkeit und Arbeitslosenversicherung in der Weimarer Republik 1918–1927* (Stuttgart, 1992).

barometer of the shift from deterrence to prevention and of the growing recognition that social programs for the respectable working classes had to be based on different principles than programs to assist the traditional poor.

In conclusion, we need to bear in mind that, although employment offices and unemployment benefits may now be the key features of state-sponsored social insurance, their origins are to be sought at the local level in the voluntary social engagement of both reform associations and municipal government, as well as in the interest politics of worker and employer organizations. Labor exchanges and labor offices evolved at the local level through the interplay between assistance to the poor and social policies for the working classes. But no matter what form they took, these institutions were an integral element of the local welfare state, and municipal officials howled mightily when they were removed from local authority in 1927.

This local innovativeness was facilitated by both the federalist structure of the empire and the particular constellation of political forces prevailing in the prewar years. National legislation – as, for example, with the Relief Residence Law – often provided merely a framework that was to be filled out by state legislation and local practice. This dynamic was intensified in peculiar ways after the turn of the century by political paralysis at the national level, which left broad fields of social policy unregulated by a Reich government that itself was insulated to a large degree from unwelcome initiatives from below. The variety of local social policy outcomes, as well as the extremely uneven character of social policies for the unemployed in the prewar years, resulted from the combination of local autonomy and the diversity of local social, economic, and political formations. In this respect, the passage of the Labor Exchange and Unemployment Insurance Law was a measure of how fundamentally the war and its consequences had burst prewar constraints on social policy.

9

Youth Welfare and the Political Alchemy of Juvenile Justice

In imperial and Weimar Germany, youth welfare was the most contentious field of preventive social welfare. Not only were its fortunes most closely identified with those of the larger welfare state idea. It was also in this domain that the socialization of liberal jurisprudence ultimately advanced the furthest, thus revealing most fully the contradictions and ambiguities of social citizenship and the preventive project.[1]

The new youth welfare was based on the recognition that waywardness could be most effectively prevented, and punishment itself perhaps rendered unnecessary, by providing corrective education to children who were neglected and endangered, but who had not yet run afoul of the law. Since the forms of social intervention required to put this preventive project into practice conflicted with traditional liberal principles of family law and social assistance, Progressive reformers were, therefore, forced to rethink the liberal social

---

[1] The literature on youth welfare has grown rapidly over the past two decades, with every contribution seeking to define itself in relation to Detlev Peukert's seminal *Grenzen der Sozialdisziplinierung. Aufstieg und Krise der deutschen Jugendfürsorge 1878 bis 1932* (Bund Verlag, 1986). The most important contributions to this literature are Edward Ross Dickinson, *The Politics of German Child Welfare from the Empire to the Federal Republic* (Harvard University Press, 1996); Dietrich Oberwittler, *Von der Strafe zur Erziehung? Jugendkriminalpolitik in England und Deutschland (1850–1920)* (Campus Verlag, 2000); Marcus Gräser, *Der blockierte Wohlfahrtsstaat. Unterschichtjugend und Jugendfürsorge in der Weimarer Republik* (Vandenhoeck & Ruprecht, 1995); Gabriel Finder, *"Education not Punishment". Juvenile Justice in Germany, 1890–1930* (Dissertation, University of Chicago, 1997); Michael Willrich, *City of Courts. Socializing Justice in Progressive Era Chicago* (Cambridge University Press, 2003); David Tanenhaus, *Juvenile Justice in the Making* (Oxford University Press, 2004); Elizabeth Harvey, *Youth and the Welfare State in Weimar Germany* (Oxford University Press, 1993); Markus Köster, *Jugend, Wohlfahrtsstaat und Gesellschaft im Wandel. Westfalen zwischen Kaiserreich und Bundesrepublik* (Schöningh, 1999); and Derek Linton, *"Who has the Youth has the Future". The Campaign to Save Young Workers in Imperial Germany* (Cambridge University Press, 1991).

contract, and in so doing they alternately challenged these liberal principles in the name of the welfare of the community, the family, and the child. The cornerstone of their approach to this problem was the idea of a child's "right to education," that is, the right to an upbringing that would insure that children developed the physical, intellectual, and moral capacities that they would need in order to fulfill the diverse social obligations that would later be expected of them as adult members of the community. This chapter will focus on the political alchemy through which youth welfare and juvenile justice reformers sought to draw out the implications of this right so that potential sanctions toward children and their families could be understood and legitimated as educational, rather than as retributive or punitive, measures and the interests of the community equated with the well-understood interests of both children and their parents.

Guardianship and the Public Interest in the Private Family

The background to the youth welfare movement was a widely perceived increase in juvenile delinquency since the 1870s. The root of this problem lay in the expanded opportunities for unskilled factory work, which allowed urban youth of both sexes an unprecedented degree of independence from traditional socializing institutions. Although these developments were an unavoidable consequence of industrialization and social change, contemporaries — both liberal and conservative — regarded new forms of working-class youth culture as the antithesis of their own cultural norms and practices, and they were especially concerned that industrial employment was destroying the idealized paternalistic relations between masters and their male apprentices, which formed the main point of reference for contemporary reflections on the youth problem. Reformers constantly spoke of the brutishness, moral degeneration, and unbridled hedonism of the young; they equated their independence with delinquency and immorality; and they feared that this explicit rejection of the principles of authority, order, and discipline was eating away at the foundations of the Christian bourgeois order and making these "half-grown punks" into the natural constituency of socialism and democracy.[2]

If this cultural crisis provided the deep background for the rise of modern youth welfare, then the proximate cause of the first innovations in this domain were infant mortality rates that were twice as high among the traditional clientele of municipal poor relief as among those at the top of the social scale.[3] The children who were most endangered belonged to several overlapping

---

[2] Oberwittler, *Von der Strafe zur Erziehung*, 26ff., 166ff., nicely articulates the cosmic significance that the educated middle classes attributed to these changes. See also Peukert, *Grenzen*; Dickinson, *The Politics of German Child Welfare*, chapters 1 and 2; and Jürgen Reulecke, "Bürgerliche Sozialreformer und Arbeiterjugend im Kaiserreich," *AfS* 22 (1982), 299–329.

[3] Jörg Vögele, "Urban Infant Mortality in Imperial Germany," *Social History of Medicine* 7:3 (1994), 401–25.

groups: orphans, illegitimate children, children supported by poor relief, and *Ziehkinder* (i.e., children who were in the paid care of someone other than a family member). Fragmented and overlapping responsibility for these children presented a problem in its own right. However, this problem was aggravated by the fact that the officials directly responsible for supervising these children – the police, male poor guardians, and ladies in the volunteer service of one or another of these municipal agencies – invariably lacked either the expertise, the authority, or the social spirit needed to help them and their mothers, while individual guardians, who had traditionally been appointed to watch over these children, lacked the time and the knowledge to effectively aid those who were most in need.

The leading innovator in this field was the physician Max Taube, who in 1883 was appointed director of the Leipzig *Ziehkinder* office.[4] Despite high mortality rates, Taube was initially reluctant to remove these children from the custody of their mothers because he feared that this would simply represent a premium on maternal irresponsibility. However, he gradually altered his position and came to believe that the real root of the problem was poverty. These children, he concluded, received such poor care because their mothers earned so little, because few if any of the fathers of these children contributed to their support, and because public supervision was so poorly organized. To ensure that none of these children were unnecessarily endangered, Taube convinced the city to appoint the director of the *Ziehkinder* office as legal guardian for all these children, and in this position he was then able to more aggressively pursue child support and more systematically monitor and assist these children – in part through the employment of paid, trained, female social workers, for which he was an early advocate.

This "collective guardianship" pioneered by Taube provided an influential example of how the centralization and professionalization of social work could be used to promote the welfare of disadvantaged groups wherever a legitimate public interest was deemed to be at stake.[5] Many people were also eager to extend these innovations to the war on juvenile delinquency and criminality, and by 1909/10 a number of cities had established either municipal youth welfare offices or other agencies to coordinate the work of the many public and private agencies active in the field. At the 1910 conference of the German Association for Poor Relief and Charity, Mainz mayor Georg Schmidt, who had led the reorganization of relief and welfare in that city, sought to spell out the rationale underlying these new agencies. Schmidt told the audience

---

[4] Max Taube, *Der Schutz der unehelichen Kinder in Leipzig. Eine Einrichtung zur Fürsorge ohne Findelhäuser* (Leipzig, 1893); Herbert Studders, *Das Taub'sche System der Ziehkinder-Überwachung in Leipzig* (Berlin, 1919); Ernst Pütter, *Das Ziehkinderwesen*, SDV, 59 (1902); and *Stenographischer Bericht über die Verhandlungen*, SDV, 62 (1902).

[5] Christian Jasper Klumker and Johannes Petersen, *Berufsvormundschaft*, SDV, 81 (1907); Georg Schmidt, *Die Organisation der Jugendfürsorge*, SDV, 92 (1910), and *Stenographischer Bericht über die Verhandlungen*, SDV, 94 (1910). Both Klumker and Spann published prolifically on professional guardianship between 1905 and World War I.

that children belonged to the state as well as to the family and that the state, therefore, had a positive obligation to act whenever a child was exposed to an immediate threat of moral endangerment. The problem was that, although the state had a political interest in acting on behalf of endangered children, and an obligation to do so, such preventive intervention could not be justified under the minimalist, deterrent poor laws. In the absence of a legislative mandate, preventive youth welfare depended on the interest and voluntary engagement of both associations and local government, with all the contingencies and limitations that this entailed.

The question, then, was how best to organize these new child protection agencies? Schmidt's plan was to unify all the diverse public social services that were concerned with the socialization and education of children within a single agency that would be administratively separate from minimalist, deterrent poor relief and thus free from its constraints. Moreover, in view of the intense fragmentation of public social services and the limitations of both individual guardianship and voluntary work, Schmidt argued that delinquency could be effectively combated only if all public and voluntary efforts in this sphere were coordinated by a single person whose authority derived from this public obligation and who was accountable to public authorities for his work: the professional guardian. Since the fulfillment of any public obligation could not be left to the discretion and limited resources of private or voluntary groups, he concluded that "everything that is a statutory obligation of public authorities should also be performed by public organisations," with voluntary welfare being correspondingly limited to only those fields that could not be considered to represent a vital public interest.[6]

Such expansive claims regarding the potential scope of public social welfare were bound to cause alarm among the representatives of voluntary welfare, who rightly feared that such a development would have marginalized them. At the conference, Frieda Duensing, the director of the German Central Bureau for Youth Welfare (*Deutsche Zentrale für Jugendfürsorge*) in Berlin, agreed with Schmidt that the community had a positive obligation to protect children, but argued that this obligation was not exhausted by state engagement in the field. Since, Duensing maintained, public social programs were often logically and chronologically dependent on the prior efforts of voluntary associations, public authorities should, she insisted, step in only on a post factum basis once innovations had become established and routinized. The task of public authorities was, she explained, to promote, rather than supplant, the work of voluntary associations, delegate the broad domain of pedagogical work to voluntary associations, and retain only an attenuated supervisory authority over these associations.[7]

---

[6] Schmidt, *Die Organisation der Jugendfürsorge*, 26.
[7] *Stenographischer Bericht über die Verhandlungen*, SDV, 94 (1910), 54ff., citation 67, and the correspondence between Polligkeit and Agnes Neuhaus from the following year in ADCV 319.4 E II.2.

Although everyone wanted to eliminate the duplication of effort and gaps in coverage that occurred when welfare programs rested primarily in the hands of voluntary associations, the various associations active in any given field were seldom willing to cooperate either with each other or with public officials.[8] While Duensing praised the interconfessional character of the Frankfurt Central Bureau for Private Welfare, she failed to realize that the Inner Mission and the Caritas Association both regarded watered-down, liberal Christianity with only slightly less contempt than socialism itself. But without a common commitment to a shared set of values, any substantial cooperation was most unlikely, and this 1910 debate prefigured what was to be the single most divisive issue in welfare politics after 1918.[9]

Juvenile Delinquency and the Socialization of Juvenile Justice

The liberal principles of deterrent public assistance were also challenged by other developments in the field of preventive youth welfare. The catalyst here was the development of reform schooling and, in particular, the desire to bring more and younger juvenile offenders within the scope of correctional education programs, particularly children who were wayward or delinquent, but who had not yet committed a punishable offense. The 1871 Criminal Code defined 12 years of age as the minimum age of criminal responsibility and required that children under this age be returned to their families. Offenders between 12 and 18 could be acquitted if they were deemed unable to understand the criminal nature of their actions, and in such cases the judge could either remand these children to their families or send them to a foster family, a house of salvation, or a reformatory, where they could be kept until they reached 21. This law was obviously unsatisfactory to those concerned with the problem of juvenile delinquency because it gave them no means of reaching children under 12, who were believed to be most impressionable and thus the best candidates for preventive measures. In 1876 the criminal code was revised to give the federal states the authority to send children aged 6–12 to a reformatory, where those deficiencies in education, discipline, and supervision that had supposedly led to their delinquency could be remedied.

Debate over the implementation of the 1876 Reich law pivoted around the question of whether the state had the right to abridge the rights of either the family or the child itself by allowing officials to send those children to reform schools who manifestly endangered or neglected, but who had not *yet* broken the law.[10] While 1878 Prussian Compulsory Education (*Zwangserziehung*)

---

[8] See the comments by Duensing and Neuhaus in *Stenographischer Bericht über die Verhandlungen*, SDV, 94 (1910), 82, 104–6.
[9] On these religious tensions in the prewar years, see Dickinson, *The Politics of German Youth Welfare*, 93–100.
[10] Polligkeit, "Das Recht des Kindes auf Erziehung," *Jahrbuch der Fürsorge* 2 (1907), 1–86, especially 3.

Law gave authorities the right to place delinquent children between the ages of 6 and 12 in either a foster family or a reformatory in order to prevent their further moral waywardness, it hewed close to the spirit of liberal jurisprudence in predicating such action on the commission of an offense.[11]

Relief officials obviously had a keen interest in these issues, and the topic was debated at the 1884 and 1885 conferences of the German Association for Poor Relief and Charity.[12] Here, Ohly warned that the consequences of the spread of juvenile delinquency were so dire that the state had to intervene in advance to reverse incipient moral degeneration, rather than to wait and punish juvenile crime on a post facto basis in the manner required by classical liberal jurisprudence. He called for state legislation that would permit local authorities to place in a foster family or reformatory children and adolescents who had not yet been convicted of a criminal offense, but whose delinquency was already manifest and whose indiscipline was so severe that they could not be controlled by their parents or the schools. Although several conference participants criticized both the principle of preventive correction and the vagueness of the concept of delinquency, the association adopted Ohly's proposal by a large margin, and this willingness to circumscribe classical liberal freedoms in the name of the welfare of both the child and the state was reflected in correctional education laws in Hesse, Baden, and Hamburg, which all went further down the path of preventive intervention than did Prussia.

The problem was that such measures could never gain broad acceptance until they came to be seen as a coherent alternative to liberal jurisprudence, rather than as ad hoc deviations that weakened its central principles (specifically the deterrent aim of punishment, the scope of parental responsibility, procedural guarantees of personal rights, and the proportionality of offense and sentence). This depended on (1) the reconceptualization of punishment as an educational measure and (2) the development of a compelling account of why the abridgements of the rights of the family that were believed to be necessary for the prevention of delinquency should be seen as enhancing the welfare of the child and not just the security of the public. These pieces of the Progressive puzzle were provided in the 1890s and early 1900s by the criminologist Hugo Appelius and the welfare expert Wilhelm Polligkeit, who, like Klumker and Spann, was associated with the Frankfurt Institute for the Common Welfare.[13]

---

[11] Dickinson, *The Politics of German Child Welfare*, 18ff., and Peukert, *Grenzen*, 68ff.

[12] I have not been able to locate the original proceedings of these meetings, and this account relies on Peukert, *Grenzen*, 116ff.

[13] Appelius, *Die Behandlung jugendlicher Verbrecher und verwahrloster Kinder. Bericht der von der Internationalen Criminalistischen Vereinigung (Gruppe Deutsches Reich) gewählten Commission* (Berlin, 1892); Polligkeit, "Das Recht des Kindes"; Polligkeit, "Strafrechtsreform und Jugendfürsorge," *Beiträge zur Kinderforschung und Heilerziehung* (1905), H. 12, 1ff.; Peukert, *Grenzen*, 72ff.; and Finder, "*Education not Punishment*," 26ff. On German criminology in this period, see Richard Wetzell, *Inventing the Criminal. A History of German Criminology 1880–1945* (University of South Carolina Press, 2000).

Juvenile Delinquency and the Socialization of Juvenile Justice

Both Appelius and Polligkeit agreed that parents had a natural right to educate their children, but they sought to reconstruct the relation between the family, the child, and the state as a set of implicit contracts so as to justify an expanded role for the state. Instead of viewing the parent-child relationship as something natural and prepolitical, they claimed that these familial rights were the correlate of the familial duty to ensure the proper physical, intellectual, and moral development of its offspring. This was crucial because, unless children possessed the capacity to distinguish right from wrong, they could not be held responsible for their transgressions, and the lack of these moral capacities substantially increased the likelihood that such children would become a burden on or a danger to society, rather than useful citizens. On this basis they concluded that, since the state had a vital interest in the education and welfare of children, it also had the responsibility to watch over the fulfillment of this contract and to step in whenever parents proved unable or unwilling to discharge their obligations to their children. Although both agreed that it was dangerous to the community and an injustice to wayward children – who were seen as victims of their own circumstances – to leave them mired in a swamp of depravity and misery, existing criminal law offered, as we have seen, little leverage in such cases.

While the 1900 Civil Code continued to predicate public guardianship on parental abuse or neglect, most endangerment was not the result of intentional abuse or neglect, but rather of social conditions that made it difficult for families to properly raise their children. Like Schmidt a few years later, Polligkeit called for a national education law that would fill the "gap" in existing legislation and provide a legal foundation for positive state action to ensure that all children received the education that they would need if they were to be able to fulfill their future obligations to the community. State supervision of juvenile education, he concluded, which was currently limited to combating parental abuse or neglect, "has to be transformed into a regular, organized, preventive surveillance" with responsibility for this public obligation to be placed in the hands of professional guardians.[14]

Appelius's proposals for the reform of juvenile justice were part of a broader penal reform movement, whose leading figure was Franz von Liszt. Liszt argued that, in view of the manifest ineffectiveness of the abstract principles of retribution and deterrence, the penal system should be reformed in accordance with its underlying aim of protecting society from crime, and he proposed that, in accordance with a more socialized conception of justice, punishment should

---

[14] Polligkeit, "Strafrechtsreform und Jugendfürsorge," 8–10, 22, 25, and "Das Recht des Kindes," 29–38, 79. Although authority over the education of children lay formally in the hands of the father or the legal guardian, Sylvia Schafer has argued that the removal of children – especially girls accused of sexual immorality – from households headed by single women often involved the implicit construction of women as agents of this paternal power, though only for the purpose of denying that they had proved themselves capable of exercising it properly. Schafer, "Between Paternal Right and Dangerous Mother: Reading Parental Responsibility in Nineteenth-Century French Civil Justice," *Journal of Family History* 23:2 (April 1998), 173–89.

be individualized on the basis of sociological and medical knowledge to maximize its specific deterrent effect. Translated into practical measures, this meant that first-time offenders who seemed likely to be deterred from future offenses should be subjected to a suspended sentence with probation, that, conversely, repeat offenders who seemed likely to benefit from rehabilitation be subjected to sentences longer than those currently imposed in order to facilitate their resocialization, and that the incorrigible be subjected to indefinite sentences, not for their own betterment, but for the protection of society.

But what of juvenile offenders? With regard to children, Appelius argued that the commission of an offense provided an opportunity to impose individualized sanctions designed not to punish or exact retribution, but rather to provide that education whose absence was believed to be the ultimate cause of their offense. As Appelius explained, "in the future, punishment for the juvenile must be detached from the exclusive domination of the idea that it is penance and retribution for his guilt and for the extent of his guilt. It should rather simultaneously and predominantly be made to serve the objective of influencing him, of directing or redirecting him to his duties to the state and to his fellow man."[15]

This did not mean, however, that delinquent children necessarily got off easier. Detlev Peukert is undoubtedly correct in arguing that the pedagogical reformulation of juvenile justice and the recognition of a public obligation to secure the child's right to education together gave rise to a new impulse to monitor and correct endangered and wayward children and that these efforts pointed – at least notionally – to a world in which the rights of these children were to be advanced through their more systematic, continuous, comprehensive, and – presumably – effective control.[16] However, Peukert seems to overstate his claim that the logic of prevention led to the quasi-totalitarian subordination of the interests of the child to those of the state. At the theoretical level, although Polligkeit did derive the child's right to education indirectly as a function of the interest of the state, he did not define this simply in terms of the state's desire to protect itself from delinquent children (for which repression alone would have sufficed), but rather in terms of the state's need for responsible, productive citizens. Similarly, Appelius insisted that parents who loved their children and wanted the best for them, but who were unable to provide the necessary supervision, would welcome the helping hand of the state in getting their wayward children back on the right track.[17] Although the preventive youth welfare programs envisioned by these reformers may well have led to the more intensive control of endangered children, this control was also combined with real assistance in the form of material support, a healthier home environment, and a concern to keep problem children out of further trouble.[18]

---

[15] Cited in Finder, "*Education not Punishment*," 37.
[16] Peukert, *Grenzen*, 72–7, 131–3.
[17] Polligkeit, "Strafrechtsreform," 10; Polligkeit, "Das Recht des Kindes," 82–3; and Appelius, *Die Behandlung jugendlicher Verbrecher*, 36–7.
[18] Dickinson, *The Politics of German Child Welfare*, 60ff., makes this point as well.

Reform schooling was not the only form of preventive youth welfare established during these years. School meal programs for needy children, day-care and after-school programs for children who would otherwise be left without supervision, and rural camps (*Ferienkolonien* or *Walderholungsstätten*) to give working-class children fresh air, healthy food, and outdoor exercise all combined assistance and discipline in their own way, with the former generally being more central to their mission than the latter, as was the case with the infant protection movement that expanded so rapidly in the prewar decade. All these programs illustrate how during the first decade of the century the liberal social contract was being refigured along Progressive lines and how the fear that any assistance beyond the deterrent existence minimum would weaken parental responsibility gradually gave way to, without ever being completely supplanted by, the principle of prevention.[19]

This development can be clearly seen in the history of school meal programs. In the 1890s, the population question emerged as one of the central political issues of the day, and it was against this background that nutrition, along with food quality and supply, acquired a new biopolitical significance in Germany and other western countries.[20] Although charitable programs to feed the hungry children of the nation's urban poor had a long tradition, what was novel about the new school meal programs for needy schoolchildren (and the school medical programs with which they were closely associated) was that they were preventive in nature and motivated more by broader concerns about social unity, national efficiency, international competitiveness, and the quantity and quality of the population than by the traditional concern to alleviate the momentary suffering of these children.

School meal programs first became the object of systematic public discussion in Germany in the second half of the 1890s. At the 1896 conference of the German Association for Poor Relief and Charity, Wilhelm Cuno argued that school meals were necessary if children were to draw the maximum benefits from compulsory primary schooling. However, most of the people attending the conference opposed the idea because they feared that such programs would diminish parental responsibility and filial piety, and they argued in classical liberal terms that the provision of meals should be limited to cases of proven

---

[19] On the infant welfare centers and the rural camp movement in Germany, see, respectively, Frohman, "Prevention, Welfare, and Citizenship: The War on Tuberculosis and Infant Mortality in Germany, 1900–1930," *CEH* 39:3 (September 2006), 431–81, and Thilo Rauch, *Die Ferienkoloniebewegung. Zur Geschichte der privaten Fürsorge im Kaiserreich* (Deutscher Universitätsverlag, 1992). Anna Plothow, "Die erste Deutsche Kinderhortkonferenz in Dresden," *BfSA* 3:8 (1911), 57–9, and Elisabeth Stürickow, "Das Charlottenburger Jugendheim," *BfSA* 5:4 (1913), 25–7, reflect the tensions between the preventive impulse and parental responsibility in the development of day-care centers in the prewar years.

[20] Matthias Weipert, *"Mehrung der Volkskraft": Die Debatte über Bevölkerung, Modernisierung und Nation 1890–1933* (Schöningh, 2006); Corinna Treitel, "Max Rubner and the Biopolitics of Rational Nutrition," *CEH* 41 (2008), 1–25; Rainer Mackensen and Jürgen Reulecke, eds., *Das Konstrukt "Bevölkerung" vor, im und nach dem "Dritten Reich"* (Verlag für Sozialwissenschaften, 2005); and Chris Otter, "The Vital City: Public Analysis, Dairies and Slaughter-Houses in Nineteenth-Century Britain," *Cultural Geographies* 13:4 (2006), 517–37.

parental negligence, where existing sanctions would ensure that such assistance did not degenerate into a premium for parental irresponsibility.[21]

Like their British counterparts, German reformers were concerned about national power and the degeneration of the population, and the passage of British legislation (1906) permitting local school authorities to provide meals to necessitous students sparked a new round of debate in Germany.[22] There was some disagreement over whether available statistics on the nutritional conditions of schoolchildren described a glass that was half full or one that was half empty, but reformers were increasingly concerned that the entire spectrum of health problems resulting from poor childhood nutrition – including subnormal height and weight, stunted or deformed skeletal development, diminished attention span and mental capacity, and greater susceptibility to disease – was creating a population that was increasingly unfit for military service, less productive, and more likely to become a burden on the productive population.[23] Although there was a broad consensus in favor of some kind of concerted action to improve the nutrition of those children who were not being adequately fed, the challenge continued to be to find a way of doing this that would not undermine that other pillar of the nation's strength: the self-reliance of individuals and families.

During the first decade of the century, the leading advocate of school meal programs in Germany was Helene Simon, a prominent social reformer who joined the Social Democrats after 1918. Simon extended Cuno's arguments by claiming that compulsory education could only achieve its aims if it were accompanied by a corresponding communal obligation to ensure that primary school students were not so mentally distracted and physically stunted by poor nutrition that they could neither profit individually from this schooling nor develop into the productive citizens envisioned by the school law. She pointed out that this obligation was also necessary to ensure that the restrictions on child labor that had been imposed in conjunction with compulsory schooling had their intended effect.[24] Simon, whose ideas closely tracked both Fabian reasoning and British legislation, presented school meal programs not as charity, but as a productive investment in the nation's human capital, and she called for the establishment of a national nutritional minimum, which would not simply prevent these children from starving, but rather would be sufficient to ensure that children would reach their full mental and physical potential. Since

---

[21] Wilhelm Cuno, *Fürsorge für arme Schulkinder*, SDV, 26 (1896), 75, 79.
[22] The most important contributions to this debate were Helene Simon, *Schule und Brot* (Hamburg, 1907); Simon, *Die Schulspeisung*, SDV, 89 (1909); *Stenographischer Bericht*, SDV, 90 (1909), 61–99; and *Die Ernährungsverhältnisse der Volksschulkinder. Vorbericht und Verhandlungen der 3. Konferenz der Zentralstelle für Volkswohlfahrt* (=*Schriften der Zentralstelle*, N.F. Heft 4, 1909).
[23] *Die Ernährungsverhältnisse der Volksschulkinder*, 121ff.
[24] Simon, *Schule und Brot*, 11–12, and *Stenographischer Bericht*, SDV, 90 (1909), 73. Simon spoke here of a communal *Nährpflicht* that corresponded to the *Lernpflicht* and *Wehrpflicht* of the individual citizen.

all needy individuals enjoyed this social "right to nutrition" by virtue of their status as citizens, she argued that the national community itself had to mandate such programs, rather than leave them to the discretion of local officials and voluntary groups, and that this had to be done as a matter of public policy outside the framework of the poor laws.[25]

Simon dismissed fears that school meal programs would weaken family responsibility as a pretext for social inaction. Not only was there little evidence that school meals were leading parents to neglect their obligations; these programs were, she argued, actually sharpening parental consciousness of their obligations by bringing a goal that otherwise exceeded their financial resources at least partly within their control. Moreover, while the defenders of deterrence maintained that meals must not be provided whenever parental fault was suspected in order to ensure that such assistance did not encourage further parental negligence, Simon insisted that the welfare of children and the public interest in their development had to take priority over deterrence and that the needs of these children had to be met regardless of parental fault.

The debate was further complicated because the question of parental neglect could not be separated from the divergent and often irreconcilable views on domesticity and women's work. A number of writers blamed the poor nutritional conditions of poor children on bad mothering and women who for selfish motives chose to work outside the home. From this perspective, the solution to the problem of inadequate childhood nutrition was to be found more in mandatory home economics schooling for working-class girls and the more intensive inculcation of domestic values than in expanded school meal programs. However, these views accorded poorly with social realities. According to a survey by the Central Bureau for Workers' Welfare Institutions, the main causes of the nutritional need of elementary schoolchildren were – in order of decreasing importance – poverty, the death of a parent, the sickness of a parent, unemployment, and maternal work outside the home, and it was this set of factors that underlay Simon's basic claim that, at bottom, the national question was a social one.[26]

This broad program of nutritional improvement was endorsed by many, even if they did not fully subscribe to Simon's reasoning. For example, Adolf Gottstein – one of the key figures in the prewar social hygiene movement – did not so much dispute her reasoning as suggest that it be expanded in a social hygienic direction to emphasize the contribution of such programs to combating degeneration and preserving the productive power of the nation.[27] On the other hand, the social hygienist Ignaz Kaup, who was Simon's most influential opponent in this debate, argued that these programs had to be justified

---

[25] Simon, *Schule und Brot*, 69ff.
[26] The results of the survey can be found in *Die Ernährungsverhältnisse der Volksschulkinder*, 8ff.
[27] Adolf Gottstein, "Volksspeisung, Schulkinderspeisung, Notstandsspeisung, Massenspeisung," in *Weyl's Handbuch der Hygiene*, 2. Aufl. (Leipzig, 1914), Ergänzungsband, Theil 2, 229–89, esp. 272–3.

primarily in populationist and productivist terms, rather than in terms of social rights; he opposed her plan to make the provision of school meals into a public responsibility on classical liberal grounds because he feared that more generous assistance provided in anything other than an individualizing, deterrent manner would open the door to a host of moral hazards; and he maintained that the only way to meet the nutritional needs of needy children without undermining parental responsibility was to keep such programs under the auspices of individualizing, deterrent poor relief, but to elevate the level of public assistance for large families so that these families could fulfill their natural obligations and thus ensure that parental negligence could no longer be confused with the effects of poverty.[28]

Although German social reformers were unable to reach a consensus on the issue, this debate nevertheless illustrates both the steady shift from deterrence to prevention and the ways in which the idea of social citizenship was being constructed after the turn of the century. Nor did the lack of national legislation slow the spread of school meal programs, which were an important field of collaboration between voluntary associations and municipal government.[29] Moreover, while support for the social mission of the school meal programs continued to grow, their fortunes were linked increasingly closely to another new social institution that achieved a new importance during the war: after-school centers for school-age children who would otherwise be without parental supervision (*Kinderhorte*). The confluence of a changing conception of children's needs with both greater material deprivation and expanded women's work led the reform community to view these centers less as a means of keeping unsupervised children off the street than as a way of nurturing the physical, intellectual, and moral development of working-class children, who were coming to be seen as needy precisely because their impoverished home environments did not provide the conditions favorable for their development. The provision of meals was a strong incentive for parents to send their children to these centers, where they would not only be fed, but also where they would learn the principles of cleanliness, order, and rational nutrition – and where the parents themselves could be drawn into the pedagogical orbit of the social reformers who operated these centers.[30]

No matter how this food was provided, school meal programs had the potential to shape the subjectivity of their beneficiaries and serve as mechanisms of social disciplining.[31] Yet these programs do not appear to have been perceived as particularly intrusive by the groups at whom they were directed.

---

[28] *Die Ernährungsverhältnisse der Volksschulkinder*, 124–5, 130.
[29] For Berlin, see Dr. Fischer, *Die ersten fünf Jahre der Berliner Schulspeisung* (Berlin, 1913).
[30] On these centers and the potential pedagogical role of meals, see Elisabet von Harnack, *Fürsorge für schulpflichtige Kinder in Kinderhorten* (Berlin, 1918), and Anna von Gierke, *25 Jahre Verein Jugendheim und 5 weitere Jahre* (Charlottenburg, 1924).
[31] James Vernon, "The Ethics of Hunger and the Assembly of Society. The Techno-Politics of the School Meal in Modern Britain," *AHR* 110:3 (June 2005), 693–725.

When we balance the potential disciplinary effect of these programs against the potential benefits of the additional food provided to those who suffered from the greatest nutritional deprivation (and the long-term benefits in terms of education, health, earning capacity, and cultural elevation that were expected to flow from this food), it seems that the balance here was struck in favor of the latter. Although we need to be wary about equating every form of social pedagogy with intrusive social disciplining, and although this balance may have changed to the extent that the nutritional, hygienic, and domestic norms promoted by the day-care centers came into conflict with the culture and habits of the working classes, the absence of a coercive capacity meant that the disciplinary potential of these programs could never be as strong as that of those programs that sought to bring the power of the state to bear in order to alter the character of older children who had already run afoul of prevailing social norms.

But it was precisely these features that have made reform schooling, juvenile courts, and the other programs for delinquent youth into the focus of most recent accounts of youth welfare and the larger Progressive project in the prewar years. The terms of the debate here were framed by Peukert, who sought to interpret the authoritarian turn in German social welfare in the 1930s as the inevitable unfolding of a repressive, exclusionary potential that was latent in the intellectual assumptions that drove the original development of the Progressive project – and who espied the first manifestations of this dystopian potential in the ideas of Appelius and Polligkeit.[32] Peukert's arguments have, however, been criticized from a variety of perspectives. First, although the crisis of correctional education later came to be seen as emblematic of the crisis of the broader Progressive project, only about half of all juvenile offenders were, in fact, sentenced to correctional education. The others were either remitted to their own families or placed in foster homes, where it seems much more likely that interventionist measures would lead to real benefits.[33] This is compatible with my own findings with regard to the impact of preventive social hygiene programs for infants and the tubercular. Second, a number of writers have convincingly argued that the intensification of surveillance and control made possible by the Progressive break with liberalism could not have provoked a systematic crisis of correctional education – if only because the reformatory establishment remained the privileged domain of confessional groups through the Weimar Republic and beyond, despite a number of high-profile experiments with Progressive pedagogy. The legitimation crisis of correctional education, they argue, was due to the disconnect between the highly authoritarian pedagogy of these institutions, which viewed discipline as the substance of rehabilitative education, and the values, experiences, and needs of urban, working-class children, who made up their primary clientele. It was, they conclude, not the Progressive modernity

---

[32] Peukert, *Grenzen*, especially 307.
[33] Gräser, *Der blockierte Wohlfahrtsstaat*, 91, and Oberwittler, *Von der Strafe zur Erziehung*, 144ff.

of the Wilhelmine and Weimar social states and the limits of social discipline that gave rise to its crisis, but rather the limits of the conservative social imagination.[34] These criticisms notwithstanding, it is important to recognize that Peukert's account of the tendency of these new agencies and institutions to colonize the family and the life-world of those caught up in the social bureaucracy nevertheless captures something essential.[35]

It is in the domain of juvenile justice that the ambiguities of preventive social welfare – predicated as it was on the systematic departure from the principles of liberal jurisprudence – can be seen most clearly. Liberal jurisprudence was based on the formal equality of free, rights-bearing subjects, and the counterpart to these individual freedoms was the threat of retribution, a threat that was, however, mediated through procedural safeguards of individual rights and graduated in proportion to the gravity of the offense. But while liberal jurisprudence insisted on viewing crime as an act of free will, the proponents of a social conception of law focused less on the act itself than on the underlying social or environmental pressures that conditioned the character of the offender.

The goal of youth welfare and juvenile justice reformers was to substitute education for punishment and thus to reclaim offenders whose waywardness was due to social conditions and deficient socialization. This strategy reflected a widely shared faith in the ability of the courts to mitigate the social problem through the careful, individualized application of new forms of social knowledge. But the realization of this goal was predicated on a complete rethinking of the strategic rationality of liberal jurisprudence. First, the substitution of education for deterrence and punishment meant that children could not enjoy the same procedural protections as adults. Second, since the goal was to individualize corrective measures in order to maximize their pedagogical effect, the greater degree of discretion that judges would have to have – in collaboration with the new social professionals – in devising reformative measures meant that socialized jurisprudence would also have to move away from the principles of determinate sentences proportionate to the offense and the uniform treatment of offenders. As a result, the discretionary power granted to youth court judges to command or prohibit a wide variety of actions, the possibility that such measures could be maintained through the entire minority of the offender (rather than the few days or weeks to which children would otherwise have been sentenced for minor transgressions), and the fact that these measures were designed to reach into the recesses of the soul, rather than simply compel

---

[34] Dickinson, *The Politics of German Child Welfare*, especially 100–5; Dickinson, "Biopolitics, Fascism, Democracy: Some Reflections on Our Discourse about 'Modernity,'" *CEH* 37 (2004), 1–48; Gräser, *Der blockierte Wohlfahrtsstaat*; and Oberwittler, *Von der Strafe zur Erziehung*.

[35] Oberwittler, *Von der Strafe zur Erziehung*, 133, notes that many later problems flowed from this condominium between Progressive reformers, who had to rely on existing voluntary institutions to put their program of correctional education into practice, and a conservative house of salvation movement, which relied increasingly on such children to keep their institutions solvent.

external conformity, meant that such sanctions could well be more intrusive than jail, even though they may have appeared as less drastic. But it was this combination measures that reassured Progressives that the new juvenile justice could strengthen the child's consciousness of his or her social obligations, rather than simply coddling juvenile offenders, and it undergirded their optimism that children would eventually come to see the coupling of material and pedagogical assistance with the veiled but nevertheless real threat of disciplinary correction as a benevolent act, rather than a punitive one.[36]

The first juvenile court in Germany was established in Frankfurt in 1908, and by 1912 there were more than 550 such courts across the country. Since correctional education was still predicated on parental neglect or juvenile delinquency, these first juvenile courts rested on the expedient of a personal union between criminal court and guardianship court judges. As a result, they retained their character as a hybrid between the pedagogical institutions envisioned by the Progressives and liberal institutions of proportionate retribution. As Frankfurt judge Karl Allmenröder observed, "this youth court should by no means deny its expiatory character, but its mission should be above all the education of the juvenile offender."[37] This explains why some juvenile justice reformers saw the youth courts as a means of overcoming traditional penology in the name of social principles, while others could, with equal justice, see the enhanced mechanisms of administrative justice as a means of making the courts into more effective means of implementing traditional penal principles.[38]

The 1900 Prussian Correctional Education Law permitted children to be sent to a correctional institution if they were delinquent due to parental neglect or if they had committed crimes for which they could not be punished because of age. But it went beyond the limits of liberal family law in also permitting correctional education in cases where the educational influence of parents, school, or other adults was inadequate to prevent the "*complete* moral corruption of the minor (emphasis added)," even if the parents themselves could not be considered neglectful. The Progressive thrust of the law was also evident in its terminology, which characterized such measures as "reformative" or "correctional" education (*Fürsorgeerziehung*), instead of the older "compulsory" education (*Zwangserziehung*).

Although this law appeared to expand the ability of public authorities to bring more children of a younger age under their guidance, the Prussian courts – in upholding the principle of subsidiarity – prevented poor relief officials from paying for such treatment unless all other measures were deemed inadequate to the task. This meant that public officials had only limited financial capacity to put such a policy into action (in the form of reform schooling or foster care

[36] Willrich, *City of Courts*.
[37] Allmenröder, "Die Tätigkeit des Frankfurter Jugendrichters," in Berthold Freudenthal, ed., *Das Jugendgericht in Frankfurt a.M.* (Springer, 1912), 1–17, citation 1.
[38] Finder, *"Education not Punishment,"* 6, speaks of the eclectic experimentalism of the early juvenile courts.

for such children), and to escape these constraints they appealed to voluntary associations to pick up the cost of aiding such children while themselves trying to make more public funds available for such purposes outside the poor relief budget.[39] Despite these limitations, the resulting shift in the age structure of the institutional population had important effects on the practice of correctional education. While younger, more pliable children were returned to their families under the supervision of public authorities, who were coming to prefer working with parents to improve the home environment over breaking up the family, reformatories became the last stop for older, more intractable children, a development that cumulatively aggravated the legitimation crisis of reform schooling.[40]

The foundation for the rehabilitative work of the juvenile courts was probation, which was made possible through the conditional suspension of criminal sentences that was introduced in many states in 1895, but only formally codified after the war. The juvenile courts relied on a battery of social and medical experts to provide judges with the detailed knowledge of the character and personal circumstances of the child that they needed to determine whether or not young offenders were good candidates for probation and, if so, what specific measures would be most appropriate. The new branch of social work devoted to carrying out these investigations, making recommendations regarding the disposition of the case, and taking over the "protective supervision" of these children before their trial and during their probationary period was known as juvenile court assistance (*Jugendgerichtshilfe*).

Juvenile court assistance opened new domains for collaboration between voluntary welfare and the local state. It required the former to submit to the regulations and routines of the latter while enhancing the authority of voluntary associations vis-à-vis the needy by permitting them to share in the authority and the power of the state. Social workers, however, played a peculiar role in this process. Although they were to serve as advocates for the best interests of the child, this advocacy took a very different form in the juvenile court, where adversarial proceedings were excluded as far as possible in hopes of persuading the child to admit his or her guilt – a step that was regarded as essential in bringing the child to collaborate in his or her own rehabilitation. Court social workers were to act as advocates for the accused children, but "not to be sure... as an advocate who will get his client off (*durchbringen*) at all costs, but rather as one who does not close himself off to the necessity of punishment when it appears in the interest of the community and the accused."[41] This argument, and with it the legitimacy of the juvenile justice system, pivoted on

---

[39] *Zwangserziehung und Armenpflege*, SDV, 64 (1903); *Stenographischer Bericht über die Verhandlungen*, SDV, 67 (1903), 16–72; and Johannes Petersen, *Die öffentliche Fürsorge für die sittlich gefährdete und die gewerblich tätige Jugend* (Leipzig, 1907).
[40] On the development of correctional education practice during these years, see Oberwittler, *Von der Strafe zur Erziehung*, 122ff., and Köster, *Jugend, Wohlfahrtsstaat und Gesellschaft*, 143ff.
[41] Merton to Polligkeit (September 28, 1913), StAF, Magistratsakten V573.

an analogy between the state and the family and on the claim that such harsh measures differed in no essential way from the corrective punishments that might be administered by a wise parent. All the ambiguities inherent in the juvenile justice system are glaringly evident in this lapidary assertion that both the public and the child could be equally well served by sentencing the child to probation or to reform school.

Probation was the quintessential penal-welfare measure, keeping the child as it did suspended between the promise of rehabilitation and the threat of punishment, and practitioners spoke in this respect of an organic connection between penal justice and rehabilitative youth welfare.[42] The juvenile courts depended on the guardianship court to ensure them a direct influence over the education of the child that they would otherwise lack, especially since the conditional suspension of a sentence by the criminal court did not by itself give welfare officials the right to intervene into the daily life of a child whose sentence had been suspended. But the issue was even more complicated. Although welfare officials in theory preferred leaving the child in the family, the problem was that they also believed that most delinquency was attributable to a poor home environment. Their response to this problem was to attempt to persuade the parents to consent to the appointment of a guardian for the child and, failing this, to begin correctional education proceedings to put pressure on the parents, whose collaboration was still regarded as essential to the success of rehabilitative education. The upshot of this was that it made the family itself into a penal-welfare object in hopes of enhancing its ability to perform its natural educational functions. As Polligkeit explained, the purpose was not to criticize parents for their failings, but rather to serve as a source of advice that would "not bear so much the character of public control as that of solicitous support (*fürsorgliches Beistehen*)."[43]

All these processes show how, in the prewar years, the preventive project was exerting a powerful gravitational force that was pulling the child protection, youth welfare, and juvenile justice movements further and further away from their original liberal moorings and toward a new, Progressive approach to the problem of juvenile delinquency. Although these innovations were justified as essential for securing the child's right to education, they were all premised on highly speculative constructions of the relation between the rights of the child, the family, and the state that ultimately turned on the possibility of making sanctions appear as pedagogical measures that were in the best interest of all three. It should not, therefore, come as a surprise that these programs could appear as a means of enhancing both the welfare of their target populations and the coercive power of public authorities and voluntary organizations, groups whose values were often at sharp odds with those of the population whom they were ostensibly trying to assist.

---

[42] Polligkeit, "Die Jugendgerichtshilfe in Frankfurt a.M., ihre Aufgaben, Organisation und Wirksamkeit," Freudenthal, ed., *Das Jugendgericht in Frankfurt a.M.*, 35–86, citation 36.
[43] Polligkeit, "Strafrechtsreform," 9–10.

10

The Social Evolution of Poor Relief, the Crisis of Voluntarism, and the Limits of Progressive Social Reform

As we saw in Chapter 3, voluntarism was the logical correlate of the limited state, and the importance of this voluntaristic impulse, as well as the pathos attached to it by the propertied classes, was reinforced by both the refusal to codify a right to assistance and the belief that personal intercourse between rich and poor was peculiarly well suited to combating the social problem as it was understood across much of the nineteenth century, that is, as a problem of individual character.[1] This combination of "providence, paternalism, and philanthropy"[2] within the framework of the limited state also defined the political rationality of public assistance in Germany from the *Vormärz* until the end of the century. At the turn of the century, though, the idea that need was due more to the structural inequalities of the bourgeois social order than to individual character failings implied to a growing number of observers that disadvantaged persons should enjoy more explicit rights to social services that would not simply keep them from starving, but rather would put them in a position to more fully realize their own potential and enjoy the rights and duties associated with political citizenship. This trend was reinforced by the greater participation of the working classes in political and social life, at both the local and the national levels, and these developments combined to set in motion a rethinking of the nature and purpose of social assistance that called into question every element of this liberal, voluntaristic paradigm.

One challenge to the voluntaristic tradition came from the formation of a new class of technically trained and increasingly professionalized administrators, who in the first decades of the empire began to displace traditional

---

[1] See Pat Thane, "Women in the British Labour Party and the Construction of State Welfare, 1906–1939," in Seth Koven and Sonya Michel, eds., *Mothers of a New World. Maternalist Politics and the Origins of Welfare States* (Routledge, 1993), 343–77, especially 358–9.
[2] Geoffrey Finlayson, *Citizen, State, and Social Welfare in Britain 1830–1990* (Oxford University Press, 1994).

notables as the backbone of local government.[3] While this new administrative class brought greater professionalism and expertise to poor relief administration, these administrators were also impatient with the foibles, inefficiencies, and dilettantism of the voluntary sector, especially its fragmentation and the waste to which this gave rise.[4] It is possible to present this conflict over charity organization as a generational conflict between older notables and the new administrative class.[5] However, one should not downplay the genuine commitment of these younger officials to the voluntaristic tradition. It is equally likely that these administrators were divided in their own minds over whether possible gains in efficiency from greater organization might be more than offset by the resulting diminution of personal engagement and solicitude on the part of philanthropic volunteers. For example, even Münsterberg, who was the very embodiment of the professional ethos and rationalizing aspirations of this new generation of relief officials, was an ardent supporter of voluntarism. As he told the 1891 conference of the German Association for Poor Relief and Charity, "it is love, which can achieve so much, but which tolerates nothing worse than compulsion and regimentation.... Love wants to act only for a specific purpose, only for one specific person, and it fails completely when it is denied the possibility of acting on behalf of this purpose or this person. The only consequence of any serious compulsion in this respect would be the substantial reduction in voluntary giving, and personal involvement would disappear almost entirely."[6]

---

[3] On the rationalization and professionalization of municipal social services during this period, see Wolfgang Krabbe, "Von der Armenpflege zur lokalen Sozial- und Gesundheitsverwaltung. Wandlungen im kommunalen Pflichtaufgabenbereich unter dem Druck der Modernisierung am Beispiel westfälischer Städte (1800–1914)," *Beiträge zur Geschichte Dortmunds und der Grafschaft Mark* 76-7 (1985), 154–215; Krabbe, *Kommunalpolitik und Industrialiserung. Die Entfaltung der städtischen Leistungsverwaltung im 19. und frühen 20. Jahrhundert* (Kohlhammer, 1985); Martin Weyer-von Schoultz, *Stadt und Gesundheit im Ruhrgebiet 1850–1929. Verstädterung und kommunale Gesundheitspolitik am Beispiel der jungen Industriestadt Gelsenkirchen* (Essen, 1994); and Hedwig Brüchert-Schunk, *Städtische Sozialpolitik vom wilhelminischen Reich bis zur Weltwirtschaftskrise. Eine sozial- und kommunalhistorische Untersuchung am Beispiel der Stadt Mainz 1890–1930* (Stuttgart, 1994); as well as the critique of this work in Friedrich Lenger, "Bürgertum und Stadtverwaltung in Rhenischen Großstädten des 19. Jahrhunderts," in Lothar Gall, ed., *Stadt und Bürgertum im neunzehnten Jahrhundert* (Munich, 1990), 97–169.

[4] See the exasperated comments by Berlin city councilman Eduard Eberty in *Die Bestrebungen der Privatwohltätigkeit und ihre Zusammenfassung, SDV,* 19 (1894), 93-4.

[5] Stephen Pielhoff, "Indirect Gift-Exchange. Mediators between 'Civil Society' and Municipal Politics in Imperial Germany," presented at the conference on "Philanthropy in History: German and American Perspectives" sponsored by the German Historical Institute in Washington (March 2006).

[6] Münsterberg, *Die Verbindung der öffentlichen und der privaten Armenpflege, SDV,* 14, (1891), 25-6. On the problems involved in coordinating the work of municipal poor relief and voluntary associations, see Münsterberg, *Die Verbindung der öffentlichen und der privaten Armenpflege, SDV,* 14, (1891); *Stenographischer Bericht über die Verhandlungen, SDV,* 15 (1891), 21ff.; Eduard Eberty and Bürgermeister Künzer, "Die Bestrebungen der Privatwohltätigkeit und ihre

The role of voluntarism within the municipal poor relief apparatus was also being challenged during these years. The growing scale and complexity of urban life, the sprawling anonymity of the new metropolises, the mobility of the urban working classes, the increasing geographical separation between rich and poor, and the concentration of the poor in the new tenements or *Mietskaserne* were all making it difficult, if not impossible, for guardians to maintain the local knowledge of and personal relations with the poor on which the Elberfeld system had depended. Nor could voluntary and honorary guardians be expected to keep current of administrative law pertaining to the relief residence system, social insurance regulations, or developments in the areas as diverse as labor law and infant hygiene. Although the introduction of paid workers into municipal poor relief was unavoidable, this led to serious friction with poor guardians, who remained the backbone of the system, but who feared that their influence and prerogatives would be thereby reduced.[7]

But the most serious challenge to the voluntaristic tradition came from the social perspective on poverty and the preventive project. In Britain, the classic site of confrontation between these two assistantial regimes was the Royal Commission appointed in 1905 to consider revisions of the poor laws. It was the confrontation with the defenders of deterrent poor relief and scientific charity within the commission that helped crystallize Beatrice Webb's conviction that the problem of poverty could only be solved through what she called the break-up of the poor laws, rather than their reform. In Germany, the relationship between deterrent poor relief, social policy, and preventive social welfare was conceptualized in terms of the "social evolution (*soziale Ausgestaltung*) of poor relief," and this issue was first systematically debated at the 1901 and 1905 conferences of the German Association for Poor relief and Charity. Although the workings of the British poor law commission are one of the great set pieces of any account of turn-of-the-century social policy in that country, this German debate has – surprisingly – never been the object of systematic study, even though it preceded its much more famous British counterpart by several years.[8]

At the 1901 conference, Frankfurt city councilor Karl Flesch, one of the leading left liberal experts on social reform matters, laid out what might be called the liberal view of the social evolution of poor relief. According to Flesch, all individuals had to rely on work, property, and the family to meet their basic needs. The purpose of poor relief was to step in when these mechanisms of

---

Zusammenfassung," *SDV*, 19 (1894), 87–117; and *Stenographischer Bericht über die Verhandlungen*, *SDV*, 20 (1894), 95–127.

[7] The most influential model for integrating paid workers into the municipal poor relief system was the district system that was identified most closely with the city of Strassburg. See Christoph Sachße, *Mütterlichkeit als Beruf. Sozialarbeit, Sozialreform und Frauenbewegung 1871–1929* (Suhrkamp, 1986), 36ff., and the sources cited there.

[8] For a more extended treatment of the British commission and the parallels between German and British thinking here, see Larry Frohman, "The Break-up of the Poor Laws – German Style: Progressivism and the Origins of the Welfare State, 1900–1918," *Comparative Studies in Society and History*, 50:4 (October 2008).

private reproduction failed, and Flesh insisted that the only way to preserve the integrity of these institutions while meeting the needs of society's more unfortunate members was to provide only a minimal level of assistance and to do so in an individualizing, discriminating, and subsidiary manner. In view of these manifest limits of individualizing poor relief, Flesch argued that the best hope for social progress was to be found in social policy legislation, which alone could strengthen the position of the working classes in the labor market and thus roll back class poverty without weakening the basic institutions of bourgeois society.

From this perspective, then, the evolution of poor relief in the direction of social rights to preventive social welfare was self-contradictory and ill advised. Not only would such a development undermine the very institutions that it was intended to support. It would involve an open-ended financial commitment that no society could afford. It was simply impossible, Flesch argued, to provide – at public expense – to every person who had only a rudimentary home, or perhaps no home at all, a home that adequately satisfied both the needs of the family and the standards of modern cultural life, rather than the minimal housing required by the poor laws. The only "social" consideration that Flesch was willing to inject into current relief practice was to distinguish between those whose poverty was due to their own faults and those who were more worthy of assistance – and to provide the latter with assistance generous enough to enable them to lead a "humane existence," rather than continue to limit such assistance to the traditional existence minimum.

This was a powerful liberal vision of social reform, one that would have brought about the gradual withering away of poor relief through the expansion of social policy legislation without altering the existing poor relief system in any significant way. However, this did not mean that there was no place for preventive social welfare in Flesch's system. Instead of asking poor relief undertake tasks that were incompatible with the minimalist, deterrent nature of this form of social assistance, Flesch argued that relief officials should instead encourage the formation of voluntary associations to serve as the agents of preventive social welfare. In contrast to statutory programs, voluntary programs could more easily discriminate between the deserving and the undeserving and maintain a proper balance between the commitment to the welfare of the underprivileged classes and the resources available to them. Drawing on the legal theorist Rudolf Ihering, Flesch envisioned a progression leading from concerned individuals via these voluntary associations to the state; to the extent that these preventive programs achieved general recognition, they would be institutionalized in state social policy legislation, but would not take the form of accretions to a poor relief system that was based on completely different principles.[9]

Flesch's arguments here illustrate the precise sense in which voluntarism was integral to the liberal state, and these beliefs should also make us quite

---

[9] Karl Flesch and Adolf Soetbeer, *Sociale Ausgestaltung der Armenpflege*, SDV, 54 (1901) and *Stenographischer Bericht über die Verhandlungen*, SDV, 56 (1901), 28–63.

wary of the approach of modern analysts of the third or nonprofit sector, who categorize associations according to whether they supplement the state, collaborate with it, or contest it through advocacy. As we can see from Flesch's account of the relation of philanthropic associations to poor relief in bourgeois society, it lay in the very essence of these associations that they shared in all three moments: supplementing a state that in good conscience could not make open-ended commitments that threatened its very foundations, collaborating with state officials who nevertheless valued the preventive programs offered through these associations and were willing to provide subsidies and other assistance outside the framework of the poor law, and advocating social policy legislation that would institutionalize these programs.[10]

The 1905 debate, however, moved in a more radical direction to argue that the principles of public assistance would have to be fundamentally rethought so that these programs could positively promote the welfare of the disadvantaged classes and thus give substance – in precisely the way that Flesch said that poor relief could not do without ceasing to be poor relief in any recognizable sense of the word – to the promise of social citizenship. At this conference the two main proponents of this broader vision of the social evolution of poor relief were Strassburg mayor Rudolf Schwander and Adolf Buehl, Münsterberg's successor as the director of the poor relief administration in Hamburg.[11] For Schwander, the purpose of public assistance was to fill the gaps in the existing economic system and step in wherever its regular operation did not permit the individual to satisfy his or her basic needs through work, property, or family.

---

[10] During these years, German reformers developed a special concept of welfare (*Wohlfahrtspflege*) to describe the diverse measures that were undertaken on a voluntary basis by government, social groups, and private individuals to meliorate the social ills that were caused by economic forces. However, the idea occupied a conceptual no-man's land. Such programs could only be distinguished from social policies by emphasizing their voluntary and individualizing aspects, while the foregrounding of this dimension put proponents in the uncomfortable position of explaining how problems that affected entire classes could be effectively combated by individualizing and discriminatory means. See *Das Programm der Wohlfahrtspflege. Vorträge gehalten auf der ersten Konferenz der Zentralstelle für Volkswohlfahrt am 21. Oktober 1907* (=*Schriften der Zentralstelle für Volkswohlfahrt*, Heft 1, 1908); *Die Zentralstelle für Volkswohlfahrt. Ihre Organisation und ihre Tätigkeitsbereich* (Berlin, 1909); Robert von Erdberg, *Die Wohlfahrtspflege. Eine sozialwissenschaftliche Studie* (Jena, 1903); and Andrew Lees, *Cities, Sin, and Social Reform in Imperial Germany* (University of Michigan Press, 2002), Chapter 9.

[11] On the local context of the Progressive policies that Schwander was here advocating on the national level, see Silke Schütter, "Von der rechtlichen Anerkennung zur Ausgrenzung der Armen. Euphorie und Scheitern eines großen kommunalpolitischen Reformprojektes Straßburgs zwischen den 1880er Jahre und der 1920er Jahren," *AfS* 46 (2006), and Bénédicte Zimmermann, "Naissance d'une politique municipal du marché du travail. Strasbourg et la question du chômage (1888–1914)," *Revue d'Alsace* 120 (1994), 209–34. On the municipal policies of the left liberals and their influence on municipal politics (often in alliance with the Social Democrats) after the turn of the century, see Alastair Thompson, *Left Liberals, the State, and Popular Politics in Wilhelmine Germany* (Oxford University Press, 2000), 109ff. and, more generally, chapters 1 and 3. Thompson (113) sees municipal government as "one of the few areas where Wilhelmine left liberalism had genuine claims to political glory."

Since most cases of need, Schwander argued, could, in fact, be traced back to failures of the economic system that did not lie within the control of the individual, it only seemed reasonable that these persons should be granted a "right to assistance" or a "right to existence,"[12] which in Buehl's words embodied the "social obligation" owed by the community to those members who were systematically disadvantaged by the functioning of its most basic institutions.[13]

Schwander insisted that responsibility for discharging this public obligation should be placed in the hands of a public agency, rather than being regarded as a matter of secondary importance that could comfortably be left to the discretion of voluntary associations, and he called for the revision of the suffrage law – along the lines of the later 1909 law – because he felt that the deterrent loss of suffrage rights was inconsistent with his understanding of the causes of poverty and his vision of social citizenship.[14] Using the recent history of school meals, youth welfare, and social hygiene programs as examples, Buehl argued that eligibility for preventive services should be cut loose from poor law definitions of need and made available without distinction to a much broader group of needy persons – by which he appears to have meant all those persons whose culture and way of life could not conform to the standards of modern hygiene and culture without such assistance. Schwander and Buehl justified their call for the entitlement to an expanded spectrum of preventive social welfare programs by playing on the slippage between political citizenship and socioeconomic disadvantagement. Alice Salomon complemented this approach by arguing that prevention was a necessary, productive investment in the nation's human capital whose scope had to be determined "from the perspective of the national welfare, that is, from the perspective of the health, strength and morality of the nation." Public officials, she insisted, should worry less about whether these programs might on occasion coddle the needy than about what needed to be done on a systematic basis to promote the welfare of the nation.[15]

This generalization of preventive social welfare to all citizens on a nondiscriminatory basis simply by virtue of their membership in the community is what Schwander and Buehl had in mind when they spoke of the social evolution of poor relief. This Progressive position differed from the liberal position marked out by Flesch in that it placed the blame for poverty squarely on the operation of the economic system, rather than the failures of individual character and private reproduction; it inferred from the failings of the economic system the existence of individual social rights and public social obligations; and it charged the public assistance system with taking direct action to remedy class poverty rather than being content to work indirectly through the impact of social policy on the market. It differed from socialism in that it sought to use

---

[12] *Die heutigen Anforderungen an die öffentliche Armenpflege*, SDV, 73 (1905), 155–6.
[13] *Stenographischer Bericht über die Verhandlungen*, SDV, 75 (1905), 92.
[14] *Die heutigen Anforderungen an die öffentliche Armenpflege*, SDV, 73 (1905) and *Stenographischer Bericht über die Verhandlungen*, SDV, 75 (1905).
[15] *Stenographischer Bericht über die Verhandlungen*, SDV, 75 (1905), 145–6.

public assistance to compensate for structural inequalities within the capitalist system rather than calling for its overthrow.

The voluntary sector was doubly marginalized by this logic. On the one hand, it was clearly impossible to solve the problem of structural, class poverty through the individualizing, discriminatory methods common to poor relief and charity, and the voluntary sector in any case lacked the resources necessary to assist an entire social class. On the other hand, once it was recognized that the public owed these obligations to all members of the disadvantaged classes, the fragmentary, incomplete, and provisional character of voluntary programs came to be seen as decisive disadvantages that easily outweighed the pioneering function attributed to them in an earlier period. The need to ensure the comprehensive, systematic satisfaction of this public obligation thus seemed to demand that these programs be placed in the hands of public agencies that were to have primary responsibility for discharging this obligation. This turn is what was meant by "collectivism," or at least collectivism in a certain sense, for the question of communal control of private property and industry through the state, which is normally what is meant by the term, remained entirely beyond the horizon of this debate. Nevertheless, this proposal was the exact inversion of the liberal state, voluntaristic, deterrent paradigm described earlier.[16]

The problem was that the Progressive vision of reformed public assistance corresponded only unevenly with actual relief practice. While Prussian legislation limited statutory assistance to the existence minimum, other states already included in their definition of need at least a minimal degree of moral, civic, and occupational education. The Federal Office of Relief Residence Affairs had also ruled that, in contrast to the older understanding of medical relief, states were obligated to provide more extensive medical treatment to the poor if such care could be expected to bring about a substantial improvement in the person's condition (or prevent a substantial deterioration). But this principle could only be applied to remedy existing need, not to prevent its occurrence in the first place, and the German Association for Poor Relief and Charity wanted to extend the poor relief existence minimum to include education and occupational training because, as one member put it, "without a certain degree of education and occupational training the individual is a completely incapable, helpless member of human society."[17]

This represented a modest, but symbolically important, expansion of the statutory responsibility of poor relief, and this, together with more extensive medical care for the poor, which had hitherto been limited to keeping them alive, was often cited as an example of the new "social" mission of poor relief. However, a 1905 survey showed that in a number of areas (including levels of monetary assistance, the expansion of the existence minimum to include

---

[16] This logic is laid out most clearly in Finlayson, *Citizen, State and Social Welfare in Britain*, Chapter 2, but see also the discussion of youth welfare in Chapter 9.
[17] Erste Sitzung der Reichs-Armengesetz-Kommission (January 10, 1913), ADCV 319.4, SKF Bl.1, Fasz. 1.

sanatorium treatment and education, and school meals) the actual practice of many cities had not yet gone nearly as far as was already permitted by existing legislation. The authors of the survey concluded that the most that one could discern was a tendency for relief authorities to provide these preventive programs, but pointed out that this trend could never become universal without a fundamental transformation of the principles of poor relief, something that was hardly likely to happen in the foreseeable future in view of the large number of cities that were hostile – or at best indifferent – toward the social evolution of poor relief. But the survey also noted that one reason why so many relief authorities did not feel constrained to expand their own work was that they were already supported by voluntary associations that had assumed responsibility, as best they could, for public obligations in the field of preventive social welfare.[18]

The climate for social reform was also decidedly inauspicious at the national level. Although Bismarck had been forced from office in 1890 because of his opposition to the social aspirations of the new emperor Wilhelm II, the "new course" in social policy under Minister of Commerce and Trade Freiherr Hans-Hermann von Berlepsch, which led to important advances across the entire field of social policy, was short lived.[19] The emperor's policy reversal in 1894/6 marked the beginning of a decade of repressive measures toward the working classes. Business and industry also began a sustained campaign against state social policies. Arguing that these programs had failed to reconcile the working classes with the existing social order and substantially increased the cost of production while encouraging the Social Democrats to make even further-reaching demands for political and economic change, industry sought to reorient German social policy along nationalist, corporatist, and productivist lines.[20] This backlash was broken only – and then only partially – by the collapse of the governing coalition and the virtual paralysis of the national government after the 1912 elections, which saw the Social Democrats emerge as the largest party in the Reichstag.

Aside from the continual tinkering with the relief residence system, the 1909 exclusion of preventive social welfare from the suffrage disabilities associated with poor relief was the only substantive modification of the poor laws undertaken during these years. However, this inaction at the national level left the cities a large degree of latitude to define need and determine, in conjunction with local voluntary associations, what would be done to assist the needy. At a certain level, there was a broad consensus in favor of municipal social reform.

---

[18] *Die heutigen Anforderungen an die öffentliche Armenpflege*, SDV, 73 (1905), 37ff.
[19] Hans-Jörg von Berlepsch, *"Neuer Kurs" im Kaiserreich? Die Arbeiterpolitik des Freiherrn von Berlepsch 1890 bis 1896* (Bonn, 1987).
[20] Dennis Sweeney, "Corporatist Discourse and Heavy Industry in Wilhelmine Germany: Factory Culture and Employer Politics in the Saar," *Comparative Studies in Society and History* 43 (2001), 701–34, and Eckart Reidegeld, *Staatliche Sozialpolitik in Deutschland. Historische Entwicklung und theoretische Analyse von den Ursprüngen bis 1918* (Westdeutscher Verlag, 1996), 252ff.

The first municipal "social commissions" had been established in 1893/5, and by 1909 such commissions had been established in sixteen cities.[21] The growing centrality of social policies to local government was reflected in the fact that the theme of first conference of the League of German Cities (1903) was their "social mission." And almost all the innovative social relief programs described in the previous pages had been created since the turn of the century through the collaboration of voluntary associations and public officials at the local level.[22] However, this was not a universal development. These innovations were clustered in a small number of commercial centers, including Berlin, Frankfurt, Mainz, Düsseldorf, Cologne, Hamburg, Dresden, and Bremen, and there were many places where local elites successfully resisted Progressive reforms.

The key question in the historiography of Wilhelmine Germany is whether in the prewar years domestic political life had led to a dead end or whether there was a possibility that, had the war not intervened, a reformist coalition would have emerged that would have been able to lead the country down a more democratic, constitutionalist path.[23] A number of works have sought to answer this question by examining the political parameters of municipal social policy, in particular the possibilities and limitations of a "social liberalism" based on a positive alliance between Progressive members of the bourgeoisie and reformist Social Democrats. However, this literature has generated more questions than answers: Why, in contrast to England, did German social liberalism never enjoy the influence at the national level that it had in local politics? Did restrictions on municipal suffrage give liberals the freedom to pursue reformist policies that they would have been unable to advocate if their position had been threatened from either the left or the right? Did pressure from the working classes encourage the liberals to move in this direction or frighten them away from such policies? Were progressive municipal social policies intended to satisfy the legitimate demands of the working classes and thus forge a closer alliance between the two or to combat Social Democracy by taking the wind out of its sails? How did the social policy programs of the different fractions and personalities in the liberal and Progressive camps differ from one another? What conditions would have been necessary in order to build meaningful political bridges to the reformist wing of the Social Democratic Party, and where, if at all, did such conditions prevail?[24]

---

[21] *SPr*, 18:26 (1908/9), col. 684, and Hugo Lindemann, *Arbeiterpolitik und Wirtschaftspflege in der deutschen Städteverwaltung* (Stuttgart, 1904), I:3–15.
[22] Franz Adickes and Otto Beutler, *Die sozialen Aufgaben der deutschen Städte* (Leipzig, 1903).
[23] See, most recently, Geoff Eley, ed., *Wilhelminism and Its Legacies. German Modernities, Imperialism, and the Meanings of Reform, 1890–1930* (Oxford University Press, 2003).
[24] Jan Palmowski, *Urban Liberalism in Imperial Germany: Frankfurt am Main, 1866–1914* (Oxford, 1999), 205ff., 238ff.; George Steinmetz, *Regulating the Social. The Welfare State and Local Politics in Imperial Germany* (Princeton University Press, 1993) 147ff.; Marcus Gräser, *Wohlfahrtsgesellschaft und Wohlfahrtsstaat. Bürgerliche Sozialreform und welfare state building in den USA und in Deutschland 1880–1940* (Vandenhoeck & Ruprecht, 2008); Dieter Langewiesche, *Liberalism in Germany* (Princeton University Press, 2000), xiv, 206ff., 218ff.;

While much of this literature has focused on Frankfurt as the city where such a social liberal coalition was most likely to coalesce, it could with equal plausibility be argued that Frankfurt represents an exception (or at best one of a number of possible developmental paths), rather than the norm. In other cities, the economic, political, cultural, and institutional factors were very different and give little reason to expect that municipal officials and voluntary associations would have moved in the direction of such a reformist alliance.[25]

Political paralysis at the national level created a space for municipal social policy and for voluntary social initiatives which thrived either because of local circumstances or because their voluntary nature left interested local groups free to proceed even in the absence of a favorable local constellation. In looking at the debate over the social evolution of poor relief and at patterns of municipal social policy, it seems clear that there is no single master narrative capable of summing up all the contradictory and asynchronous developments in the welfare sector in the years before 1914. In previous chapters, we have documented the diversity and conflict within the voluntary sector. In the domain of municipal social reform, while some cities were aggressively pursuing Progressive reforms, many others were noticeably unenthusiastic, and in 1914 there was no obvious single path along which social policy could have been expected to evolve at either the local or the national level. Consequently, the year 1914 does not constitute a natural dividing point in the history of German welfare system. Only in retrospect are we constrained to speculate on how these diverse trends might have played out had not the assassination of Archduke Francis Ferdinand set in motion a chain of events whose ultimate consequences could hardly have been foreseen.

Ralf Roth, *Gewerkschaftskartell und Sozialpolitik in Frankfurt am Main* (Waldemar Kramer, 1991); Ursula Bartelsheim, *Bürgersinn und Parteiinteresse. Kommunalpolitik in Frankfurt am Main 1848–1914* (Frankfurt am Main, 1997); and Holger J. Tober, *Deutscher Liberalismus und Sozialpolitik in der Ära des Wilhelminismus. Anschauungen der liberalen Parteien im parlamentarischen Entscheidungsprozess und in der öffentlichen Diskussion* (Husum, 1999).

[25] Hans-Ulrich Thamer, Jochen-Christoph Kaiser et al., "Kommunale Wohlfahrtspolitik zwischen 1918 und 1933 im Vergleich (Frankfurt, Leipzig, Nürnberg)," in Jürgen Reulecke, ed., *Die Stadt als Dienstleistungszentrum. Beiträge zur Geschichte der "Sozialstadt" in Deutschland im 19. und frühen 20. Jahrhunderts* (Scripta Mercaturae Verlag, 1995), 325–70; Paul Brandmann, *Leipzig zwischen Klassenkampf und Sozialreform. Kommunale Wohlfahrtspolitik zwischen 1890 und 1929* (Böhlau, 1998); Karl Heinrich Pohl, *Zwischen protestantischer Ethik und kapitalistischem Interesse: Zur Geschichte der kommunalen Arbeitsvermittlung in Bielefeld zwischen 1887 und 1914* (Bielefeld, 1991), 205ff.; Hans-Peter Jans, *Sozialpolitik und Wohlfahrtspflege in Ulm 1870–1930. Stadt, Verbände und Parteien auf dem Weg zur modernen Sozialstaatlichkeit* (Kohlhammer, 1994); and Thomas Küster, *Alte Armut und neues Bürgertum. Öffentliche und private Fürsorge in Münster von der Ära Fürstenberg bis zum Ersten Weltkrieg (1756–1914)* (Aschendorff Verlag, 1995).

11

Family, Welfare, and (Dis)order on the Home Front

Total War and the Transformation of Social Politics

The Great War wrought fundamental changes in the existing system for assisting the needy in Germany, and it was the war itself, rather than the revolution and the republic, that led to the breakthrough of the preventive social welfare programs that had developed since the turn of the century.

The initial purpose of wartime social welfare programs was to give concrete substance to the suspension of domestic politics proclaimed by the Kaiser at the outbreak of the war and to mobilize the nation's energies against all those inner enemies that might weaken resolve of the home front, on which the success of the military effort rested. In the words of Marie-Elisabeth Lüders, the liberal and feminist activist who was to become the director of the women's department in the War Ministry in the second half of the war,

> we experienced the great unity [of the nation] in a double sense. From the very first days [of the war], we had an overwhelming experience of national unity. The other unity – social unity – was something that still had to be created, and we had to take this upon ourselves and make its realization our own particular mission. The will to help one another should and had to become our inner defense because with every passing day it became clearer that victory and defeat depended no less on this inner defense than on the success of our weapons.[1]

But this experience of the unity of the nation at war was, if not exactly illusory, then certainly only provisional, and state social programs proved to be as much a source of conflict as a means of stabilizing the existing social order and maintaining the unity of the home front.

The relationship between warfare and welfare during theses years is an extremely complex problem. While the war inflected long-term trends in the development of social assistance in specific ways, it also set in motion entirely

---

[1] Marie-Elisabeth Lüders, *Das unbekannte Heer. Frauen kämpfen für Deutschland 1914–1918* (Berlin, 1936), 7.

new developments. Moreover, wartime welfare programs never represented merely a neutral, functional response to social dislocation. Rather, they were designed to ensure the reproduction of a specific social order: bourgeois society, its basic institutions, and all the gender hierarchies and other forms of status and inequality on which this society rested. The problem was that these programs unintentionally unsettled the gender hierarchies that they were supposed to reinforce, and the ensuing debates over wartime welfare policy played an important role in the gendering of social and political citizenship.

The evolution of the wartime welfare state was shaped by three broad developments in particular: the new importance with which welfare was endowed by the war; the absolute scale of need resulting from the war; and the kinds of people who became dependent on the state, the way their need was constructed, and the claims that this enabled them to make on the state.

First, the war fundamentally changed the rules of the relief game and gave welfare a new quality. Just as the totalization of war broke down the barriers between military and society, the need to mobilize society behind the war brought about a broad inversion of the political calculus of nineteenth-century deterrence and endowed preventive social welfare programs with a national, military, and social significance that largely overrode the fear of moral hazards that had limited the acceptance of these ideas in the prewar years. Within a matter of months, programs that had been contested or unthinkable before August 1914 were adopted as self-evident necessities for a national community mobilized for industrial warfare, and wartime assistance programs, which were based on principles that were completely foreign to deterrent poor relief, played a catalytic role in the terminal demise of this older assistantial regime. This is not, however, to say that the ideological construct of total war fully corresponded to reality. But it did provide a compelling rationale for the extension of preventive and therapeutic social welfare programs to the entire population, who quite literally were the embodiment of the economic, demographic, and military potential of the nation. In so doing it brought the reproductive activities of the private family into a more direct relation to the state.[2] A number of developments that we will trace in the following pages then conspired to ensure that the preventive, therapeutic welfare programs pioneered during the war would remain the primary means of assisting the needy after 1918.

Second, World War I was a demographic catastrophe for the German people, and the death of so many men, the dissipation of such a huge portion of the nation's accumulated wealth, the disruption of family life, the impaired health of the entire population, and the economic disorder of the war led to a quantum expansion of need and thus provided the most direct stimulus for the expansion of the German welfare state during the war. Between 1914 and 1918, 13,250,000 German men – more than half of all men of military age – served

---

[2] Elizabeth Domansky, "Militarization and Reproduction in World War I Germany," in Geoff Eley, ed., *Society, Culture, and the State in Germany, 1870–1930* (University of Michigan Press, 1996), 427–64.

in the armed forces. Support for the families of many of those men fell to the government, and in many larger industrial cities as much as 30–50% of the home front population depended on state support in the later years of the war. Not only did disabled veterans require state assistance in the form of pensions, medical treatment, and rehabilitative services. The war led to the death of more than 2,000,000 men on the German side alone – nearly one-third of whom left behind wives and children who were entitled to state aid. When the dust had finally settled, 721,000 men were receiving disability pensions (not counting the more than 800,000 veterans who had received lump-sum payments for disability of less than 30%); 1,600,000 persons were receiving survivors pensions (including 365,000 widows who had not remarried, 1,028,000 children, and nearly 200,000 parents supported by sons killed in the war); and another 1,000,000 former members of the middle classes, whose businesses, savings, investments, and pensions had been destroyed by the war and the inflation, were also receiving state assistance.[3]

Third, the mobilization of the nation for war meant that large segments of the population, who in normal times would never have come into contact with public assistance, or perhaps would have done so only in their capacity as poor guardians, had to depend – either temporarily or permanently – on the state to provide for their basic needs, and the constitution of these "new poor" was as much a discursive and political process as an economic one. These people could make claims on the state in ways that the traditional poor could not. As citizen-soldiers, the men who fought in the war – those who survived as well as those who did not – had sacrificed for the nation and thereby implicitly entered into a social contract that called on the nation to honor their sacrifice and make them and their families whole. This was a debt of honor that could not be paid in the currency of poor relief or charity. However, these claims, and those of the other groups of the new poor, could not be translated in any straightforward manner into entitlements to pensions or social services because wartime welfare programs were often asked to serve multiple goals that could not be easily reconciled with each other: Was the primary purpose of benefits to disabled veterans to honor their service or reintegrate them into the productive life of the nation? Was the primary purpose of separation allowances to enable women – especially those with young children – to devote themselves full time to their domestic duties or to relieve these women of their domestic duties so that they could take work in war-related industries? Should wartime welfare programs provide generous benefits in order to keep spirits high on the home front or should these benefits be minimal and means-tested in order to save money and maintain the work ethic of these dependents and survivors? To

---

[3] "Die Zahl der Kriegsbeschädigten und Kriegshinterbliebenen in Deutschland," *Wirtschaft und Statistik*, 5 (1925), 28–30; *Reichsarbeitsblatt* 12:21 (July 1932), II. Nichtamtlicher Teil: "Die Zahl der versorgungsberechtigten Kriegsbeschädigten und Kriegshinterbliebenen Deutschlands im Mai 1932," 287–91; and *Statistik des Deutschen Reiches*, Bd. 421: *Die öffentliche Fürsorge im Deutschen Reich 1927 bis 1931*, 12.

what extent could and should the distinction between the new poor, whose need was ostensibly the direct or indirect result of the war, rather than the failure of character or will, and other needy groups, especially the disreputable recipients of poor relief, be preserved? Or, conversely, to what extent should anticipated future contributions to the productive life of the nation, rather than either past sacrifice or moral failing, be made the measure of social rights? And how could these programs be designed so as to strike a viable balance between the fiscal interests of the Reich and those of the local welfare state, which quickly became the primary provider of wartime welfare services?

These differences were complicated by mobilization from below, which gave rise to an entirely new kind of social politics. By 1916, all but the most affluent found their standard of living being whipsawed between chronic shortages and rising prices. While the government called on the home front to support the war effort by persevering in the face of material deprivation and personal loss, the women who were responsible for holding together house and home, and especially women of the popular classes, who were most sensitive to the failings of state-organized provisioning, in turn called on the government to secure for them the necessities that they needed to carry out their domestic obligations. Very early on, these women began to mobilize to protest against the perceived inequalities in suffering resulting from the government's failure to hold up its end of the bargain.

By 1917, the various groups of war victims themselves began to mobilize, and the resulting conflicts pitted the different elements of the new poor against each other – and all of them against the local and national states – as they struggled in an intrinsically fluid semantic field to conquer a stable position from which to define their own needs and rights. Veterans, dependents, and survivors employed a rhetoric of sacrifice and service to justify their claims – and the rhetoric of victimization whenever they felt that the nation was not living up to its end of the wartime social contract.[4] The wives and widows of men serving in the armed forces were angry that social workers and welfare officials were using wartime welfare, which was ostensibly an entitlement grounded in the service of their male relatives to the nation, as an opportunity to monitor and discipline them, while every benefit offered to one group was automatically perceived as unjust by those groups who were not so privileged and who felt their service and sacrifice thereby devalued. The last major participant in this free-for-all were the new social experts, whose claim to apolitical expertise led to chronic conflict with a clientele that was politically empowered and endowed with new kinds of symbolic capital. Consequently, rather than acting as an engine of political integration, wartime welfare became an engine of political disaffection that served to divide the nation as much as to unite it.

---

[4] Greg Eghigian has explored the role of sacrifice and victimhood in the formation of the German welfare state in "Pain, Entitlement, and Social Citizenship in Modern Germany," in Paul Betts and Greg Eghigian, eds., *Pain and Prosperity. Reconsidering Twentieth-Century German History* (Stanford University Press, 2003), 16–34.

The cumulative impact of these conflicts was to make wartime social politics into a space of interminable trench warfare; anyone who expected that these programs would succeed in mobilizing the nation behind the war effort was quickly disabused of such ideas; and, in reality, these programs played a central role in turning the home front against the war and the state after 1916.[5]

The war led to the broad breakthrough of new ideas on social citizenship and preventive social welfare while endowing these programs with a new significance. To a large degree the Weimar welfare system simply codified an entire set of social programs that had been established during the war and passed on to a new generation the economic costs of these programs and the political and cultural conflicts that they had engendered. It is, therefore, perhaps most appropriate to see the war as a kind of "saddle" period connecting two distinctly different assistantial regimes, and this transformation will be the focus of this and the following chapter.

Female Dependence, Female Citizenship, and the Wartime Challenge to Deterrent Poor Relief

At a June 1915 meeting called to create a new organization for the welfare for pre-school-age children, Polligkeit, who would become the most important social welfare expert during the Weimar Republic, explained that in the coming years social policy would have to be a "social policy for the family."[6] This was a two-pronged statement that referred both to the need for day-care centers and social hygiene programs to directly assist needy infants and toddlers as well as to the broader need for social programs to shore up the family and thus put mothers in a position where they could carry out their maternal duties. This latter point was an obvious concern in view of the fact that the family was considered by many to be weakened, endangered, or even transformed by the absence of so many men at the front, though it was of equal relevance to the ongoing debate over the impact of women's factory work on domesticity and motherhood, a problem that would only grow more urgent as the war progressed. But the constitution of these women as "needy" objects of social concern, and the strategies adopted to remedy this need, was informed by normative visions of family, gender, domesticity, and sexuality, and this section will examine how the basic wartime welfare programs for dependents and survivors

---

[5] Belinda Davis, *Home Fires Burning. Food, Politics, and Everyday Life in World War I Berlin* (University of North Carolina Press, 2000); Wilfried Rudloff, *Die Wohlfahrtsstadt. Kommunale Ernährungs-, Fürsorge- und Wohnungspolitik am Beispiel Münchens 1910–1933* (Vandenhoeck & Ruprecht, 1998); Maureen Healy, *Vienna and the Fall of the Habsburg Empire. Total War and Everyday Life in World War I* (Cambridge University Press, 2004); and Young-sun Hong, "World War I and the German Welfare Sate: Gender, Religion, and the Paradoxes of Modernity," in Eley, ed., *Society, Culture, and the State in Germany*, 345–69.
[6] "Besprechung über den Zusammenschluss zwecks Organisation der Klein-Kinder-Fürsorge (June 30, 1915)," ADW CA/J, 58.

were designed to preserve the elementary structures of bourgeois society, the ways in which these programs tended to undermine or unsettle these norms, and the impact of these programs on both deterrent poor relief and the parameters of social and political citizenship.[7]

The family, and more specifically the male breadwinner family, was the axis around which all wartime welfare programs turned. This view of the family was based on essentialist assumptions regarding the intrinsic nurturing dispositions of women, assumptions that justified gender hierarchies within the family and a sexual division of labor between the public and the private spheres. The correlate to women's exclusion from the public sphere was the need for, and a right to, support in the form of a male breadwinner, who was also responsible for representing the private family in public affairs. Men were seen as the embodiment of authority, reason, and order, and their authority within the family was based in large part on the power that flowed from their role as breadwinner.

These assumptions regarding women's dependence, which were often grounded in discourses on their reproductive capacity and the need for its protection, had deeply influenced prewar social legislation in Germany, and during the war, the belief that the family, and the social order on which it rested, was endangered by the temporary or permanent absence of so many family fathers provided the most basic rationale for the expansion of wartime welfare programs.[8] As Klumker explained, the antiquated notion that welfare for these persons consisted exclusively or even primarily in providing them with pensions had to be rejected. Rather, he insisted, "what must be restored to the family is that which it is lacking: but that is not primarily money, but rather the direction and leadership of the family head."[9] This idea was also shared by the women's movement, which felt empowered by its role in putting these principles into practice. In the words of Helene Simon, "pensions and monetary donations are not sufficient to ward off the decline of the family that has been robbed of its head. The purpose of social welfare is to stand in for the protector, advisor and educator so far as and so long as the economic, moral,

---

[7] There are a number of important works on gender, welfare, and the home front in World War I Germany. See, in addition to the works by Davis, Domansky and Hong cited above, Karen Hagemann and Stefanie Schüler-Springorum, eds., *Home/Front. The Military, War and Gender in Twentieth-Century Germany* (Berg, 2002); Birthe Kundrus, *Kriegerfrauen. Familienpolitik und Geschlechterverhältnisse im Ersten und Zweiten Weltkrieg* (Hans Christians Verlag, 1995); and Ute Daniel, *The War from Within. German Working-Class Women in the First Word War* (Berg, 1997).

[8] Susan Pedersen has demonstrated the role that wartime welfare programs played in consolidating the breadwinner model and the forms of hierarchy and dependence it entailed in Britain. See Pedersen, "Gender, Welfare, and Citizenship in Britain during the Great War," *AHR* 95:4 (October 1990), 983–1006, and *Family, Dependence, and the Origins of the Welfare State. Britain and France 1914–1945* (Cambridge University Press, 1993).

[9] Sitzung des Zentralausschusses [des Deutschen Vereins für Armenpflege und Wohltätigkeit] am 22. und 23. Januar 1915, IfG 226 (2).

and psychological independence [of the family] has not yet been established and secured."[10] The terms *Kriegerfrauen* and *Kriegskinder* were widely used to describe those persons who were regarded as needy precisely because of the absence of a male authority figure and breadwinner.[11]

Military service was the foundation for male political citizenship. Although women were the object and beneficiary of these wartime social welfare programs, they were eligible not in their own right, but rather as dependents of men. The expectations were that these social welfare programs would be a temporary substitute for the absent husband, that they would enable these *Kriegerfrauen* to maintain the household and continue to perform their domestic and reproductive labors, and that men would assume their natural roles as family head and breadwinner when they returned from the front. The home front was a rhetorical construct that reflected the distinction between a martial, rational, aggressive, public male space and a maternal, nurturing, domestic, female space, a space that was at once geographical, social, and political, and the continued prosecution of the war depended, quite literally, on maintaining the stability of the "home" front and all that it symbolized.

If *Kriegerfrauen* enjoyed an entitlement to welfare programs by virtue of the military service of their breadwinner, this was not an unlimited or unconditional right, and in return for these benefits women were obligated to contribute their all to the war effort within their own proper sphere. The obligations instituted by state social welfare programs created an opening through which social workers could monitor and discipline these women and children and promote more modern, rational approaches to the entire spectrum of maternal tasks. However, to the extent that the successful prosecution of the war was regarded as being dependent on better mothering, these tasks assumed a new quality, moving out of the private realm and becoming public matters of national import. As this happened, women too moved at least partly out of the political shadow of their husbands and fathers and entered into a more direct relation with the state that was no longer mediated entirely through these men. Thus, one of the unintended effects of wartime welfare and the mobilization of women for war was the creation of a new space in which the idea of female citizenship could be explored.

Wartime welfare was not only paternalist in the sense of seeking to sustain the basic institutions of a patriarchal social order. It was also a maternalist

---

[10] Helene Simon, "Ueber Versorgung und Fürsorge," *SPr* 31:33–5 (August 1922), cols. 857–60, 894–6, 939–40, especially 894.

[11] There was a broad debate on causes of the perceived increase in juvenile delinquency during the war and the best means of combating it. See Edward Ross Dickinson, *The Politics of German Child Welfare from the Empire to the Federal Republic* (Harvard University Press, 1996), 113ff.; Eve Rosenhaft, "Restoring Moral Order on the Home Front. Compulsory Savings Plans for Young Workers in Germany, 1916–19," in Frans Coetzee and Marilyn Shevin-Coetzee, eds., *Authority, Identity and the Social History of the Great War* (Berghahn Books, 1995), 81–109; and Andrew Donson, *Youth in the Fatherless Land: War Pedagogy, Nationalism, and Authority in Germany, 1914–1918* (forthcoming).

project. These programs presumed that those character traits and virtues that were believed to be the spiritual expression of women's biological nature had a unique value for the greater society, and they were also to a large degree the product of women's agency.[12] But maternalism was intrinsically ambiguous, and the question was whether women's sacrifice, the value of their factory work and other public labors, or their contribution to the biological and social reproduction of the nation could become the basis for women's citizenship and the refiguration of the gender order along maternalist lines? As one woman wrote to the League of German Women's Associations,

out there, the men were doing something important; every worker was a hero. Everyone expected this of him, and, look, he was something only because it was expected. What resounding camaraderie, what ambition of each to outdo the other.... Who would have thought about what women could achieve? Achievement? Make a positive contribution? *Ach nein.* Sacrifice, wait, be patient, every woman for herself alone in her small, lonely household.... Nowhere have I heard women speaking to other women about their needs and the liberation from them, nowhere "we women." Nowhere. We are also valuable beings. I've bitterly suffered from this, as have almost all, and I repeat once again: as a female, it was as if I were extinguished – and this in a time that was so filled with masculine figures and their deeds![13]

Wartime welfare and the payment of benefits directly to women for their maternal labors, even if they were only eligible for such assistance by virtue of the military service of men, raised a host of questions regarding the relation between women's work, domesticity, and citizenship. Statutory programs may have guaranteed assistance to married women, but the question of whether women enjoyed this entitlement by virtue of their dependence on absent men or by virtue of their service to the nation remained a bit more open than many people would have liked, though recent literature has been circumspect in its assessment of the contribution of the war to women's emancipation in Germany.[14]

The foundation of wartime welfare were the separation allowances (*Familienunterstützung*) paid to the dependents of men serving in the military.[15]

---

[12] For an account of maternalism and its influence on welfare policy, see Seth Koven and Sonya Michel, "Introduction," Koven and Michel, eds., *Mothers of a New World. Maternalist Politics and the Origins of Welfare States* (Routledge, 1993), 1–42.

[13] HLA: 45-188/2 (November 1914).

[14] See Margaret Higonnet and Patrice Higonnet, "The Double Helix," in Margaret Higonnet et al., eds., *Behind the Lines. Gender and the Two World Wars* (Yale University Press, 1987), 31–47; Daniel, *The War from Within*; Reinhard Sieder, "Behind the Lines: Working-Class Family Life in Wartime Vienna," in Richard Wall and Jay Winter, eds., *The Upheaval of War. Family, Work and Welfare in Europe, 1914–1918* (Cambridge University Press, 1988), 109–38; and Domansky, "Militarization and Reproduction in World War I Germany."

[15] These were paid on the basis of an 1888 law that was updated on August 4, 1914 and revised several times during the course of the war. E. Friedeberg and Siddy Wronsky, eds., *Handbuch der Kriegsfürsorge im Deutschen Reich* (Berlin, 1917), 32–60, reprint the successive revisions and the important decrees regulating the implementation of the law.

These allowances were paid to the needy wives and children of these soldiers by special local delivery agencies (*Lieferungsverbände*), which were geographically coextensive with municipal or rural district governments, and these delivery agencies were to be reimbursed by the Reich for their expenditures. The purpose of these allowances was to facilitate the maintenance of an "orderly household" and to ensure that "all of those concerns that his dependents are not being adequately cared for, which might impair his nervous strength, are kept away from the family breadwinner as he faces the enemy." Aside from the fact that eligibility was contingent on female dependence, rather than female contribution, the most important feature of these separation allowances was that they were entirely independent of poor relief and were to entail none of the disabilities associated with public assistance. The social dimension of the law, that is, the subordination of the traditional emphasis on combating dependence to the maintenance of the lifestyle of the recipients, was also reflected in the way that need was to be determined. Government decrees repeatedly explained that local officials were to be flexible and generous in determining need and not adhere to the principles of poor relief. The government prohibited the delivery agencies from taking into account other forms of assistance, such as charitable aid or assistance from the employers of their husbands, in determining whether or not these women were eligible for allowances, and it even permitted – again in contrast to poor relief – officials to overlook the possession of a small amount of capital or the ownership of a small piece of real estate in determining need "if its preservation seems necessary for the family." In response to numerous complaints from these soldiers' wives, in October 1915 the Prussian government issued a decree that explained that "it is urgently necessary to investigate need in a manner that is free from all narrowmindedness." Although many applications had been turned down because these women were deemed capable of supporting themselves, this decree explained that these women generally had small children to care for and that, ability to work notwithstanding, maternal duties had to be given priority over paid employment.[16]

During the war, separation allowances were revised in two directions: the scope of persons covered by the law was expanded and the allowances themselves were increased. The one point of real controversy was what to do for the illegitimate children of these men. This was an issue of considerable importance both in principle and in practice since an estimated 1 million such children had fathers serving in the military. The law governing separation allowances, as amended in August 1914, had for the first time constructed a familial relationship between illegitimate children and their fathers, though it did so in the narrowest possible terms. While Progressive youth welfare reformers called for the extension of benefits to these children, such proposals were opposed by a broad spectrum of other groups, including religious organizations, which

---

[16] All of these quotations are taken from the 1914/15 Prussian regulations reprinted in Friedeberg and Wronsky, *Kriegsfürsorge*, 42–3. Also see the "Zusammenstellung der Grundsätze über die Anwendung des Gesetzes..." (April 19, 1915), BA RAdI 12091 Bl. 376ff.

complained that ignoring differences between legitimate and illegitimate children would undermine marriage and the family.[17] Across 1914/15, the Reich government tried to tack between military/political necessities and conservative principles by making it substantially easier to bring illegitimate children within the protective scope of the law, without, however, accepting their outright equality with the children of marital unions. Reich officials insisted that, for the purpose of the separation allowance law, the eligibility of these children had to depend on the recognition by the father of his obligation to support the child. But they also sought to make this easier by agreeing that this paternal obligation could be established by a letter from the soldier to the mother and that it could even be inferred from the fact that the man had voluntarily supported the child in the past.[18] This seemed to be the best compromise that could be reached given the existing balance of political power, and an estimated 340,000 children were covered by the January 1916 Bundesrat decree that formalized the policies that had been promulgated on an ad hoc basis since August 1914. Progressives such as Klumker characterized this as an important innovation that, at least in part, placed the welfare of these children above both the private interest in the regulation of property claims within the family and an exaggerated and narrow-minded conservative interest in upholding marriage and family – no matter what the cost to children born outside this framework.[19]

Allowances were initially set at 9 marks monthly for women (12 marks in winter) and 6 marks for children. In spring 1915 the winter rates became the base rate, and in September 1915 rates were raised to 15.0 and 7.5 marks, respectively. Allowances also included free medical care for those women and children not covered by sickness insurance. However, the program generated widespread dissatisfaction on the part of both administrators and beneficiaries. Despite repeated pronouncements from Berlin, local administrators often took anything but a flexible approach in assessing need, especially in their insistence that able-bodied women could not be considered needy. In addition, there were widespread complaints that generous separation allowances had made many women financially better off than before the war and that, with ready cash in their pockets and free from the guiding hands of husbands, these women were on occasion abandoning themselves to luxury and other forms of improper behavior.[20]

Part of the problem was that the law required municipal officials to grant the full amount of the allowance as soon as even a minimal amount of unmet

---

[17] Christian Jasper Klumker, "Kriegsunterstützung und uneheliche Kinder," *ZfA* 15:10-11 (October/November 1914), 287-95; Klumker, "Kriegswaisenrente für uneheliche Kinder," *Die Frauenfrage* 18:2 (January 16, 1916), 9-10; and the materials in ADCV 319.4 SKF: B II 3.
[18] "Zusammenstellung der Grundsätze über die Anwendung des Gesetzes... (April 19, 1915)," BA RAdI 12091 Bl. 380, and Friedeberg and Wronsky, *Kriegsfürsorge*, 41-2.
[19] Klumker, "Kriegsunterstützung und uneheliche Kinder," 288-9.
[20] See, for example, the two letters from Magdeburg Oberpräsident von Hegel (March 1 and April 29, 1915), BA RAdI 12093.

need had been established. This meant that allowances and other sources of income could together exceed the needs of these *Kriegerfrauen*, at least in the eyes of the officials who administered the programs. Not only was there an obvious conflict between the aims of separation allowances and the principles of deterrent poor relief. Blanket eligibility for separation allowances also created a cleavage among the prewar recipients of poor relief, and it did not seem entirely just that such families should suddenly find themselves so much better off when other persons remained dependent on poor relief simply because no male relative had been drafted. And what was to become of these persons when the war was over? Were they to be forced back upon public assistance, or did somehow military service permanently cleanse them of their previous social stigma?

While a steady stream of complaints pushed the government in the direction of across-the-board increases in allowance rates, local officials complained that such a policy was providing too much assistance to some without ensuring that everyone's basic needs were met. Even worse, such schematic increases were not capable of keeping up with the rising cost of living, and, despite the September 1915 increase, by the fall of the following year, the government was under pressure to establish uniform minimum incomes to which all soldiers' wives would be entitled. The League of German Cities, however, objected to such a policy, warning that another round of across-the-board increases would place an even greater burden on their already-overburdened finances. The league feared that the practice of excluding all or part of the earnings of these soldiers' wives in calculating their need was breeding covetousness, and the organization insisted that the only way to do justice to all was to leave municipal officials free to match assistance more precisely with proven need.[21]

This conflict between across-the-board increases and individualized assistance reflected fundamental differences in the way that need was viewed and rights constructed by various groups, and the debate over the reform of separation allowances established a pattern that was to endure until the Nazis made it too dangerous to complain about insufficient state assistance. In this instance, the administration decided that, for reasons of military and political necessity, it had to give priority to reducing the widespread complaints from *Kriegerfrauen*. A January 1916 Bundesrat decree established minimum income levels (graduated according to locale and cost of living) below which need was to be presumed, and women whose incomes were above these levels could still qualify for allowances if justified by their specific circumstances. But despite these requirements, the administration recognized that the elimination of these complaints would largely depend on the way the law was applied at the local level, and it warned the state governments that they would have to "repeatedly and expressly" admonish local delivery agencies, which had a strong financial incentive to limit benefits, that they were obligated to be positively disposed to these women, especially since the rising cost of living since the beginning of the

[21] Berlin Mayor Wermuth to Reich Chancellor (December 27, 1915), BA RAdI 12095 Bl. 2ff.

war meant that many women whose applications had originally been rejected now qualified for allowances.[22]

But separation allowances were only the subterranean foundation, so to speak, of the wartime welfare system. Already in August 1914, the Reich Interior Minister issued a decree requiring local government to set up wartime welfare programs (*Kriegswohlfahrtspflege* in the narrow sense) for "all persons who become needy as a consequence of the war." This assistance was not to entail any of the legal disabilities of poor relief or to be limited to the poor relief existence minimum.[23] The goal of wartime welfare was to combat the churning of class structures and preserve the standard of living and social position that people had occupied before the war, that is, "to the extent possible the preservation of the domestic conditions (*Hausstand*) of the soldier and the appropriate maintenance of his dependents."[24] This new "social existence minimum" became the measure of need which the delivery agencies were obligated to relieve.[25]

While separation allowances were themselves set so low that dependents could not make ends meet if they had no other source of income, this was done in the expectation that local government would step in to supplement Reich payments.[26] While these supplements – which generally amounted to 50–100% of Reich separation allowances – gave local government a minimal ability to adapt assistance rates to local circumstances, the fiscal concerns of local government often played a greater role in determining local supplements than did considerations of need or equity. The result was widespread dissatisfaction with both the absolute level of assistance and the huge differences in assistance rates from place to place.

Wartime welfare represented an immense, open-ended, and ultimately unsustainable commitment that the Reich entered into on behalf of local government (though it should be noted that local spending for wartime welfare was partly offset by substantial decreases in local poor relief costs).[27] Although

---

[22] Letter from Reich Chancellor (January 25, 1916), BA RAdI 12095 Bl. 209ff. See RAdI 12094 for the petitions and discussions leading up to the January decree and the criticisms of the proposed law by the various parties.

[23] Interior Ministry circular (August 28, 1914), BA R43F 2411. For the adjudication of this separation between poor relief and wartime welfare, see the ruling of the Federal Office of Relief Residence Affairs (March 27, 1915), BA BAdI 1281 Bl. 4097ff., which defined wartime welfare as all assistance required because of the military service of the breadwinner.

[24] "Zusammenstellung der Grundsätze über die Anwendung des Gesetzes...," Bl. 379.

[25] See, for example, Badischer Heimatdank, *Bericht über die Sitzung des Badischen Landesausschusses der Kriegshinterbliebenenfürsorge am Samstag, 27. Oktober 1917* (Karlsruhe, 1918), 15–16, and Friedeberg and Wronsky, *Kriegsfürsorge*, 111.

[26] See the memorandum dated February 26, 1913, LAB A Rep 044, 1644. All the cities in Greater Berlin, for example, agreed to add a 100% supplement to Reich separation allowances and to provide the same benefits to illegitimate children living in the same household.

[27] On the asymmetry between what local government was obligated to pay out and what the Reich was obligated to reimburse, see "Zusammenstellung der Grundsätze über die Anwendung des Gesetzes...," Bl. 379.

the Reich may have had no choice but to make such a promise, and although it certainly did so in the expectation that the war would be brief and prices stable, as the war dragged on and social dislocation mounted, the gap between what the Reich administration promised and what local government was able to deliver grew to gigantic proportions. Over the course of the war the failure to realize the ambitious aims of wartime welfare increasingly undermined the legitimacy of the government in the eyes of the population that depended on these programs for their basic necessities, and this conflict was to permeate every public welfare program between 1914 and 1924 and beyond.[28]

It is virtually impossible to get a firm fix on the real value of wartime welfare and pensions over any sustained period of time because the rising cost of living constantly outpaced increases in government assistance rates. The most relevant statistical indicator here is the standard of living index, which rose from 100 in 1913 to 103 in 1914, 129 in 1915, 170 in 1916, 253 in 1917, and 313 in 1918.[29] These problems are illustrated by a fall 1916 study that the Saxon government undertook in order to get a better measure of the actual needs of military dependents. Here, Saxon officials established a list of the quantities of the basic foodstuffs required to provide a modest, but sufficient, diet for *Kriegerfrauen*, and they then added a 25% supplement for housing, clothing, and other needs. Local officials were simply to plug in local prices to determine local assistance rates. What Saxon officials found was that, although women needed 35.00–39.32 marks per month to meet their basic needs, Reich separation allowances amounted to only 15 marks per month at that point. While the Reich allowed a flat rate of 7.50 marks per child, the Saxon survey also determined that infants and toddlers needed a minimum of 9.75–11.57 marks per month to meet their basic needs, while older children needed 19.50–22.75 marks. Ministry officials noted that Reich separation allowances were not sufficient even for the countryside, where prices were lower and people lived more simply, and they estimated that the city of Dresden would have to increase its own spending by 135% above its current level in order to meet the minimum needs of military dependents – a figure that allows us to estimate the magnitude of need that was not being met even before inflation and the cost of living began to spiral out of control. And, as Saxon officials conceded, all these calculations were to a certain extent artificial because many basic foodstuffs were simply not available at these prices.[30]

While there was widespread agreement in the fall of 1916 that something had to be done before winter to bring separation allowances and municipal

---

[28] Letters from the Saxon Ministry of Foreign Affairs (January 31, 1918) and the State Secretary in the Reich Interior Ministry (March 28, 1918), BA RAdI 12106 Bl. 253ff., 258ff.

[29] Jürgen Kocka, *Facing Total War* (Berg, 1984), 22.

[30] Sächsisches Ministerium der auswärtigen Angelegenheiten to Reichsamt des Innern (September 15, 1916), BA RAdI 12097. Roger Chickering provides a good account of these problems and the other challenges of wartime society in *The Great War and Urban Life in Germany. Freiburg, 1914–1918* (Cambridge University Press, 2007), especially 438ff.

Female Dependence, Female Citizenship, and the Wartime Challenge 219

supplements more into line with the real cost of living, opinion was divided as to the best way to proceed. In addition to the usual reservations about across-the-board increases, there was a new concern that the generous assistance that had been paid to military dependents to boost the morale of men at the front was demoralizing these *Kriegerfrauen*. For example, one official from rural West Prussia complained that, because current rates were already more than adequate for many military dependents living in rural areas, women and children who had traditionally helped out with the potato harvest had simply invoked their "right" to state assistance and decided to stay at home. This magistrate complained that "numerous" women were either taking their allowances to the bank or wasting them on such luxuries as clothing, toys, train travel, and better food, something that he noted was generating bitterness on the part of those women who lived in similar circumstances but who, for whatever reasons, were not eligible for such public largesse. He concluded that military morale "would not be any worse if from the very beginning allowances had been lower and the right to support had not been so insistently preached to the people from every direction."[31] This question of the rights and duties of *Kriegerfrauen* was to become a major issue across 1917/18 as these women came to be seen as an important untapped source of labor for the war economy.

Despite such complaints, the real inadequacy of separation allowances in most every other part of the country and political pressure from every direction led the Reich to increase separation allowances to 20 marks per month (10 marks for children) in November 1916.[32] But this increase only made prevailing separation allowances marginally less inadequate, and whatever benefits it might have brought were vastly outweighed by the sheer impossibility of obtaining food at any price across the winter of 1916/17. By mid-1917, there were again widespread calls for yet another increase in allowance rates. Although public officials generally conceded the legitimacy of these demands, they objected to yet another across-the-board increase, arguing that the entire system had become dysfunctional. While inadequate benefits undermined public faith in the goodwill of local officials and fueled the widespread calls for expanded entitlements, across-the-board benefits, these officials argued, served only to further demoralize these *Kriegerfrauen* while excessively increasing the total cost of assistance to military dependents and forcing local delivery agencies to bear a disproportionate cost of this wasteful policy. The only way out of this vicious circle, they argued, was to give local officials greater latitude in setting allowance rates and at the same time to fundamentally reform the way

---

[31] Landrat des Kreises Berent to Regierungspräsident Danzig (November 22, 1916), BA RAdI 12099.

[32] Reich spending on its share of separation allowances had risen from 27 million marks per month in August 1914 to 65 million in January 1915, 90 million in July 1915, and 129 million in December 1915, and it was expected to increase to over 170 million (or more than 2 billion marks annually) after the November 1916 increase. "Wirtschaftspolitische Wochenschau" (December 2, 1916), BA RAdI 12099.

these programs were financed in order to relieve some of the financial pressure on local officials.³³ These arguments ultimately carried the day, and in November 1917 the Bundesrat issued a decree that returned a substantial degree of control to local officials by requiring delivery agencies to increase separation allowances by an amount that was deemed appropriate to local circumstances (but by at least 5 marks) with the Reich, rather than the local delivery agencies, bearing the cost of this increase.³⁴

Kriegerfrauen and the Politics of National Obligation

The battles of Verdun and the Somme brought an end to the nineteenth century and forced all the belligerent powers to find new ways of organizing themselves for war. These were battles of attrition whose outcome depended to a large degree on the quantity of men and materiel that each side could throw against the other and their ability to mobilize the productive forces of the nation to feed these mass armies and produce the weapons of industrialized warfare. In Germany, this change was marked by the appointment of a new military high command under generals Hindenburg and Ludendorff and the adoption of the Hindenburg Plan, which called for the total mobilization of labor and industry in order to bring about, within a matter of months, the quantum increase in military production that the new commanders believed necessary to win the war. The December 1916 Auxiliary Labor Law, which was pushed through the Reichstag by the military against the opposition of industry, was one of the pillars of this strategy. It rendered the entire male population aged 18–60 liable for state service in either the army or designated war industries. In exchange, a series of concessions was made to labor concerning collective bargaining and industrial codetermination. This law marked a major step toward the development of parliamentary government and the integration of the working classes into the German state.³⁵

Although the original draft of the law had also called for the compulsory mobilization of women, this provision was ultimately dropped. However, women were still regarded as an important untapped source of labor that could free up men for service at the front. The question was how – without undermining the commitment to motherhood and the preservation of the home front – to draw these women into the industrial workforce.

---

[33] K. Staatsministerium des Innern to K. Staatsministerium [Bavaria] (September 7, 1917), BA RAdI 12102, Bl. 262ff.; Staatsekretär des Innern to Staatsekretär des Reichsschatzamts (October 15, 1917), and the letter dated October 16, 1917, both in BA RAdI 12103 Bl. 87ff. and 168ff.; and Bavarian Staatsministerium to Reichsamt des Innern (January 29, 1918), BA RAdI 12105, Bl. 219.

[34] Circulars from Reich Chancellor (October 23 and November 3, 1917), BA RAdI 12103, Bl. 151 and 299f. These problems continued to worsen through 1917/18. However, there is little to be gained by following these debates through their final iteration during the last weeks of the war.

[35] Gerald Feldman, *Army, Industry and Labor in Germany, 1914–1918* (Princeton University Press, 1966), 150ff.

Even before the passage of the Auxiliary Labor Law, General Wilhelm Groener, the head of the War Office, had met with leaders of the women's movement to discuss the problems involved in mobilizing women for the war economy. These women explained to Groener that social welfare programs were the key to achieving this goal. Not only did women have to be educated about the national importance of their work and learn the skills and habits that were necessary for factory labor. Steps also had to be taken to protect women's reproductive health and to ease the constraints of domestic responsibility that hindered women from taking such jobs. In December 1916 the National Committee for Women's War Work (*Nationaler Ausschuß für Frauenarbeit im Kriege*) was established to coordinate the work of the major women's and welfare organizations to support these goals. Within the War Office itself, a Women's Department was established with two major divisions: one acting as a labor office or labor exchange for women and the other responsible for social services for working women, including *Kriegerfrauen*. Both of these departments were headed by Lüders, and both this administrative structure and this personal union between the two departments were replicated at the level of the military districts.[36]

This recognition of the national importance of social work by the War Ministry was something of a victory for the women's movement, though the degree to which the creation of the Women's Department (which was sometimes known as the "Pacifier Department") reflected a change in men's attitudes should not be overestimated. At the first meeting of the National Committee, Groener emphasized the importance of social work in steeling the population behind the men at the front and creating an "an absolute will to prevail." However, he also emphasized that the overriding goal was to increase military production, and he reminded the National Committee "that it is not a question of providing social welfare for its own sake, but rather one of doing so for the sake of greater production."[37] In practice, the work of this welfare department consisted of encouraging war industries to make special accommodations for working mothers, including providing rooms where women workers could nurse their children, creating factory day-care programs (whose schedules would be more attuned to the needs of working mothers) and cafeterias, instituting half-day shifts, and hiring factory social workers to watch over

---

[36] Lüders, *Das unbekannte Heer*; Young-sun Hong, "Gender and the Politics of Welfare Reform in World War I Germany," *SH* 17 (May 1992), 251–270; Daniel, *The War from Within*, 73ff.; Catherine Elaine Boyd, *Nationaler Frauendienst: Middle-Class Women in the Service of the Fatherland, 1914–1918* (Dissertation, University of Georgia, 1979), 120ff.; and Gertrud Bäumer, "Was verdient von der Tätigkeit der Frauenreferate beim Kriegsamt und den Kriegsamtsstellen in die Friedensarbeit übernommen zu werden?" in *Gekürzter Bericht über die Tagung der Freien Vereinigung für Kriegswohlfahrt am 1. und 2. Dezember 1917 in Hamburg*, 32–46.

[37] "Niederschrift über die 1. Sitzung des Nationalen Ausschusses für Frauenarbeit im Kriege" (January 29, 1917), ADCV CA XIX 15. Groener also admitted that women's performance in the factories had been "truly excellent (*wirklich ausgezeichnet*)," and he conceded that "women had shown themselves to be capable of much more strenuous work than had previously been assumed."

the welfare of these women. This often also meant pressuring local associations to abandon their discriminatory policies against unmarried mothers and their children and give up many long-standing restrictions that they had put in place in what they saw as an attempt to ensure that these facilities would not weaken parental responsibility.[38]

The Hindenburg Plan and the Auxiliary Labor Law both reflected the ascendancy of the military over civilian officials, and the new priority of military production over the earlier concern to conserve the family was also apparent in Groener's charge to the National Committee, much to the consternation of broad segments of the social reform community. In March 1917, the government issued a decree on separation allowances that reflected these new priorities. This decree allowed local officials to withhold allowances from *Kriegerfrauen* who refused to accept appropriate work if they were physically fit for such work and not constrained by their household obligations. This decree effectively altered the definition of need employed by local delivery agencies and, at least in theory, circumscribed the rights of *Kriegerfrauen* more narrowly. The basic problem was that this decree did not spell out what was meant by a woman being "constrained" by household duties. A number of women's organizations protested that women with young children to care for could not be considered "socially" available for work.[39] Moreover, the unions complained that forcing *Kriegerfrauen* to work by threatening to withhold their allowances was discriminatory and represented an attempt to introduce by military decree an obligation that had been specifically excluded from the Auxiliary Labor Law. If the labor shortage was so dire as to justify the abridgement of the rights of needy *Kriegerfrauen*, they argued, then a work obligation should be introduced for *all* women, not just those who depended on state support. However, the administration refused to back away from the new policy because, given the current military situation, it did not think that it was unreasonable to ask greater sacrifices from *Kriegerfrauen* and other citizens, especially if these sacrifices were made more palatable by expanded social services.[40]

In 1917/18, the war economy was of paramount importance, and public officials were much more interested in drawing *Kriegerfrauen* into war work than in punishing them for shirking. However, the instrumentalization of social work to eliminate obstacles to women's factory work would not have increased the number of women working in war industries if these women would have thereby lost their eligibility for separation allowances. Since the various ruses

---

[38] For an example of these older attitudes, see Elisabeth Stürickow, "Das Charlottenburger Jugendheim," *BfSA* 5:4 (April 1, 1913), 25–6.
[39] "Eingabe betreffend Familienunterstützung an arbeitende Frauen (June 4, 1917)" and the response by the Reich Chancellor (August 14, 1917) in HLA 186/1.
[40] See the letters from the Generalkommission der Gewerkschaften Deutschlands (March 21, 1917) and the response by the Reich Chancellor (April 4, 1917) in BA RAdI 12100 and the second letter from the Generalkomission (November 22, 1917) in BA RAdI 12104.

that *Kriegerfrauen* relied on to engage in remunerative work without losing their allowances tended to disrupt production, both employers and local officials supported the idea of permitting *Kriegerfrauen* to keep some percentage (most often 50%) of their earnings without incurring any reduction in their benefits. This policy, together with the tangible benefits of working in war industries (high wages, supplementary food rations, and easier access to scarce food through factory cafeterias), gave these women a strong incentive to move into the paid workforce, and this policy was finally codified shortly before the end of the war.[41]

However, two contradictory discourses on women were woven around this policy. On the one hand, *Kriegerfrauen* were often depicted as unpatriotic slackers. In view of the deteriorating military situation, many officials were deeply offended at the very idea that these women might be permitted to sit on their hands.[42] They saw such idleness as the end product of the excessive and corrosive insistence on the rights of *Kriegerfrauen* – to the neglect of the equally weighty obligation to give their all for the war effort. In the words of a press release issued by the chancellor's office in the summer of 1918,

> to the obligation of the Reich... corresponds the duty of each individual in these difficult times to employ all of her powers for the welfare of the fatherland. Now, where everything depends on even the most minimal amount of labor power, no one can and should simply put their hands in their laps, not even *Kriegerfrauen*. Everyone must, to the extent allowed by her domestic and physical conditions, take up employment. We can not and will not tolerate idlers when everything is at stake.

Or, in the somewhat terser phrasing of an earlier draft of this release, "we don't want to breed idle women."[43]

On the other hand, the social reform community was concerned that the instrumentalization of welfare for the sake of the war economy had gone too far and was undermining, rather than conserving, the family.[44] These reformers were also skeptical of the claim that the protection of the family inevitably bred idleness. A 1917 survey showed that nearly three-quarters of the women employed in munitions factories and public transportation in Frankfurt were, in fact, *Kriegerfrauen*, many of whom had one or two young children. Polligkeit insisted that this survey definitively refuted the notion that these women preferred a life of idleness and leisure to earning their bread by the

---

[41] Reich Chancellor to Bremen Senate (September 22, 1918), BA RAdI 12109. There is extensive correspondence on this issue in RAdI 12107–9. Women did, however, continue to face many problems in moving into the paid workforce. See Daniel, *The War from Within*.

[42] Bavarian Staatsrat to the Reichsamt des Innern (July 11, 1917) and Reich Chancellor to Generalkommission der Gewerkschaften Deutschlands (August 14, 1917), BA RAdI 12102, Bl. 77–8, 157.

[43] BA RAdI 12107 Bl. 260ff.

[44] "Arbeitspflicht und Unterstützungsanspruch der Kriegerfrauen," *SPr* 27:8 (1918), cols. 114–15, and Polligkeit's report of the same title in *Bericht über die Tagung der Freien Vereinigung für Kriegswohlfahrt (September 23, 1917)*, 8–16.

sweat of their brow, and he pointed out that generous separation allowances were not keeping these *Kriegerfrauen* from accepting factory work.[45] But, at least at this point in the war, these reformers were reconciled to the necessity of women's work, and they supported the combination of pressure and incentives to draw *Kriegerfrauen* into the industrial workforce.

Motherhood, Work, and the Grounds of Citizenship

The most privileged objects of welfarist solicitude were not *Kriegerfrauen*, but war widows and orphans.[46] Here, the basic problem was how to ensure that these women could reconcile the conflicting imperatives of financially supporting the fatherless family and ensuring the proper upbringing of the children. Survivors pensions were not adequate to support these women in the absence of property or other resources, and some, such as Klumker, questioned whether they should be, citing the moral and psychological value of work, especially for those widows who were young and able to work.[47] Before the war, working-class women had been expected to work if their husbands died – both to maintain their own self-reliance and to minimize the burden on the public purse. However, it was less easy to make this argument for war widows, especially for women with young children to care for, and most certainly not for women from the better classes, and the death of so many men and the corresponding increase in concern for the future of the population shifted the pendulum even further in the direction from work to motherhood. The problem was that neither of the most obvious solutions – requiring widows to work or providing them with pensions so that they would not have to do so – was able to resolve this conflict, and the debates over this issue ate away at all of cultural superstructures that had heretofore masked the ideological fault lines running through the breadwinner family construct – either by depriving the

---

[45] Wilhelm Polligkeit, *Die Kriegsnot der aufsichtslosen Kleinkinder* (=*Schriften des Deutschen Ausschusses für Kleinkinderfürsorge*, Heft 1, 1917), 10–11.

[46] On welfare for survivors during and after the war, see the following: Hermann Luppe, ed., *Das Wesen und die Aufgaben der Kriegshinterbliebenenfürsorge im Deutsche Reiche* (Leipzig, 1917); Friedeberg and Wronsky, *Kriegsfürsorge, Hinterbliebenenfürsorge. Mittheilungen aus der Arbeit der Zentrale für private Fürsorge in Berlin* (1915); Badisher Heimatdank, *Bericht über die Sitzung...*, Nationalstiftung für die Hinterbliebenen der im Kriege Gefallenen, ed., *Leitfaden der Kriegshinterbliebenenfürsorge*, 2. Aufl. (Berlin, 1919); Oskar Weigert and Lothar Richter, eds., *Die Versorgung und die soziale Fürsorge für Kriegsbeschädigte und Kriegshinterbliebene* (Berlin, 1921), the *Schriften des Arbeitsausschusses der Kriegerwitwen- und -Waisenfürsorge*, especially Heft 9: *Stand und künftige Entwicklung der Kriegerwitwen- u. -Waisenfürsorge* (1918); *Soziale Kriegshinterbliebenenfürsorge. Mitteilungen der Nationalstiftung...* Bd. 1–4 (1916–20); and Karin Hausen, "The German Nation's Obligations to the Heroes' Widows of World War I," in Higonnet et al., eds., *Behind the Lines*, 126–40.

[47] Klumker, "Die Hinterbliebenen unserer gefallenen Krieger," *ZfA* 15:12 (December 1914), 353–8.

breadwinner function of its gender specificity or by separating motherhood and reproduction from the bourgeois family altogether.[48]

Under the 1906 Military Survivors Law, war widows and orphans were entitled to pensions equaling a percentage of the pensions for which fully disabled veterans would have qualified.[49] This system of graduating pensions according to military rank reflected older notions of social status and military authority, and it was out of step with the idea of a nation in arms and with the need to maintain the stability of the "home" front. In March 1915, the Reichstag had approved a motion calling on the administration to reform the military pension system on "social" principles so that these pensions would more accurately reflect the prewar income and social position of those soldiers who died in the line of duty. Although the administration insisted that the systematic reform of military pensions would have to be deferred until the end of hostilities, a number of provisional measures were implemented in hopes of counteracting the precipitous decline in income and status resulting from the death of the family head. Here, too, the major point of contention was whether illegitimate children, who were not mentioned in the 1906 law, should be eligible for survivors benefits. This led to an acrimonious dispute between Progressive reformers and the defenders of marriage and the family, especially the Catholic charities. But the immediate concern to maintain troop morale and the long-term concern with the size and quality of the population combined with Progressive arguments to effect a limited shift in policy, with the administration ultimately agreeing to extend survivors pensions to illegitimate children on the same basis as with separation allowances.[50]

Pensions may have been the basis of public assistance to military survivors, but they were by no means the only, or even the most important, element, and, as the casualty toll steadily mounted across 1915, public debate over the goals and methods of social welfare for war widows and their children sprawled across all the central issues through which the position of women in society and the state was defined. At the first major conference on the topic, there was broad agreement that the tear in the fabric of the family could not be repaired

---

[48] Who were these war widows? According to one study, most of the war dead were skilled workers or members of the lower middle classes; war widows were overwhelmingly under 30, and 90% were under 35; half of all war orphans were under 6; two-thirds of all war widows had one to three children (with only 10% being childless); two-thirds of these widows and 25% of their children needed medical care because they suffered from serious health problems; and only one-third of these women had worked before or during marriage, mostly as maids or factory workers or in commerce. *Hinterbliebenenfürsorge. Mittheilungen aus der Arbeit der Zentrale für private Fürsorge in Berlin*, 37ff.

[49] Dr. Grosse, "Die rechtlichen Grundlagen der Rentenfürsorge des Reiches für die Kriegshinterbliebenen," in Luppe, ed., *Das Wesen und Aufgaben der Kriegshinterbliebenenfürsorge*, 6ff.

[50] Bernhard Würmeling, "Versorgung von unehelichen Kindern gefallener Kriegsteilnehmer," *Concordia. Zeitschrift der Zentralstelle für Volkswohlfahrt* 23:2 (January 15, 1916), 17–22, which gives an overview of the arguments and the contemporary literature, and ADCV 319.4 BII, 3, which contains extensive correspondence relating to this issue.

by material assistance alone and that helping these women learn to become self-reliant, productive members of the community would require the development of entirely new forms of pedagogical social welfare.[51] However, these debates also uncovered virtually all the limitations and contradictions latent in the plan to use wartime welfare to preserve the breadwinner family.

For Klumker, the task was to reclaim these damaged and needy women and children for the nation through education and vocational training. By education, Klumker meant two things. On the one hand, the war had deprived the family of its head, who embodied the principle of authority. This was the necessary complement to the nurturing capacity of the woman and the cornerstone of the moral education of the child, and it was not a gap that could be filled by even the most skillful and devoted mother. On the other hand, these widows were faced with a bewildering array of problems involved in winding up the legal affairs of their deceased husbands, putting their households on a firm economic foundation, and securing a proper education for their children. These were tasks that traditionally lay within the purview of the head of the family, and it seemed clear that in making choices regarding such matters war widows would need to rely on the counsel of others.[52]

The central question, though, was what could and should be done to help these women balance between their maternal duties and their need to support their families, and the answer to this question depended, in turn, on how one understood these activities. Since it seemed clear that many war widows would have to take on paid employment after the war (if they had not done so before), several representatives of the women's movement took the opportunity to call for the elevation of women's work. Josephine Levy-Rathenau, for example, took up a long-standing demand of the women's movement in arguing that vocational training for war widows was desirable for both material and ethical reasons. The feeling of being able to provide for oneself and one's family without being dependent on others would, she argued, be a source of satisfaction to these widows – and, by implication, to all women – and she added that, from the standpoint of national economics, it was important to have skilled women workers who created wealth rather than simply consuming it.[53]

The key word here was "skilled." The need to acquire such skills pointed to the centrality of vocational advising and training, and such elevated feelings, and a comparable level of compensation, could hardly be expected from unskilled labor, especially the cottage labor on which many mothers had historically relied.[54] But such training depended on coming to see women's factory

---

[51] *Soziale Fürsorge für Kriegerwitwen und Kriegerwaisen*, SDV, 103 (1915).
[52] *Soziale Fürsorge für Kriegerwitwen und Kriegerwaisen*, SDV, 103 (1915), 6–11.
[53] *Soziale Fürsorge für Kriegerwitwen und Kriegerwaisen*, SDV, 103 (1915), 44.
[54] Cottage labor had been a hot topic for social reformers before the war, and during the war the focus naturally shifted to cottage labor for war widows, though without raising any fundamentally new issues (beyond a concern that military pensions would further depress wages for these women and other pensionless women engaged in this kind of work).

work as a true vocation endowed with moral meaning, rather than as a second-best alternative to maternal work within the home, and on properly remunerating it as such. This solution to the war widow problem pointed beyond the breadwinner model by abrogating the gender specificity of breadwinning. Women had traditionally been paid less than men for the same work on the presumption that their work was simply a supplement to the family wage of the breadwinner husband, while this presumed right to support from someone else diminished their "need" for a wage that would enable them to fully support themselves. However, as Levy-Rathenau argued, in order to gain financial independence, war widows, and women more generally, would have to be remunerated according to the value of their work, rather than on the basis of the diminished need ascribed to them by the breadwinner model.[55]

The question of cottage labor also attracted the critical attention of the Social Democratic women's press. In a terse series of articles that appeared in the wake of this conference, the anonymous author argued that capitalism had colonized the working-class home and that the imperative to extract surplus labor was robbing women of both their reproductive capacity and the time and energy required to properly raise their children. The idyll of cottage labor as a means of reconciling work and motherhood was, the author (possibly Clara Zetkin) argued, an illusion that was no more viable for war widows than it had ever been for working-class women:

Cottage labor leaves behind only the deceptive appearance of the coexistence of motherhood and paid labor. But in reality it completely destroys the preconditions for this coexistence because it too is based on the principle of surplus value – and nothing but surplus value! To suggest that war widows should, in principle, take up cottage labor – in its present form and apart from certain exceptions – amounts to nothing other than abandoning these welfare recipients to a form of production in which the working conditions are the most unfavorable and, as a result, to make their maternal vocation even more difficult.[56]

At the conference several prominent members of the women's movement, including both Gertrud Bäumer and Paula Müller, the conservative chair of the German Protestant Women's League, rose to defend skilled women's work as a true vocation. Müller, for example, defended the right of women not only to a job, but to a vocation or profession and to appropriate remuneration for this work, arguing that one could aspire to the ideal of exclusive devotion to family life only if economic preconditions permitted such a choice. The right to choose one's vocation was an essential aspect of personal freedom, and Müller argued that such work, even outside the home, did not contradict women's "essence."

[55] Levy-Rathenau, *Frauenerwerb und Kriegerwitwe. Referate erstattet auf der 2. Tagung des Hauptausschuses der Kriegerwitwen- und –Waisenfürsorge* (=*Schriften des Arbeitsausschusses der Kriegerwitwen- und –Waisenfürsorge*, Heft 1, 1916), 4.
[56] "Zwei Grundfragen der sozialen Fürsorge für Kriegerwitwen und Kriegerwaisen," *Die Gleichheit* 25:17–18, 20, 22, 24, 26 (May/September 1915), 109–10, 125–6, 142–3, 158–9, 174–5, citation 175.

Such reasoning pointed toward the overturning of the breadwinner model precisely because those women who pursued such a skilled vocation would have little need for those things that were ostensibly provided by the male family head. However, even within the liberal wing of the women's movement, such conclusions, and all other such demands for equal education, employment, and rights, had generally been deflected by the belief that such advances would find their ultimate meaning in a more elevated and spiritualized version of motherhood. At the conference, Müller herself insisted that, in contrast to women, the vocation of *mothers*, and especially the mothers of young children, was to be found in the family because in most such cases work outside the home impaired their ability to care for and educate their children and was thus an evil to be avoided. This argument led, in turn, back to cottage labor (under appropriate safeguards and with better pay) and part-time work as the only option that did not conflict with their maternal obligations, though it was far from clear that such work could ever provide the financial security that mothers would need either to create a proper home or to find the personal satisfaction that came from other kinds of work.[57]

Other representatives of the women's movement attempted to square the circle of work and motherhood by finding a way to justify public support that would be sufficient to enable mothers to devote themselves full time to the care of their young children (though this commitment was limited at times by the belief that not all women were qualified for the tasks of motherhood).[58] For example, Käthe Gaebel, the director of the cottage labor department of the Social Reform Association, argued that domestic maternal labor itself deserved such compensation because motherhood was a public office or responsibility that was exercised in the national interest.[59] This implied that women could stake a claim to the rights of social citizenship on the basis of the public value of their maternal labor, and it also raised the questions of why, if their work was considered valuable enough to merit compensation by the state, such compensation should be limited to the wartime death of the family breadwinner and why women should not also have a voice in running the affairs of state? In contrast, Helene Simon justified the idea of a mother's pension program not because of the public character of such work, but rather because of its essentially private, domestic, and certainly prepolitical character. For Simon, motherhood was the essential embodiment of precisely that kind of unalienated labor (*"ein Beruf jenseits allen Wettbewerbs"*) that could only be performed by women who were sheltered from the alienating forces of public, economic life by a male breadwinner, whose protection was the correlate of their own dependence. Making it possible for mothers to remain within the private home memorialized the status of the male breadwinner who had died in battle by

---

[57] *Soziale Fürsorge für Kriegerwitwen und Kriegerwaisen*, SDV, 103 (1915), 115–23.
[58] See, for example, the comments of Frau Prof. Schönflies in "Niederschrift der Besprechung über Kriegshinterbliebenenfürsorge (June 18, 1915), StANürnberg C 25/I F Reg. 1067, Bd. 1.
[59] *Soziale Fürsorge für Kriegerwitwen und Kriegerwaisen*, SDV, 103 (1915), 123–6.

perpetuating the dependence of these women. As Simon argued, the nation had a sacred obligation "to the fallen warrior, whose pride had been his home and his ability to spare his wife – through his own labors – the need to work herself" so that she could devote herself completely to home and child. This was not paid labor, but rather an honorarium for refraining therefrom, with the state acting in a paternalist manner to assume the obligations of the absent breadwinner.[60]

The intrinsic contradictions of maternalist ideology and paternalist policies, together with the inbuilt linkages to questions of work, family, reproduction, and citizenship, made it impossible to bring definitive closure to this principled debate over the scope of social welfare for war widows. But the attempt to think through these issues revealed the unsettling, and potentially subversive, implications of wartime welfare for the domestic, gender, and social order. For wartime welfare programs to preserve the breadwinner family, they had to find a way of satisfactorily combining work and motherhood. But every suggestion as to how this circle might be successfully squared tended to call the breadwinner family into question, except for Simon's, which was unacceptable because the suggestion that mothers of young children not be required to work at all entailed unforeseeable financial costs and moral hazards.

The inability to resolve these questions of principle did not, however, pose an insuperable obstacle to the development of effective programs for these women, and in 1915 the Central Committee for the Welfare of War Widows and Orphans was founded as a national coordinating and policy body in the field.[61] Social programs for war widows embraced a wide variety of areas, including vocational counseling and training for war widows and assistance finding appropriate work; securing health care; advising widows on the sale or operation of businesses run by their husbands and on questions relating to inheritances, debt, and other financial and legal matters; helping widows establish their pension rights and otherwise bringing order to their household finances; arranging the whole spectrum of social services for children, including sanatorium care, kindergarten and day care, and reform schooling; helping

---

[60] *Soziale Fürsorge für Kriegerwitwen und Kriegerwaisen, SDV*, 103 (1915), 28–9.

[61] *Zur Theorie und Praxis der Kriegshinterbliebenenfürsorge* (=*Schriften des Arbeitsausschusses der Kriegerwitwen- und – Waisenfürsorge*, Heft 3, 1916). The organizational development of social programs for military survivors is a complex story that cannot be fully told here. The key actors were the *Nationalstiftung für die Hinterbliebenen der im Kriege Gefallenen* (a nationwide fundraising body), the Central Committee (*Hauptausschuß der Kriegerwitwen- und – Waisenfürsorge*), and the network of welfare centers created at the local level beginning in 1916 to coordinate the work of the public and private agencies active in the field. The key sources here are *Stand und künftige Entwicklung; Probleme der Kriegshinterbliebenenfürsorge* (=*Schriften des Arbeitsausschusses der Kriegerwitwen- und – Waisenfürsorge*, Heft 6, 1917), especially the presentation by Herman Luppe; and Gerda Simons, "Die Entwicklung de sozialen Kriegsbeschädigten- und Kriegshinterbliebenenfürsorge," *SPr* 29:33–4 (1920), cols. 775–7, 804–6. These local organizations were carried over into the Weimar Republic where they – along with similar organizations created for disabled veterans – were incorporated into the newly created municipal welfare offices.

decide what vocations would be appropriate for war orphans, negotiating apprenticeships or other arrangements, and supervising the children during their training period; counseling women who sought to flee the countryside after the death of their husbands; and negotiating with landlords and local government regarding housing, rent, and rent subsidies. It is impossible to exhaustively describe the scope of these social programs for these women and their children. In fact, this inability to plan for every conceivable eventuality was one of the reasons why social work schools insisted that their students had to have a broad knowledge of social sciences and social policy, for without such an education they would be unable to act independently of those men who did.

Disabled Veterans and the Contradictions of Therapeutic Welfare

While other belligerent countries granted pensions to disabled veterans primarily in recognition of their service and sacrifice, the German military pension system followed the principles of the social insurance system in linking benefits to disability, and the country eagerly adopted advances in orthopedics and preventive social welfare in the expectation that these men could thereby be made into productive members of society for whom work would be the foundation of masculine identity, authority within the family, citizenship, and economic security.[62] Progressives favored this approach because they felt that the individualized graduation of benefits according to the degree and nature of (dis)ability was the most democratic solution, one that they hoped would abolish the divisive distinctions between the various groups of the new poor while stimulating individual self-help and national reconstruction. The problem was that this approach to military pensions also gave rise to a conflict between disabled veterans, who insisted that their sacrifice had given them a privileged claim on the gratitude and resources of the nation, state and local officials, who were charged with representing the fiscal interests of the nation, and medical and social experts, who couched their productivist priorities in a language of social service and apolitical expertise. It is not clear whether these conflicts could have been resolved under the best of circumstances. But under the extreme conditions of World War I, the lack of the requisite degree of trust needed to transcend all of these potential conflicts inverted the anticipated

---

[62] On pension and social programs for German veterans, see Michael Geyer, "Ein Vorbote des Wohlfahrtsstaates. Die Kriegsopferversorgung in Frankreich, Deutschland und Großbritannien nach dem Ersten Weltkrieg," *GuG* 9 (1983), 230–77; Greg Eghigian, *Making Security Social. Disability, Insurance, and the Birth of the Social Entitlement State in Germany* (University of Michigan Press, 2000); Deborah Cohen, *The War Come Home. Disabled Veterans in Britain and Germany, 1914–1939* (University of California Press, 2001); Klaus-Dieter Thomann, "Die medizinische und soziale Fürsorge für die Kriegsversehrten in der ersten Phase des Krieges 1914/15," in Wolfgang Eckart and Christoph Gradmann, eds., *Die Medizin und der Erste Weltkrieg* (Centaurus, 1996), 183–96; and Heather Perry, *Recycling the Disabled: Army, Medicine, and Society in World War I Germany* (forthcoming).

synergies between the welfare of disabled veterans and that of the nation as a whole, and the history of these programs can, to a substantial degree, be told in terms of the unfolding under the pressure of events of these contradictions.

Military pensions were graduated according to the degree of disability and set at such a level that only completely disabled veterans could live from their pensions alone. While the military was responsible only for providing medical treatment for war-related injuries, these core medical services were surrounded by a web of supplementary rehabilitative programs known as welfare for the "war damaged" (*Kriegsbeschädigtenfürsorge*) that were run by voluntary associations to facilitate the transition from the military hospital to the workplace. Beginning in 1915, welfare centers for disabled veterans were founded at the district and state levels to coordinate – under the leadership of public officials – the work of the many different organizations active in the field.[63] They worked increasingly closely with military pension offices and eventually took over from the police and the military responsibility for the investigation of personal and family circumstances that was necessary in order to establish claims for supplemental pensions and other social services. At the national level, the National Committee for the Welfare of Disabled Veterans (*Reichsausschuß für Kriegsbeschädigtenfürsorge*, founded in September 1915) brought together social reformers, the leading welfare and charity organizations, representatives of the relevant Reich and state ministries, and local welfare officials to establish guidelines for the work of local welfare centers.[64]

While disabled veterans – and all the new poor – phrased their demand for public recognition of their sacrifice and suffering in the language of rights, the social service organizations and public officials represented in the National Committee rejected the idea of allowing the veterans themselves to participate in its work, claiming that these demands were a sign of the growing covetousness and egoism bred by wartime welfare itself. This refusal, however, set in motion a vicious circle that led veterans groups to demand in an even more insistent manner rights, representation, and self-determination, rather than charity and tutelage. As one veteran phrased the issue in May 1918, the main reason why these men were dissatisfied with the existing arrangements was not so much the quality of these programs as the fact that they had no voice in the process:

People work to find appropriate places for veterans in commerce and industry. That is all well and good. However, ladies and gentlemen, whether these efforts succeed or fail in any particular instance, whether or not the individual disabled veteran receives what is his due is not important. What disabled veterans want is not only that they

[63] Their work was funded by the Reich, local government, the voluntary organizations themselves, and the Ludendorff-Spende, a nationwide organization that was established to raise money for this purpose.
[64] On the founding and structure of the organization, see the excerpt from the *Sächsische Staatszeitung* in BA RAM 8861. Extensive documentation of the work of the Reichsausschuß can be found in BA RAM 8864.

are taken care of. They feel like little children when higher-ups decide what is to be done to and for them. They themselves want to be responsible for what happens to them. They themselves want to have some control over their positions in public life and the economy.... We don't want adult men to become merely the object of legislation. Rather every individual must play an active role in making these decisions.[65]

Ultimately, what the speaker wanted was public recognition that "disabled veterans also have a valuable role to play in society (daß... *der Kriegsbeschädigte im Staate etwas gilt*)." However, this conflict over the right to representation within the policymaking bodies of the wartime welfare state was not resolved until after the revolution.

In conclusion, the wartime welfare system for veterans, dependents, and survivors proved to be extremely important for the fortunes of German society at war and for the long-term development of the German welfare system. First, it helped preserve the breadwinner model across a period when it was under pressure from many directions, even as it revealed the limitations of this model. This may help explain one apparent anomaly: why scholars have had so much difficulty demonstrating that the Great War had as great a positive impact on the emancipation of German women as was long believed to be the case. Second, wartime welfare was the first instance of using welfare to promote something resembling income maintenance, even if it never quite succeeded in sustaining a social existence minimum. But the new poor were different from the old poor, and the May 1920 Reich Pension Law and the 1924 National Social Welfare Law represented a hybrid between the income maintenance and preventive social welfare programs that had been created during the war, rather than new departures.[66] Third, these wartime welfare programs fulfilled their mission of uniting the home front behind the war at best only in part. Despite the commitment to preserving prewar status and income, wartime welfare was never in a position to fully compensate for chronic shortages and a steadily rising cost of living, and these inadequacies amplified social conflict on the home front, rather than dampening it. Lastly, the Weimar welfare system also inherited all the political conflicts engendered by wartime welfare, and these conflicts were complicated by disputes among the organizations representing veterans, survivors, and the other new poor – groups that were united in their opposition to the anti-democratic tutelage of the new social bureaucracy, but deeply divided against one another as to the meaning of the war, the revolution, and the republic.[67]

---

[65] "Bericht des Oberwachmeisters Zufall über die öffentliche Versammlung... (May 11, 1918)," BA RMdI 13089, Bl. 102ff.

[66] *RGBl.*, 1920, I, 989–1019, and 1924, I, 100ff. The 1924 law is reprinted in Julia Dünner, ed., *Reichsfürsorgerecht* (Munich, 1924), 1ff.

[67] Geyer, "Ein Vorbote des Wohlfahrsstaates," and Ewald Frie, "Vorbild oder Spiegelbild? Kriegsbeschädigtenfürsorge in Deutschland 1914–1919," in Wolfgang Michalka, ed., *Der Erste Weltkrieg. Wirkung – Wahrnehmung – Analyse* (Munich, 1994), 563–80.

12

Wartime Youth Welfare and the Progressive Refiguring of the Social Contract

From Prevention to Promotion: Rethinking the Political Rationality of Social Assistance

In his famous 1961 essay on "The Welfare State in Historical Perspective," Asa Briggs drew a distinction between what he called the "social service state," which guaranteed individuals and families a minimum income irrespective of their position in the labor market and provided a degree of security against such contingencies as sickness, old age, and unemployment, and the "welfare state," which went beyond securing this minimum to ensure that all citizens enjoyed a fair share in the resources of the nation, a share that would permit them to realize their individual potential without being constrained by preventable illness, want, and ignorance.[1] In this chapter I will argue that wartime youth welfare programs served as one of the mediums for the articulation of a new, distinctly Progressive approach to the problem of social inequality that provided the theoretical foundation for the twentieth-century German welfare state along the lines described by Briggs. Although the key ideas here had already been advanced in the debate over the social evolution of poor relief, the war transformed the political rationality of social assistance in a way that made the active promotion of the welfare of needy and endangered individuals appear more important than avoiding the moral hazards traditionally associated with any assistance that exceeded the deterrent existence minimum.

One of the most important of the new preventive social welfare programs was the maternity allowance (*Wochenhilfe*) program that was established by the Bundesrat in December 1914.[2] In responding to the problem of providing for new mothers and their children, the Bundesrat at first hewed to a conservative line in restricting maternity allowances to self-insured women and

---

[1] Asa Briggs, "The Welfare State in Historical Perspective," in *The Collected Essays of Asa Briggs* (University of Illinois Press, 1985), II:177–211, especially 183ff.
[2] W. Winkelmann, ed., *Die Kriegswochenhilfe* (Bielefeld, 1915).

married women whose husbands had belonged to one of the sickness insurance funds before the war and who were now serving in the military. However, this policy was attacked from two directions. Population and military concerns led many conservatives who condemned single motherhood to see the children of extramarital liaisons in a new light and to argue that more vigorous steps had to be taken to ensure that they grew up to be healthy, productive, and law-abiding citizens.[3] On the other hand, critics on the left argued that eligibility for maternity assistance should be expanded for reasons of equity, rather than out of military considerations.[4]

The administration was soon forced to revise its position on maternity allowances. The new policy, which was laid out in an April 1915 decree, extended maternity allowances to all women earning less than 1,500 marks annually, including unmarried mothers if – again, as with separation allowances – the father was serving in the military and recognized his paternal obligation in a formal or informal manner. It also brought substantial improvements in the level of maternity benefits as compared with prewar maternity provisions of the social insurance system. However, while the infant protection movement was disappointed that the law did not prohibit women from working during the first three months after giving birth, Catholics were even more unhappy with the extension of maternity benefits to unmarried women. Agnes Neuhaus, the chair of the influential Catholic Welfare Association for Girls, Women and Children, admitted that single mothers had to be helped if only because their poverty placed them in even greater moral danger, but she regretted that the law had made no distinction between legitimate and illegitimate children. However, she did regard it as a minor victory that the idea of creating a maternity insurance program had been dropped and that maternity allowances were to be provided through the sickness insurance funds. Her own preference would have been to create a maternity insurance program that would be restricted to married women while providing maternity assistance to unmarried mothers through poor relief authorities, where the absence of a right to benefits would have put the charities in a better position to exert a moral influence over these women. But her top priority remained "to avoid anything that might unsettle the foundations of legitimate marriage."[5]

---

[3] For example, Leo Langstein, "Die Aufgaben der Säuglings- und Kleinkinderschutz im Deutschen Reiche," *Zeitschrift für Säuglingsschutz* (1916), 393–8, and Edward Ross Dickinson, *The Politics of German Child Welfare from the Empire to the Federal Republic* (Harvard University Press, 1996), 121–4.

[4] Friedrich Kleeis, "Die Fortführung der Mutterschaftsfürsorge," *Die Gleichheit* 26:3 (October 19, 1915), and Dr. Bornstein in *Bericht der elften Tagung Deutscher Berufsvormünder in Berlin am 19. und 20. September 1917* (=Zur Frage der Berufsvormundschaft, Heft 11), 34.

[5] Memorandum by Carl von Behr-Pinnow and Fritz Rott (December 8, 1916), ADCV 319.4 SKF EV III, 1 and letter from Neuhaus to Fräulein Eder (May 10, 1915), Ibid., B II, 3. On the further development of infant welfare programs through World War I and beyond, see Larry Frohman, "Prevention, Welfare, and Citizenship: The War on Tuberculosis and Infant Mortality in Germany, 1900–1930," *CEH* 39:3 (September 2006), 431–81.

Early childhood welfare (*Kleinkinderfürsorge*, for children aged 1–6) first emerged as a distinct area of social concern during the war. While the infant protection movement had made reformers more conscious of the specific hygienic dangers faced by pre-school-age children, such as rickets, tuberculosis, and other diseases that were more likely to cause long-term damage to the child than to result in immediate death, these growing concerns about the physical development of young children were paralleled by a new understanding of the importance of these early years for their mental and moral development. This new sensitivity to the specific needs of this age group came at just the moment when the absence of so many fathers and the spread of women's factory work was leaving more and more children without adequate supervision and care at the very moment in their lives when, according to experts, they most needed such nurturing.[6]

In describing the scope and mission of early childhood welfare, Polligkeit argued that, despite past success in reclaiming delinquent children, in the future youth welfare would have to adopt a more proactive approach. Since, he argued, "effective prevention is only possible when we take positive steps to insure that every child receives the requisite education," child welfare would have to shift its focus away from combating existing need and, instead, work to ensure that all children received the care that they needed to prevent need from occurring in the first place. This would involve, he continued, abandoning the assumption that the poor were somehow different from their social betters and eliminating the socially discriminatory distinction between youth *welfare* (*Jugendfürsorge*) programs for endangered and delinquent children and youth *cultivation* (*Jugendpflege*) programs for "normal" children who suffered from no manifest disadvantages in order to make the entire juvenile population the uniform object of normalizing social intervention. "In addition to rescue work for endangered and delinquent children," Polligkeit explained, "we need public and voluntary institutions whose goal is to insure that every child receives a basic education" simply by virtue of their status as members of the community.[7]

---

[6] Gustav Tugendreich, "Die Fürsorge für Kleinkinder," in Deutsche Zentrale für Jugendfürsorge, ed., *Kleinkinder in der Grossstadt* (Berlin, 1910), 3–12; Hildegard Böhme, "Vorbericht," Deutsche Zentrale für Jugendfürsorge, ed., *Gesamtbericht der Tagung in Frankfurt a.M. am 7., 8. und 9. Oktober 1915* (Berlin, 1916), 1ff.; Wilhelm Polligkeit, *Die Kriegsnot aufsichtsloser Kinder* (=*Schriften des Deutschen Ausschusses für Kleinkinderfürsorge*, Heft 1, 1917); Adolf Gottstein, *Die gesundheitliche Kleinkinderfürsorge und der Krieg* (=*Schriften des Deutschen Ausschusses für Kleinkinderfürsorge*, Heft 3, 1917); and Tugendreich, "Der Ausbau der Kleinkinderfürsorge," in *Fortschritte des Kinderschutzes und der Jugendfürsorge* Heft 2 (1917), 3–22.

[7] Polligkeit, "Kriegstagung der Jugendfürsorge," *Mitteilungen der Deutschen Zentrale für Jugendfürsorge* 10:4–5 (October 1, 1915), 1–3. On youth cultivation, Edward Ross Dickinson, "Citizenship, Vocational Training, and Reaction: Continuation Schooling and the Prussian 'Youth Cultivation' Decree of 1911," *European History Quarterly* 29:1 (1999), 109–47, and Derek Linton, *"Who has the Youth has the Future." The Campaign to Save Young Workers in Imperial Germany* (Cambridge University Press, 1991).

The most important early childhood welfare programs were day-care centers (*Krippen*, kindergartens), which were designed to give pre-school-age working-class children the all-important physical care, emotional nurturing, and intellectual stimulation that working mothers could not provide, and maternal advice centers (*Mütterberatungsstellen*), which were often combined with the infant welfare centers that had spread rapidly since 1905.[8] Several key concerns dominated the work of the German Committee for the Welfare of Pre-School-Age Children, which was established in April 1916 as a national coordinating body, and the practical work of the diverse local groups active in the field.[9] Above all, these organizations emphasized how, by giving rise to a general form of distress that affected the entire nation, rather than just the poorer classes, the war had made need into a national concern and transformed assistance to needy children into a "self-evident national and social obligation," rather than an act of charity undertaken by the propertied for the benefit of the popular or underprivileged classes. This meant, as Lili Droescher (the director of the Pestalozzi-Fröbel-Haus and one of the leading figures in the kindergarten movement) explained in 1917, that social workers would have to free themselves from the idea that all that the nation owed its needy children was primitive housing and meager material assistance and, instead, establish day-care centers and other programs that would ensure that working-class children grew up under conditions that would encourage the full development of their natural abilities.[10]

The same ideas also dominated the broader debates over youth welfare reform, which also struggled with the task of redefining the nature of public obligations to the young and devising a politically acceptable organizational mechanism for discharging these duties. The leading Progressive youth welfare reformers during these years – Klumker, Polligkeit, Aloys Fischer, and Kurt Blaum – all argued that the society had a positive obligation to actively promote the fitness of all children for their multiple roles in adult life, and they insisted that society could no longer wait until children had succumbed to some form of need before acting. As Fischer, one of the leading pedagogues of the period, argued in his keynote address to the most important wartime youth welfare conference, youth welfare was one of the most important means by which a society insured the education and socialization of its young and thus

---

[8] Ludwig Pallat, "Zusammenfassung der Ergebnisse des Kursus" (September 23, 1916), GStAPrK, I. HA, Rep. 76, VII neu, Sekt. 1A IV, Nr. 24; Lili Droescher, "Wie sollen und können Tagesheime dem Erziehungsnotstand von Kleinkindern abhelfen?" in *Gesamtbericht der Tagung*, 52–65; Polligkeit, "Gutachten" concerning the activity of the Committee (December 19, 1916), BA R86 2396; and the materials in ADCV 319.4 SKF E VIII, 6.
[9] Deutsche Zentrale für Jugendfürsorge, ed., *Gesamtbericht der Tagung*. The committee sponsored several important conferences and training courses during the second half of the war, as well as an important exhibition on early childhood welfare.
[10] Droescher, *Die Erziehungsaufgaben der Volkskindergärten im Kriege* (=Deutscher Ausschuß für Kleinkinderfürsorge, Kleine Schriften 2, 1917), 6, 8 in GStAPrK, I. HA, Rep. 76, VII neu, Sekt. 1A IV, Nr. 24, and *Nachrichtendienst über Kleinkinderfürsorge*, 27 (December 1918), 109.

its own reproduction. The community, he argued, must develop "a consciousness of collective responsibility [with regard to this obligation]. We must feel and be convinced that we are all implicated in the need of every child and therefore obligated to help remedy this need... whenever there is anywhere in the fatherland a child who is endangered or who has succumbed to such danger." Such a positive obligation – both individual and collective – for the welfare of others reflected a Progressive understanding of the social contract that was entirely foreign to the intellectual world of classical liberalism. But while this sense of collective obligation and solidaristic responsibility for the welfare of all individual children had propelled the piecemeal formation of voluntary associations in previous decades, this process had now entered a new stage, Fischer noted, in which the community itself had become aware of this obligation. The transformation of this sense of social obligation from a private to a public matter meant that youth welfare work would henceforth have to make a conscious, systematic effort to secure the rights of all children because "we can not be indifferent as to whether or not proper and sufficient measures are taken to insure the welfare of a child who is disadvantaged through no fault of his own." And since the lack of coordination among voluntary organizations, their freedom to choose their causes and their clientele, and their limited resources meant that voluntary welfare would always be contingent, incomplete, and unable to ensure that all children could be systematically monitored and assisted in a timely manner, the community itself would have to assume primary responsibility for securing the rights and welfare of all its children.[11] The public youth welfare office was to be the institutional embodiment of this commitment. As Blaum, a prominent young welfare reformer who had done his apprenticeship in the Strassburg social administration and who was to later serve as Frankfurt mayor from 1945 to 1946, explained, the mission of these offices was to "insure that every child and youth who is in need of protection and supervision benefits from the requisite social welfare in a timely and certain manner in every part of the land and at all times."[12]

It was easy to justify this expanded vision of welfare in terms of population policy and wartime exigency, and one can multiply at will statements calculating how many millions of infants had died because of preventable diseases in previous decades and how many more divisions could have been put into the field by more ambitious infant and youth welfare programs. However, many Progressive youth welfare reformers were more circumspect here. Blaum, for example, explained in 1917 that the state did not exist for its army, but rather for its citizens, and that, similarly, the purpose of youth welfare was not to keep children healthy "just so that they can one day become brave soldiers,

[11] Aloys Fischer, "Gemeinschaftsarbeit und Persönlichkeitspflege in der Jugendfürsorge," in Deutscher Verein für Armenpflege und Wohltätigkeit, ed., *Jugendämter als Träger der öffentlichen Jugendfürsorge im Reiche. Bericht über die Verhandlungen des deutschen Jugendfürsorgetages am 20. und 21. September 1918 in Berlin* (Berlin, 1919), 11–25, citations 18–19.

[12] Kurt Blaum, "Ein Reichsgesetz über Jugendämter," in *Jugendämter als Träger der öffentlichen Jugendfürsorge*, 58.

but rather so that they can successfully meet all the dangers in the struggle for life – which naturally also include military prowess." Thus, he continued, the primary rationale for youth welfare lay in the fact that "we find ourselves constrained – if we wish to see our race develop further – to preserve and promote the health, intellectual development and morality of all life that is born or that should be born and to snuff out all of the dangers that threaten this life, if not to prevent them from arising in the first place."[13] This is not to say that the population question and the war did not figure in the thinking of the Progressives, for these were points that Blaum and Klumker readily noted. However, as Klumker explained, the connection between war and welfare was only an external and contingent one. The basic insights of the child protection movement dated back to the turn of the century, when the declining birthrate had not yet become a major issue, and the oft-cited problem of wartime social distress, he noted, simply represented a special case of more general social problems that were linked to the rise of industrial society.[14]

It was at this point, at the very latest, that Catholics began to voice their many concerns regarding public youth welfare. Catholic charities were obsessed with the possibility that they would simply be frozen out by professional guardians, who would take all children under their own wings and leave Catholic organizations to wither on the vine. Moreover, they argued, there was simply no way that people who were paid to concern themselves with the welfare of children could gain the trust of these children to the same degree as those who did so voluntarily or exercise the same personal influence over them. And even if professional guardians could, by some chance, evince the same warmth and concern for their wards as voluntary individual guardians, any form of statutory guardianship was a non-starter for the Catholics if it could not guarantee that Catholic children would have Catholic guardians.

But Catholic charities were also skeptical about these developments because they believed that the very idea of public guardianship was incompatible with the natural right and duty of parents to provide for the bodily and spiritual welfare of children. If the family was unable to discharge this obligation, then responsibility then fell to the religious community, whose right to secure the salvation of its members could not be abridged by secular law.[15] But at that point, Catholic charities simply lacked the organizational depth needed to meet the challenge of public welfare.

State, Society, and the Corporatist Turn in the Social Sector

This confrontation between Progressives and the defenders of the prerogatives of the church charities (and of voluntary welfare more generally) was brought

---

[13] *Bericht der elften Tagung Deutscher Berufsvormünder*, 56.
[14] Klumker, "Die Notwendigkeit des Ausbaues," in *Jugendämter als Träger der öffentlichen Jugendfürsorge*, 30–1.
[15] Lorenz Werthmann, "Grundsätzliches über staatliche Wohlfahrtspflege und freie Caritas," *Caritas* 23:10–12 (July–September 1918), 199–205.

to a head in the second half of the war by the unavoidable encounter with the wartime welfare state in two areas: the national regulation of voluntary charity by the government and the debate over a proposed Prussian youth welfare law.

The expansion of state social programs during the war forced the church charities to modernize in order to better defend their traditional values and practices. This process can be followed most clearly in the case of the Caritas Association. The war was leading to the creation of a vast public welfare bureaucracy and the formation of central coordinating agencies in every field of social work, and the Caritas Association feared that this organizational centralization and consolidation was leaving less and less room for specifically Catholic charity. This danger was especially acute in those instances where, on the pretext of expertise or efficiency, these offices were beginning to directly assist persons who applied to them for help, rather than simply passing them on to existing associations.[16]

The Catholic charities responded to this challenge by constructing a much denser network of local Caritas organizations that mirrored the structure of these official agencies while trying to create both specialized organizations of their own and training a new cadre of social workers to ensure that there would be an appropriate Catholic agency to provide spiritual and material succor to all members of the faith, no matter what their specific need.[17] As we have seen, the Caritas Association had achieved only limited recognition and influence before the war. However, in the summer of 1916, the Conference of German Bishops designated the organization as the official representative of the church in the welfare field. This gave the Caritas Association greater prestige and influence over other Catholic charities and enabled it to play a greater role in coordinating and encouraging the activity of individual Catholic charities while permitting them to speak with a single, more authoritative voice in representing Catholic interests vis-à-vis government and other voluntary organizations.[18]

Even before the war there had been no shortage of complaints that there were too many small, often amateurish voluntary organizations – replete with officers, administrative costs, and membership drives – engaged in wasteful

---

[16] Constantin Noppel, *Denkschrift über den Ausbau der katholischen Caritasorganisation* (Freiburg, 1915), 9. The Inner Mission was also affected by these forces. See Jochen-Christoph Kaiser, *Sozialer Protestantismus im 20. Jahrhundert. Beiträge zur Geschichte der Inneren Mission 1914–1945* (Oldenbourg, 1989).

[17] For example, when the government floated a plan to centralize care for war orphans under the authority of the Red Cross in the summer of 1915, the various national Catholic organizations active in the youth welfare field came together to form a Central Office for Catholic War Orphans to ensure that all Catholic war orphans would be placed with Catholic foster families or in Catholic institutions so that none of these children would be lost to the faith. "Vertraulicher Bericht über die Gründung einer Zentralstelle für katholische Kriegswaisenpflege" (August 3, 1915), ADCV 319.4 BII.

[18] See "Bericht über die zweite Sitzung des Zentralrates des Caritasverbandes für das katholische Deutschland" (July 4–5, 1917) and "Bericht über die Sitzung des Zentralvorstandes und Zentralrates des Deutschen Caritasverbandes" (July 25/October 7, 1918), AKFD Mappe Deutscher Caritasverband, and Deutscher Caritasverband, ed., *Denkschriften und Standpunkte der Caritas in Deutschland*, Bd. I: *Die Zeit von 1897 bis 1949* (Lambertus, 1997), passim.

competition with one another. With the outbreak of the war, literally hundreds of new associations sprouted into existence, especially in the larger cities. By one estimate, some six hundred wartime charities were established in Berlin alone. These new associations often duplicated the work of existing associations; they were not always operated by people with the best credentials; and in some cases these new wartime charities were little more than thinly veiled scams. In July 1915, the Bundesrat issued a decree requiring the approval of the federal states for all war-related fundraising activities within their borders. However, it quickly proved difficult to distinguish between those charitable activities that were related to the war and those that devoted to more general purposes, and in February 1917 a second decree was issued allowing the states to supervise all charitable or patriotic associations.[19] Although this second decree specifically exempted all organizations that had been founded before the start of the war and had little concrete impact on the established welfare organizations, it stirred up fears of state regimentation of voluntary welfare and forced them to give greater consideration to how they might collaborate with one another to fend off further public supervision.[20]

Numerous conferences, both large and small, were devoted to this question in 1917/18, but debate tended to circle around a limited number of issues and alternatives.[21] Representatives of the voluntary sector feared both state regimentation and the potential instrumentalization of such authority for political ends, especially since there was no hard-and-fast way to distinguish judgments concerning the competence of a particular organization from those concerning the merits of the cause it served, and the potential benefits of greater collaboration were limited by the insistence that any centralization or rationalization would have to emanate from the organizations themselves.

A number of Progressives, including Polligkeit, Blaum, Hermann Luppe (deputy mayor of Frankfurt, then mayor of Nuremberg, and a nationally recognized expert on municipal welfare), and Siddy Wronsky (a prominent Jewish social work expert), called for the formation of municipal central

---

[19] *RGBl.* (1915), 449–50, and *RGBl.* (1917), 14347.
[20] Deborah Cohen, *The War Come Home. Disabled Veterans in Britain and Germany, 1914–1939* (University of California Press, 2001), 71ff., argues that these measures were the first step in a systematic campaign by public officials to eliminate the influence of voluntary associations, at least in the care of disabled veterans.
[21] The most important sources for this debate are *Stenographischer Bericht über die Verhandlungen, SDV*, 107 (1918), 114–99, 227–9; "Das Zusammenarbeiten der Wohlfahrtsvereine," *Schriften der Zentralstelle für Volkswohlfahrt*, N.F. Heft 14, 4–92; Deutscher Caritasverband, *Soll die Staatsaufsicht über die freie Wohlfahrtspflege in die Friedenszeit hinübergenommen werden?* (Freiburg, 1917); Werthmann, "Grundsätzliches über staatliche Wohlfahrtspflege und freie Caritas"; Friedrich Zahn, *Staatliche Aufsicht über die freiwillige Wohlfahrtspflege?* (=*Archiv der Hamburgischen Gesellschaft für Wohltätigkeit*, Heft 8, 1916); the reports by Albert Levy and Friedrich Zahn in *Gekürzter Bericht über die Tagung der Freien Vereinigung für Kriegswohlfahrt* (December 9–10, 1916), 3–12 and 12–26, respectively; two essays by Polligkeit in *Concordia* 24:1–2 (January 1 and 15, 1917); and the materials in ADCV CA XX 31a.

organizations – modeled on the municipal centrals for war welfare – that would bring together all local voluntary associations under the leadership of public officials while preserving the full autonomy of these associations. However, this "mixed public-private organization" could only serve as a model for collaboration as long as public officials did not insist on leading voluntary organizations in a direction that they did not wish to go, or on preventing from following their own inclinations, and it was the introduction of the Prussian youth welfare law in the summer of 1918 that forced the issue.

The proposed Prussian law codified many of the new practices that had been adopted at the municipal level since the turn of the century. It mandated the establishment of youth welfare offices and charged them with protecting children of all ages from the many dangers that they faced. These offices were to assume the duties of the local orphans council, act as guardian over all illegitimate children, supervise the care of foster children, participate in the assistance of poor children, and work with provincial authorities in correctional education. By permitting local poor boards to include the cost of education and vocational training, the law would have marked an important step away from the old poor law existence minimum. In carrying out these duties, the youth welfare offices were to collaborate with voluntary associations while respecting their independence, and to facilitate this collaboration the governing boards of the local offices were to include representatives from the voluntary sector alongside official members.

By 1918, the confluence of prewar reform trends and the new wartime concern for child welfare virtually assured the passage of youth welfare legislation, if not at the Reich level, where such proposals had been consistently blocked by the Finance Ministry, then at the state level. The question was whether initiative would lie with the officials in the new agencies or with the voluntary sector.[22] At the last major youth welfare conference before the revolution, Blaum and Friedrich Siegmund-Schultze, who later became the first director of the Berlin youth welfare office, floated ideas on how voluntary charity might be integrated into the governing bodies of the proposed youth welfare offices.[23] However, these proposals involved making compromises that Catholic charities could not accept. Their main objection was that the Prussian law did not provide what they considered to be sufficient guarantees against being squeezed out by public officials, and the Catholic charities focused on ensuring that the youth welfare offices would have as little discretionary authority as possible. However, without such authority, the youth welfare offices could hardly become the public socialization agencies that Klumker envisioned. The Prussian law was revised as it made its way through the legislative process, and the Catholic

---

[22] On the political context of 1917/18, see Dickinson, *The Politics of German Child Welfare*, 127–38.
[23] Blaum in *Bericht der elften Tagung Deutscher Berufsvormünder*, 70–3, and Siegmund-Schultze, "Wie kann die freie Liebestätigkeit zu einem vollen Erfolg der Jugendämter beitragen?" in *Jugendämter als Träger*, 157–70.

charities ultimately decided to support the law less because they approved of its thrust than because in its final form it promised to limit the influence of urban liberalism.[24]

The revolution interrupted consideration of the Prussian law, and by the early 1920s the question of youth welfare legislation had shifted from the states to the Reich. There are two points, though, that need to be made about this unfinished Prussian debate. First, the war years were crucial in defining the Progressive vision of modern social welfare, the new conception of social citizenship on which it rested, and the institutional changes that would be needed to put this program into practice. However, the growing clarity of these Progressive ideas provoked a sharp reaction on the part of Catholic charities, and their defense of the natural rights of the family and the religious community, and the conception of subsidiarity that it implied, was a direct response to these Progressive reform proposals.

Second, this principle of subsidiarity could only be institutionalized within a corporatist system of governance that would regulate relations among the various voluntary organizations (and between the voluntary sector as a whole and its public counterparts) without limiting their freedom of action within their own domains. The creation of such a system would have (re)privatized public welfare and thus hollowed out the authority of democratically elected government. This was, of course, exactly what the confessional organizations wanted, especially after the revolution. The problem, though, was that the political, religious, and economic conflicts of the age made it impossible to settle on a stable system for delimiting the rights and prerogatives of the main stakeholders. The Weimar years were a turbulent time, with culture wars in the welfare sector contributing in important ways to the ultimate crisis of the republic before the Nazis tried to impose their own solution by force. German social welfare politics wobbled wildly between these two poles in the years between 1918 and 1945. It was not until the discrediting of political extremes on the right and the left in the aftermath of World War II and the acceptance of the Catholic principle of subsidiarity during the years of Christian Democratic dominance after 1945 that something resembling a stable modus vivendi was reached that became the foundation for the pillarized system of social welfare in the Federal Republic.[25]

---

[24] Neuhaus in *Jugendämter als Träger*, 174ff.; *Denkschrift des DCV zum preußischen Jugendfürsorgegesetz-Entwurf* (Freiburg, 1918); "Besprechung des preußischen Gesetzentwurfes über Jugendämter und Berufsvormundschaft" (undated); and "Beratung mit dem Landeshauptman von Westfalen" (January 1918), both in ADCV 319.4 SKF EII, 2, Fasz. 1.

[25] On this and the following, see Young-sun Hong, *Welfare, Modernity and the Weimar State, 1919–1933* (Princeton University Press, 1998), and Dickinson, *The Politics of German Youth Welfare*, 139ff.

Conclusion

The End of Poor Relief and the Invention of Welfare

Wartime welfare created a number of quandaries for poor relief officials. Simply because a son or husband was drafted, people who for years may have depended on poor relief fortuitously became eligible for much more generous wartime welfare. It was hard for relief officials to justify why these families should suddenly be treated in a preferential manner, or why other, equally needy families should not, and they were disturbed at the prospect that this preferential status might endure beyond the end of the war. They feared that the suspension of the poor laws during the war would unleash a massive wave of migration by the poor from the countryside to the cities and thus bring about a permanent geographical shift in the distribution of poor relief costs. They struggled to balance the demands of economy and the principle of deterrence against the government's policy of using wartime welfare as a means of preserving social and political stability on the home front. And they were worried that the constant harping on rights and the increasing willingness to depend on the assistance of others without any loss of social status or civic rights were weakening the self-reliance of the population. Although these questions exercised relief officials at the time, in the long run they proved to be issues of minor concern because other developments were challenging deterrent poor relief in more fundamental ways.

The mobilization of the nation for war meant that large segments of the population – including the recipients of separation allowances and wartime welfare, disabled veterans and their families, social insurance beneficiaries, and the many members of the middle classes whose economic position was permanently undermined by inflation, shortages, disability, and death – came to depend either temporarily or permanently on the state to provide for their basic needs. These were people who in normal times would never have come into contact with public assistance, and they could make claims on the state in ways that the traditional poor could not. In addition, the increasingly total nature of the war made it virtually impossible to distinguish between the general population and those persons deserving of special privileges because of their contribution to the war. As one commentator explained, "in the last analysis every member of the population is a veteran. There is hardly anyone whose actions and labors did not strengthen and sustain the resistance of the German people."[1] As a result, poor relief diminished in both absolute and relative importance as a larger and larger proportion of the entire population was brought under the umbrella of wartime income maintenance and preventive social welfare programs.[2] Just as importantly, this proved to be a one-way door. Not only did these developments create a huge constituency in favor of the continuation of preventive and curative social welfare programs; to the extent that these programs came to be seen as crucial to the long-term tasks of reconstruction, there was little possibility that poor relief would recover its prewar position after 1918.

The assistantial vacuum that was left behind by the hollowing out of deterrent poor relief during the war was quickly filled as reformers renewed their call for the further expansion of preventive welfare in order to give real substance to the rights associated with the Progressive social contract. In 1919, Heinrich Ruland – the chair of the German Association for Poor Relief and Charity – in 1919 spoke of a "social obligation of human society to insure the most humane existence for all its members and, therefore, to seek out in every sphere of poverty the roots of this evil and to stamp them out," rather than to wait until people had fallen into poverty or succumbed to other forms of need before acting, as had been the case as long as social assistance was dominated by the principles of deterrence and less eligibility. The correlate of this social duty was the endowment of all citizens with social rights to that assistance necessary for them to become full members of the community, that is, to quote Ruland, "the moral right of every person who is threatened by poverty to the timely social assistance of his compatriots in order to avoid poverty, in order to ensure that the endangered person remains a full member of the community and does not become dependent on the help of others." From this perspective, it was necessary to jettison the concept of poor relief altogether – precisely because the need to relieve poverty implied the failure to prevent its occurrence in the first place – and to replace it with a form of social assistance that better captured the new commitment to prevention, individual social rights, and the respect for the dignity of the needy that flowed from them.[3] It was in this spirit – and against the background of a revolution whose eventual outcome was still uncertain – that the German Association for Poor Relief and Charity, which for nearly four decades had been the institutional home of urban liberalism and the

---

[1] Prof. S. P. Altmann in *Stenographischer Bericht über die Verhandlungen*, SDV, 107 (1917), 67.

[2] *Die Armenpflege nach dem Kriege*, SDV, 105 (1916), 70ff. There are no reliable numbers on the number of people supported by wartime welfare, but one-third seems like a reasonable estimate. As of November 1915, it was estimated that 4 million families with 11 million persons were being supported by wartime welfare, and the number continued to rise through the end of the war. BA BAdI 12094, Bl. 213.

[3] Heinrich Ruland, "Soziale Ausgestaltung der Armenpflege und Reichsgesetzgebung," *ZfA* 20:1–3 (January/March 1919), 1–8, citation 4.

primary advocate of the rationalization of deterrent poor relief and scientific charity, changed its name in 1919 to the German Association for Public and Private Welfare (*öffentliche und private Fürsorge*).[4]

Progressive welfare reformers argued that the poor relief existence minimum should be supplanted by what they called a "social" existence minimum that would ensure that needy persons could realize their potential and thus become good citizens and productive members of the community, rather than continue to vegetate in a state of unproductive poverty, disease, and delinquency, where they would be a burden on society. As one social reformer phrased the issue, the goal of preventive social welfare was the "elevation of everyone to a certain norm, the establishment of standards of assistance that actually contribute to increasing the productive power of the German people. Only when humane and productivist (*kraftsteigernd*) measures and programs based on social and population-political considerations are established for the totality of the population" would the future of the nation be secure.[5] These ideas had first been advanced in Germany at the turn of the century under the rubric of the social evolution of poor relief. What was different at the end of World War I was that the exigencies of war and the challenges of national reconstruction, reinforced by the wave of democratic sentiment sweeping the country, gave long-standing Progressive reform ideas a political resonance that burst the prewar limits on social reform.

Making this move meant, as Klumker had argued, ceasing to use ostensible moral failing and moral worthiness as the basic criteria for determining assistance and focusing instead on the nature of individual need and the kinds of assistance that would be needed to restore the economic independence of the person. Many people, however, were reluctant to completely abandon deterrent poor relief, and they argued that it would have to be retained as an ultimate refuge for a small residuum of what were termed (following Klumker) "hopelessly uneconomical" persons, who forfeited the right to preventive welfare not by falling into need in the first place, but rather by rejecting assistance that was offered to them or by subverting such efforts through wanton acts of improvidence and irresponsibility.[6] These were the deadbeat dads, malingerers, hard-core vagrants, and prostitutes whom relief officials had been trying to get a handle on for decades. They would be the residual clientele of the workhouse and the police.

However, the social rights enjoyed by the citizens of the new social welfare state were not unlimited, and social services did not come with no strings

---

[4] The British Charity Organization Society, by contrast, rebuffed a similar postwar proposal and only changed its name to the Family Welfare Association in 1946. A. M. McBriar, *An Edwardian Mixed Doubles. The Bosanquets versus the Webbs. A Study in British Social Policy 1890–1929* (Oxford University Press, 1987), 359.

[5] Altmann, *Stenographischer Bericht über die Verhandlungen*, SDV, 107 (1917), 68.

[6] See the discussion among Polligkeit, Ruland, and Luppe in *Die Armenpflege nach dem Kriege*, SDV, 105 (1916), 108ff.

attached. It was not so much that the Progressives wished to overthrow work ethic, family, and property as that they believed that more radical forms of social intervention and regulation were necessary to produce the familial subjects on which these ideals and institutions rested. Within the Progressive social contract, the counterpart to the duty of society to prevent need, and to the social rights of the needy to such assistance, was the duty of the needy to help themselves. As Polligkeit explained, "the right to subsistence and to work, to health care and education, is inconceivable without the express emphasis on the corresponding duties. One can even say that, without the express emphasis that each individual is obligated according to his powers to support himself through the application of his labor power, to stay healthy, and to educate his children, the granting of a right to assistance is inconceivable."[7] Those who argue that all the evils of the modern welfare state stem from its separation of social rights from social obligations miss this key point.[8]

But the breakthrough of the preventive project also posed two problems that were to be of fundamental importance for the subsequent history of the welfare state. The first was that of maintaining a proper balance between the social rights and the social obligations of the individual. The second was that of ensuring that the greater leeway for intervening into the private sphere that made possible preventive intervention in fact empowered the beneficiaries of these programs and enhanced their welfare, rather than leading to their more intensive coercion. Although I have tried to address this issue and show how emancipation and discipline were joined at the hip, there is no single answer to these questions, because the conflicts between rights and duties were resolved in many different ways depending on time and context. To provide a historical answer to this theoretical question would be to write an impossible history of the welfare state in the twentieth century.

The liberal defenders of deterrent poor relief did not simply roll over and die at the end of World War I. Nor did the Weimar welfare system put all these Progressive principles into practice in a wholesale manner. The parlous state of postwar finances alone constituted an insurmountable obstacle to the systematic implementation of these ideas. But by the end of the war the idea of preventive social welfare, and the Progressive political theory on which it was based, had achieved a critical mass of acceptance within the social reform community, and it was the language of welfare, rather than the language of deterrence, that defined the terms of debate in the postwar years. There were many who continued to champion deterrent poor relief, if only as the appropriate means of providing for those incorrigible and hopelessly uneconomical persons who failed to hold up their end of the Progressive social contract. But the defenders of the old assistantial regime were being pushed further and

---

[7] Polligkeit, "Die Neuorientierung und Neugestaltung des Deutschen Vereins für Armenpflege und Wohltätigkeit," *ZfA* 20:4–6 (1919), 106–16, citation 107.

[8] Gertrude Himmelfarb, *Poverty and Compassion. The Moral Imagination of the Late Victorians* (Random House, 1991), 384.

Conclusion

further onto the defensive by the massive social dislocation of the war, the equally massive challenges of reconstruction, and the social aspirations of the new republic.

The first half of this book was devoted to reconstructing the formation of deterrent poor relief and situating it in the broader history of nineteenth-century bourgeois society. The second half, though, has been woven around two other narratives. The one is the rise of the social perspective on poverty, the development of preventive social welfare, and the emergence of a Progressive political theory that allowed prevention to appear as a coherent, compelling alternative to deterrent poor relief. The other is the mirror image of the first: the progressive hollowing out of deterrent relief between the 1890s and 1918. It was during World War I that these two arcs definitively crossed, and it is this peculiar dialectic that enables us to speak of both the break-up of the poor laws and the evolution of the welfare state out of nineteenth-century poor relief. But the problems of the postwar German welfare state, the language of reform, and the nature of social politics were no longer those of the prewar world, and thus it makes sense to bring this work to a close on the cusp between one assistantial regime and its successor.

Sources and Abbreviations

Bibliographical Note

A full bibliography of all the secondary literature consulted in the composition of this work has been omitted for reasons of space. The reader will find full bibliographical information on all works cited in the initial citation of the work within each of the individual chapters.

Archives

ADCV	Archiv des Deutschen Caritasverbandes
ADW	Archiv des Diakonischen Werkes
AKFD	Archiv des Katholischen Frauenvereins Deutschland
BA	Bundesarchiv
GStAPrKB	Geheimes Staatsarchiv Preussischer Kulturbesitz
HLA	Helene Lange Archiv
IfG	Archiv des Instituts für Gemeinwohl
LAB	Landesarchiv Berlin
StAF	Stadtarchiv Frankfurt

Publications

AfS	Archiv für Sozialgeschichte
AHR	American Historical Review
BfSA	Blätter für Soziale Arbeit
CEH	Central European History
GuG	Geschichte und Gesellschaft
HZ	Historische Zeitschrift
IRSH	International Review of Social History
JMH	Journal of Modern History
RGBl	Reichs-Gesetzesblatt
SDV	Schriften des Deutschen Vereins für Armenpflege und Wohltätigkeit (later Schriften des Deutschen Vereins für öffentliche und private Fürsorge)

SH	Social History
SPr	Soziale Praxis und Archiv für Volkswohlfahrt
VSWG	Vierteljahrschrift für Sozial- und Wirtschaftsgeschichte
ZfA	Zeitschrift für das Armenwesen
ZfS	Zeitschrift für Sozialreform

Index

Abel, Wilhelm, 18
Allmenröder, Karl, 193
Alsace-Lorraine, 86, 106
Anti-Socialist Law, 102
Appelius, Hugo, 184, 185, 186, 191
Asociality, 5, 16, 17, 31, 55, 144, 169, 172
Association of German Evangelical Women (Deutsch-Evangelischer Frauenbund, DEF), 116, 122
Associations (Voluntary), 2, 9, 50, 53, 78, 116, 127, 163, 165, 168, 174, 194, 199, 203, 205, 231, 237, 241, 242
  and state-society relations, 8, 56, 57, 58, 68, 75, 199
  Collaboration with local state, 8, 190, 204
  Competitive proliferation of, 7, 8, 56, 113
  Progressive views on state and association, 182
Austria, 35, 44, 46, 99
Auxiliary Labor Law (1916), 220, 221, 222

Barth, Theodor, 110
Bäumer, Gertrud, 124, 151, 227
Begging, vagrancy, vagabondage, 11, 14, 15, 16, 20, 21, 23, 24, 29, 30, 31, 41, 42, 48, 63, 88, 92, 96, 98, 161, 162, 163, 170, 171
  as heart of early modern social problem, 11, 16, 43
  as negation of middle-class values, 161, 162
  Catholic attitudes toward, 21, 28
  Children, 46
  Impact of poor laws on, 162, 164
  Impact of stations on, 167, 168
  Integration of beggars into local community, 11, 21, 37
  Presumptive criminality of, 15, 16, 20, 25, 38, 39, 45, 70, 89, 166, 170
  Prussian law on, 82, 84
  Workhouse as means of combatting, 5, 32, 35, 36, 40, 41
Berlepsch, Freiherr Hans-Hermann von, 203
Bismarck, Otto von, 99, 102, 103, 113, 141, 203
Blaum, Kurt, 237, 240, 241
Bodelschwingh, Friedrich von, 115, 116, 164, 166, 168. *See also* Migrant relief
Böhmert, Viktor, 78, 79, 96, 105, 106, 108
Bosanquet, Bernard, 143
Bourgeois women's movement (*see also* Social work), 7, 113, 133, 151
  Affinities to liberalism, 116
Brandts, Franz, 135
Brandts, Max, 135, 136, 138
Bridewell, 35
Briggs, Asa, 233, 235
Bucer, Martin, 26
Buehl, Adolf, 200, 201
Büsch, Johann Georg, 48

Calvinism, 5, 20, 25, 26, 27, 29, 34, 116
Cameralism, 34, 39, 40, 41, 46, 52
Castel, Robert, 43
Catholicism, 5, 7, 13, 18, 19, 20, 24, 28, 29, 30, 44, 113, 138, 162, 166, 225, 238, 239, 241, 242
  Association of German Catholic Social Workers (Verein der deutschen katholischen Sozialbeamtinnen), 133

251

Catholicism (*cont.*)
  Caritas Association, 138, 183, 239
  Catholic Welfare Association for Girls, Women and Children (*Katholischer Fürsorgeverein für Frauen, Mädchen und Kinder*), 234
  Charity as good works, 13, 14, 15, 25, 28
  Elisabeth associations, 133
  Relation to public poor relief, 18, 136
  St. Vincent de Paul associations, 133
Cauer, Minna, 121
Center Party (Catholic), 134
Central Association for the Welfare of the Laboring Classes, 75, 76, 78
Central Bureau for Private Welfare (Centrale für private Fürsorge), 147, 151
Central Bureau for Workers' Welfare Institutions, 189
Central Committee for the Welfare of War Widows and Orphans, 229
Charity, 1, 2, 5, 6, 7, 20, 22, 23, 29, 38, 41, 53, 55, 59, 64, 77, 78, 79, 89, 91, 92, 93, 94, 95, 105, 115, 116, 121, 134, 135, 136, 137, 138, 139, 141, 145, 147, 151, 152, 164, 165, 166, 173, 174, 188, 197, 202, 208, 231, 236, 238, 239, 241
  "Indiscriminate", 11, 13, 14, 18, 92, 96, 98
  Emergence as object of public policy, 11, 17, 24
  Historicity of, 1, 5
  Late medieval regulation of, 12, 14, 15, 16
  Limitations of voluntary welfare, 182, 183, 197, 201, 202, 237
  Medieval Catholic theory and practice, 16
  Organization, 96, 98, 121, 241
  Relations between donors and recipients, 4
  Scientific, 92, 96, 115, 198, 245
  State coordination and regulation, 98, 241
  Superiority over poor relief, 57, 69, 82, 182
Church discipline, 26, 27, 34
Churchill, Winston, 159
Citizenship, 2, 7, 55, 83, 86, 113, 143, 148, 196, 201, 207, 211, 212, 213, 230
  Social citizenship, 6, 141, 142, 143, 145, 147, 149, 151, 179, 190, 200, 201, 210, 228, 242
  Women's citizenship, 213, 229, 230
Civil society, 1, 5, 8, 50, 53, 55, 56, 57, 60, 64, 70, 71, 84

Cologne, 27, 59, 97, 135, 177, 204
Commercial and Industrial Code (Prussia, 1845), 74, 76, 203
Communism, 67
Confessionalization, 29
Congress of German National Economists, 77, 96
Conservatism, 64, 65, 66, 68, 69, 70, 71, 74, 78, 79, 85, 95, 97, 100, 101, 102, 103, 110, 111, 115, 116, 151, 164, 165, 180, 192, 215, 227, 233, 234
Corporatism, 9, 26, 56, 70, 203, 242
Correctional education. *See* Youth welfare
Council of Trent, 28
Counter-Reformation, 29
Criminal Code (Reich, Prussia), 84, 170, 171, 183
Croly, Herbert, 112
Cuno, Wilhelm, 187, 188

Deacons (Deaconesses), 25, 26, 27, 66, 115, 116
Deserving (Undeserving) Poor, 4, 11, 13, 17, 18, 23, 25, 30, 31, 34, 36, 48, 70, 79, 90, 91, 92, 163, 199, 245
Disability, 49, 72, 103, 104, 106, 107, 146, 208, 230, 231, 243
Doell, Albert, 162
Douglas, Mary, 43
Droescher, Lili, 236
Duensing, Frieda, 182, 183

Education through work (Arbeitserziehung), 40
Elberfeld system, 6, 97, 98, 115, 127, 136, 139, 142, 198
  Vincent associations as model, 136
Emergency work programs (Notstandsarbeiten), 175, 176
Emminghaus, Arwed, 78
Endowed foundations (Stiftungen), 14, 22, 27, 41, 47, 59, 90, 133
Enlightenment, 35, 43, 44, 45, 64
Erfurt Program, 138
Eugenics, 144

Fabian, 188
Fallati, Johannes, 77
Family, 6, 13, 17, 22, 23, 47, 58, 65, 73, 81, 94, 111, 116, 125, 126, 146, 158, 194, 195, 198, 199, 200, 207, 222, 224, 226, 230, 231

Index

as focus of social intervention, 7, 65, 93, 113, 155, 157, 210, 211
as ideal for Christian conservatives, 69, 70, 71, 135, 137, 215
as point of intersection between individual, market and social, 154
Bourgeois, 88, 117, 225
Breadwinner family, 7, 102, 105, 106, 107, 135, 153, 154, 155, 171, 211, 212, 214, 224, 226, 227, 228, 229, 232
Desertion, non-support, slacking, 154
Endangered by World War I, 210, 211, 212, 225, 226
Failure as cause of poverty, 4, 65, 67, 154, 156
Familial subjects, 8, 107, 154, 246
Family care for foster children and orphans, 45, 183, 184
Family responsibility as goal of social work, 63, 64, 173
Fear of weakening, 89, 187, 188, 189, 190, 222, 223
Mutual support obligations, 23, 59, 91, 169
Private sphere and relation to state, 154, 179, 180, 181, 182, 183, 184, 185, 192, 193, 195, 207, 211, 238, 242
Federal Office of Relief Residence Affairs, 87, 202
Fischer, Aloys, 236
Flesch, Karl, 202
Fliedner, Theodor, 66, 116
Foucault, Michel, 3, 17, 34, 36, 50, 89
Frankfurt, 35, 64, 75, 77, 97, 129, 130, 137, 146, 183, 193, 198, 204, 205, 223, 240
Free trade, 64, 77
Freedom of movement, trade and marriage, 76, 80, 82, 83, 87, 99, 110, 163
French Revolution, 59
Fröbel, Friedrich, 118
Fröhlich, Cyprian, 137

Gaebel, Käthe, 228
Gall, Lothar, 18, 71
Gefährdetenfürsorge, 171
General Charity Association (Württemberg), 57
General German Women's Association (Allgemeiner Deutscher Frauenverein, ADF), 119, 120, 128
Gérando, Joseph-Marie de, 92, 93
German Association for Poor Relief and Charity (Deutscher Verein für Armenpflege und Wohltätigkeit), 97, 105, 106, 110, 115, 128, 129, 133, 151, 156, 162, 163, 172, 181, 184, 187, 197, 198, 202, 244
German Association of Women Social Work Professionals (Deutscher Verband der Sozialbeamtinnen), 133
German Central Bureau for Youth Welfare (Deutsche Zentrale für Jugendfürsorge, 182
German Committee for the Welfare of Pre-School-Age Children, 236
Gesamt-Verband Deutscher Verpflegungsstationen, 165
Ghent system, 177
Girls' and Women's Group for Social Assistance, 121
Göttingen, 46
Gräser, Marcus, 127
Groener, Wilhelm, 221, 222

Habermas, Jürgen, 47
Hamburg, 50, 52, 66, 67, 91, 97, 130, 184, 200, 204, 221
Workhouse, 35, 37
Hertling, Georg von, 134
Hesse, 85, 184
Hindenburg, Paul von, 220
Hitze, Franz, 134
Holy Roman Empire, 12, 14, 21, 46, 59
Homelessness, 43, 85, 164, 169
Hong, Young-sun, 9
Hospitals, 14, 22, 28, 29, 33, 34, 59
Houses of salvation, 65, 66, 67, 68, 183
Howard, John, 44
Huber, Victor Aimé, 70
Humanism, 19, 34
Hygiene, 6, 121, 122, 132, 150, 156, 198, 201. *See also* Social hygiene

Ihering, Rudolf, 199
Industry schools, 45, 49, 60
Infant mortality, 157, 180, 237
Infant welfare, 131, 137, 187, 191, 198, 210, 218, 234, 235, 236
Inner Mission, 64, 65, 66, 67, 68, 69, 70, 115, 116, 137, 183
Institut für Gemeinwohl, 147
Institute for the Common Welfare, 147, 151, 184

Jesuits, 29
Joblessness. *See* Unemmployment assistance

Joseph II (Emperor of Austria), 44
Juvenile courts, Juvenile delinquency, Juvenile justice. *See* Youth welfare

Kant, Immanuel, 80
Kaup, Ignaz, 189
Ketteler, Wilhelm Emmanuel von, 134
Kindergarten, day-care, 66, 75, 118, 132, 187, 190, 191, 210, 221, 229, 236
Klumker, Christian Jasper, 147, 151, 184, 211, 215, 224, 226, 238, 241, 245

Labor colonies, Labor exchanges. *See* Unemployment assistance
Lammers, August, 78
Lange, Helene, 119, 128
League for the Protection of Mothers, 151
League of German Cities, 204, 216
League of German Labor Exchanges (Verband Deutscher Arbeitsnachweise), 175
League of German Women's Associations (Bund Deutscher Frauenvereine, BDF), 120, 122, 213
Leisnig, 23, 25
Lette, Adolf, 76, 78
Levy-Rathenau, Josephine, 226, 227
Lewis, Jane, 126
Liber vagatorum (The Book of Vagabonds and Beggars), 16
Liberalism, 8, 50, 51, 64, 68, 71–79, 80, 99, 103, 114, 115, 143, 180, 204, 206, 228, 242, 244
  and personal freedoms, 99
  and the exhaustion of early modern paternalism, 5, 44, 50
  and the social evolution of poor relief, 198, 199, 201
  Associationalism and the social question, 72–77
  Commitment to deterrence, 7, 183, 190, 246
  Individualism, 143, 173, 192, 196
  Integralness of voluntarism to liberal state, 55, 199, 202
  Left liberalism, 72, 97, 110, 151, 198. *See also* Progressivism
  Liberal governmentality, 50
  Liberal Protestantism, 115, 116, 183
  National Liberalism, 72, 97, 151
  New Liberalism (Britain), 150
  Opposition to charity, 77
  Opposition to statutory relief, 78–79, 95
  Social ideals, 18, 71
  Social liberalism, 204, 205
  View of society and market as self-regulating, 53
  Views on the role of the state, 54, 58, 102, 179, 193
Lischke, Elberfeld Oberbürgermeister, 95
Liszt, Franz von, 185
Ludendorff, Erich von, 220
Lüders, Marie-Elisabeth, 206, 221
Luppe, Hermann, 240
Luther, Martin, 16, 19, 20, 23
Lutheranism, 5, 18, 25, 68, 71, 164
  and poor relief, 5, 18, 21, 22, 25, 26, 27, 34, 41, 84
  Attitude towards work, 19, 20, 38
Lyon, 35

Malthus, Thomas Robert, 43, 51, 61, 147
Marxism, 61, 138
Maternal advice centers, 236
Maternalism, 128, 212
Maternity allowance, 233, 234
Merton, Wilhelm, 147
Migrant relief. *See* Unemployment assistance
Monarchical principle, 57
Moral reform, 5, 6, 55, 63, 64, 66, 80, 89, 141
Morality movement (Sittlichkeitsbewegung), 115, 161, 172
Müller, Paula, 227
Munich, 35, 48, 130, 137
Municipal government (Local state)
  as key domain of social politics, 8, 9, 101, 114, 115, 141, 142, 175, 178, 196, 209, 214, 217, 218, 236, 241
  Collaboration with voluntary organisations, 194, 199
Münster, 28, 59, 97
Münsterberg, Emil, 122, 145, 197, 200
Mutual assistance funds, mutualism. *See* Social insurance

Napoleon Bonaparte, 53, 57
National Committee for the Welfare of Disabled Veterans (Reichsausschuß der Kriegsbeschädigtenfürsorge, 221, 222, 231
National Committee for Women's War Work (Nationaler Ausschuß für Frauenarbeit im Kriege), 221
National Social Association, 151
National Social Welfare Law (1924), 232
Natural rights, 45, 134, 242
Naumann, Friedrich, 147, 151

Need. *See* Poverty
Netherlands, 12, 26, 35
Neuhaus, Agnes, 234
Nipperdey, Thomas, 53
North German Confederation, 78, 99
Nuremberg, 14, 15, 21, 23, 35, 240

Oestreich, Gerhard, 1, 2
Ohly, Albrecht, 156, 184
On the Condition of Labor (encyclical), 135
Otto-Peters, Louise, 118

Pauperism, 5, 6, 20, 43, 48, 49, 53–64, 67, 71, 75, 77, 80, 85, 87, 96, 98, 99, 172
Peace of Westphalia, 35, 41
Pestalozzi, Johann Heinrich, 45, 118
Peukert, Detlev, 1, 152, 186, 191
Pietism, 44, 45, 65, 67, 68
Police ordinances, 3, 21
Polligkeit, Wilhelm, 184, 185, 186, 191, 195, 210, 223, 235, 236, 240, 246
Poor guardian (Armenpfleger), 47, 88, 89, 90, 91, 93, 94, 95, 129, 139, 181, 195, 198, 208
    Workers serving as, 139
Poor laws, 5, 6, 10, 32, 38, 41, 44, 59, 80, 85, 100, 101, 102, 109, 142, 163, 182, 189, 198, 199, 200, 201, 203, 241, 243. *See also* Relief Residence Law (system)
    Baden, 85, 86
    Bavaria, 85, 86, 106
    Break-up of, 7, 198, 247
    Home law (Heimatrecht), 85, 86, 100
    North German Confederation, 87
    Prussia (1842, 1855), 85, 203
    Royal Commission on the Reform of the Poor Laws (Britain), 198
Poor relief
    Calvinist reorganisation of (16th century), 27
    Catholic reorganisation of (16th century), 29
    Existence minimum, 6, 90, 187, 199, 202, 217, 232, 233, 241, 245
    Hollowing out by preventive social welfare, 7, 143, 175, 187, 203, 207, 214, 216, 219, 238, 247
    Individualization, 28, 48, 79, 92, 139, 216
    Individualized personal help, 69, 79, 89, 94, 125, 144, 153, 161
    Lutheran reorganisation of (16th century), 25
    Secularization of, 25, 41, 59

Social evolution, 7, 143, 198, 200, 201, 203, 205, 233, 245
Social existence minimum, 217, 245
Population, 3, 8, 11, 28, 38, 41, 61, 81, 85, 146, 160, 162, 164, 173, 176, 194, 220, 221, 234, 243
    as basis of state power, 6, 39, 40, 51, 148, 149, 207
    Consequences of World War I, 207
    Overpopulation, 42, 59, 62, 81, 82
    Percentage considered needy or receiving relief, 13, 62, 89, 96, 106
    Population question at turn of 20th century, 187, 188, 190, 224, 225, 237, 245
    Trends and size, 18, 19, 30, 38, 42, 61, 109, 112, 160
Poverty, 12
    Desacralization of, 5, 146
    Family size as cause, 90, 106, 152
    Illness as cause, 13, 23, 48, 49, 60, 72, 90, 101, 104, 107, 108, 145, 148, 189, 215, 233, 234
    Individualist, voluntarist perspective on, 6, 31, 63, 107, 139, 143, 148, 159, 172, 173, 196, 209, 245
    Old age as cause, 13, 23, 72, 76, 104, 107, 146, 152, 233
    Social perspective on, 6, 98, 150, 158, 159, 198, 247
Prevention. *See* Social welfare – preventive (soziale Fürsorge)
Preventive detention (Bewahrung), 172
Probation, 186, 194
Progressive People's Party (Fortschrittliche Volkspartei), 151
Progressivism, 147, 152, 184, 191, 193, 196, 201, 202, 204, 205, 214, 225, 233, 238, 242, 246
    Principles, 152
    Productivist approach to veterans' welfare, 230
    Rethinking of classical liberalism, 7, 149, 150, 172, 179, 187, 191, 237, 244
    Socialization of liberal jurisprudence, 179, 184, 192, 193, 195
Property, 10, 12, 13, 41, 51, 61, 63, 64, 66, 73, 78, 79, 126, 133, 134, 138, 198, 200, 202, 215, 224, 246
Prostitution, 63, 67, 115, 137, 144, 161, 170, 245
Protestantism, 18, 19, 20, 24, 27, 28, 29, 30, 64, 65, 66, 67, 68, 69, 70, 71, 115, 116, 124, 134, 135, 162, 165, 166, 227

Prussia, 40, 68, 74, 75, 78, 80, 86, 87, 90, 99, 100, 110, 111, 129, 131, 132, 139, 160, 163, 168, 174, 183, 184, 193, 202, 214, 219, 239, 241, 242
  Eastern Prussia as area of out-migration, 6, 82, 107, 168
  General Code (Allgemeines Landrecht), 58
  Poor laws, 85
  Settlement laws, 83
Public sphere, 8, 47, 53, 56, 76, 113, 120, 211
Pullan, Brian, 18, 29

Radical Association (Freisinnige Vereinigung), 151
Reich Pension Law (1920), 232
Relief Residence Law (1870), 87
  1894 and 1908 revisions, 111
Relief residence system, 83, 84, 86, 99, 100, 101, 106, 110, 111, 162, 168, 198, 203
Repp, Kevin, 151, 152
Rickert, Heinrich, 78
Rousseau, Jean-Jacques, 118
Ruland, Heinrich, 244

Salomon, Alice, 122, 123, 124, 125, 132, 201
Savings, 60, 72, 75, 108, 208
Schmidt, Georg, 3, 181, 182, 185
Schmoller, Gustav, 145
School meals, 191, 201, 203
Schuckmann, State Minister von, 82
Schulze-Delitzsch, Hermann, 78
Schwander, Rudolf, 200, 201
Schwerin, Jeannette, 121, 122
Separation allowances, 208, 213, 214, 215, 216, 217, 218, 219, 222, 224, 225, 234, 243
Settlement laws, 21, 80
  Prussia, 83
  Southern Germany, 81, 86
Seven Years' War (1756–63), 43
Sexual immorality, 161, 172
Seyffardt, Ludwig Friedrich, 87, 172
Sieveking, Amalie, 66
Simon, Helene, 188, 189, 211, 228, 229
Smith, Adam, 80
Social contract, 6, 149, 150, 180, 187, 208, 209, 237, 244, 246
Social control, 3, 162, 175
Social Democracy, 7, 102, 110, 113, 125, 126, 138, 139, 150, 151, 175, 188, 203, 204
  Arbeiterwohlfahrt, 135, 140

Social discipline, 1–5, 9, 23, 27, 29, 33, 34, 39, 94, 113, 127, 152, 187, 190, 192, 246
Social governance (governmentality), 5, 8, 33, 44, 50, 56, 169
Social hygiene, 129, 132, 144, 148, 149, 157, 189, 191, 201, 210
Social insurance, 1, 8, 73, 100, 101, 102, 103, 105, 107, 108, 109, 135, 141, 152, 153, 173, 178, 198, 230, 234, 243
  Accident insurance, 103, 104
  Disability and old age insurance, 104, 108
  Mutual assistance funds, 72, 73, 74, 75, 76, 102, 104, 114, 118, 139
  Sickness insurance, 104
  Unemployment insurance, 142, 159, 169, 173, 176, 177, 178
Social policy, 1, 5, 8, 9, 36, 39, 44, 50, 74, 77, 97, 100, 103, 113, 134, 136, 144, 146, 155, 168, 169, 174, 175, 178, 198, 199, 200, 201, 203, 204, 205, 210, 230
Social rights, 6, 7, 149, 150, 173, 190, 199, 201, 209, 244, 245, 246
  Right to assistance, 4, 48, 196, 201, 246
  Right to education, 180, 185, 186, 195
  Right to health, 157
  Right to nutrition, 189
  Right to work, 51, 138, 176
  Social obligations, 6, 123, 150, 157, 193, 201, 236, 237, 244, 246
Social welfare (soziale Fürsorge), prevention, 1, 2, 6, 7, 8, 10, 13, 46, 48, 52, 87, 110, 113, 121, 131, 141, 142, 147, 148, 149, 150, 152, 153, 154, 157, 171, 173, 179, 182, 192, 198, 199, 201, 203, 206, 207, 208, 210, 221, 225, 226, 229, 230, 231, 232, 233, 237, 244, 245, 246, 247. *See also* Poverty–Social perspective on, Progressivism, Social work, Youth welfare, Unemployment assistance, Migrant relief, Wartime welfare, War widows, Welfare state
Social work. *See also* Bourgeois women's movement, 126, 127, 155, 194
  Conference of Social Women's Schools, 131
  Conflict with Prussian officials over social work training, 132
  Entry of women into municipal poor relief, 131
  Social women's (social work) schools, 123, 131, 132, 230
  World view, 126
Society for Ethical Culture, 151

Index

Society for Maternal Charity, 57
Soldiers' wives (Kriegerfrauen), 212, 216, 218, 219, 220, 221, 222, 223, 224
Spann, Othmar, 146, 147, 184
St. Vincent de Paul, 29
Steinmetz, George, 175
Strassburg, 26, 129, 137, 200, 237
Subsidiarity, 23, 47, 242, 244
Suffrage, 70
   Municipal suffrage restrictions, 204
   Suffrage rights and poor relief, 92, 99, 110, 201, 203
   Women's suffrage, 128
Supplemental corrective detention, 170

Taube, Max, 181
Thirty Years' War, 29, 38, 42
Tuberculosis, 131, 157, 235

Unemployment assistance, 178
   Labor colonies, 164, 166, 167, 173
   Labor exchanges, 142, 158, 159, 163, 166, 168, 172, 173, 174, 175, 177, 221
   Migrant relief, 115, 169

Varnbüler, Karl Gottlob von, 100, 101
Verwahrlosung, 65, 75
Veterans assistance programs, 208, 225, 230, 231, 232, 243
Vincent association, 136
Visiting, 23, 47, 49, 66, 67, 93, 127, 136
Vives, Juan Luis, 20, 34
Voght, Caspar, 48
Völter, Ludwig, 65, 71
Voluntarism, 8, 125, 126, 132, 133, 196, 197, 198, 199, 202, 205, 240, 241. *See also* Association
Voluntary and honorary office (Ehrenamt), 91, 95, 198
Voluntary welfare. *See* Charity
Von der Heydt, Daniel, 90, 91

Wagemann, Ludwig Gerhard, 46
Wages, 18, 19, 30, 48, 51, 72, 104, 120, 127, 133, 144, 156, 160, 176, 223, 226, 227
Wagnitz, Heinrich Balthasar, 44
Waisenhausstreit, 45
Walker, Mack, 85
War widows, 224, 225, 226, 227, 229
Wartime welfare (Kriegswohlfahrtspflege), 207, 208, 209, 210, 211, 212, 213, 217, 218, 226, 229, 231, 232, 239, 243

Webb, Beatrice, 198
Weber, Max, 17
Weimar Republic, 9, 172, 191, 210
Welfare state, 7, 9, 74, 126, 141, 142, 149, 154, 169, 178, 179, 204, 207, 209, 233, 246, 247
Werthmann, Lorenz, 136
Wichern, Johann Hinrich (*see also* Inner Mission), 66–70, 116
   on relation of church charity and poor relief, 68–70
Wilhelm II, Emperor, 18, 203
Wirth, Max, 78
Work stations. *See* Unemployment assistance
Workers' Welfare (Arbeiterwohl), 135
Workhouse (house of correction), 5, 20, 44, 45, 47, 49, 52, 84, 85, 88, 89, 95, 100, 138, 157, 166, 167, 172, 245
   Amsterdam, 35
   Enlightenment critique of, 45
   in 1600s, 41
   Number of persons confined, 40
World War I, 4, 7, 96, 100, 117, 122, 128, 129, 138, 142, 162, 207, 230, 242, 245, 246, 247
Wronsky, Siddy, 215, 240
Württemberg, 57, 59, 85, 86, 163

Youth, 46, 47, 48, 64, 65, 67, 69
Youth welfare, 46, 122, 132, 154, 157, 195, 201, 214, 238, 241, 242
   Correctional education, 49, 135, 183, 184, 191, 193, 194, 195, 241
   Correctional Education Law (Prussia), 193
   Early childhood welfare (Kleinkinderfürsorge), 235, 236
   Guardianship (professional), 181, 182, 185, 238
   Hamburg, 49
   Juvenile delinquency, 143, 145, 146, 148, 180, 181, 182, 183, 184, 193, 195, 245
   Juvenile justice (courts), 157, 185, 186, 191, 192, 193, 194, 195
   Orphans, 22, 33, 40, 45, 181, 224, 225, 229, 230, 241
   Youth welfare law (Prussia), 239, 241
   Youth welfare offices, 181, 237, 241

Zetkin, Clara, 227
Zollverein, 75